HISTORY OF CRIME AND CRIMINAL JUSTICE
David R. Johnson and Jeffrey S. Adler, Series Editors

# COPS AND KIDS

*Policing Juvenile Delinquency in*
*Urban America, 1890–1940*

## DAVID B. WOLCOTT

The Ohio State University Press
Columbus

Library of Congress Cataloging-in-Publication Data
Wolcott, David B.
Cops and kids : policing juvenile delinquency in urban America,
1890–1940 / David B. Wolcott.
     p. cm.—(History of crime and criminal justice series)
Includes bibliographical references and index.
ISBN 0–8142–1002–3 (cloth : alk. paper)—ISBN 0–8142–9080–9 (cd-
rom) 1. Juvenile justice, Administration of—United States—History. 2.
Police questioning—United States—History. 3. Juvenile delinquents—Civil
rights—United States—History. 4. Juvenile delinquency—United States—
History. I. Title. II. Series.
     HV9104.W64 2005
     364.36'09730904—dc22
                    2005011588

Cover design by Dan O'Dair.
Type set in Adobe Garamond.
Printed by Thomson-Shore, Inc.

9 8 7 6 5 4 3 2 1

# CONTENTS

# ILLUSTRATIONS

## FIGURES

## TABLES

# ACKNOWLEDGMENTS

I n the long maturation of this book, I have benefited greatly from the assistance and generosity of many people. In thinking about delinquency, I am convinced that it takes an engaged and supportive community to help raise a child through the troubles of adolescence. The same could be said for an intellectual project such as this one.

My greatest professional debt is to Steven Schlossman, my dissertation advisor at Carnegie Mellon University. Without his example and persistence in challenging me, this book would not have been possible. Other faculty members from my time at Carnegie Mellon also made tremendous contributions. Peter Stearns, John Modell, and David W. Miller helped me find direction for this project, encouraged me to think in terms of the big picture, and helped rescue me from the dangers of imprecision. In addition, the Carnegie Mellon Department of History provided consistent financial support. The intellectual community there was also wonderfully encouraging. Mary Lindemann, Kate Lynch, Scott Sandage, and the late Eugene Levy generously offered advice and guidance. Equally important, my thinking was shaped by a remarkable group of fellow graduate students and adjunct faculty, including J. Trent Alexander (who helped introduce a neophyte to quantitative history and statistical software), Jennifer Bannister Alexander, Jared Day, Tom Buchanan, Jim Longhurst, Mike Neiberg, Jon Silver, Jeff Suzik, Jennifer Trost, and Carl Zimring.

A larger community of scholars have also helped to shape this book. Jeffrey Adler, Wilbur Miller, Joseph Spillane, and an anonymous reader for The Ohio State University Press each read versions of the manuscript and helped make it a much better book. David Tanenhaus facilitated my journeys to Chicago and shared ideas about juvenile justice. I have also benefited from feedback offered at institutions and conferences where I have presented portions of this project: the history departments at Miami University and The Ohio State University, and the annual meetings of the Organization of American Historians, the History of Education Society, and especially the Social Science History Association (where the "crime gang," including Mary

Beth Emmerichs and Joanne Klein, have been discussing this project with me for years). At The Ohio State University Press, Heather Lee Miller has consistently advocated and guided this book.

My current professional home, Miami University in Oxford, Ohio, has also been extremely supportive. Our department head, Charlotte Goldy, has championed me and helped provide the job stability necessary to complete this project. In addition, colleagues, including Drew Cayton and Allan Winkler, welcomed my wife Elizabeth and me to small-town academic life.

In the course of this project, I have been aided by librarians and archivists at Carnegie Mellon University's Hunt Library (particularly Sue Collins and Gerri Kruglak), Miami University's King Library, the Detroit Public Library's Burton Historical Collection, the Archives of Labor History and Urban Affairs at Wayne State University, the Archives of Industrial Society at the University of Pittsburgh, the Chicago Historical Society, the University of Illinois at Chicago's Special Collections Department, the University of Chicago's Regenstein Library, and the Chicago Public Library's Municipal Reference Library.

Earlier versions of parts of this book appeared as "'The Cop Will Get You': The Police and Discretionary Juvenile Justice, 1890–1940," *Journal of Social History* 35 (Winter 2001): 349–71; "Juvenile Justice before Juvenile Court: Cops, Courts, and Kids in Turn-of-the-Century Detroit," *Social Science History* 27 (Spring 2003): 109–36. I am grateful for permission to incorporate this material here.

In the end, my family made this project possible. My parents, Frank and Cindy Wolcott, always supported me even when they were skeptical about my seemingly endless education. Likewise, my parents-in-law, George and Miriam Roemich, demonstrated eternal optimism and enthusiasm. My brother, Stephen Wolcott, has been an intellectual companion for many years (and has provided thoughtful last-minute feedback on a tricky chapter of this book). Finally, I thank my wife, Elizabeth Roemich Wolcott, for her love and friendship and constant belief in me even when I didn't believe in myself. And I thank our daughter, Eleanor, whose impending birth motivated me to complete this project and whose babyhood has given me new insight into what children are all about.

# INTRODUCTION
# A Police-Centered Story of Juvenile Justice

When most modern Americans think of police officers and juvenile delinquents in past decades, the first image that comes to mind is that of Officer Krupke, the tough street cop in the1957 Broadway musical and 1961 film, *West Side Story*. A big, gruff, uniformed officer, Krupke constantly pounded his nightstick in his hand, chased the young gang members at the center of the story away from their street corner hangouts, and threatened repeatedly to "run [them] in" if they didn't cooperate. On the one hand, Krupke embodies the notion that police officers could and would use intimidation, arrest, and physical discipline to maintain order on their beats in U.S. cities. On the other hand, he was not very effective. The boys he threatened did not take him seriously, and he could not prevent the violence that drove the story. Audiences remember Krupke not because he was a particularly important character, but because of a song about him, "Gee, Officer Krupke," which satirizes prevailing attitudes about juvenile delinquency. In the song, the boys recount the many times that Krupke has "run them in," only to be released by soft-hearted judges, psychiatrists, and social workers who forgive the boys' misbehaviors on the basis on their own pet theories of delinquency. The song reminds us that tough cops like Krupke had to work with an array of other professionals, and were often subordinate to them. Even though the Krupke of the song's narrative keeps trying to discipline the boys, they always know that they could get away with anything. At the end of the song, the boys declare, "Gee Officer Krupke, Krup you!"[1]

Today this image of Officer Krupke as both intimidating and impotent perhaps arouses mixed reactions. An older generation may feel some nostalgia for an earlier time when police officers could personally correct recalcitrant youth. In contrast, those more interested in due process or in children's welfare than in immediate solutions may believe that it is just as well that

1

officers like Krupke are restrained. For the most part, however, today's Americans assume that police have only a limited role in dealing with young offenders. Police officers may run them in, but judges, probation officers, and social workers decide how best to handle them.

This current arrangement—and the assumptions behind it—grew out of the particular circumstances of the United States at the turn of the twentieth century and the success of social reformers during that time. Between the 1880s and the 1910s, child welfare advocates, social settlement workers, and legal professionals sought consciously to lessen the power of the police over young people. This goal was one aspect of more wide-ranging campaigns to protect young people from the dangers of urban-industrial life. These reform campaigns regarded delinquent behavior as a symptom of the social disloca-tions that urban environments fostered among working-class and immigrant youth. Reformers also maintained that existing criminal justice institutions exacerbated delinquency by treating young offenders as if they were adults. As a solution, many reformers advocated the creation of separate juvenile courts. Juvenile court, they argued, would not only segregate children and youth from adult criminal courts and jails, but would also provide treatment to help eliminate the social and environmental sources of delinquency. Lobbying from these reform movements led the state of Illinois to create the world's first juvenile court in 1899 for Cook County (Chicago) and con-tributed heavily to the creation of similar institutions in most other U.S. cities in the ensuing twenty years. For the remainder of the twentieth centu-ry, juvenile courts separate from and parallel to criminal courts for adults have been the primary mechanisms of justice for juveniles. Moreover, although not everyone agreed with it, the abstract idea that young offenders needed protection and guidance represented at least the starting point for subsequent thinking about delinquency. In the contest to shape institutions and discourse, progressive reformers won.[2]

Most of the scholarship on the history of juvenile justice has focused on the origins of this separate system and the ideas it exemplified, examining the founding and early years of juvenile courts between 1899 and 1925.[3] By con-centrating on reform movements and juvenile courts, however, this scholar-ship has overlooked a key question: how was juvenile behavior regulated on an everyday basis *outside* of the courts? In other words, how did the real Officer Krupkes deal with delinquency?

To borrow a model from the legal scholars Lawrence Friedman and Robert Percival's study of turn-of-the-century Alameda County, California, we might imagine criminal justice as a wedding cake, in which the cases were divided into informal graduated layers. Applied to juvenile justice, at the top layer we would find a small portion of cases that result in long-term confinement or the transfer of juvenile offenders into adult criminal courts. In the larger middle layer would be routine delinquency cases, mainly involving theft or disorderly behavior, adjudicated in juvenile courts. At the bottom, largest, layer would be a wide range of complaints about juvenile misbehavior handled by the police or other ground-level treatment agencies. Almost all juvenile cases would enter the system at the bottom layer, but successively fewer would proceed to each of the higher layers.[4]

If we think of the justice system as a wedding cake, then we realize that much of the real action of regulating delinquency took place on the bottom layer, prior to and outside of the official operations of juvenile court. Examining decisions made as close to the action as possible—by police on the streets and in the station houses—clarifies our understanding of how law enforcement officials sought to manage youthful misbehavior from day to day. Observing the interactions between cops and kids from the bottom up is precisely the goal of this book. And the story that emerges may be surprising. Both before and after the creation of juvenile courts, the police did not function simply as foils to young offenders nor did they function as oppressors, but instead they used their authority in complicated ways to try to correct the behavior of youths. Day-to-day interactions between cops and kids represented a form of discipline, started legal mechanisms in motion, and shaped the ensuing operations of the courts. Furthermore, while juvenile courts had been intended to remove this authority from the police, they did not accomplish this goal. After the turn of the century, the police became less central to juvenile justice at a formal policy level, but in practice they remained key players who often initiated the process of regulating juvenile delinquency.

Examining how police handled young offenders presents problems of both scale and evidence. This story is a national one about what happened on a neighborhood and street level. For that reason, it derives much of its information about ideas of delinquency and juvenile justice from national sources: periodicals, conference proceedings of both child welfare workers and police, and publications from fields such as sociology, social work, and law enforcement. At the same time, it derives much of its information about what happened on a neighborhood and street level from local sources such as police records, annual reports of police departments and correctional agencies, court records, and interviews with young offenders.

Drawn mainly from Chicago, Detroit, and Los Angeles, these local sources suggest distinct strategies that these cities used to deal with delinquency. All three locations share a great deal in common. Each experienced remarkable growth in both industry and population, Chicago and Detroit at the turn of the twentieth century and Los Angeles somewhat later, between the 1920s and 1940s. All three cities underwent sharp demographic changes due to the migration first of Europeans, then of African Americans during the era of World War I, then of Latinos and Mexicans between the 1920s and 1940s in Los Angeles. In all three cases, these urban transformations seemed to generate visible increases in crime and, especially, juvenile delinquency. Yet all three cities offer something distinct and important as locations for closer examination. Chicago, as the home of the first and foremost juvenile court, represents the standard model against which all other histories of juvenile justice must be compared. Even there, police played a crucial but rarely noticed role. Detroit might be regarded as a control, a city much like Chicago, yet one that followed a different path in juvenile justice and one that provides insight into a more typical trajectory for a city that was not on the cutting edge of reform. And examining Los Angeles at a slightly later point in time illuminates how juvenile justice evolved in a similar context but in a period when the influence of the progressive juvenile court had been superseded by new models of crime and delinquency, and new demands on the justice system.

Across these locations and over time, the factors that shaped police officers' actions display remarkable continuity. For much of their history, American police are best understood not as agents of public policy or of the will of their departments but as individual "officers of the neighborhood."[5] Municipal governments in the United States founded police departments only in the middle of the nineteenth century, and well into the twentieth century officers operated primarily at their own discretion rather than on the basis of department policies, rules, regulations, or training. The duties of policemen involved mainly walking a beat, dealing with a host of minor problems, responding to complaints, and serving as roving general magistrates. Thus, public demands, everyday encounters with citizens, and their own discretion shaped the actions of individual officers. Regardless of whether we look at the 1890s or the 1940s, police decisions when dealing with youthful misbehavior were often based on a general sense of public interests and on the specifics of interactions with kids and complainants. In contrast to the treatment-oriented approach of progressive reformers, the police disciplined youth in a manner consistent with public expectations and their personal perspectives, often jaded by years of walking a beat and dealing with young miscreants.[6]

Likewise, juvenile delinquency also demonstrated fundamental continuities as well. Boys constituted the large majority of young offenders and represented the main source of concern for most observers. Police officers, court officials, and even many social reformers conceptualized juvenile crime and delinquency primarily as a male problem. Moreover, youthful misbehaviors also changed little over time. Boys' offenses remained opportunistic, precocious, and for the most part, relatively mild; girls' offenses continued to involve violations of moral standards or their families' expectations. To be sure, rates of arrest, the offenses for which young people would be arrested, and the demographics of these youths would all change over time. Rather than indicating clearly that juvenile crime increased or worsened in degree, however, these measures evidence the ways in which the both urban environments and the legal mechanisms for dealing with young offenders were transformed.

How police dealt with young offenders—and how juvenile justice operated more generally—would change in subtle but significant ways between 1890 and 1940. Not surprisingly, the creation and evolution of juvenile courts contributed heavily to those changes. In fact, the history of juvenile courts provides the framework for organizing the story of cops and kids. This story divides loosely into three parts. It begins by examining how police disciplined young offenders before the creation of juvenile courts, until roughly 1900. Then, it considers how the policing of delinquency evolved during the height of juvenile courts' influence, between the 1900s and the 1920s. Finally, it analyzes how policing young offenders changed between the 1920s and the early 1940s as enthusiasm for juvenile courts plateaued but new ideals of preventing crime and new demands for tougher policing reshaped the justice system.

In addition to juvenile courts, two other factors also drove changes in how police dealt with youth. First, a gradual, painful process of professionalization transformed American police beginning as early as the 1890s, blossoming in the 1910s, and lasting through at least World War II. These changes themselves were rooted in even broader changes in urban life and municipal government. In the late nineteenth and early twentieth centuries, at the peak of the industrial revolution and the gradual transfer of industry from rural to urban settings, U.S. cities experienced massive growth. Many cities doubled in size from decade to decade, and this population explosion brought both sharp social dislocation and the potential for increased crime. By the turn of the twentieth century, municipal leaders increasingly found the old generalist model of policing inadequate to maintain order, and pressured police to organize themselves better to meet the new situation. In fits and starts, different cities' departments adopted organizational models from business and from social welfare agencies so that, by the 1930s, the most advanced among them had become more capable of effective policing.[7]

Second, the newly expanded population of U.S. cities was also very different than before. Between the 1880s and the 1900s, a flood of immigrants from southern and eastern Europe fueled American urban growth. Police—composed at the time mainly of men of northern European ancestry—monitored a population increasingly distinct from themselves in ethnicity. By the 1920s, World War I and federal immigration restrictions slowed this flow of foreign arrivals to a trickle, but African Americans moving from the South to the North took their place. In addition, western cities like Los Angeles experienced a profound influx of Mexican migrants in this same period. In short, social changes brought on by urbanization and migration to the cities—both foreign and internal—forced police to deal with a rapidly changing population. Disparities of ethnicity and race emerged sharply in the policing of youth. Newcomers had long been the primary subjects of law enforcement, but this was especially the case in the early twentieth century.[8]

The emergence of official juvenile courts, the professionalization of the police, and the transformation of urban populations all contributed to shifts in handling young offenders. Juvenile courts have been central to our understandings of the history of juvenile justice, but, in many ways, the decisions of the police—the policies of departments and the discretionary choices of individual officers—made the system run. The police determined in large part how to intervene with children and youth, whether to make arrests, where to detain kids, whether to refer kids to courts, and what sorts of experiences young people had in the legal system. Their treatment of young offenders shaped the options available to other institutions. Further, their decisions were governed not so much by policy but by their sense of popular demands and by daily encounters with the public. By focusing on the police, we can also see how the treatment of young offenders evolved over a fifty-year period of sharp change in American urban life.

More generally, the story of cops and kids also opens a window into how thinking about youth and youthful misbehavior changed over time. The experiences of American youth were transformed in the late nineteenth and early twentieth centuries as more and more young people spent more time in school and made transitions to work later and later. New intellectual formulations for understanding the teenage years as a vulnerable passage from childhood to adulthood also emerged at the turn of the twentieth century.[9] Examining how police dealt with young offenders allows us to see these evolving models of youth in a new light by illuminating the everyday way of dealing with adolescents who were *not* making the transition to adulthood in a socially approved fashion. The working concept of juvenile offenders maintained by the police (and apparently, by a segment of the general public) developed rapidly over this period. In the 1890s, before the rise of juvenile courts, police thought of them mainly as public nuisances or habitual truants.

In the 1900s and 1910s, at the height of juvenile court influence, police partly accepted the reform movements' formulations and regarded them as victims of social dislocation amenable to guidance. But from the mid-1920s
onward, this perspective was tempered by a simultaneous view that juvenile
offenders were likely to become young criminals. By the late 1930s, the concerns of law enforcement increasingly shaped the operations of juvenile justice. On the eve of World War II, the police were clearly winning the ongoing
contest to shape institutions and discourse surrounding juvenile delinquency.

And as police dealt with increasingly diverse urban youth populations,
efficiently implementing this crime control perspective fostered conflicts with
the communities policed. The transformation of juvenile justice by the late
1930s illuminates the historical precedents for abiding tensions between
America's police and minorities that have characterized the latter half of the
twentieth century. These tensions are rooted in part in competing ideas of
delinquency that emerged in the latter half of the nineteenth century.

# ⇥ 1 ⇤

# Competing Ideas of Delinquency

Police Officer Edward J. Talbot had a reputation as "the toughest man on Harrison Street," itself a rough district in 1890s Chicago. Judge Richard S. Tuthill knew Talbot as the arresting officer for some of the worst characters brought before him. Tuthill was surprised then when Talbot also appeared in court on behalf of a little boy, arrested for vagrancy and sleeping on the streets. At the hearing, Talbot seemed angry, maybe even drunk, but obtained permission to question the boy anyway. Talbot asked the boy why he did not sleep in the Palmer House (a first-rate hotel), or in a cheaper lodging, or in a flophouse where he could find a bunk for just a nickel. To each question, the boy answered that he did not have any money. At that point Talbot declared that he was angry not at the boy, but at a city that would jail boys for being poor. "Judge," Talbot reportedly asked, "let me have that boy. We won't be back, we assure you." Tuthill had few choices other than imposing a fine that the boy could not pay or sending him to a workhouse, so he agreed to place him under Talbot's supervision. After this incident, Tuthill noticed that Talbot regularly interceded in court for boys. The two gradually developed a friendly working relationship in which the judge actively sought Talbot's advice on dealing with troublesome youth. Tuthill maintained that Talbot had a way of correcting boys without degrading them; he did not know of a single one of Talbot's charges who got into more serious trouble.[1]

Talbot took it upon himself to supervise vagrant boys and street children in Chicago's central business district in the 1890s and 1900s. Like many police officers, he was of Irish descent. Born in Ireland during the Great Famine, he migrated to Chicago as a teenager and worked as a policeman for the better part of his adult life until he retired in 1912. While he performed regular beat patrols, Talbot devoted his real energies to helping newsboys,

9

boot blacks, and vagrant children working and living on the streets. In the 1890s, Talbot organized a "Waif's Mission" for street boys in a back room above a grocery store. In exchange for sweeping the sidewalks, the grocer let the boys sleep on cots and come and go as they wished. Other neighborhood storekeepers provided coffee and food. At holidays, Talbot partnered with prominent local merchants to give the boys a grand turkey dinner. On occasion, Talbot brought boys to his own home for a bath and a meal and gave them clothes belonging to his son.[2]

Boys reciprocated by obeying the law and by helping Talbot solve neighborhood crimes. The grocer who hosted the Waif's Mission never noticed anything missing from his shop, in spite of ample opportunity for boys to take what they wanted. In addition, when petty thefts and purse snatchings were reported on Talbot's beat, he turned to his boys for information. The newsboys and street waifs would tell Talbot who was responsible, and he would admonish the culprits to return what they had stolen. Talbot reportedly let kids keep a little something for themselves. According to his son, "[H]e said the most he ever remembered anyone losing out of a pocketbook was a quarter or a dime and what the heck the poor lad was hungry. And, he said, people got their pocket-books back with what was left, and surely [he] didn't think anyone could object to buying the kid a sandwich."[3]

Talbot dealt every day with behavior that might be labeled "juvenile delinquency," but he did not see his boys as delinquents. He saw them as boys who worked and sometimes lived on the streets, who were poor, whose experiences were not all that different from his own as an Irish immigrant. Violating the law by sleeping in the streets or by committing petty theft did not make boys "delinquent"; these acts were simply reasonable choices given the limited options available. The best ways to help boys, according to Talbot, were to treat them fairly and to address their most immediate practical needs by providing food, lodging, and guidance.

Talbot worked during the same decades that child welfare and juvenile justice reform swept Chicago; yet he did not see eye-to-eye with the reformers. Accustomed to exercising their own discretion to resolve neighborhood problems, police officers like Talbot sometimes resented the interference of social welfare advocates and court officials. He expressed hostility toward reformers who, at conferences, criticized his methods of dealing with youth. He questioned the dedication of people whom he characterized as "bright-crime do-gooders," and he "wasn't too enthused" about the creation of juvenile court in 1899.[4] At the same time, no evidence indicates that Talbot had an official role in the juvenile court system after 1899, so the feeling may have been mutual.

Tensions between social reformers and policemen like Talbot can be attributed to a number of sources. First, they differed in class backgrounds. Many juvenile court advocates came from middle-class or elite backgrounds; they were lawyers, professionals, philanthropists, clubwomen.[5] In contrast, policemen tended to be first- and second-generation immigrants from working-class backgrounds who often moved back and forth between policing and other semiskilled occupations.[6] Second, they differed by gender; the most prominent turn-of-the-century social reformers—Jane Addams, Louise de Koven Bowen, Julia Lathrop, among others—were women. They brought a maternalist ideology to child welfare reforms and designed many of their programs primarily to save girls.[7] In contrast, Chicago police officers were all male before 1915. Policemen like Talbot saw their approach to youth as being most appropriate for boys. Talbot himself clashed with reformers because he would only take care of boys, declaring that charitable agencies could have the girls because there was no room for them mixed with his boys.[8]

More importantly, they disagreed over ideas of delinquency. Both sides accepted the basic concept that children were less culpable for illegal or immoral behavior than were adults and that they were more malleable and amenable to reform. They did not agree, however, on how the concept should be applied. Social reformers tended to define delinquency broadly, as a complex of behaviors—crime, truancy, promiscuity, incorrigibility—all resulting from the dual impacts of a degrading urban social environment and a troublesome family life. Their prescriptions for improvement required not only responding to a child's behavior but also ameliorating the worst conditions in society and remaking each family to reflect a supportive ideal. In contrast, policemen tended to define delinquency more narrowly as particular misbehaviors like petty theft that represented rational (albeit ill-advised) reactions to their specific circumstances. Their prescriptions involved immediate, practical responses based on personal intervention.

The meaning of "juvenile delinquency," its sources, and prescriptions for minimizing it are all influenced substantially by who is seeking to define it. In other words, delinquency is in the eye of the beholder. Furthermore, ideas of delinquency change over time, depending on social circumstances, popular interpretations, and youthful behavior. While historical studies almost invariably examine *how* ideas of delinquency changed over time, too often they assume that a single, more-or-less monolithic idea prevailed at any particular time. Dominant ideas simply evolved in light of evolving circumstances and often reflected the interests of their advocates.[9] Only more recent scholarship has begun to suggest that different ideas competed with one another. Experts—court officials, social reformers, and probation officers—

held interests that only sometimes complemented one another and thus had to balance their goals to determine what shape institutional responses would take.[10]

The competition among ideas of delinquency also included nonexperts such as police officers, men who had to deal with the practical problems of youthful misbehavior on a daily basis. Although perhaps not as articulate and certainly not as widely publicized as reformers, the words and actions of police officers show that they too developed their own understandings of delinquency, understandings that were often at odds with those of progressive reformers. Furthermore, the interests of the police were also at odds with those of progressives. If reformers prioritized rescuing children from potential delinquency, police prioritized maintaining public order and discouraging criminal behavior. A great deal of historical literature on juvenile delinquency and juvenile justice examines the ideas and interests of reformers who created new institutions for children. However, the ideas and interests of their competition, the police, have received far less attention.

The competition over ideas of delinquency is most evident at the turn of the twentieth century. In the nineteenth-century United States, social reformers had largely shaped these ideas, locating the sources of delinquency in the increasingly urban environments where many children and youth lived. By the dawn of the twentieth century, these ideas culminated in the creation of juvenile courts, which promised ambitiously to confront the root causes of delinquency by transforming children's social environments. The turn of the century, however, saw the height of competition with the ideas and interests of the police, who retained very different concepts of delinquency and remained ambivalent about juvenile court and social reform more generally. If the environmental theories of reformers and juvenile court advocates implied that they should meet delinquency by improving children's familial and social conditions, the experience-based approach of police implied that they should combat delinquency via personal intervention and immediate discipline.

## ENVIRONMENTAL MODELS OF DELINQUENCY AND THE ORIGINS OF JUVENILE COURT

At the turn of the twentieth century, scholars' and social reformers' thinking about delinquency emerged from an ongoing reconceptualization of childhood and youth. During much of the preceding decades, the experiences of youth had been sharply differentiated by class and ethnicity. For a small strata—generally the white male children of emerging commercial and professional classes—childhood and youth were periods of preparation and training for adult lives. Schooling was important, but by the mid-teenage years, young men were gradually integrated into adult occupations via clerkships, apprenticeships, and entry-level jobs. For most others—especially the offspring of immigrants and workers living in cities—much of childhood and youth entailed laboring in shops, on the streets, or in factories, perhaps learning a trade, and scrambling to find enjoyment where they could. From a young age, they were expected to contribute to their families' economic survival. For both groups, the years between roughly ages ten and sixteen were understood as a time when young people began to assume adult responsibilities.[11] This model began to change, however, around the end of the nineteenth century. According to historian David Macleod, urban middle and upper classes came to believe in a notion of "sheltered childhood" in which children were to be "set apart, protected from adult concerns, their activities carefully age-graded."[12]

As applied to youths in their teens, this new model was justified by the concept of "adolescence," first articulated fully by psychologist G. Stanley Hall in 1904 and popularized rapidly in the ensuing years. According to Hall and his followers, adolescents were in the midst of a turbulent transition from childhood to adulthood, and therefore needed to be protected from assuming the responsibilities of adulthood too early. Ideally, teens were expected to live at home, receive extended schooling, and avoid paid labor. Although these models were developed with middle and upper classes in mind, turn-of-the-century social reformers and child welfare workers also applied them to working-class and immigrant youth. Progressive thinkers seized on the nascent idea of adolescence and used it to justify a range of initiatives to shelter children from the harmful impact of urban-industrial life. From child labor laws to compulsory education to curfews to juvenile courts, they devised new initiatives to protect not only their own upper-middle-class children but also the children of the working and immigrant classes as well.[13]

From the perspective of an expanding and increasingly professional cohort of charitable workers and activists, the day-to-day experiences of working-class youth working, living, and playing on the streets of U.S. cities looked a lot like juvenile delinquency. Moreover, they understood the urban social and familial environment in which children grew up to be the source of this delinquency. Speaking to like-minded peers at the 1903 annual meeting of the National Conference of Charities and Corrections, Mornay Williams, president of the New York Juvenile Asylum, summarized this thinking by arguing that a "street boy" was "literally a product of his environment." Lax parenting, tenement housing, and the freedom inherent in the streets drove boys to lives of petty crime.[14] Working-class and ethnic families, it was further claimed, did not guide their children's social and moral development. Alcohol in particular was thought to render many parents unable to supervise their offspring. One commentator argued that boys worked and played in the streets to avoid their parents' "intoxication . . . , surliness of temper, and want of appreciation."[15] Another observer questioned whether many mothers who drank had "ever seriously considered the responsibilities of maternity?"[16] Reformers also concerned themselves with the ways in which street trades such as selling newspapers and blacking boots encouraged boys to misbehave. Myron Adams of Buffalo, New York, asserted that the life of "the semi-vagrant and truant newsboy is . . . one of the best known schools of vagrancy and crime."[17] With proper discipline and training, Williams believed that street children might become "upright and moral citizens," but if an urchin was ignored or punished, he would grow up to be "dull, embruted [sic], cunning but not clever, hateful and hating others—a criminal in little."[18]

Reformers in Chicago, which represented the urban industrial transformation of America at its most extreme, dominated this national discourse about the problem of delinquency. Chicago was the economic center of the upper Midwest and experienced rapid industrialization, fueled by businesses such as steel production and meat processing. It was also the Midwest's focal point for tremendous foreign immigration, and received new migrants from all over the world. As a result, its population grew astronomically, increasing by at least half a million people each decade between 1880 and 1910. The city's housing could not come close to accommodating such growth, so hundreds of thousands of new arrivals found themselves living together in dangerously crowded tenements. Working low-wage jobs, many migrants had little hope for anything better. In short, Chicago's industrial boom coexisted with severe social and economic dislocation.[19]

This context fostered exactly the sort of environment thought to contribute to delinquency but also helped create an unusually active social welfare community to address it. As early as 1883, the Chicago Women's Club—a group of female philanthropists, often the wives and daughters of the businessmen and professionals who profited from Chicago's growth—became involved in social reform. In 1889, two young women—Jane Addams and Ellen Gates Starr—founded the Hull House Social Settlement, a home in one of Chicago's worst immigrant slums where reformers sponsored social services, engaged in community organizing, and lived among the people they sought to help. Hull House fostered an entire generation of professional reformers and became a focal point for the "child-saving" movement to create a separate juvenile court. These organizations—alongside Catholic and Protestant charities—established an institutional structure for lobbying to protect children and nurtured individual reformers such as Addams, Louise de Koven Bowen, and Julia Lathrop. While perhaps more archetypal than typical, the Chicago experience has shaped much of subsequent thinking about the history of juvenile justice.[20]

Chicago's "child-savers" also built upon almost a century of earlier reforms. Dating from the 1820s, a diverse array of people characterized by historian Paul Boyer as "churchmen, moralists, members of old elites, and even well-to-do and upwardly aspiring city dwellers," all sharing similar concerns that the transformation of U.S. cities during their own era fostered juvenile crime and delinquency, began to take action. Some private organizations established their own correctional institutions, as did the Society for the Prevention of Pauperism when it founded the New York House of Refuge in 1825. Others campaigned successfully for publicly supported reform schools that flourished between the 1840s and 1870s. Still others favored relocating urban street waifs to the countryside and placing them with rural farm families, as did the Children's Aid Society founded by activist Charles Loring Brace in 1853. This group transported as many as 90,000 youths westward on so-called "orphan trains" between 1853 and 1893. Regardless of their practical differences, the solutions developed by nineteenth-century reformers all shared similar understandings of delinquency. They all viewed delinquency as a broad range of misbehaviors, far broader than simple violations of the law. These misbehaviors resulted from the corrupting influence of the urban social environment and the failures of their families. And they all fundamentally agreed that juvenile misbehaviors could be addressed by removing young people from the environments and families that generated problems and by offering the affectionate discipline of a simulated family as an alternative.[21]

Turn-of-the-twentieth-century social reformers distinguished themselves from their predecessors by demonstrating a profound faith in the ability of science to solve social problems and in the ability of government to achieve positive change. Rather than remove young offenders from the urban environments that generated delinquency, they intended to fix them. According to historian Victoria Getis, Progressive Era reformers employed a scientific method based on observation and classification intended to get at the roots of social problems. They expected that local, state, and federal governments (under the direction of trained experts such as themselves) would then use the resulting information to implement reforms. While later critics have charged that progressive reformers sought to impose their own values on children and their families, reformers would have defined their goals as rationally and dis-interestedly improving society.[22]

Chicago reformers embraced firmly a model of delinquency rooted in the goal of protecting childhood in spite of a degrading social environment. Julia Lathrop, a Hull House activist who went on to become head of the U.S. Children's Bureau, matter-of-factly declared her belief that a "sheltered child-hood" should be universal, asserting "childhood is the period for education and should be spent neither in idleness nor in labor."[23] The reality, however, was far different from this ideal. In the eyes of Jane Addams, youth were more likely to face the drudgery of the factory floor or the moral hazards of unsu-pervised play.[24] Timothy Hurley, president of a Catholic charity, the Chicago Visitation and Aid Society, and later chief probation officer for the juvenile court, extended this logic one step further by foretelling a bleak future for mis-guided youth. He asked, "What chance was there for these poor little waifs of fortune, these human derelicts, drifting, rudderless, upon the turbid stream of life? If they walked the streets, as they usually did, they became steeped in the very dregs of degradation. . . . What could one expect from such conditions except the result that was inevitable—the ultimate outlawry of the child?"[25]

Social scientific study of delinquency by Chicago reformers also located the problem firmly in the urban environment. In their 1912 inquiry, for exam-ple, Hull House– and University of Chicago–affiliated social investigators Sophonisba Breckinridge and Edith Abbott found that delinquency could be correlated with a combination of observable elements: immigrant status, poverty, death or illness of one or both parents, and neglect by schools, churches, and civic society more generally. The investigators' environmental perspective is most apparent in how they constructed their studies, collecting quantifiable data on questions such as delinquent children's family income, "parental condition" (whether or not each parent was living and present), and nationality, but little on delinquent behaviors, and all but no data that might be applicable to alternative interpretations of delinquency rooted in heredity or psychology.[26]

These same sorts of observers maintained that the police worsened the social environment rather than improved it. At the turn of the century, repeated investigations of big-city police departments (including New York City's famous 1894 Lexow Committee and multiple inquiries into the Chicago police) charged that officers routinely lacked discipline, drank on duty, and neglected their assignments. At worst, police officers were alleged to protect crime, gambling, and prostitution, and to line their pockets in the process.[27] On this basis, reformers charged, the general lack of discipline

among the police created circumstances in which they treated young offenders cruelly and arbitrarily. In an 1884 exposé of Chicago law enforcement
practices, activist (and later, Illinois governor) John Peter Altgeld reported
that the police detained hundreds of boys each year as vagrants for sleeping
in sheds or stables. Altgeld argued that the police arrested these boys "just to
keep them out of mischief." Upon arrest, police officers treated adolescents
"precisely like the old offender with a heinous crime." Cops handcuffed boys
and detained them overnight at police stations before requiring them to
appear in front of a magistrate in the morning.[28] Denver's Judge Ben B.
Lindsey, the most famous proponent of juvenile courts of his day, similarly
argued in 1905 that police and criminal courts dealt with young offenders
"based on a doctrine of fear, degradation, and punishment." As a result, he
felt, boys came to despise police and the law.[29]

Chicago reformers sought most immediately to change the judicial instruments that dealt with children. By the 1890s, courts in Illinois and nationwide faced mounting criticism not only for failing to address the root causes
of delinquency but also for failing to protect them from the justice system
itself, for arraigning delinquent children alongside adults under the same
criminal codes and then placing them all in the same correctional facilities.
Furthermore, although nineteenth-century reformers had sought to create
new institutions to handle young offenders differently than adults, they had
achieved only limited success. Reform schools and "placing out agencies"
coexisted with criminal courts and police, and children and youth could fall
under the jurisdiction of either. The number of reform schools multiplied
after 1850, but still fewer than sixty operated in the United States in 1890.[30]
Over 9,000 boys ages sixteen and under were institutionalized in reform
schools nationwide in 1890, but at least 2,000 served their sentences in state
prisons and county jails, and an untold number awaited court hearings in local
jails and lockups.[31]

In Illinois, which did not operate a correctional facility specifically for
juveniles in the late nineteenth century, local officials generated criticism by
routinely housing boys awaiting hearings or convicted of minor offenses in
county jails or, in Chicago, in the city's house of correction (known as the
Bridewell). Commentators complained ritualistically that courts and jails
indiscriminately mixed adolescent and adult offenders, exposing juveniles to
older and more experienced criminals who taught them to become more
skilled in crime. Judge Richard S. Tuthill argued, "No matter how young . . .
the State kept these little ones in police cells and jails among the worst men
and women to be found in the vilest parts of the city and town. Under such
treatment they developed rapidly, and the natural result was that they were

thus educated in crime and when discharged were well fitted to become expert criminals and outlaws who have crowded our jails and penitentiaries." Timothy Hurley further argued, "Before the bar of a criminal court there was no difference, from the viewpoint of the law, between the adult and the infant." To him, penal institutions represented "so many hatcheries for criminals."[32]

In response to the apparent failings of existing institutions, many cities and states began to make special provision for juvenile offenders. As early as 1877, states such as New York enacted legislation requiring police to separate children from adult offenders in jails and in criminal courts.[33] Others modified their correctional facilities. In 1897, the city of Chicago and the Chicago Board of Education established the John Worthy School for boys detained at the house of correction. This school separated boys from adult criminals and compelled them to attend classes. Outside of five hours per day of schooling, however, boys remained, according to reformer Lucy Flower, in "absolute idleness" under the supervision of the Bridewell's guards. In addition, their cases were still heard in adult court and boys and girls remained subject to adult punishments.[34] These half-measures did not resolve the fundamental problem that children remained subject to disparate laws and correctional possibilities, determined as much by jurisdiction, circumstances, and luck as by any conscious intent to offer treatment and reform.

The creation of special courts for young offenders helped to systematize their treatment by coordinating previously separate processes: investigation, detention, court hearing, probation, and institutional placement. At the behest of a range of Chicago activists working in conjunction—members of the Chicago Women's Club, Hull House residents, Catholic and Protestant charities, and the Chicago Bar Association—the Illinois legislature passed the Illinois Juvenile Court Act, inaugurating the first official juvenile court in Cook County (Chicago) in 1899. As the idea spread, almost every state provided for some sort of juvenile court by 1920.[35]

Juvenile courts had two fundamental goals. First, they were intended to remove children and youth from criminal proceedings. Instead, young offenders—typically defined during this period as boys age sixteen or younger and girls age seventeen and under—were to be processed in courts designed exclusively for them. Second, the courts were intended to eliminate the sources of delinquency and help reform individual delinquents.[36]

Juvenile courts embodied an extraordinary Progressive Era optimism about addressing the root causes of delinquency. Unlike traditional criminal courts, juvenile courts introduced diagnostic and preventive goals into legal proceedings. Rather than focus primarily on a juvenile's offense, juvenile courts provided a forum for wide-ranging inquiries into children's misbehavior. Adolescents could be brought to the attention of courts not only via arrest but also by petitions submitted by parents, schools, or any reputable citizen. This procedure encouraged agencies to refer children to court as a preventive measure, not just for specific criminal offenses. Upon receiving a complaint, juvenile court officials could investigate a child's home and family in order to understand the underlying circumstances of his or her delinquency. In so doing, court officials also enjoyed the opportunity to inquire into the larger social environment contributing to delinquency.[37]

Juvenile court advocates' prescriptions for change were to address apparent social and familial problems. If at all possible, juvenile courts sought to place children under the supervision of probation officers, who were intended to inquire into the circumstances of home and family, offer specific plans to resolve problems that contributed to delinquency, and maintain ongoing contact to ensure that their plans were executed. Probation and juvenile courts more generally were even supposed to be more economical than traditional punishments because they addressed the fundamental sources of crime and thereby prevented future offenses. Probation, according to Buffalo reformer Frederic Almy, "save[d] both dollars and men."[38]

In short, according to its most vociferous advocates, juvenile court was intended to create a new relationship between the child and the state. Assuming that social environments were at the root of delinquency, juvenile court sought to address the individual consequences of detrimental surroundings. As Hurley characterized it, juvenile court represented "a return to paternalism. It is the acknowledgement by the State of its relationship as the parent to every child within its borders." Similarly, the early Cook County Juvenile Court Judge Julian W. Mack argued that the main principle of the court was "that the child who has begun to go wrong, who is incorrigible, who has broken a law or an ordinance, is to be taken in hand by the state, not as an enemy but as a protector, as the ultimate guardian." Most famously, Denver Judge Ben Lindsey presented himself as a "pal" to the children before him and maintained that his approach succeeded not only in discouraging delinquency but also in winning the cooperation of his city's boys. Juvenile courts were to provide delinquents with affectional discipline, addressing the offender rather than the offense and resolving the social and familial sources of delinquency. They embodied an effort to use the authority of the legal system to modify the surroundings in which troublesome children grew up in U.S. cities.[39]

# THE POLICE RESPONSE TO DELINQUENCY AND JUVENILE COURT

Even as environmental models of delinquency were being institutionalized in the juvenile court, these ideas were by no means universally accepted by the wider public or by law enforcement officials assigned to implement them. Many—such as the police—who dealt with young offenders on a regular basis regarded delinquency in straightforward legalistic terms. They believed that delinquency was normal behavior for adolescents and a reasonable response to urban life. According to this view, boys would simply be boys. From the police perspective, young offenders were best understood as rowdy street children or disruptive youth who broke the law, not as victims of their environments or as born criminals. To the police and many urban residents, delinquency was natural, if not desirable.

These contrary views of delinquency were rooted in the experiences and interests of those who embraced them. Unlike reformers, police officers often came from backgrounds comparable to the children they policed. As a result, they could see their own childhood and youthful experiences reflected in the delinquents and could easily regard their behavior as ordinary. Furthermore, police pursued different interests than reformers. Juvenile court advocates sought to protect young offenders from the justice system and to use the power of social scientific investigation and the state to reform them. Police, in contrast, had more prosaic goals. First and foremost, they sought to minimize crime and maintain public order; only second did they intend to aid young offenders.

The origins and structure of police departments shaped the criteria that officers used to discipline young offenders. In the United States, police departments were established in the middle of the nineteenth century as one of the first active arms of municipal governments, partly in response to the rioting and crime that plagued cities. Full-time police forces were established in Boston in 1838, in New York in 1845, in Chicago in 1855, and in Detroit in 1866.[40] These organizations were not the centralized law enforcement agencies of today. Instead, police officers operated with tremendous autonomy and performed an extraordinarily wide variety of functions. These included inspecting streetlights and sewers, clearing roadways of obstructions, finding lost children, lodging vagrants, controlling animals (especially dogs), protecting the sick and injured, and, quite regularly, dealing with troublesome youths who crossed their paths.[41]

With this job orientation, debates over the reasons why children committed delinquencies often seemed irrelevant to police, both beat officers and leaders. The sources of delinquency mattered less than practical responses. On the one hand, because police embraced neither environmental models nor the perspective of social reformers, they were profoundly ambivalent about juvenile courts and reluctant to participate in courts' protective modes of treatment. On the other hand, many police nonetheless saw juvenile delinquency as less severe and qualitatively different than adult crime. At the turn of the twentieth century, police tended to view delinquent acts as the results of rash, impulsive decisions, and preferred to respond by making youths aware of the consequences of their actions.

Viewing young offenders as being disruptive but essentially harmless had deep roots in nineteenth-century American culture. This perspective allowed observers to see young people's admirable qualities as well as their troublesome ones. The novelist Horatio Alger's characters—street boys like Ragged Dick who rose from rags to riches—have come to represent the American ideal of achieving success based on individual initiative.[42] Observers also found praiseworthy qualities in real street children. Newspapers, for example, often commended their newsboys. In 1900, for example, the *Detroit Free Press* characterized one group of its newsboys as "strongly representative of juvenile energy, enterprise, and hustle. . . . Wideawake [*sic*], industrious, and studious, these boys are credited with more than the average amount of intelligence and business ability."[43] Similarly, street children embodied nobility and honesty for some observers within the social welfare community. In 1898, Mrs. E. E. Williamson told the National Conference on Charities and Corrections, "these street boys . . . sometimes make our best and noblest citizens." She recounted the graciousness of street boys she had known and their refusal to accept charity.[44]

Sharing this perspective, policemen like Chicago cop Edward Talbot preferred to intervene personally with disruptive boys rather than expose them to either the court system or social welfare reformers. To his mind, boys would benefit more from friendly discipline than from the unfeeling law. Well before the creation of juvenile court or separate children's detention facilities in Chicago, Talbot sought to prevent boys who had been arrested from sharing jail cells with adults. If he could, he arranged for boys to be kept in separate cells, away from other prisoners, and if regular detention facilities were too crowded, he would place boys in the adjoining women's quarters. In the 1890s, Talbot also made deals with boys detained at the John Worthy School, offering them early release in exchange for reports of good behavior from their teachers and supervisors. This practice—sanctioned by judges who signed Talbot's writs of release—allowed him to use incentives to coerce better discipline from boys and perhaps had a deeper impact than extended detention. The creation of juvenile court, however, superseded Talbot's more personal methods of intervention, and he found himself frustrated both with institutional changes that excluded him and with "the type of people who were becoming part of it."[45]

Although Talbot apparently had no official role after juvenile court was established in July 1899, he still retained enough stature to be called to assist when ten boys escaped from detention that December. Before the escape, Talbot reportedly told the officer in charge to take off his uniform, to put his gun in a drawer, and not to let the boys know that he was a police officer because they would want to challenge him. The officer, however, disregarded Talbot's advice and, in a moment of inattention, a group of boys attacked him with broken chair legs, stole his gun and nightstick, and escaped. Talbot ultimately used his influence to locate the boys and helped recapture them and recover the gun. In this case at least, relying on the official authority of a uniform and a nightstick led to trouble, but personal intervention—based in previously established respect—resolved the problem.[46]

As Talbot's response suggests, the creation of juvenile court elicited profoundly mixed responses among law enforcement officials. Many—to a greater or lesser degree—supported neither the environmental understandings of delinquency underlying juvenile court nor the main theoretical alternative, theories of crime rooted in biology and heredity derived from the ideas of Italian criminologist Cesare Lombroso. As Chief Jerome E. Richards of Memphis, Tennessee, told his colleagues at the 1900 meeting of the International Association of Chiefs of Police (IACP), he found useful elements in both biological and social theories of crime: "I am convinced that much weight is to be attached to hereditary conditions but I am just as firm in my conviction that early environment is responsible for more crime than the sins of the parents." However, policemen did not regard the sources of delinquency as their primary concern. "Scientists," Richards asserted, "may wrangle over theories as to the origin of crime and write learned and profound technical papers as to its growth and development [but] the policeman and the peace officer have nothing to do with this element of the question." His real interest was elsewhere. "It is more the remedy than the cause which demands our attention." Chief Thomas F. Farnan of Baltimore likewise answered the question of whether crime was a disease by suggesting that the whole issue was irrelevant. He stated, "It seems idle to discuss the origin of crime."[47]

If, as many law enforcement officials believed, delinquents were best understood as rowdy youths who violated the law, then the main purpose of police was to discourage these behaviors as much as possible. In their eyes, the best way to deter crime was to increase the likelihood of punishment. This position echoed through their public statements in the first decade of the 1900s. For example, Police Chief Benjamin Murphy of Jersey City, New Jersey, told his IACP colleagues in 1901, "It is the duty of the police to keep the criminal classes under such strict surveillance that it will be difficult for them to commit crime and avoid arrest and punishment. A knowledge of a certainty of punishment has a wholesome restraint upon the community at large and forces the criminal to behave themselves, thus very materially aiding the police in the line of their duty."[48] Although officials such as Richards, Farnan, and Murphy were aware of current thinking about the nature of crime and delinquency, they explicitly rejected environmental and hereditary models in favor of advocating more diligent law enforcement as the most effective response to crime, regardless of its sources.

Although even the toughest cops had some sympathy for young offenders, they also worried that juvenile courts and probation undermined their ability to enforce the law. Chief W. H. H. Rodenbaugh of Norristown, Pennsylvania, suggested that crime could best be prevented by setting boys straight while they were still young, and attributed most juvenile offenses to negligent parenting rather than boys' own depravity. That said, he also believed that well-intentioned laws to protect juvenile offenders hampered police abilities to discipline them. The 1901 passage of an act to protect juveniles had, according to Rodenbaugh, taught teenage boys to disrespect the law. "The threat of a night in the lock-up used to be a powerful factor in controlling [disorderly boys], and seldom, indeed, did we have to actually carry out the threat. Since the passage of the act in 1901, however, the youngsters have learned that they cannot be placed in the lock-up; . . . they have no fear of the probation officer, and are openly defiant of the police." In spite of his complaints, Rodenbaugh disagreed more with the execution of the laws than their intention; he suggested that juvenile laws might be made effective if the state could establish "proper places of detention" that could provide friendly treatment but still inspire some fear of punishment.[49]

Some police criticism of juvenile courts betrays a sense of professional injury, that the duty of police officers to deal with young offenders had been usurped by probation officers. Joshua B. Gray, chief of the Central Railroad Police in Jersey City, New Jersey, asserted that he did not understand why police were assumed to be "incompetent" to work with children. He questioned, "why should the young offender be committed to the care of the probation officer in preference to the policeman?" Police officers walking a beat, in his view, had every opportunity to get to know teenage offenders, while probation officers had little experience and no right to interfere. Expressing a professional resentment akin to that of Edward Talbot, Gray maintained that advocates of the "juvenile movement" may "have done more harm than good by carrying their pet theory to extremes."[50]

Other police leaders argued straightforwardly that juvenile court and probation encouraged juvenile crime and undermined the police. They, like commentator James M. Buckley, believed the main reason for "the present epidemic of crime" was "the irregularity and uncertainty of the administration of justice [which] has diminished reverence for the law." For example, purporting to offer his IACP colleagues an even-handed assessment of probation in his state, Chief Henry Cowles of New Haven, Connecticut, argued that sympathy and leniency "gives the incorrigible boy and wayward girl an opportunity to commit further offenses with practically no restraint." Releasing boys on probation, according to Cowles, created contempt for the law and encouraged them to commit further burglaries because there would be no consequences. According to Cowles, boys had no fear and little respect for probation officers. Boys would arrive for probation meetings on roller skates and "rush up the iron stairs hooting and shouting, making more noise than a tribe of wild Indians." Likewise, sympathetic judges who failed to support the police and laughed off boys' misbehavior as childish pranks also undermined respect for the law. Cowles concluded that "the present probation system is a farce and I believe it has tended to increase rather than decrease the number of young criminals."[51]

To be sure, police hostility toward juvenile court was by no means universal. Cowles's remarks at the 1911 IACP meeting sparked an unusually heated discussion, with a number of police chiefs vociferously disagreeing and endorsing probation laws in their jurisdictions. Many, however, reacted more against the harsh tone of Cowles's comments than against his specific criticisms. Chief Perry D. Knapp of Toledo, Ohio, in a sentiment echoed by a number of other leaders, advocated some understanding for young offenders, suggesting that a little sympathy could make the difference between success and a life of crime. Knapp posited that if, as a boy, he had been arrested for stealing apples, he might have ended up in prison rather than as a police chief.[52]

Sympathy for boys was a common refrain in early-twentieth-century police statements about juvenile delinquency. Like Knapp, they tended to look back nostalgically on their own youths, recalling how friendly discipline from parents or other authority figures had helped them, and frequently cited policemen of their own time for lacking compassion for boys. Chief William Moore of Binghamton, New York, argued, "I have seen enough to know that boys are not properly or wisely treated by police officers; that they are wholly ignored when they could profitably be given a little considerate attention; and harshly dealt with to no good purpose, when a display of thoughtfulness might, and doubtless would, accomplish wonders." Instead, he maintained, policemen should establish friendships with boys. "Boys respond readily to kindness, and they are not ungrateful, and the officer who succeeds in gaining their confidence and friendship, will find it easy to restrain them for the commission of many [crimes]. Moreover, he will make them his allies instead of his foes."[53]

It was but a short step for some police officers to go from feeling this sympathy for boys to tentatively supporting juvenile courts. Their avuncular sense of protectiveness paralleled juvenile courts' paternal goals of saving youth. In the early 1900s, a handful of police leaders saw the creation of juvenile court as a potential step in the right direction. At the 1903 IACP meeting, St. Louis Chief of Detectives William Desmond acknowledged, "one of the most difficult and delicate problems confronting the officers of the law has been how to deal with the juvenile offenders; what to do with the child who has committed such a breach of public decorum as would in an adult require and demand punishment." Juvenile court offered a potential solution, albeit one still in an experimental stage. Unlike many other officers, Desmond did not see juvenile court as challenging or excluding police, but instead complementing them and providing them a means of contributing. He believed "the police have an important part to play in this experiment. They will of necessity be largely relied upon to discover the fit and proper subject for judicial investigation and to furnish the appropriate evidence for the exercise of judicial discretion."[54]

Most early-twentieth-century police seem ultimately to have responded to juvenile court and child saving with ambivalence. They could support the goal of protecting young offenders who had not yet become hardened in their ways, but they remained skeptical about social reformers' theoretical perspectives and methods. J. N. Tillard, chief of police in Altoona, Pennsylvania, exemplified this ambivalence. In some of the most thoughtful papers presented to the IACP, he struggled with the questions of when and how police should intervene with disruptive children. On the one hand, Tillard acknowledged in a 1907 speech, many people believed that in order to save children from themselves and from lax parental authority the police officer should enforce curfew laws and restrain rambunctious youth. On the other hand, others remained "mortally offended" if police sought to "curb the exuberance of the malicious child," denouncing the officer as a "brute." In short, Tillard realized that curfew laws (his particular concern) and juvenile justice more generally trapped police between a rock and a hard place, creating contradictory expectations that they should both aggressively restrain children and grant them more leeway than an adult who acted similarly. Tillard's tone also suggests animosity toward the reformers who put police in this position, an animosity consistent with police attitudes more generally. He argued that "the good people who are most active in the support of laws for the restraint of children would themselves resent what must necessarily be crude attempts on the part of the policeman to execute the laws of which they would make him the agent." In the end, Tillard proposed what he saw as a workable solution. He suggested a distinction between responses to "potential vice" and to "potential crime." The former would be efforts to save the individual from himself, and in the case of the child, would be the responsibility of the home. The latter would be efforts to prevent the individual from "injuring his neighbor"; only that would be the responsibility of the police.[55]

In 1916, Tillard again addressed his colleagues on the same subject, this time highly critical of juvenile courts but nonetheless arguing for a balanced and sympathetic approach to juvenile offenders. He asserted "there is but little question but that juvenile crime has largely increased in my jurisdiction since the establishment of the juvenile court, and that this increase has been attributable to this feeling of immunity is admitted on all sides." Parents, he argued, took advantage of the court's leniency and encouraged their children to commit crimes and disrespect the police. One boy who had been before juvenile court a number of times had recently shot a police officer to death; another group of boys, already on probation, had recently been arrested for a string of burglaries. They had reportedly tried to kill the arresting officers, each carrying "several revolvers strapped to their waists." As a result of such breakdowns, Tillard proclaimed that his "whole being rebels against . . . such loose and silly methods of management as have come under my observation since the establishment of the juvenile court in my county." That said, Tillard also maintained that he still had "profound faith in the fundamental principle involved" in juvenile court and strongly opposed "purely punitive" responses. Instead, he argued for a balanced approach, one that incorporated sympathy for the relatively harmless young offender, yet one that also had sufficient teeth to restrain dangerous recidivists.[56]

Police—both rank-and-file cops like Edward Talbot and leaders like J. N. Tillard—remained ambivalent about juvenile court in its early decades. Juvenile court advocates placed them in an awkward position, simultaneously asking them to enforce more elaborate laws regarding children and criticizing police methods. Moreover, the perceived leniency of juvenile court seemed to undermine the ability of police to discipline young offenders. At the same time, however, most policemen shared juvenile court's implicit sympathy for youth and wanted to find methods of dealing with them more protectively and more supportively than they would adult criminals.

## COMPETING IDEAS

Different concepts of delinquency and different interests were at the heart of the disagreement. Late-nineteenth- and early-twentieth-century social reformers and juvenile court advocates saw delinquency as a symptom of a degrading urban-industrial environment. The delinquent youth was a victim of social change. In response, they prescribed adjusting the particular social environment in which a child lived, placing him or her on probation, working with parents, improving home life, and trying to minimize the conditions in that child's life that contributed to delinquency. For the police, however, these discussions of the sources of delinquency were irrelevant. To the extent that they thought about causes at all, police tended to see delinquency as natural behavior. The delinquent youth, while disadvantaged, misbehaved because he or she lacked discipline and did not appreciate the consequences of his or her actions. Rather than worry about definitions, police assumed that they knew delinquency when they saw it. Thus, the question for them was not what caused delinquency, but what to do about it. Some police wanted to get tough on juvenile misbehavior, seeing it as little different from that of adults. Most, however, sympathized with young offenders, preferring to intervene personally with troublesome youth and to exercise friendly discipline that would teach them not to misbehave again. If reform school and juvenile court embodied an ideal of affectional discipline, then cops embraced a goal of personal intervention and immediate individual correction. As the subsequent chapters demonstrate, this model of personal intervention sometimes complemented the emerging system of juvenile justice, sometimes contradicted it, and profoundly shaped it.

# ❧2❧

# Growing Up and Getting in Trouble in Turn-of-the-Century Detroit

fter arresting them for a string of burglaries, police characterized Cecil Hollier (age fifteen) and Charles Kert (age thirteen) as "the boldest little thugs in Detroit." Both boys confessed to entering and robbing at least seven homes over the Christmas and New Year's holidays in 1906, stealing an array of watches, jewelry, and opera glasses and spending their money on "good things to eat." The boys admitted that their modus operandi was quite simple—they found houses unlocked, walked in, and helped themselves. They were finally caught on January 2 when a neighbor saw them stashing loot in a barn off an alley in the rear of their street and reported them to the police.[1]

The two boy burglars became a minor sensation in January 1907. Young Charles was "inclined to tears" and allowed to go home to his parents to await trial, but the older Cecil acted defiant toward the police and was held in jail in lieu of a $50 bond. He also made the most of his moment of celebrity. Having already garnered front-page headlines for their arrest, Cecil boldly declared that he would "get even" with the neighbor who notified the police. In ensuing days, he remained in the headlines as his mother wrote letters to all the local newspapers declaring that he had been a quiet, well-behaved boy until he began imitating a popular dime novel "gentleman burglar" named A. J. Raffles. Cecil's mother particularly blamed the *Detroit News* (which had reprinted Raffles stories in 1906) for Cecil's crimes. Cecil, in turn, denied the whole story to a reporter for the *News*, only to reignite the controversy by confirming his mother's account the next day for the rival *Detroit Free Press*. He again cited the Raffles stories as "one of the things that got me started in the burglary business."[2]

Cecil and Charles encapsulate the confusion surrounding juvenile delinquents in late-nineteenth- and early-twentieth-century U.S. cities. Were they bold little thugs, young desperadoes, as the newspapers of the day called them?[3] Cecil certainly sought to play the part, issuing daring statements and encouraging the newspaper sensation around him, yet his behavior betrays an element of play-acting as well, as if he were assuming a role of a rakish criminal that he thought he should. Or was Charles more typical, a boy who had stolen impulsively when opportunity presented itself but had broken down in tears when confronted with his offense? The popular literature and newspapers of the time were filled with contrasting images of young offenders, characterizing them simultaneously and contradictorily as young desperadoes, habitual truants who could easily be led astray, victims of their environment, born criminals, and/or plucky, admirable children of the city. Just who was the turn-of-the-century delinquent?

Historical studies have surprisingly little to say about juvenile delinquents themselves, and even less to say about their misbehaviors. Studies of delinquency tend to focus on ideas of delinquency and the development of institutions to treat it, less so on the children involved and less still on their behaviors.[4] Thus, we know very little about the misconduct of boys in the past. Many of the founding works in the history of juvenile justice establish that children in reform schools, juvenile courts, and other treatment facilities for youth were largely from immigrant and working-class families. They devote little attention, however, to the specific acts that brought children to the attention of these institutions.[5] Other scholars who are more interested in how institutions for juveniles operated—and hence, in the relationship between their lofty rhetoric and reality—also provide a more substantive sense of who their subjects were. We know that boys mainly encountered juvenile institutions for a range of offenses against property. Violations of public order also were common, but violence was rare. Still, these works do not foreground delinquency per se, nor do they establish the distinctiveness of children's offenses by comparing them with those of adults.[6] In fact, we know much more about female offenders than male, in spite of the fact that girls constituted a distinct minority of delinquents. Girls who got in trouble exemplified new economic, social, and sexual opportunities available to urban young women in the early twentieth century. These girls tended to be in late adolescence, often employed, often seeking to live independently, often willing to experiment with sexual relationships. "Delinquency" was a label that families, reformers, and public officials applied to socially precocious and/or sexually active young women whom they sought to protect from the perceived risks of their behavior.[7]

Particularly for boys, however, the questions remain open of just who became delinquents and what behaviors constituted delinquency. We have especially little systematic knowledge about delinquency for the period before the creation of juvenile court. If early-twentieth-century social change helped define female delinquency, then how did the rapid industrialization and urbanization of the late nineteenth century help to shape boys' experiences and misbehaviors? Scholars might well ask the same question as did people at the time: just who was the turn-of-the-century delinquent?

Examining juvenile delinquency in Detroit in the 1890s and 1900s offers one way to address these issues. Detroit was emblematic of other flourishing northern cities. With its rapid transformation into an industrial center and its sudden population growth, Detroit embodied the emergence of an urbanized America and the conditions believed to generate delinquency. Between 1880 and 1900 (even before the emergence of large-scale auto manufacturing), heavy industry superseded the commerce and smaller, consumer-oriented production that had provided the basis of Detroit's economy since the 1830s. This industrial growth both attracted and was fueled by a population explosion as immigrants from Europe and rural America came to Detroit to work in the new factories. Detroit's population ballooned from roughly 116,000 in 1880, to 285,000 in 1900, and to 993,000 in 1920.[8] At the same time, factors that distinguish Detroit also make it a useful subject for a case study of delinquency. Precisely because it was *not* at the forefront of the child-saving movement, Detroit probably provides a better example of the everyday policing of juveniles than do cities like Chicago, Boston, or Denver, where well-organized child advocacy groups more strongly influenced public policy. In fact, Detroit was comparatively late to establish a juvenile court in 1907.[9]

This chapter addresses three sets of questions. First, how can we measure juvenile delinquent behavior as a historical phenomenon (and how did the nature of the law enforcement agencies shape what behaviors came to be considered delinquency)? Second, who got arrested (and thus became "delinquent")? And third, what were they arrested for, and hence, what misbehaviors constituted delinquency?

## DETERMINING DELINQUENCY: ARREST DATA AND THE DETROIT POLICE

Measuring juvenile delinquency is problematic. The most common methods to analyze the nature of criminal or delinquent behavior in the past are to use the records of correctional institutions[10] or of juvenile courts.[11] Both methods are limited, however, and in fairness, scholars using these sources do not purport to measure delinquency; they analyze the behaviors that brought subjects to institutions. The records of correctional institutions (reform schools, reformatories, and the like) focus on a relatively stratified sample of juvenile offenders—those who not only committed an offense but were referred to a court, adjudicated delinquent, and institutionalized. If we think of the justice system as a wedding cake, in which cases are divided into graduated layers, children and youth who were committed to reform schools would probably represent the highest—and smallest—layer. A similar difficulty applies to using the records of juvenile courts as a measure of delinquency. Children in juvenile court would represent the second highest strata in juvenile justice, just one layer below kids in reform school. Below them would be a still larger layer of children arrested or against whom some formal action had been taken, and below them would be the largest layer, all delinquent behavior, whether or not authorities discovered it. Because the sum total of delinquency will probably always be an unknowable dark figure, the best way to examine typical delinquent behavior in the past is to look at the next layer up, children arrested or whose behavior generated a formal complaint.

Criminologists and criminal justice scholars studying juvenile crime in the modern world also encounter problems of measuring delinquency. Rarely would they use data from correctional institutions or courts to measure crime. Instead, they use two different standard measures. The first, the Federal Bureau of Investigation's Uniform Crime Reports, published since the early 1930s, count crimes known to police (as a result of complaints or victim reports and confirmed by police, regardless of whether or not they led to arrest). The second is the National Crime Victimization Survey (NCVS), initiated in 1973, an ongoing survey conducted by the U.S. Census Bureau to measure how many households have been victims of crime in the previous year, regardless of whether crimes were reported to police. Both methods have inherent flaws when it comes to counting juveniles. Because both seek to capture the extent of crime, whether or not a perpetrator is known, they do not include information on the age of the perpetrator, so it is difficult if not impossible to distinguish juvenile offenses from the larger universe of crime. As a result, criminologists also turn to arrest data to measure juvenile crime today. Arrest data, however, are limited too. They only include those juvenile offenders who were arrested, and they are shaped by the actions of the arresting agency. Nonetheless, they consistently record age and thus provide some measure of the lowest layer possible of juvenile offenses.[12]

From both historical and contemporary perspectives, arrests seem to be the best single measure of juvenile crime. Surviving records of arrests in Detroit allow a detailed analysis of whom the police apprehended, for what offense, and how they were processed by the court system. My analysis of delinquency relies on a systematic sample of 20 percent (every fifth case) of all boys between the ages of eight and sixteen arrested by the Detroit Police Department at six data points: 1890, 1893, 1896, 1900, 1903, and 1906.[13] This database also includes information on every arrest of a girl between ages ten and seventeen in the same six years.[14] I selected these particular years in order to capture the operation of justice for juveniles before the creation of Detroit's juvenile court. Arrest records, of course, provide only a rough measure of offenses. They do, however, indicate who were treated as delinquents, and what behaviors were considered delinquent. Furthermore, as historians such as Eric Monkkonen and Eugene Watts have argued, arrest records also represent a good measure of police activity.[15] That is how I use arrest records here—as documentation of which children and youths were regarded as delinquents, of what behaviors became defined as being delinquency, and of how police sought to regulate it.

The nature of the Detroit Police Department and its officers obviously shaped both their interactions with youth and the resulting arrest records. Like departments in Boston, New York, and other cities, the Detroit Police Department had been created in 1865 in order to curtail the threat of mob violence. In reality, the job of a nineteenth-century police officer was almost never so dramatic as putting down a riot. Police of the time functioned primarily to maintain public order and to protect property. The policeman's actual work most often involved walking a beat, ensuring the security of homes and shops, and resolving everyday disputes. In Detroit in particular, police officers tended to concentrate their efforts in downtown business districts and in affluent residential neighborhoods, making sure that doors were locked after hours, monitoring suspicious characters, and supervising brothels, saloons, and gambling dens where transient or criminal populations might gather.[16]

The Detroit police might best be described through a portrait in numbers. Rather astonishingly, the size of the Detroit Police Department kept pace with the growth of the city, increasing from 178 officers in 1880 to 1,340 in 1916. As a result, the ratio of police officers to Detroit residents remained relatively constant during a period of remarkable urban growth, ranging between a low of 1.43 officers per 1,000 citizens to a high of 1.95 per 1,000. The steady growth of the police is explained partly by a low rate of turnover. The share of recruits filling vacated positions was rarely more than 20 percent in any given year between 1880 and 1910, and usually well under 10 percent. (In comparison, auto manufacturers often experienced annual turnover in excess of 200 percent prior to World War I). Low turnover rates among officers were connected to long terms of service, averaging over ten years between 1880 and 1909.[17] The resulting police department was a surprisingly consistent organization during a period when other cities' police underwent much greater upheaval. The Detroit police obviously offered attractive and steady employment, or its officers would have found work elsewhere. Moreover, even as the department actively sought to hire men to fill new positions, recruits could depend on a core of veteran officers for guidance. Low turnover and long terms of service ensured institutional continuity.

Police officers tended to be recruited from a particular element of the Detroit community. They were, as historian Rebecca Reed puts it, "overwhelmingly male, white, working class, and native born." The Detroit police were exclusively male until they hired their first policewomen in 1921. They hired their first black officer in 1883 and a handful more after 1900, but these positions tended to be token gestures aimed at satisfying Detroit's then-small black community.[18] The typical police officer was a young white man of working-class background. Job criteria were based more on physical stature than job skills. New recruits had to be at least 5'9" tall, at least 140 pounds, and between ages twenty-three and thirty. Their average age at the time of hire was in the late twenties, as the upper age limit was often disregarded in practice. Recruits also tended to be family men. Approximately 61 percent were married when they were hired, and of those who were married, the vast majority had children. In terms of occupation, the largest share of recruits had been employed previously in semiskilled blue-collar jobs such as factory operative, and a substantial share also came from skilled jobs such as carpentry and machine work. Officers tended to be born in the United States more often than the Detroit population. In 1900, approximately 64 percent of Detroiters were born in the United States, while 84 percent of new police recruits hired between 1880 and 1918 were native-born. In short, Detroit police officers were not unrepresentative of the city as a whole, but they most closely represented one component of the city's population: young, white, male, native-born, working-class family men.[19]

Police had plenty of opportunities to encounter children and teenagers on the streets. Their main duty was to maintain strict vigilance against crime and disorder as they walked prescribed beats around the city. As historians such as Mark Haller and Alexander von Hoffman have shown, police officers served as roving magistrates, maintaining public order through informal interactions with urban residents.[20] In so doing, police interacted with youth on an everyday basis. Their contacts, however, did not necessarily involve formal law enforcement responsibilities. For example, police regularly aided youths injured in accidents involving wagons, trains, and public transportation. They investigated what caused the accidents, took wounded children home, and ensured that they received medical aid.[21] In addition, the police recovered lost children. When parents became separated from their offspring, they often turned to police for help. Urban residents also occasionally found abandoned infants on their doorsteps and reported their discoveries to police, who transported the babies to foundling homes for care. Police precinct houses often served as way stations for small children waiting to be returned home or sent to more permanent placement.[22] The police, it should be noted, performed some of these services grudgingly. Police spokesmen characterized lost children as causing the police "much trouble," and occasionally issued to the newspapers "hints on when and when not to call the police," suggesting that constant petty demands from citizens rendered a policeman's life "not a very happy one."[23]

Reflected in the work of police officers, we begin to see which children and what behaviors were defined as being delinquent in turn-of-the-century Detroit. Their arrest practices allow us to measure delinquency. We should be aware, however, that their backgrounds and perspectives may have shaped the choices that contributed to arrest practices. Police officers mainly represented one element of the diverse Detroit population. While they came from working-class backgrounds not dissimilar from Detroit's youth, differences in nativity and ethnicity between them and the young people they policed may have contributed to an undercurrent of tension that sometimes arose between the two sides. It is ironic that, in spite of the social distances between them, the police nonetheless assumed a responsibility to keep children and youth out of trouble.

## WHO WERE DETROIT'S DELINQUENTS?

Using arrest records of the turn-of-the-century Detroit police, we can develop one way to measure delinquency. Children who were arrested should be understood in relationship to two sets of questions. First, how did juvenile offenders compare with adults? What can the policing of delinquency reveal about the differences between juvenile and adult crime? Second, how can we characterize children and youths who were arrested? In terms of nativity? Race? Occupation? Age? Their place in their life course? How did they compare with children and youth who were *not* arrested? How can delinquents illuminate more generally the experience of young people growing up in an industrial city?

It is no great surprise that arresting juveniles constituted a relatively minor aspect of the larger operation of policing Detroit. The nineteenth- and early-twentieth-century Detroit police, like police elsewhere, had a variety of means of disciplining children and youth who fell short of arrest. They could issue warnings, recover and return stolen property, or intimidate potential offenders simply by walking their beats. When they did make arrests, they mainly arrested adults. In the six sampled years between 1890 and 1906, boys between ages eight and sixteen comprised only 9 percent of total male arrests; girls between ten and seventeen comprised 5 percent of total female arrests.[24] While the police arrested 54 of every 1,000 males in Detroit's total population, they arrested only 27 of every 1,000 boys between eight and sixteen. Similarly, police arrested over 7.8 of every 1,000 women in the total population, but only 2.6 of every 1,000 girls between ten and seventeen.[25]

Turn-of-the-century Detroit was a city of newcomers, both to the city and to the United States, and juveniles who were arrested were no exception. Detroit experienced tremendous in-migration of people who had come to pursue jobs in the city's growing industries. As a transportation hub on the Great Lakes and the Canadian border, Detroit also saw tremendous short-term population movement in and out of the city. As a result, the city's population in 1900 was an ethnic polyglot. According to the U.S. census, only about 21 percent of Detroit residents were whites born in the United States to native-born parents. Forty-three percent were second-generation immigrants born in the U.S. to foreign-born parents, 34 percent were first-generation immigrants born abroad who had themselves immigrated, and 1.2 percent were blacks. Over three-quarters of the population, as historian Olivier Zunz observes, could be labeled as ethnic in some sense. Most substantial among these ethnic groups were concentrations of Canadians, British, Germans, Polish, and Russian Jews, each of which developed their own geographic clusters and communities. At the turn of the century, Detroit was very much divided by ethnicity.[26]

The children of immigrants have traditionally been blamed for delinquency. Historian Robert Conot, for example, describes Detroit's immigrant neighborhoods as places where "children were so numerous that they traveled in swarms. . . . Lacking playgrounds or supervision, they congealed into neighborhood gangs, in which the older boys served as fathers to the younger. Many of the gangs practiced organized thievery."[27] The demographic reality was more complex than Conot suggests. As was also the case nationwide, the ratio of children and teenagers (ages nineteen and under) to adults in Detroit's population dropped sharply at the turn of the century, from seventy-six young people for 100 adults in 1890 to just fifty-two in 1920.[28] Observers nonetheless saw young people constantly on the streets, going to and from work, selling newspapers or peddling other wares, delivering messages, playing in vacant lots or thoroughfares, supervising their younger brothers and sisters while their parents worked in shops or factories.

The perception that Detroit swarmed with children was possible because the proportion of young people to adults varied substantially by nativity. In 1900, roughly eighty-three native whites with native parents ages nineteen and younger lived in Detroit for every 100 adults of the same nativity, a ratio close to the seventy young people for every 100 adults that characterized the city as a whole. These ratios are very different, though, among other groups. On the one hand, there were only fifteen young people per 100 adults among the foreign-born, and forty-five young people among African Americans. On the other hand, among native-born whites of foreign parents—the children of immigrants so often blamed for delinquency—there were 157 young people for every 100 adults.[29] In short, two different patterns are apparent in 1900. Young people were uncommon among foreign-born immigrants and among African Americans (who were also likely to have relocated from the South or Canada). In contrast, among second-generation immigrants, young people outnumbered adults by half again, in spite of the overall trend toward lower proportions of children in the population. No wonder they were blamed for delinquency. For middle-class observers whose family sizes had steadily decreased in the nineteenth century, the streets probably *did* seem to swarm with the children of immigrants.

Were children of immigrants most likely to be arrested for delinquent offenses? Yes and no. The majority (51 percent) of boys age eight to sixteen arrested between 1890 and 1906 were native-born whites with foreign-born parents, as were the largest portion (41 percent) of girls between ten and seventeen. That said, 62 percent of children and youth within those age ranges in Detroit in 1900 fell into this category. While second-generation Americans were the largest share of delinquents arrested, they were nonetheless underrepresented in terms of their population. The nativity of offenders might better be understood via rates of arrest. Children of immigrants were arrested in modest numbers in comparison to their population, approximately 23 per 1,000 boys and 2 per 1,000 girls. Arrest rates for both second-generation boys and girls were lower than those for Detroit juveniles as a whole and, for girls, were the lowest among any nativity, lower even than those for native-born whites (see table 2.1).

Instead, adolescents who had themselves migrated or whose nativity made them stand out experienced arrest much more often. Foreign-born whites were arrested at rates strikingly higher than those of other groups, roughly 41

**Table 2.1**

Detroit Juvenile Arrest Rates, 1890–1906, by Nativity

|  | Boys, Ages 8–16 | Girls, Ages 10–17 |
| --- | --- | --- |
| Native-born white, native parents | 20.90 | 2.40 |
| Native-born white, foreign parents | 22.54 | 1.75 |
| Foreign-born white | 41.38 | 3.35 |
| African American | 116.33 | 20.22 |
| TOTAL | 27.08 | 2.57 |

Source: Calculated from Detroit juvenile arrest database. Data represent juveniles at first arrest; subsequent arrests have been eliminated in order to count individuals only once. Population comparisons are from U.S. Census Office, *12th Census; 1900 Population*, 128.

per 1,000 boys and 3 per 1,000 girls. In addition, police arrested African Americans at astonishing rates, 116 per 1,000 boys (better than four times the rate for the city as a whole) and 20 per 1,000 girls (almost eight times that for the city). Presenting African American arrests in rates per 1,000 exaggerates the actual numbers; only about 500 black teenagers (boys and girls) lived in Detroit in 1900. However, arrest rates reveal just how much more likely African Americans were to be arrested than any other group. Early-twentieth-century sociologists influenced by environmental models believed that migrants committed more delinquencies due to the difficulties they faced adjusting to urban life and due to the problems of transferring traditional community-based controlling institutions to the new urban setting.[30] However, given the nature of the evidence, there is no easy way to determine if African American (and, to a lesser extent, immigrant) youth actually committed more offenses or if police just arrested them more often. Other than nativity and race, little distinguished immigrant and African American youth who were arrested from other juveniles; their offenses and ages paralleled those of other juvenile arrestees. It is clear, though, that children and youth of these groups were more likely than their peers to be *treated* as juvenile delinquents.

Looking at young offenders in terms of age, schooling, and work suggests that their experiences paralleled those of Detroit's working-class youth more generally. The life course of those who were arrested has striking parallels to those who were not. Just as notably, arrestees came from similar class and occupational backgrounds as the police who arrested them.

The prevalence of crime by age follows a well-known curve, rising sharply to a peak in the late teenage years and following subsequently a long steady decline. In the modern-day United States, people in their late teens and early

**Table 2.2**

Occupational Structure of Boys Arrested in Detroit, 1890–1906

| Occupational Structure | Boys, Ages 8–14 | | Boys, Ages 15–16 | | Total Boys | |
|---|---|---|---|---|---|---|
| Occupation | 16% | | 77% | | 45% | |
|   Low white collar | | 0% | | 3% | | 1% |
|   Skilled | | 0% | | 8% | | 4% |
|   Semiskilled | | 1% | | 5% | | 3% |
|   Unskilled | | 7% | | 55% | | 30% |
|   Juvenile jobs | | 8% | | 6% | | 7% |
| No occupation | 84% | | 23% | | 55% | |
|   Schoolboy | | 55% | | 7% | | 33% |
|   None | | 29% | | 16% | | 22% |
| TOTAL | 100% | | 100% | | 100% | |
| | $N = 407$ | | $N = 361$ | | $N = 768$ | |

Source: Detroit juvenile arrest database. Data represent only boys at first arrest; subsequent arrests have been eliminated in order to count boys only once.

twenties commit crimes at higher rates than any other age group. As criminologists Travis Hirschi and Michael Gottredson declare, "one of the few facts agreed upon in criminology is the age distribution of crime."[31] The age-crime curve seems to be shaped by the modern experience of adolescence. Youth commit more crimes in their late teens not only as they become more adult physically, but also as they achieve greater independence, leaving school, finding employment, and establishing independent living arrangements.[32]

Arrests of juveniles in Detroit between 1890 and 1906 support this pattern. Police arrested relatively few boys between ages eight and fourteen—just 18 per 1,000—but arrested boys between fifteen and sixteen at a far higher rate—59 per 1,000. In fact, the police arrested fifteen- and sixteen-year-olds at a rate greater than that of the total male population (54 per 1,000). Girls' arrests followed a similar curve. The police arrested only 1.2 girls per 1,000 between ages ten and fourteen but 4.9 per 1,000 between fifteen and seventeen.

Patterns of age and arrest also conformed to patterns of schooling and work, patterns that paralleled those of the children of the working class generally. In the 1890s and 1900s, high school was not yet a common experience. Detroit teenagers generally stayed in school through the age of fourteen, but many dropped out after reaching the legal end of compulsory education at fifteen.[33] Eighty-six percent of boys and 83 percent of girls between the ages of ten and fourteen attended school in 1900, but only 20 percent of boys and

**Table 2.3**

Occupational Structure of Girls Arrested in Detroit, 1890–1906

| Occupational Structure | Girls, Ages 10–14 | | Girls, Ages 15–17 | | Total Girls | |
|---|---|---|---|---|---|---|
| Occupation | 15% | | 68% | | 53% | |
| Low white collar | | 0% | | 2% | | 2% |
| Skilled | | 0% | | 5% | | 3% |
| Servant | | 14% | | 47% | | 37% |
| Prostitute | | 0% | | 11% | | 8% |
| Other semiskilled | | 1% | | 3% | | 3% |
| No occupation | 85% | | 31% | | 47% | |
| Schoolgirl | | 49% | | 4% | | 17% |
| None | | 36% | | 27% | | 30% |
| TOTAL | 100% | | 99% | | 100% | |
| | *N* = 92 | | *N* = 229 | | *N* = 321 | |

Source: Detroit juvenile arrest database. Data represent only girls at first arrest; subsequent arrests have been eliminated in order to count girls only once.

22 percent of girls between fifteen and nineteen were enrolled.[34] Police records, which were designed for adult offenders, did not indicate whether people arrested were in school, but they did list some juveniles' occupations as "schoolboy" or "schoolgirl." The police labeled 55 percent of eight- to fourteen-year-old boys and 49 percent of ten- to fourteen-year-old girls as schoolchildren; by contrast, only 7 percent of fifteen- to sixteen-year-old boys and 4 percent of fifteen- to seventeen-year-old girls were in school (tables 2.2 and 2.3). These data should be taken as low estimates of school attendance, for they include only those who told the police that they were schoolchildren. It seems clear, however, that like most Detroit adolescents, juveniles who were arrested were enrolled in school only as long as they were obligated, and that many had dropped out by age fifteen or sixteen.

Teenagers in Detroit generally left school to enter the job market. Younger children often worked in order to contribute to their families' economies. According to the 1900 U.S. census, a substantial number of younger teenagers in Detroit already had jobs—24 percent of boys and 20 percent of girls between ages ten and fifteen. Few families (particularly not the families of industrial workers and immigrants) could make ends meet on the income of one adult male wage earner. As Zunz argues, "Whenever a family needed additional income, the solution was to put the children to work, even at the expense of their schooling." The percentage of youths employed, however, increased dramatically around age fifteen. By the time they had become young adults, most had left school for full-time work. Eighty-eight percent of men and 49 percent of women between ages sixteen and twenty-four were employed. For older children, leaving school and finding employment also meant something different than for youngsters. Not only did it allow them to contribute to the family economy, it also represented one of the biggest steps in the transition to adulthood.[35]

The occupations that police attributed to children whom they arrested reveal where these kids were in the transition to adulthood. Obviously, the one-word labels supplied by the police ("laborer," "newsboy") are problematic data sources. They reflect snap judgments made by the police as they filled out arrest blotters, and certainly cannot encompass the multiplicity of things that kids did (work, go to school, play). Nonetheless, these data do reveal what police perceived to be the arrestee's characteristic occupation in that moment. According to the police records, very few juveniles arrested under the age of fifteen were employed (tables 2.2 and 2.3). Those under fifteen who did work most often had jobs associated with juveniles such as hawking newspapers on the streets or delivering messages. These jobs required them to work in public, easily in view of watchful police officers. Young girls had even fewer employment options; if they worked, they were almost always servants. While servants did not by nature attract police attention, they did work under the often-suspicious eyes of employers. In each case, these children were uniquely vulnerable to arrest.

In contrast, most fifteen- to sixteen-year-old boys who were arrested did have occupations listed. They were characterized mainly as unskilled laborers rather than as performing distinctly juvenile jobs. Other boys pursued a variety of more adult occupations: low white-collar work (clerks), semiskilled jobs (making cigars, driving horse teams), and even some skilled labor (stove mounting, meat cutting; see table 2.2). Based on their ages, it seems likely that most boys in more specialized occupations were in reality apprenticed, helpers, or just starting out in their careers. Their overwhelming concentration in blue-collar labor also suggests that they came from working-class backgrounds comparable to the Detroit police; it was merely their youth that accounted for their concentration in the least-skilled occupations. Mid-teen boys who were arrested often left school and began to earn money in blue-collar jobs, but this did not differentiate them from the larger population of Detroit. Instead, they were in the midst of a fairly typical transition from being children to becoming adults.

Girls who were arrested also encapsulated a typical but awkward transition to adulthood. Like boys, most female arrestees between fifteen and seventeen were employed, although they were concentrated in a narrower range of occupations than boys; 47 percent were labeled "servants." Domestic service was among the few employment options available to girls, especially immigrants and daughters of immigrants, and was a typical first job for them. At the same time, service created conditions that could lead some girls to commit (or be blamed for) minor crimes. Easy access to their employers' homes and goods tempted some to steal, while having an income, modest as it might be, permitted others to enjoy new amusements that could lead to drinking and disorderly behavior.[36] Surprisingly, though, many of the other jobs increasingly typical of young women at the turn of the century (e.g., working as salesgirls, waitresses, or factory operatives) are rarely cited in police arrest records. Instead, the police cited 11 percent of the fifteen- to seventeen-year-old girls whom they arrested as "prostitutes." In an era when full-time prostitution was on the wane and brothels faced widespread opposition, it seems unlikely that selling sex represented so many girls' main occupation. Instead, these data reflect how police labeled girls. Police may well have mistaken other sorts of working girls, out for a good time at dance halls or amusement parks, sometimes allowing men to "treat" them in exchange for sexual favors, for prostitutes. Being arrested for public disorderliness, and being mislabeled a prostitute, was apparently one of the risks faced by young women in the midst of a problematic transition to adulthood.[37]

In short, children and teens arrested in turn-of-the-century Detroit were pretty typical of urban working-class youth. They encapsulated the same preponderance of second-generation immigrants, difficulties of children who were immigrants themselves, and life-course transition from schooling to work. These juveniles stand out not because they were so different from their peers but because, unlike most of their peers, they got in trouble with the police.

## What Constituted Delinquency?

In addition to showing who delinquents were, arrest records also indicate what behaviors constituted delinquency. Arrests, however, cannot be regarded as a straightforward measure of crime. Instead, a number of factors contributed to any decision to make an arrest. First, policemen relied heavily on their personal discretion. Walking beats, turn-of-the-century police officers received little guidance from central administrators and were largely on their own to decide whether to arrest young offenders. Second, their department's mission of maintaining public order and protecting property nonetheless provided a subtext for any decision individual officers made. Third, the interests

**Table 2.4**

Offenses Charged against Detroit Males, 1890–1906

| Type of Offense | Boys, Ages 8–14[a] | Boys, Ages 15–16[a] | Total Boys[a] | All Males[b] |
|---|---|---|---|---|
| Public order | 8% | 33% | 19% | 69% |
| Crime | 67% | 65% | 66% | 29% |
|   Person | 9% | 9% | 9% | 7% |
|   Property | 58% | 56% | 57% | 22% |
| Status | 25% | 3% | 15% | 1% |
| TOTAL | 100% | 101% | 100% | 99% |
| | N = 420 | N = 370 | N = 790 | N = 45,723 |

Sources: DPD, *Annual Reports,* 1891; 1894; 1896; 1901; 1904; 1907. The Annual Report covering 1896 is unavailable, so data from the previous year were substituted.
Note: Totals may not equal 100 due to rounding.
[a]From Detroit juvenile arrest database.
[b]Includes juveniles as well as adults.

of the public also influenced arrest decisions. This occurred not only in some vague, indirect way but in a concrete, everyday manner. Public complaints and choices whether or not to file charges specifically shaped police decision making. Modern sociological studies (in which participant-observers rode along with police officers and watched them do their jobs) indicate that situational variables such as the race, gender, and demeanor of the alleged delinquent influence arrest decisions. No factor mattered more, though, than whether encounters with youth were initiated by the police or by complainants and the demands of victims. The same turns out to be true of police decisions in turn-of-the-century Detroit.[38] In short, arrest records do provide some measure of delinquency, but they also reflect the interests and perceptions of the individual officer, the police department, and the public. They might best be understood as a measure of delinquency that at least one party considered sufficiently serious to take action.

For the turn-of-the-century Detroit police, juveniles posed a different set of problems than did adults. The two groups were arrested for very different reasons. Nineteenth-century police mainly arrested people for victimless crimes, or "public order" offenses such as disorderly conduct—drinking too much and becoming overly boisterous in the streets at night.[39] Detroit was no exception. Between 1890 and 1906, the Detroit police charged over two-thirds of all men arrested with disrupting public order. By contrast, less than one boy in five was arrested for a public order offense (table 2.4).

Furthermore, the younger boys were, the less likely police were to arrest them on public order charges. Police arrested 33 percent of fifteen- to sixteen-year-olds for violating public order, but detained only 8 percent of eight- to fourteen-year-olds on these charges.[40] This disparity reveals age-based differences both in boys' misbehavior and in policing. On the one hand, younger boys were least likely to get drunk in public, to behave boisterously, and thereby to attract police attention in the same ways as did adults. On the other hand, officers who might have gladly arrested rowdies in their mid-teens may have been more willing to accommodate the hijinks of younger children. When cops found kids drunk, they targeted those who sold them the liquor, not the kids themselves. For example, in 1907 when police encountered an unusual number of intoxicated boys—a fifteen-year-old in an alley in a drunken stupor, a thirteen-year-old brought to a police station a few hours later in a similar condition—they did not press charges against them. Instead, they detailed officers to find the saloonkeepers who sold them drinks. Likewise, judges and prosecutors publicly declared their intention to give saloonkeepers convicted of selling liquor to minors the maximum penalty allowed under the law.[41]

Whereas adults were typically arrested for public order offenses, two out of three boys arrested were charged with crimes (table 2.4). In particular, crimes against property (larceny and burglary, most often) accounted for 57 percent of boys' arrests. The same was true of both eight- to fourteen-year-olds and fifteen- to sixteen-year-olds. Property offenses constituted the most typical form of delinquency for boys in turn-of-the-century Detroit.

How serious were these crimes? The newspapers of the day reveled in the exploits of juvenile criminals, often portraying boy burglars like Cecil Hollier and Charles Kert as "young desperadoes." Boys often encouraged this image of themselves by adopting a contemptuous attitude toward the police and in court. Cecil, for example, exulted in the attention he received after his arrest.[42] Likewise, a group of eight teenagers arrested for breaking into a freight car and stealing canned strawberries and pineapple all seemed to think their arrest was a pretty good joke. They were described as laughing and playing in the courtroom, indifferent to what could befall them.[43] Twelve-year-old Anthony Oppor displayed a similarly hostile disposition. Along with two other boys (both age thirteen), Anthony had broken into a number of homes and stolen the lead pipe, then tried to sell it to a junk dealer. Anthony and one companion were convicted when the other confessed to the crime. All this was pretty routine, but Anthony garnered headlines for his behavior upon sentencing to a reform school. His mother rushed to him to say good-bye, but the boy reportedly "finished rolling a cigarette, lighted it, and blew a cloud of smoke in his mother's face. 'Aw, you go to hell,' he growled, and turned away."[44] In none of these cases did boys commit delinquencies of any great severity, but their attitudes generated attention. By acting as if they were precociously criminal, they convinced newspapers to portray them as young desperadoes.

Boys' offenses, however, are better understood as impulsive thefts. Characterizing them as young desperadoes exaggerates the severity and planning of their behavior. Complaints to the police blamed boys for pilfering cigarettes, candy, toys, and fruit from shops, stealing unattended bicycles, and removing bottles and building supplies from yards and vacant lots, but they rarely accused boys of taking property of great value.[45] Boys most typically stole things when the chance presented itself. Even major thefts resulted from the combination of impulse and opportunity. Fourteen-year-old Burrill Winters, for example, stole an automobile in 1907—a particularly significant offense at time when cars were not yet common—when he discovered it sitting unattended in front of a hotel. After driving around all day, he was found sitting in the parked car and arrested. A visitor from Grand Rapids, Burrill claimed that he owned his own car there that he missed (a dubious assertion), and "just wanted to run one for a while" (more likely). Even small boys committed thefts of opportunity. Two brothers, ages six and nine, made front-page headlines when they stole a horse and wagon from the Eastern Market.[46] Most typically, boys committed property offenses spontaneously when they stumbled into easy opportunities.

When did police confront these young offenders? As a rule, police rarely had the luck to observe a crime in progress. Instead, they intervened after citizens reported a problem to them. In particular, complaints from victims of thefts, burglaries, or assaults provided the impetus for most police interactions with kids. Small shopkeepers, for example, frequently reported petty thefts by boys. In 1896, William Boyne informed the police that five boys had stolen four pineapples from the front of his store. Boyne named all five boys he suspected.[47] Similarly, on Christmas Eve of 1897, Robert Leming notified the police when three boys (ages fifteen to seventeen) stole a pair of gloves from his store in the middle of the afternoon. Leming did not know the boys but said he would recognize the oldest if he saw him.[48] Citizens similarly demanded police action when boys burglarized their homes. Annie Landofski, for example, reported that two boys had entered her home and stolen $10.00. Her complaint resulted in at least one arrest.[49] Police even pursued cases on more tenuous suspicions. In 1897, for example, the police nearly arrested one boy when his neighbor, Mary Neis, reported that he had stolen five ducks from her home. In this case, however, the investigating officers found that the ducks had hidden under her house and released the suspect.[50]

A wave of newspaper thefts exemplifies how citizen demands shaped police actions. In 1907, stealing newspapers from news dealers, drop-off points, and even individual homes became such a problem that the *Detroit Free Press* pressured the police to work with them "to a keep a systematic lookout for thieves." Typically, newspaper employees would leave bundles of papers at locations which had already been targeted, stay and watch the papers, then if boys tried to steal them, catch them in the act and turn them over to the police. Arrests were meant, according to one *Free Press* article, to "serve as warnings . . . to all other boys and young men who have been stealing newspapers. All complaints will be followed up, further arrests made if possible, and vigorous prosecution will be made of all cases that can be proven."[51] In these cases, aggrieved parties (here, news dealers and the newspaper) grew offended at a particular crime, filed complaints, drove police to take action, and thereby helped shape what misbehaviors would be construed as delinquent.

Juvenile violence—especially shooting—also attracted a great deal of public attention. In 1907, for example, the *Detroit Free Press* declared that "the practice of carrying firearms has reached such alarming proportions among the youth . . . of the city that the police of the Chene Street station have instituted a crusade against it and it is probable that wholesale arrests of juveniles with desperado tendencies will follow." As evidence, it offered the case of fourteen-year-old Robert Markee, who was apprehended standing on a street corner, "blazing unconcernedly away at nothing in particular." The police sought to take guns out of boys' hands in order to avoid incidents like that involving Henry Krapenka, a fourteen-year-old who shot a sixteen-year-old girl. Henry had been playing at being a western gunslinger when the girl came with the message from his mother that he was out past his bedtime, and he shot her with a .22-caliber revolver. She survived but Henry was arrested. From his jail cell, he bragged that "I was just leadin' me gang of brave men through the wilderness . . . when this girl comes up and tells me that I'm wanted to home. Do you think I could stand for that? Naw."[52] Like many other boys, Robert and Henry played at being criminals. They acted the part by recklessly firing real guns in public and, in Henry's case, bragging to the press when they were caught. Pretending to be desperadoes made them actual public menaces, but this menace resulted from casual disregard for the consequences of their actions, not criminal intent to cause harm.

In spite of attention paid to them, violent young offenders were rare. Offenses against persons (e.g., assault or robbery) accounted for less than one in ten boys' arrests (see table 2.4). In fact, arrests for offenses against persons were uncommon for adults as well. Between 1890 and 1906, offenses against persons accounted for only 7 percent of arrests of all males; in this period, the Detroit Police Department never made more than ten arrests for homicide in any given year.[53] Even when police did arrest boys for offenses against persons, the legal terminology tends to overstate the severity of their behavior. Boys did not often use physical force to commit robbery. Instead, they preferred to pick the pockets of victims (usually women) who seemed unlikely to resist.[54] On occasion boys robbed other boys, but they usually employed only the *threat* of force. A boy named Otto Toth, for example, informed the police that two youths had stopped him on the street and robbed him of 75 cents, but they had not caused him any physical harm.[55] At most 8 percent of boys could be considered "armed" at the time of arrest.[56]

That said, arrests only represent a partial measure of violence by juveniles in turn-of-the-century U.S. cities. In the vast majority of arrests for assault (84 percent), a child or youth was only charged if a victim brought an official complaint to the courts, which instructed the police to make an arrest; police rarely arrested youths for assault or other violent offenses on their own.[57] Formal complaints could occasionally lead to arrests of boys as young as age six for assault and battery. Likely more often, though, police would release boys whom they could have arrested for assault if no one filed a complaint and no serious harm was done. For example, when in 1899, seven-year-old Rube McMillen struck six-year-old Fred Stock on the head with a stove poker, the police took Fred to a doctor, but they did not bother to arrest his attacker.[58] Among older youth, police also eschewed official sanction if assaults only resulted in minor injuries. Although John Petzykowski, age fifteen, shot Joseph Tamouski, also fifteen, the wound was not serious and the police made no arrests.[59] Even shootings of adults could be overlooked if they were accidental. For example, as she was walking in the middle of the afternoon, Mrs. Agnes Wojewoda was shot in the right hand by thirteen-year-old Henry Bender, who had been playing with a rifle. She had her wound dressed and made no complaint to the police, who only learned of the affair hours later. They investigated, decided the shooting was accidental, and opted not to charge Henry.[60]

Altogether, low-level violence seems to have been fairly pervasive among youth in turn-of-the-century Detroit, but it did not often pass the threshold necessary to result in arrest. Police acted to curb juvenile violence when victims filed complaints, when serious injuries resulted, or when childish indifference to other peoples' lives and limbs became so ubiquitous that they had to crack down. For run-of-the-mill fights and accidental shootings, however, they mainly let boys resolve their own disputes and go about their business.

In contrast, police placed a higher priority on correcting misbehaviors that would be labeled "status offenses" today—offenses defined by the status of being juveniles. The police arrested 15 percent of boys on charges of "truancy," "incorrigibility," or being "juvenile disorderly persons." They particularly used these charges as a means of policing younger boys; status offenses constituted only 2 percent of arrests of fifteen- to sixteen-year-olds, but 25 percent of arrests of eight- to fourteen-year-olds.[61] Many boys who were arrested as status offenders are best understood as habitual truants—boys who absented themselves from school or from home. Twelve-year-old Irving S., for example, was charged with habitual truancy in 1902 for refusing to attend classes, in spite of a warning from his principal and a truant officer. His excuse? "I don't want to go."[62] More broadly, the police made status offense arrests to discipline children whom they believed to be on the verge of delinquency. Historian Robert Conot reports that the police "used truancy laws to round up juveniles suspected of delinquency."[63] Specifically, police used status offense charges to impose an informal curfew. They made 39 percent of "truancy" arrests between 8:00 P.M. and 2:00 A.M., well outside of school hours.[64] Police did so because they recognized that status offenses could bleed over into more serious crimes. In 1902, sixteen-year-old Leo B. was arrested along with two other boys for stealing brass patterns valued at $25. Leo had already been arrested "a number of times" for truancy, twice for vagrancy, and twice for simple larceny.[65] While these earlier arrests obviously failed to teach Leo a lesson, police presumably hoped that in other cases they might succeed. Much like arresting adults for violating public order, arresting boys for status offenses allowed the police to intervene with kids and detain them for behavior that portended further trouble.

Looking closely at juvenile arrests reveals a pattern of how young offenders developed and how police dealt with them at different ages. Younger boys, between ages eight and fourteen, were arrested for a preponderance of status offenses. Their delinquencies tended to be kid stuff like avoiding school and home, and the police treated them accordingly, arresting them, warning them, and hoping they would not offend again. In contrast, older boys, ages fifteen and sixteen, were arrested for a preponderance of public order offenses. They were becoming more like adults and their offenses reflected that. For both age groups, however, the majority of arrests were for criminal offenses, particularly property crimes. These arrests seem to have resulted less from police initiative than from the complaints of victims. For the turn-of-the-century urban public, property crimes constituted the juvenile misbehaviors that really mattered, required a response, and were understood to constitute delinquency.

In comparison, arrests of girls reveal patterns of offending and policing

### Table 2.5 Offenses
Offenses Charged against Detroit Females, 1890–1906

| Type of Offense | Girls, Ages 10–14[a] | Girls, Ages 15–17[a] | Total Girls[a] | All Females[b] |
|---|---|---|---|---|
| Public order | 7% | 29% | 23% | 80% |
| Crime | 51% | 29% | 35% | 18% |
|    Person | 15% | 6% | 8% | 6% |
|    Property | 36% | 23% | 27% | 12% |
| Status | 42% | 42% | 42% | 2% |
| TOTAL | 100% | 100% | 100% | 100% |
|  | N = 94 | N = 236 | N = 330 | N = 6746 |

Sources: DPD, *Annual Reports,* 1891; 1894; 1896; 1901; 1904; 1907. The Annual Report covering 1896 is unavailable, so data from the previous year were substituted.
[a]From Detroit juvenile arrest database.
[b]Includes juveniles as well as adults.

shaped by the different experiences of young women growing up in a turn-of-the-century city. Girls' arrests were rare between 1890 and 1906, so they should be interpreted as relatively unique phenomena. Police arrested ten- to seventeen-year-old girls at a rate (2.6 per 1,000) just one-tenth that of boys (27 per 1,000).

When police did arrest girls, they often did so with the intent of protecting them as much as policing them. Status offenses accounted for 42 percent of girls' arrests, representing their largest single offense category and more than twice as large a share as among boys (table 2.5). The police also arrested ten- to fourteen- and fifteen- to seventeen-year-old girls for status offenses equally often. As with boys, arrests for status offenses could serve as an informal curfew; the police detained 40 percent of girls on "truancy" between 8:00 P.M. and 2:00 A.M.[66] The numbers, however, only begin to suggest the real function of status offenses for girls. Police and courts used charges like truancy, running away, and incorrigibility as euphemisms to justify rescuing girls from promiscuity. As young women enjoyed more independence at the turn of the twentieth century, they also seemed to many observers to place themselves at greater risk for moral corruption.

One example illustrates the larger pattern. The Detroit police apprehended Edith Cope, described as "a pretty little brunette of 15 years," after an unnamed relative filed a complaint that she had run away from her mother's home. Edith confessed that she spent nights at home only occasionally. She spent most of her time "hanging around" a bowling alley with lots of boys, and she "admitted that she preferred their society to that of her mother." Edith had violated the law by more-or-less running away, but the real reason for concern was the possibility that she engaged in illicit sexual activity with the boys at the bowling alley. Police arrested girls like Edith for status offenses to save them from dangers that they brought upon themselves.[67]

Police also arrested girls in order to rescue them from others. During the early twentieth century, reformers and the press often depicted girls as being threatened by "white slavery." According to widespread accounts, girls and young women alone in big cities were at risk of being seduced by unscrupulous men, then being forced to work in brothels, or of simply being kidnapped and sold into prostitution. The *Detroit Free Press*, for example, regularly published accounts of speeches by correctional officials proclaiming that "traffic in white slaves" thrived in Detroit, particularly due to the influence of dance halls and cheap theaters that started girls "on the road to ruin."[68] The so-called white slavery scare can be explained in part as a myth of the time invented to help explain the more liberal sexual standards (and sometime, casual prostitution) that accompanied new opportunities for women. However, white slavery seemed to be very real to early-twentieth-century observers, and the Detroit police vigorously sought to save girls from it. In one week in 1907, for example, they rescued six girls from "resorts" (a euphemism for "brothel"). In particular, upon discovering Bertha Konlezka (age seventeen) and Hattie Jubbe (age sixteen) at a Saginaw establishment, the police took them into custody. The girls, however, may not have wanted to be rescued. They refused to give their correct names, perhaps afraid of being sent home, as they ultimately were. Other girls may have invoked the white slavery scare to defend their own decisions. One "rather pretty blonde" seventeen-year-old, arrested in a rooming house with an adult boyfriend, claimed that she had been seduced and deceived into relocating to Detroit from her Ontario home.[69] The rhetoric of white slavery applied a simple narrative of victimization to a more complicated reality, and most police officers probably knew this at the time. At least in their public statements, police took advantage of the white slavery scare to justify removing girls from situations that, in their eyes, could only do girls harm.

Arrests of girls yield at least one other surprise. Criminal offenses also constituted over one-third of girls' arrests (see table 2.5). In particular, arrests on criminal charges were concentrated among younger girls. Among ten- to fourteen-year-olds, crimes accounted for 51 percent of arrests, in comparison to 29 percent of arrests of fifteen- to seventeen-year-olds. Although the numbers involved are small, these findings suggest an important pattern about how girls were policed. The Detroit police arrested very few girls under age fifteen (perhaps believing that indiscretions by young girls should be handled informally), but when they did, it was more often than not for property offenses. Often, again, police arrested these girls at the request of complainants. Eleven-year-old "flaxen-haired" Mamie Krause was arrested in a department store when Mrs. G. W. Burlinghame caught little Mamie trying to remove money from her handbag. The same store had suffered as many as twenty robberies in the previous three weeks, and when Mamie was finally caught, she was transferred immediately to police custody. Several women subsequently came forward and identified Mamie as a little girl whom they had encountered in the store on days they were robbed. Although police may have hesitated normally to arrest little girls, criminal cases differed in that victims pressed charges and left them little choice.[70]

In sum, property crimes, truancy, and running away were the offenses that constituted "juvenile delinquency" in turn-of-the-century Detroit. Children and youths were rarely the young desperadoes portrayed in the press (and which some pretended to be). Instead, they were teenagers charged with the minor offenses that were a defining characteristic of unsupervised urban youth. Their arrests reflected the general mandate of the Detroit police to preserve public order. Which particular misbehaviors required intervention, however, were determined by a combination of two separate forces. On the one hand, oftentimes complaints by the public and by victims directed police attention to the specific juvenile offenses—particularly against property— and led to arrests. On the other hand, police also used their discretion to arrest juveniles—particularly for status offenses—in order to discipline and protect them in the present and, with luck, to help prevent them from getting into more serious trouble in the future.

## Controlling Public Nuisances

The question of who was the turn-of-the-century delinquent perplexed observers at the time and has remained an often unanswered issue at the center of historical studies of juvenile justice. Delinquency in the past is difficult to measure for at least three reasons. First, its nature was not an objective constant but instead a subjective issue defined by observers. What constituted delinquency could therefore change over time and from observer to observer. Second, like crime, a certain amount of delinquent behavior never came to official attention, so we can never count its full extent. The total amount of delinquency will always remain a dark figure. Third, the best contemporary measures of crime—crimes known to police and victimization surveys—did not exist prior to the 1930s, and even if they did would not have distinguished offenders by age. Thus, for both contemporary and historical purposes, arrests of juveniles provide the most useful substitute measures. Counting arrests tabulates the law enforcement response most immediate to an offense and reveals which children and what behaviors were *treated* as delinquent. Arrests, however, should be used with caution as a measure of delinquency. Each decision to arrest a juvenile was shaped by the larger mission of the police agency, the demands of the public, and the discretion of the officers involved.

Juveniles who were arrested in turn-of-the-century Detroit were very similar to other children in the population. In fact, they exemplify the process and the potential pitfalls of growing up in an urban-industrial environment. Like Detroit's population as a whole, second-generation immigrants constituted the largest share of juvenile arrestees. However, first-generation immigrants and African Americans had markedly higher rates of arrest than did other groups. It seems probable that having migrated themselves somehow increased their likelihood of getting in trouble. Arrests also paralleled patterns of development for children and youths in industrial cities. Younger children were arrested at very low rates, large portions were enrolled in school, and only a few were listed as having an occupation. A transition, however, took place in the mid-teen years. Older youths were arrested at markedly higher rates, most had left school, and many listed occupations. These teens were already well on their way to adulthood. Arrestees were mainly distinguished from their peers by the fact that they were arrested. However, being arrested also suggests that this early transition to adulthood could be hazardous. Many had freedoms approaching those of adults but had the judgment of youth, and therefore found ways to get in trouble.

The behaviors that got juveniles in trouble were very different from those of adults. Overall, police arrested juveniles at rates roughly half those of the total population. Moreover, police rarely arrested juveniles for the public order violations typical of adults. Instead, police much more often arrested juveniles for status offenses in order to discipline and protect them. They arrested boys (particularly younger boys) as truants and "juvenile disorderlies" in order to discourage them from committing more serious offenses in the future; they arrested girls on the same charges in order to rescue them from seduction or moral hazards of their own making. Most often, police arrested juveniles for minor crimes. Although children sometimes portrayed themselves as young desperadoes, the reality of their offenses was much more prosaic. Juveniles mainly stole things impulsively when opportunity arose. The demands of complainants and victims, more so than the severity of the crimes, help explain why these offenses led to arrest. For the public at the turn of the century, and therefore for the police, low-level property crimes represented the main form of delinquency requiring intervention.

# ❧ 3 ❧

# Juvenile Justice before
# Juvenile Court:
## DETROIT, 1890–1908

T wo "street urchins," ages thirteen and eleven, stood trembling before
the desk sergeant at Detroit's central police station, holding (of all
things) a mandolin and a violin. They had been brought to the station for performing outside of saloons for patrons' spare change. As the
sergeant prepared to book them for vagrancy, one of the officers suggested that
they perform in front of the assembled police in exchange for their liberty. As
the boys removed their instruments from their cases, the plainclothes men and
blue-coated officers, "unaccustomed to the sound of music in such a place,"
gathered around them. The boys, reportedly aware that their freedom was on
the line, played "so cleverly" that the tough gray-haired sergeant had to
remove his glasses to wipe the moisture from them. At that point, he sent them
to the truant squad's office, where both their father and the police department's chief truant officer, Lieutenant Charles Breault, were already waiting.
After "exacting a promise that they would never frequent saloons again,"
Breault sent both boys home, frightened but relieved.[1]

In this particular instance, the police were probably having a bit of fun with
the boys. After all, the boys' father and the truant officer were upstairs waiting while they performed. However, this incident also illustrates how the
Detroit police dealt with young offenders at the turn of the twentieth century. On the one hand, the police apprehended the two boys for a trivial offense
and intimidated them at the police station. On the other hand, rather than
proceeding officially, the truant officer talked to them and turned them over
to their father. The police disciplined young offenders informally.

In Detroit, these practices were personified by Breault, the lieutenant in charge of this case. A veteran officer who had been a member of the police department since 1884, Breault had been appointed to lead the truant squad in 1898. During his tenure, the truant squad assumed the duty of investigating all complaints and arrests involving juveniles before prosecution, and determining how to proceed with each case. Breault decided children's cases following a general rule that "if found to be their first offense the parents are notified in order that they may correct them themselves. If found to be old offenders complaints are made in . . . court and they are tried according to law."[2] In essence, Breault and his truant officers sought to provide young offenders with a distinctive form of justice. They disciplined and corrected youths in a manner that reflected their age and vulnerability, and partially shielded them from the moral and physical hazards of courts and jails.

This protective model of justice for juveniles, however, is a far cry from that attributed to the police by social reformers at the turn of the twentieth century. Before the creation of juvenile courts, activists claimed that police used fear, intimidation, and arbitrary arrest to deal with youth. Likewise, critics believed that criminal courts were no better, arraigning delinquent children alongside adults and then placing them all in the same correctional facilities.[3] From this perspective, police and criminal courts were obligated under the law to treat young offenders no differently from adults and, in practice, were all too eager to punish youth harshly for any offenses. The "old way" to handle a young offender, according to these reformers, was to "arrest him and lock him up" because "a thief's a thief no matter if he is a kid."[4]

Was the "old way" in juvenile justice really this punitive? Or did a model akin to Breault's friendly discipline prevail more generally? From an empirical standpoint, the legal treatment of juvenile offenders in the late nineteenth century, before the creation of juvenile court, remains a mystery. Historians have generally accepted without much evidence the reformers' claim that, prior to the 1899 opening of Cook County (Chicago) Juvenile Court, the criminal justice system failed to distinguish juveniles from adults. Examples like Breault (or Edward Talbot in Chicago) were merely exceptions.[5]

The central question yet to be addressed is just how were children and youths treated in police stations and in courtrooms before the juvenile court? According to legal scholar Thomas Bernard, the lack of provisions distinguishing adolescent offenders from adults presented turn-of-the-century courts with a dilemma: they could either sentence juveniles as adults, thereby imposing excessive punishments, or they could let juveniles go with a discharge or suspended sentence, thereby failing to discipline them at all and encouraging them to commit further crimes. In the words of Detroit Judge

Henry Hulbert, courts dealing with children had only the options of employing either "punitive remedies provided for adults"—sending offenders to jail—or "extreme laxity"—discharging boys or not arresting them in the first place.[6]

This dichotomy, however, oversimplifies the options available to the police and the courts, and ignores the existence of officers like Breault. Looking closely again at Detroit at the turn of the century offers insight into how justice for juveniles actually operated in urban America before the creation of juvenile court. In Detroit, most initial decisions about how to discipline offending children and adolescents were made by the police and by low-level criminal courts, just as they were in cases involving adults. However, turn-of-the-century police and courts had more complex interactions with delinquent youth than their contemporary critics or modern scholars have acknowledged. The law may have made little official distinction between juveniles and adults, but the police and courts certainly did. Kids were arrested for very different sets of offenses than adults and experienced the justice system in very different ways. At several key stages in the legal process, Detroit police and courts segregated children and adolescents—at least in part—from the harshest elements of criminal justice. This segregation took three forms. First, the police often steered youth—both boys and girls—through the criminal courts in a manner that was sensitive to their age, and they sought every opportunity to correct juvenile misbehavior themselves. That is (to use a modern term), the police regularly "diverted" certain groups of offenders from further penetration into the justice system. Second, when juveniles were exposed to the same courtrooms and jails as adults, the police and courts found ways to ameliorate the harshness of their experiences. Third, the police and courts offered rudimentary protections and rehabilitative services for young offenders. In short, before the creation of the Wayne County Juvenile Court in 1907, offending youth in Detroit faced the same legal system as did adults, but the police and courts operated a more informal, protective version of justice for juveniles.

## MECHANISMS OF JUSTICE FOR JUVENILES

Detroit was comparatively late to establish its juvenile court, not doing so until 1907. After Chicago opened its pioneering institution in 1899, similar juvenile courts were created in 1902 in Cleveland, Buffalo, Milwaukee, Baltimore, and New York, and in 1903 in nineteen cities, including Pittsburgh, Philadelphia, San Francisco, and Los Angeles. The Denver juvenile court, which had been operating informally under Judge Ben Lindsey since 1899, also gained official legal status in 1903. In Detroit, the process moved more slowly than elsewhere. Child welfare advocates there followed the example of other major cities and advocated a juvenile court as early as 1902 but only convinced the Michigan State Legislature to establish one in 1905. Even then, the state supreme court found the initial plan unconstitutional, and not until late 1907 did Michigan devise a juvenile justice system that could overcome legal challenges.[7]

This is not to say that Detroit's children faced precisely the same system of justice as did adults. The state of Michigan made relatively extensive provisions in the nineteenth century to deal with juvenile delinquency, which in Detroit and elsewhere accompanied the rapid growth of industrial cities. Michigan founded a reform school for boys at Lansing in 1856 "as a place for the reformation of wayward boys by means of suitable and appropriate employment and instruction in some trade, coupled with a good common school education." A similar school was established for girls at Adrian in 1879.[8]

In addition, Michigan was one of the first states to offer probation services, appointing "county agents" to supervise children in trouble with the law beginning in 1873. Courts were to notify these agents (one per county) whenever a criminal complaint was made against a boy under age sixteen and a girl under seventeen. The agents then investigated the case (noting the familial and social circumstances that contributed to delinquency), reported to the judge, and recommended a disposition. In addition, they monitored juveniles on parole from state correctional institutions. Practical problems, however, limited county agents' ability to supervise young offenders. Caseloads in urban districts such as Wayne County, where the Detroit police alone arrested more than one thousand juveniles per year in the 1890s, substantially exceeded the number of children that agents could conscientiously address. Moreover, because county agents were appointed by the governor, the position saw frequent turnover and some political appointees were not interested in working with juveniles. According to one analyst, "the County Agents . . . in no way changed the procedures in the arrest, detention, and trials of juvenile offenders."[9]

Surprisingly, the organizations with the most specific, ground-level duties of handling young miscreants were big-city police. In the late nineteenth century, the Detroit police enforced state compulsory education laws. Under an 1883 regulation, Michigan required all children between the ages of seven and fifteen to attend school at least four months per year. Any child who skipped school, disobeyed teachers, or frequented public places during school hours could be arrested for truancy.[10] In 1883, the police appointed three officers to a full-time "truant squad" to enforce these laws; they added a fourth in 1884 and continued to increase the number in subsequent years.[11] Responding to reports from teachers, school principals, and parents, as well as intervening with children they saw loitering on the streets, truant officers resolved a median of 514 cases per year between 1890 and 1896, and also made over five thousand "unofficial visits" yearly to children and parents.[12]

Police justified their work with children as part of their larger mission to control crime and disorder. Officers in the truant squad shared the widely held belief that "truancy is the germ from which much delinquency grows." By fighting truancy, the police hoped to prevent future crime against persons and property. Sergeant Henry Shomaker stated, "It is from this class of boys that many of our criminals will come unless they are properly cared for and looked after when young." As a remedy, he argued that "proper control" during school hours would prevent many boys "from becoming criminals who otherwise would drift into crime and eventually find lodgment in our criminal institutions."[13]

Parents and children, however, occasionally resisted police intervention. Working-class and immigrant parents, often ambivalent about compulsory education, sometimes supported their children's truancies. Some parents saw greater economic advantage in sending their children to work, while others just had little time, inclination, or ability to restrain their offspring. Both children and parents typically resented whoever tried to enforce school attendance laws, mocking truant officers as "hooky cops." Sometimes parents were openly hostile. In one instance when a truant officer attempted to apprehend a fourteen-year-old boy at his home and the boy's mother answered the door, she attacked the officer with a stove poker, hitting him several times in the shoulders before fleeing (the boy avoided arrest for the moment, but a warrant was issued for both him and his mother).[14]

Arrest—for both the general patrolmen and the specialized truant officers—proved to be the most visible lever to manipulate juvenile offenders. Arrest practices reveal not only how delinquency was defined, but what was done about it by police and by courts. Returning to the same sample of juveniles arrested by the Detroit police between 1890 and 1906 employed in chapter 2 provides a basis for analyzing just how children and youth were treated in police stations and in courtrooms before the juvenile court. These arrest data also reveal the outcomes of individual complaints, and thus disclose how justice for juveniles operated at the lowest level.[15] Was there really a stark dichotomy between punitive remedies and extreme laxity, as Judge Hulbert argued, or was something more complicated going on, as Breault's example implies?

A superficial examination of the dispositions of boys' arrests seems to support the position of reformers like Judge Hulbert that courts had few options for dealing with young offenders other than to send them home or to send them to jail. On the one hand, 37 percent of eight- to sixteen-year-old boys arrested between 1890 and 1906 were discharged for one reason or another.[16] In addition, 27 percent of boys arrested were found guilty but given suspended sentences. Thus, 64 percent of boys arrested never penetrated past the courts into the correctional system.[17] On the other hand, 19 percent of boys who were arrested were found guilty and, like adults, were given the choice of paying a fine or serving time in the Detroit House of Corrections.[18] Only 9 percent were sentenced to juvenile reform schools and the remaining 8 percent faced a variety of other dispositions.

The situation was almost as stark for girls. On the one hand, 60 percent of ten- to seventeen-year-old girls arrested between 1890 and 1906 were sent home with either a discharge or a suspended sentence, while on the other hand 12 percent were found guilty and, like adults, were given the choice of paying a fine or serving time in the Detroit House of Corrections.[19] The police and courts were somewhat more aggressive in applying juvenile-specific sentences to girls than to boys, however, sending almost 14 percent to the reform school at Adrian and another 11 percent to private correctional facilities such as the Catholic Church–operated House of the Good Shepherd.[20]

Summarizing the outcomes of arrests does not tell the whole story, however. Criminal justice systems of the late nineteenth century were not undifferentiated wholes, but were instead comprised of distinct levels where different officials were in charge and different outcomes possible. As stated earlier, institutions of criminal justice resembled a layered cake in which a bottom layer of police supported upper layers of courts, and together they made a whole dessert. Following arrest, defendants progressed from one layer to another, a process that shaped the outcome of a case. This was true for juveniles as well as adults.

Where in the system cases were decided mattered in their outcomes. In Detroit, dispositions were made at three different levels and, at each level, a different set of options was available and a different set of concerns applied. At the first level, the police themselves decided how to proceed with cases. While they could not impose formal penalties such as fines or jail terms, they could discharge some prisoners or refer them to other law enforcement or charitable agencies. The police transferred most routine cases to a second level, the police courts, in which elected justices (not police officers) presided. The police courts decided all misdemeanor cases and, therefore, a large majority of all arrests. They could impose fines of up to $100 or jail terms of up to three months; with the approval of a higher court, they could also commit juveniles to reform schools. Procedure in the police courts typically followed a routine pattern of an arrest, a brief detention, a courtroom hearing, possibly jail, and, finally, release—a pattern of quick and dirty adjudication that Friedman and Percival call "rough justice." Cases only proceeded to the third level, the recorder's court, for formal trial and disposition when they involved felonies or appeals of police court decisions.[21]

Thus, examining how justice for juveniles operated at each level reveals a process far more complex and nuanced than is apparent from the aggregate outcomes of arrests. Juvenile justice before juvenile court should be understood not just in terms of outcomes but also in terms of how each mechanism of justice handled young offenders.

## DIVERSION, PROTECTIVE JUSTICE, AND ROUGH JUSTICE, 1890–96

Even before the juvenile court movement, the police and criminal courts found ways to treat young offenders differently than adults. These procedures changed over time, however, as legal institutions evolved from applying criminal justice mechanisms in juvenile cases to experimenting with new and separate mechanisms for kids. To track that evolution, it is useful to consider the turn-of-the-century era in two separate periods: the years between 1890 and 1896 and the years between 1900 and 1906.

In the 1890s, the Detroit police and courts segregated at least some young offenders from the roughest elements of turn-of-the-century justice. Particularly at the lower levels of the court system—the levels encountered immediately after arrest—criminal justice agencies treated many boys in a manner that they deemed appropriate to their age and, to an extent, protected them from dangers inherent in courts and jails. For many delinquent youth, the Detroit police and courts operated a rudimentary form of "diversion"—a modern tactic of deciding juvenile cases without court involvement by referring offenders to nonpunitive social or therapeutic agencies.[22]

The Detroit police exercised a hidden, sheltering decision-making authority over every juvenile arrest. Between 1890 and 1896, police disposed of a substantial number of boys' cases—24 percent—at the station house without ever transferring them to the courts, instead attributing these dispositions to the superintendent of police (see table 3.1). By contrast, according to aggregate data published by the Detroit Police Department, the police disposed of only 9 percent of total arrests on their own in the same period.[23] Moreover, when the police decided juvenile cases, they did so almost immediately. A median of just one day separated arrest and final disposition, so the police would have typically decided a child's case on the same day as arrest or after a single night in jail. As a rule, the police dispensed justice to juveniles on their own initiative mainly on the basis of the charge against them. While the police rarely decided arrests for public order offenses on their own, they did determine the disposition in the majority of status offense cases (58 percent) and in an important minority of criminal cases (19 percent). In so doing, they used arrest as an elaborate reprimand, seeking to use brief visits to the police station house to instill a vague discipline in young offenders, or at least deter them from further offenses.

Comparing how the police disposed of juvenile arrests by the offense charged reveals why youths often did not penetrate far into the judicial system. When the police arrested boys for status offenses, they preferred to decide these cases at their own discretion, referring status offenders to the police courts or recorder's court only if they were "juvenile disorderly persons" or had been arrested many times before. Instead, they mainly directed unsupervised and runaway boys back home. Of the juvenile male status cases that the police decided, they discharged 54 percent, the majority to parents or relatives.[24] A warning or reprimand from the cops, this practice implied, might help guardians manage their wayward sons better in the future. The police also sent a handful to authorities in other cities, putting at least one on "a boat for Cleveland."[25]

When the police did not send status offenders home, they enrolled them in an ungraded public school (41 percent).[26] This "truant school," operated by the Detroit Board of Education, represented the only treatment-oriented option available to police without court involvement. Referrals to it were reserved for younger and more amenable boys; all but one of the boys assigned to it were between ages eight and fourteen. The purpose of the school was to segregate "the bad boy problem" from the "normal school population," while at the same time offering the most difficult children basic academic instruction. The truant school did not maintain twenty-four-hour custody of boys. It did, however, require daily attendance and the two public school teachers who operated it supervised their boys very closely.[27] In addition, police officers visited and observed truant boys outside of school hours. Hence, assignment to the truant school marked the boys whom police officers would monitor closely in the future. The police saw the truant school as a mechanism to implement their general notion that fighting truancy in the present would help prevent crime in the future. According to Sergeant Henry Shomaker, "as the school increases in numbers, juvenile crime decreases. This fact establishes the usefulness of the school, as it prevents boys from becoming criminals, and at the same time educates them."[28]

While the police made the final decisions in a smaller share of boys' arrests

**Table 3.1**

Detroit Agencies Disposing of Boys' Arrests, 1890–96, by Offense

| Agency | Public Order Offense | Criminal Offense | Status Offense | TOTAL |
|---|---|---|---|---|
| Superintendent of Police | 9% | 19% | 58% | 24% |
| Police Court | 89% | 75% | 25% | 69% |
| Recorder's Court | 2% | 6% | 17% | 7% |
| TOTAL | 100% | 100% | 100% | 100% |
| | $N = 56$ | $N = 246$ | $N = 64$ | $N = 366$ |

Source: Detroit juvenile arrest database

for criminal offenses (about one in five), these cases reveal another key factor shaping dispositions. As a rule, police discharged boys arrested for crimes against property or persons when complainants refused to prosecute. Complaints generally initiated police action in the first place, but without victims' continued cooperation, the police could not pursue a case in the courts and had little incentive to do so. Thus, when police decided boys' criminal arrests, they discharged fully 91 percent without further legal action.[29] Victims apparently regarded some offenses as important enough to report, but not important enough to pursue. Some complainants settled for the return of stolen property. Mrs. Jennice McMillan, for example, reported that several young boys had unlocked the front door of her store and taken a box of cigars and tobacco. The police recovered the items and arrested three of the boys, but Mrs. McMillan chose not to pursue the case once she reclaimed her goods. Similarly, parents often refused to press charges against children who stole from them. Anthony Berlik, for example, informed the police in 1896 that his son Frank, age twelve or thirteen, had stolen $25 from his house, but he declined to prosecute after police officers caught the boy and recovered most of the money.[30] While most crime victims filed charges, some expected an encounter with the police to frighten the offenders enough to mend their ways and not require further immersion in the justice system. Having police confront and threaten a child was, in their view, punishment enough to discourage future offenses.

When police dealt with young female offenders in the 1890s, they acted on their own initiative even more regularly, deciding 44 percent of girls' cases at the station house (see table 3.2). As with boys, the police decided these cases

quickly; a median of only one day separated arrest and disposition. The decision not to prosecute seems to have been based upon the offenses girls were
accused of, not their ages. The police decided two out of every three girls'
arrests for status offenses, but far fewer when girls were accused of committing crimes or violating public order. Although the police rarely disposed of
cases involving girls accused of crimes, when they did, they resolved them in
the same fashion as those involving boys, discharging fourteen of sixteen
because victims decided not to prosecute. In 1897, for example, C. W.
Sweenie reported that two "little girls" between ages ten and fifteen had come
into his store and stolen six toys worth 60 cents. The police found the girls,
but Sweenie opted not to proceed with the case.[31]

When police decided girls' arrests for status offenses, they followed a different pattern than with boys because the implications of girls' misbehaviors
differed. In the late-nineteenth-century city, young women accused of being
truants, runaways, or disorderly persons were seen to have, at a minimum,
made themselves vulnerable to moral or sexual corruption. More often than
not (in 58 percent of cases), police responded by discharging girls following
arrests and, as they almost invariably noted, taking them home to their parents or relatives.[32] The police generally considered families, rather than the
courts, suited best to discipline delinquent girls.

Quite often, however, police referred girls to private custodial agencies—
Catholic or Protestant homes such as the House of the Good Shepherd or the
Open Door Society (36 percent).[33] These institutions typically sheltered girls
who were pregnant or suspected of immoral conduct. Referrals to them
required the eventual approval of a police court, the recorder's court, or a state
judge, but police made the initial decision to commit upon parents' requests.
In contrast to the short-term dispositions otherwise available to the police,
girls could be committed to the House of the Good Shepherd for a term
equal to what they might spend at a public reform school.[34] Committals to
these custodial institutions represented a much more punitive outcome of
police intervention in girls' cases than did referrals to the noncustodial truant
school in boys' cases. Arrests for truancy or other status offenses thus allowed
the police to exercise considerable control over girls they perceived as placing
themselves at risk.

These cases reveal the particular importance that turn-of-the-twentieth-
century police ascribed to protecting girls and young women. Like many
contemporaries—social reformers, juvenile court advocates, oftentimes
parents—their ideals of domestic sexually innocent young women were challenged by the realities of urban America. They were concerned that the new
employment, commercial amusements, and independence that girls enjoyed

**Table 3.2**

Detroit Agencies Disposing of Girls' Arrests, 1890–96, by Offense

| Agency | Public Order Offense | Criminal Offense | Status Offense | TOTAL |
|---|---|---|---|---|
| Superintendent of Police | 24% | 25% | 67% | 44% |
| Police Court | 73% | 70% | 33% | 54% |
| Recorder's Court | 3% | 5% | 0% | 2% |
| TOTAL | 100% | 100% | 100% | 100% |
| | $N = 37$ | $N = 64$ | $N = 82$ | $N = 183$ |

Source: Detroit juvenile arrest database.

increasingly could also contribute to moral corruption.[35] For once, the perspective of male police officers aligned with that of predominantly female reformers. In trying to protect girls, however, the Detroit police sometimes overstepped their bounds. For example, in 1907, the widely publicized kidnapping of twenty-year-old Helen Ferenczy was resolved after a twelve-hour disappearance when truant squad officers admitted that *they* were responsible. Acting on orders from Lt. Breault, two officers had apprehended Helen and taken her to the House of the Good Shepherd. Helen had moved out of her father's home and shared an apartment with a girlfriend. The father, together with his parish priest, visited Breault and told him that Helen was "under-age" and "leading a wayward life." Breault admitted that the truant squad received "scores of cases every month" in which parents or other family members asked them to "take girls to various institutions in the city," and apparently they complied routinely. The Ferenczy case came to light because she was over the age at which the truant squad had any authority and because her half-day disappearance had been noted in the press (although the newspaper coverage does not indicate when or even if she was released). This case was unique, but it demonstrated that the standard practice of the truant squad was to arrest young women for their own protection at the insistence of their families and to turn them over to private correctional facilities with little opportunity to defend themselves. And while the Ferenczy case generated a brief flurry of public outrage that the police disregarded girls' rights, it does not seem to have impacted their standard operating procedures.[36]

The Detroit police implicitly understood their intervention into children's cases and lives as a protective form of justice. By adjudicating a substantial share of boys' and girls' arrests themselves, via discharge, via referrals to the truant school, and via placement in private correctional facilities such as the

House of the Good Shepherd, they sought to safeguard young offenders—to divert them from penetrating far into the legal system. Rather than automatically sending those whom they arrested to the courts and jails, they instead released them to parents or agencies they regarded as capable of delivering education and guidance. For these delinquent youth, the Detroit police preempted the courts and operated their own system of de facto juvenile justice.

This protective justice was not for all juveniles, however. The police directed the majority of boys (69 percent; see table 3.1) and girls (54 percent; see table 3.2) whom they arrested to the second level of the justice system—the police courts. These courts processed the great majority of juveniles accused of public order offenses (89 percent of boys, 80 percent of girls) and of crimes (75 percent of boys, 76 percent of girls). In the police courts, children could expect "rough justice" intended for more mature offenders. Boys were confined before trial in the city jail together with adults; only girls and very young children enjoyed separate detention facilities. Moreover, hearings took place in public courtrooms that did not separate children from older offenders.[37] The police courts decided juvenile cases quickly (although not as quickly as did the police); the median time from arrest to disposition was four days for both boys and girls. While the rapid pace of dispositions prevented prolonged detention in jail prior to a court hearing, it also limited opportunities for a county agent to investigate a child's case and propose appropriate treatment.

How rough this "rough justice" was, however, varied by age, particularly for boys. While the police courts acknowledged few official distinctions among offenders, their dispositions were shaped largely by how old boys were. Police courts usually found juveniles guilty of something. They discharged only 26 percent of boys arrested.[38] Boys between eight and fourteen, however, were discharged more often than boys ages fifteen and sixteen (29 percent versus 22).[39] Age distinctions were more apparent in suspended sentences. The police courts granted suspended sentences to 45 percent of eight- to fourteen-year-olds but only 31 percent of fifteen- to sixteen-year-olds.[40] By suspending a juvenile's sentence, the courts established a legal record against him and created leverage to coerce proper behavior from him in the future. When young Raymond Moore was convicted of stealing lead pipe from an unoccupied home, the court released him with a suspended sentence "in view of [his] extreme youth" in spite of the fact that his father and his "colored" lawyer continually disrupted the proceedings. The judge left him with a warning that, "It will go hard for you . . . if I hear any further complaints about you!"[41] For the moment, though, the court did not penalize him or boys like him beyond the time they had already spent in jail. Like the diversionary tactics of the police, discharges and suspended sentences functioned as mechanisms for the police courts to scare, warn, and release boys, particularly younger ones. A few days of jail time, this practice suggests, might deter them from future delinquencies.

Both the police and the courts seemed to embrace a model of relatively immediate discipline and deterrence. When the police brought two boys into Judge James Phelan's court for "hitching" on streetcars, he declared that imposing a fine "would mean . . . distress to the breadwinners of your families." Instead, he declared "I want you mothers to go out with the officer and the boys. The officer will show you where there are two nice straps, and I want you both to give your boys three lashes each." The mothers resisted initially, but complied in the end, and each boy reportedly "promised to be good."[42] In the eyes of police, some courts, and many working-class parents, immediate corporal punishment was a far more effective means of correcting young offenders than were more official legal responses. Of course, this model of immediate discipline and deterrence only went so far. When fourteen-year-old James Kotwalt was arrested after being seen "climbing out of a . . . box car with a bag of plunder which he could hardly carry" just a month after being given a suspended sentence for a similar offense, the police apparently decided that he had used up his opportunities, declared that he was "an incorrigible," and returned him to the courts.[43]

The police courts largely reserved incarceration for older boys. They gave 24 percent of boys the choice of paying a fine or serving time at the House of Correction, together with offenders of all ages.[44] Again, however, this practice varied significantly by age. The police courts sentenced 42 percent of fifteen- and sixteen-year-olds to fines or the House of Correction, but only 11 percent of eight- to fourteen-year-olds. While boys as young as ten received fines and jail sentences, they were the exceptions—the "young desperadoes" envisioned by the popular press. Typically, youths sent to jail had committed crimes against property or persons, or offenses against public order. If they or their parents could not pay the fine (typically $5) they were sent to jail, usually for thirty days.[45]

At the House of Correction, boys experienced a prison-industry regimen designed to reform inmates through hard labor while also paying for itself. The boys worked alongside adult prisoners who had been committed for terms as long as two years. According to Superintendent John L. McDonnell, the boys sentenced to the House of Correction were worse than the men. "They are better versed in criminal knowledge than most of the men we get," he asserted. "The judges send the boys here only as a last resort. Their parents can't control them, they defy the policemen, they have no respect for court warnings, and they are sent here. They are the hardest prisoners we have to handle."[46]

In spite of McDonnell's rhetoric, boys at the House of Correction appear to have been treated less harshly than adults. Their average sentence of roughly a month was much shorter than the three months typical of the institution as a whole. In addition, boys were separated from other prisoners during the workday and were offered academic classes at night.[47] Committal to the House of Correction represented a short, sharp punishment intended to correct the worst juvenile offenders, but even that sentence provided youths some protections based upon their age.

While the police courts were known for "rough justice," they also sought to exercise a "protective justice" over a select group of juvenile offenders by committing them to the Michigan Industrial School for Boys at Lansing. Ten percent of the boys who appeared in police court were sentenced to the Industrial School. Lansing accepted very few boys older than age fifteen, so while the police courts sent 14 percent of eight- to fourteen-year-old boys to the Industrial School, they only committed 4 percent of fifteen- to sixteen-year-olds. The professed goal of the Industrial School was to help boys, not to punish them. Rather than delivering short, sharp punishment as did the House of Correction, a commitment to Lansing placed young offenders in long-term—and ostensibly rehabilitative—custody. In the 1890s, boys served an average term of between eighteen and twenty-four months; legally, they could be required to remain until their seventeenth birthdays. In theory, a lengthy sentence allowed the school to teach the boys to live an "honest life" by providing a rudimentary education and training in manual skills.[48]

The police courts were much more likely to send "habitual truants" to Lansing than criminal offenders. They committed 69 percent of status offenders to the Industrial School, in contrast to only 6 percent of boys accused of other offenses.[49] These were boys like Carl B., whose school principal testified that he continually skipped school, and John B., who had already been arrested three times for running away from home. In addition, boys were sometimes sentenced to reform school in order to protect them from abuse. For example, one African American boy was arrested and called before the police court in 1902 when his father accused him of being a juvenile disorderly person, "habitually truant from home." Upon examination, the boy explained that he ran away because his parents "beat him so" and the court found marks on his body to confirm his story. The justice committed him to Lansing as a "juvenile disorderly," not to punish him but to separate him from his father.[50]

The recorder's court, the highest local court in Detroit, handled only a few boys, and it too exercised "protective justice." Only 7 percent of boys who were arrested in Detroit in the 1890s reached the recorder's court (table 3.1). In several ways, juvenile proceedings there differed substantially from other courts. Boys' cases progressed slowly, averaging thirty-one days from arrest to disposition. Although recorder's court heard an occasional juvenile felony case, more notable was that 17 percent of status offense cases reached recorder's court for final disposition. These cases reached recorder's court not because they involved serious crimes—status offenses were certainly the least of the behaviors that it dealt with—but because they were on appeal. After James Roberts, for example, was convicted in the police courts of being a "truant and all around bad boy," his mother appealed his five-year sentence to Lansing to the recorder's court. There, she argued that her son was no worse than many other boys, asserting "if you are going to send all the boy cigarette fiends up you will have to send a lot of them."[51] The recorder's court, however, rarely overturned lower court decisions, so for boys, the result of a hearing there was frequently institutionalization. Twenty-six percent of boys—and 45 percent of boy status offenders—were committed to Lansing (as was James in the end).[52] Thus, a main function of recorder's court in juvenile cases was to confirm rulings of lower courts by authorizing commitments to reform school.

Overall, the Detroit courts imposed a very different mix of punishments on younger boys, who were disproportionately status offenders, than they did on older boys, who more often committed crimes. Rather than sending the younger boys to the House of Correction to mingle with adult criminals, as they often did with older teenagers, the courts sent younger, more vulnerable youth to Lansing for long-term custodial training. Ironically, efforts to protect young offenders resulted in the lengthiest incarcerations. The isolation and duration of a commitment to Lansing surely marked it in most boys' minds as a much more severe type of punishment than a short-term jolt in jail.

Girls in court faced a similar mix of rough and protective versions of justice. Three of every five did not face any punishment at all, being either discharged (32 percent) or having their sentence suspended (28 percent).[53] In contrast, almost one-fourth faced a fine or jail (24 percent), and one in seven was sentenced to the reform school at Adrian (16 percent). As with boys, sentences varied with age; the courts were somewhat more likely to sentence older girls to fines or jail and more likely to send younger girls to reform school. More fundamentally, however, the courts decided girls' dispositions based on the offense accused. Girls in court for crimes against property or persons were usually discharged or had their sentences suspended.[54] The petty thefts and scuffles that brought teenage girls into court were treated less seriously than any other offense. In contrast, the courts gave a small majority (54 percent) of girls accused of violating public order the choice of a fine or jail.[55] These charges—drunkenness or disorderly conduct, perhaps sometimes euphemisms for prostitution—warranted the most adult penalties. Finally, the courts sent more than half (52 percent) of the girls accused of status offenses to Adrian. In the eyes of the courts, for a girl to be a "juvenile disorderly" implied a potential for moral ruin that only long-term institutionalization could correct. For example, when Judge Phelan convicted two sixteen-year-olds and sentenced them to Adrian until age twenty-one, he further lectured their parents: "If you can't keep your children from going to places where they shouldn't go, you might better cut off their legs. It would be far better for them to be virtuous cripples than the certain kind of women they are likely to become if they continue in the way they are going."[56] For girls, more so than for boys, the courts understood some offenses as an indication of their moral trajectory, and if deemed necessary, exercised legal authority to redirect them.

In sum, the justice system in 1890s Detroit made little official distinction between juveniles and adults. Arrests exposed juveniles to institutions of criminal justice that, as standard procedure, detained many adolescents alongside adults as they awaited hearings, paraded them through public courtrooms, and not infrequently imposed adult-scale jail sentences. In practice, however, police and court procedures differentiated substantially between children and adults. In a crude way, the police and courts sought to impose appropriate treatment, either punitive or rehabilitative, on individual young offenders. They found ways to divert many delinquents from the criminal justice system, rapidly removing children from jails and sending them home to their parents or to schools specifically intended to discipline them. Furthermore, the courts factored into their decisions youths' ages and the relatively minor nature of their offenses, again diverting many younger boys and girls from formal corrections and softening the experience of "rough justice" for those sentenced to the House of Correction. Ironically, it was when the courts sought most self-consciously to rescue and rehabilitate youths that the system became most punitive, institutionalizing comparatively innocent and younger boys and girls for long periods in the state reform school. Nonetheless, the point remains that the police and courts in Detroit attempted to ameliorate children's encounters with the criminal justice system and to divert them into a less punitive, unofficial system of juvenile justice.

# Toward the Founding of Juvenile Court, 1900–1906

Although Detroit was slow to establish a juvenile court, its police and courts nonetheless experimented with new methods of distinguishing more systematically between juvenile and adult offenders in the years between 1900 and 1906. Beginning around 1900, the police and courts in Detroit initiated new practices for dealing with young offenders akin to those imposed in other cities by juvenile courts, but without a juvenile court law. The police took steps to segregate young offenders from the criminal justice system more consistently than in the past. Their treatment of youths also became increasingly graded by age. Likewise, criminal courts began to separate young offenders from adults (and even from youths in their mid-teens) and to offer them specialized, age-appropriate treatment. The creation of juvenile court in 1907 mainly made official the growing separation of juvenile offenders from the criminal justice system.

At the turn of the century, the police department's truant squad assumed expanded duties, seeking to intervene with potential offenders in order to prevent delinquency and to keep them out of the courts entirely. In essence, the unofficial practice of diversion became part of the truant squad's official duties. Charles Breault's 1898 promotion to lead the truant squad signaled the extension of its role. While his predecessor had described his job narrowly in terms of corralling young offenders, Breault argued expansively that the purpose of truancy work was both to educate children and to prevent crime. "If the [compulsory education] law is strictly enforced it would save children from truancy and associating with criminals and produce a great educational improvement and save the city and state a large expense in prosecuting criminals," he stated in his first annual report. Not surprisingly, the truant squad's school-related work increased dramatically. Between 1900 and 1906, the number of official warnings it issued to children found not attending school increased from 310 to 947, investigations of complaints from school officials increased from 997 to 4,497, and visits to parents rose from 7,830 to 13,567.[57]

Under Breault, the truant squad also assumed the new duty of determining the initial dispositions of all juvenile offenders. In 1898, the police department directed that all complaints involving persons age sixteen or under should be "referred to the Truant Office to be investigated before prosecution." The truant squad would then decide how to proceed with each and every case prior to official arrest. As a result, the truant squad became a filter through which young offenders passed upon their entrance into the justice system. On the one hand, this arrangement allowed the truant squad to develop familiarity and even ongoing relationships with some repeat offenders. When, for example, a beat officer brought three boys into the central station carrying "a big gunny sack filled with heavy brass casings," Breault recognized them immediately and greeted them with a friendly inquiry, "And what have you been doing now?" The response—"Aw, we was just swimmin' an' we found some brass by an old house and the cop pinched us"—apparently did not convince Breault of their innocence. He had the boys arrested, explaining to a reporter that they were regular visitors to the police station who would steal almost anything they could move. In contrast, these nominal investigations also gave Breault and his men the authority to release first-time offenders when they believed it appropriate. The two young musicians mentioned earlier, arrested for playing their instruments outside of saloons, might have faced a court hearing in addition to police chastisement without the truant squad to intervene.[58] Much as individual police officers in Detroit had traditionally done, the truant squad continued to dispose of juvenile offenders using warnings and reprimands under the guise of friendly investigation. Now, however, the truant squad had official status as a special juvenile detachment; more importantly, its officers did not necessarily have to make an arrest. Thus, the truant squad carried out a new mandate to keep juveniles (first offenders, at least) away from jails and criminal courts.

The new methods that the Detroit police began using to handle delinquency were reflected in a decline in juvenile arrest rates. After making approximately 30 arrests per 1,000 boys ages eight to sixteen between 1890 and 1896, the police arrested only 25 per 1,000 between 1900 and 1906.[59] The decline in juvenile arrest rates was relatively consistent with arrests in the city as a whole; the arrest rate for all males in Detroit dropped sharply from the 1890s to the 1900s.[60] That said, the policy of the truant squad to release rather than to arrest younger and first-time offenders contributed substantially to boys' declining arrest rate. The rate of arrest for boys ages fifteen and sixteen actually rose from 57 to 61 per 1,000, but the arrest rate for boys between eight and fourteen dropped from 23 to 15 per 1,000. Boys' arrest rates declined virtually across the board, regardless of nativity. The arrest rate for native white boys with native white parents dropped from 24 per 1,000 in the 1890s to 19 in the 1900s; for first-generation immigrants, it dropped from 47 to 35 per 1,000; for African Americans, it dropped from 134 to 102 per 1,000. Only for second-generation immigrants did the arrest rate remain flat at about 22 per 1,000.

Girls and young women experienced a similar pattern of declining arrest rates, albeit involving smaller numbers. After making approximately 3.4

arrests per 1,000 girls ages ten to seventeen between 1890 and 1896, the police arrested only 2.0 per 1,000 between 1900 and 1906.[61] As with boys, the sharpest decline took place among the youngest age groups. The rate of arrest for girls between ages fifteen and seventeen dropped from 5.7 to 4.2 per 1,000, while the arrest rate for girls between ten and fourteen dropped from 1.9 to 0.6 per 1,000.[62]

The sharp plunge in arrests for both younger boys and younger girls accounted for the overall decline in juvenile arrests. The drop in arrests of younger children resulted, in turn, from the truant squad's policy of investigating and releasing first-time offenders. According to the Detroit Police Department's official data, between 1905 and 1907 only 67 percent of juveniles accused of crimes were arrested, and of these only 47 percent went to trial. In the end, therefore, less than one-third (31 percent) of youths accused of offenses were ever prosecuted.[63] The truant squad increasingly disciplined younger offenders without making arrests or taking official action. In short, it expanded the use of diversion.

Procedures for handling juveniles after arrest also changed following the turn of the century. While the Michigan legislature did not immediately embrace the movement to establish juvenile courts, in 1901 it did provide that children under age sixteen should not be detained in the same jail cells or tried in the same courts as adults. In response, the police courts in Detroit set aside one morning a week—first Monday, later Saturday—to hear juvenile cases exclusively. This procedure did not fully segregate young offenders from adults—according to one critic, it was "practically impossible to keep [children] entirely apart from the contaminating influence of the police court"—but it did represent another layer of protection for adolescents in the adult criminal courts.[64]

After the turn of the century, Detroit's courts continued to offer juveniles both "rough justice" and "protective justice." Overall, the dispositions of boys' cases by the police court and the recorder's court between 1900 and 1906 remained very similar to the patterns between 1890 and 1896.[65] As had been the case earlier, the courts discharged about one-quarter of the boys who appeared before them. They also offered the option of paying a fine or serving a sentence at the House of Correction for about one quarter and sent about one in ten to the reform school at Lansing.[66] In committing juveniles to correctional institutions, the courts continued to draw a sharp line between older and younger adolescents. On one hand, between 1900 and 1906, they gave 40 percent of boys ages fifteen and sixteen the choice of a fine or a jail term, in comparison to 10 percent of boys between ages eight and fourteen. On the other hand, they committed 20 percent of the younger group to Lansing, in contrast to 2 percent of the older.

By contrast, the dispositions of girls' cases by the police court and the recorder's court between 1900 and 1906 shifted toward favoring reform school. The courts continued to discharge roughly three girls of every ten, and to suspend sentences on another one in four. [67] Committals to reform school increased substantially, however, almost doubling from 15 percent of girls in court in the 1890s to 28 percent in the 1900s. Institutionalization of girls between ages fifteen and seventeen increased slightly—from 16 percent in the 1890s to 23 percent in the 1900s—but the bulk of the change was accounted for by institutionalization of girls between ten and fourteen, which increased from 14 percent to 48 percent in the 1900s. [68] The police arrested fewer girls in the 1900s and fewer reached the courts, but when they did the courts apparently determined that the situation called for institutionalization, a solution intended to be rehabilitative but that was in practice highly restrictive.

Most surprisingly, however, the courts in the early 1900s began to experiment with new sentences that reflected an entirely different penal strategy. The share of boys' arrests resulting in suspended sentences dipped from 38 percent in the 1890s to 30 percent in the 1900s as a new disposition—probation—became an option. Probation accounted for 4 percent of sentences in the latter period. The change was more apparent among younger boys. The portion of eight- to fourteen-year-olds granted suspended sentences dropped from 43 to 33 percent. [69] Instead, the courts placed 9 percent of this age group on probation, letting them return to their communities under court supervision. [70]

Judge William F. Connolly of the recorder's court led the move toward using probation. In 1905, he began to defer sentences on young, first-time offenders, placing them at liberty with the proviso that they report once a week to J. Morris Fisher, the superintendent of a private home for boys. Each boy was made to understand that "if at any time his conduct is unsatisfactory, . . . he will be rearrested and sentenced to the statutory limit of imprisonment." All but one succeeded in an initial cohort of twenty-seven boys, according to Judge Connolly, showing "signs of reformation and a desire to become useful citizens." [71] The *Detroit Free Press* praised Fisher and Connolly for saving many Detroit youngsters from lives of crime. According to one account, when Connolly released one seventeen-year-old after the youth had stayed out of trouble for one probationary year and found a steady job, the boy declared, "Judge, I want to thank you for what you have done for me." [72] In short, Detroit's criminal courts informally emulated the practice of juvenile courts elsewhere, placing the youngest and most amenable offenders under probationary supervision rather than incarcerating them or discharging them, and at least seeking to provide direction that would help them grow into better adults. Connolly certainly advocated an official juvenile court; he believed "a juvenile court by statute would be an improvement on this improvised probation system, and would provide more efficient machinery for keeping track of the offenders who are at large on parole." Nonetheless, his court already performed the same function as a juvenile court.[73]

One of the main platforms of the Progressive Era child-saving movement was to protect juveniles from exposure to the hazards found in criminal courts and jails. In some ways, the police and courts in Detroit had already achieved that goal before the creation of juvenile court in 1907. Because the truant squad was authorized to investigate all juvenile offenses and to filter juveniles out of the criminal justice system prior to arrest, the arrest rates for boys and girls below age fifteen dropped dramatically after the turn of the century. In addition, the criminal courts segregated younger boys from older offenders, increasingly imposed theoretically protective dispositions on girls, and, most notably, began to experiment with noncustodial dispositions aimed at rehabilitation. The police and the courts had begun to develop a more explicit form of diversion and a more truly protective justice for children. Even before the creation of juvenile court, several of the central goals of progressive child savers had already been incorporated into Detroit's system of criminal justice.

## Unofficial Juvenile Justice

In turn-of-the-century Detroit, the police and the courts demonstrated something of split personality in dealing with adolescent offenders. On the one hand, these agencies treated teenage and preteen boys harshly. The police were—as their critics charged—willing and eager to round up kids, arrest them, and detain them alongside adults. In addition, the courts could place boys found guilty of minor violations in jail or in long-term correctional institutions. On the other hand, the police and courts also created ad hoc methods of separating juveniles from the harshest elements of criminal justice. The police regularly warned boys and released them to their parents, in effect diverting them from official contact with the courts, while the courts themselves disproportionately suspended sentences against younger boys. Even the offenders sentenced to the Detroit House of Correction served shorter terms than adults and enjoyed special treatment. Furthermore, efforts by the police and courts to segregate young offenders from the formal mechanisms of criminal justice expanded after 1898. The police department's truant squad increasingly filtered delinquent boys out of the system prior to arrest and the courts introduced an unofficial system of probation. The 1907 addition of a juvenile court to these arrangements represented less a major structural innovation than a rationalization and expansion of existing experimental practices.

In contrast to reformers' assertions, the "old way" of handling young offenders before the creation of juvenile court was not merely a dichotomous choice between severe punishment and excessive leniency. Instead, the police and criminal courts employed complex practices to discipline youth in a manner that they considered roughly appropriate to their age and offense. To a large extent, the informal protective model of justice exemplified by Charles Breault prevailed in turn-of-the-century Detroit. This model would begin to change, however, with the 1907 creation of juvenile court.

# ⇥4↦

# The Widening Net of
# Juvenile Justice, 1908–19

uring his tenure as commissioner of the Detroit Metropolitan
Police between 1916 and 1918, James R. Couzens sought to
remake his department. To the public, he was perhaps best known
for demanding that his police vigorously enforce vice laws. Couzens's real
contributions lay elsewhere, though. On the one hand, he reorganized the
Detroit police operationally, seeking to apply administrative efficiency to
police work. On the other hand, he also urged the Detroit police to engage
in social welfare work with children. In 1917, Couzens asserted that his
reforms had produced a revolutionary change in public attitudes toward the
police, particularly in the minds of the young. He claimed "there exists no
more in the heart of the child the fear of the big blue-coated policemen. They
have learned by the kindly care he gives them that he is not a frightful mon-
ster waiting to catch and punish them or carry them away to some dreadful
place, but that his mission is to guard and protect them."[1]

Couzens imported a business-like sensibility to policing. Born in 1872, he
established himself in Detroit professional circles as the chief clerk for a
prominent coal company and, in 1902, parlayed this position into becoming
business manager for the newly established Ford Motor Company. In the
early years, he acted as Henry Ford's de facto partner. As general manager and,
later, vice president of the corporation, Couzens oversaw the company's day-
to-day operations, providing a business discipline that balanced the more
mercurial Ford. By 1914, Couzens had helped initiate Ford's profit-sharing
and minimum wage policies. His initial investment also made him fabulous-
ly wealthy and, after he and Ford parted ways, allowed him to pursue a career
in public service. He served first as Detroit police commissioner, then from

1919 to 1922 as mayor and, from 1922 to 1936, as a U.S. senator from Michigan. In his time as police commissioner, Couzens sought to apply many of the same principles that had succeeded at Ford to policing: establishing performance standards, utilizing labor efficiently, conducting statistical analysis, and dividing the work into specialized tasks. In spite of the potential impersonality of such an approach, Couzens regarded his reforms as consistent with another goal, child-friendly policing.[2]

Couzens's reforms in Detroit exemplified a national movement to improve municipal policing in the 1910s. Police in turn-of-the-twentieth-century U.S. cities had been criticized for their links to urban political machines, their openly partisan hiring practices, and their failure to enforce vice laws. The alternative, critics argued, was that police should become more "professional" by centralizing their organizational structures in order to minimize the influence of politics and hiring distinguished administrators from outside their departments (such as Couzens) so that chiefs would be independent of existing relationships. With better organization and leadership, police departments could adopt higher standards for job applicants, institute civil service rules, and devote more energy to investigating and punishing crime. As these proposals suggest, police reform emerged from a strain of progressivism associated with an emerging business class. Inspired by the new principles of scientific management articulated by Frederick Winslow Taylor, police reform aimed at achieving an ideal of "efficiency" in municipal administration. According to historian Samuel Walker, reform initiatives could be seen in any number of U.S. cities in the early twentieth century, but during Couzens's administration, "the spirit of police reform soared highest in Detroit."[3]

But a different strain of progressive reform, one that idealized using the state to expand the provision of social welfare services, also shaped the policing of youth. This strain of reform was rooted in environmental understandings of the hazards that could befall young people, and following the turn of the twentieth century, gave rise to new social welfare and child welfare professions intended to aid youths. This strain of reform inspired the creation of juvenile court—in Chicago in 1899 and in Detroit by 1907—and fostered a new way of thinking about young offenders as needing protection rather than punishment. This strain of progressivism also provided a model for police reform, and is also evident in the Detroit police under James Couzens.[4]

Both sets of reforms had consequences that were perhaps unanticipated. As a number of scholars have noted, administrative reforms have the potential to widen or strengthen the net of the criminal justice system. James Austin and Barry Krisberg have suggested that the justice system "can be conceptualized as a net or series of nets functioning to regulate and control personal behavior." As a justice system becomes more efficient, it can cast a wider net (increasing the proportion of people ensnared) or create a stronger net (increasing the state's capacity to control individuals). This phenomenon occurs both when intended (as in efforts to increase the likelihood or severity with which criminals would be punished) and when not intended (as in efforts to divert offenders from the criminal justice system that actually place more people under alternative sorts of correctional supervision).[5] If this model were applied to police reform of the 1910s, then it would only be logical to see a wider and stronger net of police authority. And given the explicit attention that Couzens devoted to children, it would be no surprise to see it extend the authority that police exercised over young offenders.

In Detroit (and other cities as well), the combination of administrative and social reform enhanced state power and promoted more systematic and extensive criminal justice intervention with children and youth. Rather than keep young offenders out of the judicial system, as had been the priority earlier, the creation of an official mechanism to deal with delinquents—juvenile court—prompted the police to bring more and more of them in. Furthermore, the administrative reform of police departments also contributed to more frequent and more proactive police intervention with young offenders and potential offenders. In short, by the late 1910s, urban police cast a much wider and stronger net over children and youth than they had twenty years earlier.

## DETROIT'S JUVENILE COURT

When in 1907 the Michigan legislature established a juvenile court for Wayne County (including the city of Detroit), the representatives probably did not imagine it to be a substantial departure from the current form of juvenile justice. Instead, it was regarded as a logical culmination of existing trends toward reform that would simply rationalize and formalize mechanisms already in place. By the early 1900s, Detroit truant officers investigated young offenders prior to arrests and court hearings, state law provided that they be detained and tried separately from adults, county agents nominally supervised those who were convicted, and a handful of Detroit judges offered informal probation.

From the perspective of Michigan child welfare advocates, however, these measures were insufficient. According to critics such as Richard A. Bolt, a Detroit settlement house resident involved in "boys' work," court procedures for juveniles remained fundamentally unchanged before 1907. Adult offenders reportedly were brought through courtrooms in handcuffs while youths were being tried, and many young boys and girls stayed in the courtroom to watch the proceedings. County agents, in the eyes of reformers, mainly collaborated with the magistrates to determine proper sentences. Finally, even though juveniles were separated from older offenders, those convicted could stay in the county jail as long as two weeks before being transferred to the Industrial School at Lansing.[6] As early as the 1900 meeting of the Michigan State Board of Charities and Corrections, child welfare advocates proposed that Michigan should follow the example of Illinois and create separate courts for children. The state legislature ultimately agreed in 1905, establishing juvenile courts in larger counties by designating a circuit judge or circuit court commissioner to act as juvenile judge. The constitutionality of the 1905 law was challenged in court, however, and the state supreme court overturned the initial juvenile act as an unlawful delegation of judicial powers. In spite of this setback, charitable groups continued to agitate for an official juvenile court. For example, the Social Conference Club breathed new life into the cause early in 1907 by bringing well-known Cook County, Illinois, Judge Julian Mack to Detroit to deliver a "strong and convincing address" about the benefits of juvenile courts.[7]

When, in the spring of 1907, Michigan state legislators again took up the issue of a juvenile court, they approached it as a rational reform of the existing system. They proposed a new bill that satisfied constitutional objections by providing for probate judges (rather than circuit court judges) to sit in separate juvenile sessions and thereby locating juvenile hearings in noncriminal courts. This new act sailed through the state house judiciary committee and general assembly. In addition, more specific enabling legislation for Detroit—which provided for a full-time judge, a separate juvenile detention facility, and as many as five full-time probation officers—passed with little greater difficulty in May.[8]

Who should be the chief probation officer turned out to be a larger public issue, as child welfare advocates and the press insisted that a "man of high character," one with "keen insight into child nature" should be chosen. Ultimately, the new juvenile court opened for business on July 25, 1907, with the police truant squad's Lieutenant Charles Breault serving as chief probation officer and helping to ensure a smooth transition from the old system to the new. The biggest difficulty the court encountered was gentle ribbing from newspapers for replacing an earlier practice in which truant officers dragged "little Willie" into court with a new practice in which "Willie's mother now gets a nice command, all printed in style, with a big gold seal on the bottom." All in all, the creation of a Detroit juvenile court, coming as it did eight years after the first such institution in Chicago, encountered very little opposition.[9]

Michigan's juvenile court law altered the legal structures that shaped police contacts with children in Detroit. No longer were the police supposed to decide on their own whether to dispose of cases involving "delinquent, dependent, and neglected children." The new law dictated that whenever a boy under the age of seventeen or a girl under eighteen was arrested, the arresting officer was to take him or her before juvenile court and file a formal petition. Upon this complaint, probation officers (initially, members of the truant squad) were to investigate the facts both of the case and of the child's life. If detention was necessary, police officers were to hold adolescents at juvenile custodial facilities separate from the police stations or the city jail. Once the child had been transferred to juvenile court, the court assumed responsibility for investigating the allegations and determining the disposition of his or her case.[10]

In practice, the early juvenile court in Detroit under Judge Morse Rohnert operated with surprising informality. Rohnert apparently adopted the model advocated by Denver's Ben Lindsey that a judge should act as a "friend in court" to the boys brought before him, using the proceedings to diagnose and treat the sources of delinquency. This model closely resembled the discretionary standards already utilized by truant squad investigators. And with truant officers serving double duty as probation officers, the nature of investigations probably changed little. From the start, a series of newspaper reports on juvenile court portrayed boys (and it was mostly boys) brought before the court as a motley array of delinquents and the judge as a kindly avuncular figure, gently questioning the boys, bantering with them, and correcting them. Rohnert reportedly knew each boy by name and publicly expressed his pride when they "made good."[11]

In the courtroom, Rohnert used the power to institutionalize boys and the authority to grant leniency to coerce good behavior and truthfulness. For example, one young boy, Leo, was brought before Judge Rohnert, and forthrightly admitted stealing bushels of wheat from a freight car and reselling them for the money. Because of his honesty, Rohnert decided to give him "one more chance to make a man of [him]self." Balancing leniency and discipline, Rohnert instructed him to "report to Lieut. Breault at police headquarters every Sunday morning. The first time you don't he'll have you arrested and brought back here and to prison you'll go."[12]

Rohnert described his court in language that would have appealed to child welfare reformers, characterizing its purpose as rescuing and redirecting young offenders, and saving reform school for incorrigible repeaters. "The object of the juvenile court," he argued, "is not to make criminals but to save, if possible, those who have gone wrong, and punish those who persist in wrong-doing." It was not unusual for newspapers to report that "Frank Lerchenfeldt, who had demonstrated himself an all around bad boy, was the only one of 60 juvenile court subjects to be sent to reform school by Judge Rohnert yesterday." Frank had been caught breaking into a warehouse, but released on probation. He "repaid the court's confidence" by holding up a boy with a knife and stealing $4. Two patterns emerge from this example. On the one hand, anecdotal but extensive evidence suggests that, after a hearing, the early Detroit juvenile court released the vast majority of young offenders with a warning or probation. On the other hand, the court regarded persistent offenses as the main criterion for determining which boys to send to reform school. Repeat offenders drew Rohnert's ire. "The boys," he remarked publicly, "think because we have been lenient with them in hopes they will appreciate it, that they can do what they please. We are not going to change the policy of offering every inducement to boys to be good; but when they get unruly out to Lansing they will go."[13]

Detroit police officers openly supported the new juvenile court. In light of the ambivalence of police elsewhere, this enthusiasm might seem surprising. However, the police could not argue with juvenile court's results. As one truant officer declared, "We don't have our regular juvenile thieves any more since Judge Morse Rohnert has the whole clan under his wing."[14] Perhaps more importantly, the methods of police truant officers under Breault and the juvenile court under Rohnert were quite consistent. Both utilized investigation, guidance, and leniency to correct first-time or minor offenders, and harsh repercussions for repeaters. The early Detroit juvenile court represented a more official extension of the juvenile justice policies already employed by the Detroit police.

In late 1908, however, problems with facilities brought negative public attention onto the court. In these early years, the court lacked a detention facility specifically for juveniles, so instead held boys prior to hearings in a large refurbished room on the second floor of the County Building. Twice in the fall of 1908, boys tried but failed to escape from the detention room, the second time returning because Judge Rohnert happened to be passing outside and saw two boys on the outer window ledge. Then in October, three boys between ages twelve and fifteen awaiting hearings did go free by piling furniture near the door of the room and climbing through the transom above it. In response, the county board of auditors agreed to hire a guard, a basic security measure that Rohnert claimed to have long advocated.[15]

But the controversy did not end there. A number of Detroit citizens used the boys' escapes to criticize the juvenile court more generally. A prominent Protestant minister, the Reverend William Bryan Forbush, declared that the lack of a proper detention facility was an outrage that degraded boys. Joseph L. Hudson, president of Hudson's Department Store and a leader of the civic-reforming Detroit Municipal League, argued that keeping boys together in an unsupervised detention room defeated the purpose of juvenile court. The present arrangements, Hudson suggested, allowed boys to associate with other boys "more advanced in evil ways" who would have a harmful impact on the comparatively innocent. The solution would be to construct a "big institution that would satisfactorily care for all the boys under suitable supervision."[16]

The escapes fostered a public debate over whether to revise the juvenile law and set the stage for a significant elaboration of the juvenile court. In particular, George H. Carlisle, the stenographer in Judge Rohnert's court, used the occasion to campaign openly in late fall and winter of 1908 and 1909 for an extension of juvenile court (as well as a possible seat on the bench). Carlisle made a series of speeches praising what the court had accomplished so far and calling it to have more extensive authority to deal with parents and adults as well as juveniles.[17] Finally in 1909, the state legislature responded by setting aside funds to improve the court's facilities, first to rent and remodel a home for temporary detention and then to construct the new Juvenile Court Building and Detention Home, which would ultimately open in 1916.[18]

Equally important, in September 1909, the state legislature appointed Henry S. Hulbert to succeed Rohnert as probate judge in charge of juvenile court (bypassing Carlisle). Judge Hulbert brought a more coherent philosophy to the juvenile bench than did Judge Rohnert. Rather than simply using juvenile court as an arena for informal dispositions, Hulbert saw it as performing dual functions in the community. On the one hand, it was to be "the protector of the child" from the harmful influences his or her social environment. On the other hand, it was to be "the protector of society from the actual infringement of children upon its necessary rights." To accomplish this, he foresaw an alliance between the court and its probation officers, the police, the school, and the home to work together to achieve both ends. In short, the Detroit court gradually assembled the tools and the rationale to work proactively with young offenders.[19]

At first, juvenile court in Detroit operated along the same informal lines as had the earlier system maintained by the truant squads and courts, conducting informal investigations of young offenders and casually imposing correction. For that reason, it gained the support of police. The juvenile court also added something new to the mix—a more official mechanism for administering juvenile justice. Despite its sometimes-casual operation, its existence endorsed and helped encourage more extensive intervention with young offenders. Under Judge Hulbert in particular, it sought to become a forum for coordinated efforts to handle delinquency by a range of interested agencies. The result was a juvenile justice system increasingly willing and able to intervene with youth.

## JUVENILE ARRESTS UNDER THE NEW JUVENILE JUSTICE

In the years following the creation of the Wayne County Juvenile Court, the police and legal system did in fact intervene more often in children's lives. As we shall see, rates of arrest increased sharply. The creation of juvenile court also changed the nature of information about juvenile delinquency. As part of their efforts to protect children, juvenile courts sought to maintain the anonymity of young offenders. From day one, the Michigan Juvenile Court Law required that delinquent cases not be documented outside of the court record.[20] Seemingly as a result, after mid-1907, stories of juvenile crime disappeared from Detroit newspapers. Likewise, the Detroit police gradually ceased to record juvenile arrests alongside adults in their "Record of Arrests." Thus, after 1907, it is no longer possible to utilize a database of juvenile arrests. Instead, the most systematic information on young offenders comes from aggregate tables published by the Detroit Police Department's truant squad as part of its annual reports, beginning in 1898. These reports do not provide the level of detail as did the earlier records, but they do at least permit year-by-year tracking of juvenile arrests.

As measured by reported arrests, police intervention in juveniles' lives indeed increased following the creation of juvenile court. The rate of arrests for boys between ages nine and sixteen climbed erratically upward in the early decades of the twentieth century. After resting at approximately 24 arrests per 1,000 boys per year between 1898 and 1908, the arrest rate for boys spiked to 31 per 1,000 in 1909 and 1910 (the first years that the juvenile court was fully operational) and 39 per 1,000 in 1911. Boys' arrest rate dipped in the mid-1910s, but then rose again sharply during World War I and remained between 39 and 48 arrests per 1,000 for the subsequent decade (see figure 4.1). Juvenile court provided police with a specialized and appropriate mechanism to handle young offenders and, in response, police became more willing to make arrests.

Subtle signals further suggest that police became more willing to intervene in boys' lives. Even before the creation of juvenile court, police arrested a substantial portion of boys for status offenses, actions such as truancy or incorri-

**Figure 4.1**

Boys' arrest rates in Detroit, 1898–1927

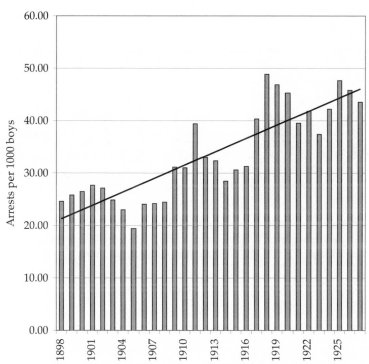

Sources: DPD, *Annual Reports* (1898–1927); U.S. Census Office, *11th Census: Population 1890,* 119; U.S. Bureau of the Census, *12th Census. Population,* 128; U.S. Bureau of the Census, *13th Census: Population 1910,* 453; U.S. Bureau of the Census, *14th Census, Population* (1920), 293; U.S. Bureau of the Census, *15th Census: 1930; Population,* vol. II, 729.
Note: For most years, arrests were reported and rates were calculated for boys ages nine to sixteen. However, for 1898–1903, arrests were reported and rates were calculated for boys ages nine to fifteen; for 1904–7, rates refer to boys ages ten to fifteen.

gibility which were not crimes but were considered signs that youth might grow up to become criminals. When police officers arrested youngsters for status offenses, they sought to take action in the youngsters' own interests, to redirect them from a path that seemingly led to a life of crime. Then, between 1908 and 1910, immediately following the creation of juvenile court, the police temporarily stopped bothering to specify boys' actual violations and instead labeled virtually every boy arrested as a "juvenile delinquent." In effect, police characterized almost all young offenders as status offenders. Of

**Figure 4.2**

Boys' Arrest Rates in Detroit, 1898–1919, by Offense Category.

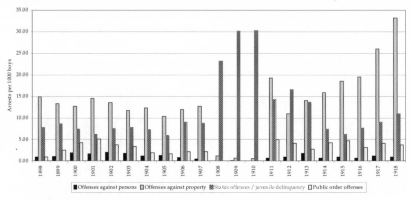

Sources: See figure 4.1.

Note: For most years, arrests were reported and rates were calculated for boys ages nine to sixteen. However, for 1898–1903, arrests were reported and rates were calculated for boys ages nine to fifteen; for 1904–7, rates refer to boys ages ten to fifteen.

the 31 arrests per 1,000 boys in 1909, thirty were charged with "delinquency" (see figure 4.2). Using terminology that distinguished between juvenile and adult offenders, and that glossed over the criminality of youths' offenses, implicitly affirmed the emerging police agenda of intervening with at-risk youth in order to do them good. When in 1911 the police resumed identifying the specific offenses for which they arrested boys, the rate of status offense arrests remained almost double what it had been before 1907. The police made over 16 status offense arrests per 1,000 boys in 1912, as compared to an earlier peak of 9 per 1,000 in 1906. In the same years, the rates of arrests for offenses against property and against persons remained more or less at their earlier level. The increase in arrests for status offenses helped to drive the overall rise in boys' rates of arrest. And the increase in status offense arrests suggests that the Detroit police at least in part implemented the new interventionist ethic promulgated by the juvenile court movement.

Arrest almost certainly introduced boys into juvenile court, particularly in the early years after the court's founding. Between 1909 and 1913, the police truant squad continued to investigate juveniles following arrest, but it ultimately referred 87 percent of boys arrested to juvenile court. This enormous share suggests that the spike in boys' arrests in the same years was driven partly by an effort to bring boys into juvenile court. These astronomical levels could not last forever (as arrest rates increased, sheer numbers strained the court's resources), but they remained quite high. The portion of boys arrested who were petitioned to juvenile court leveled off to 61 percent between 1914 and 1918, and dropped to an average of 51 percent between 1920 and 1940.[21] Petitioning even half of boys arrested, however, represents a reversal of earlier policies of doing everything possible to keep young offenders out of court. With juvenile court available, police no longer needed to segregate young offenders from the criminal courts. Instead the new institution fostered an expansion in the use of judicial procedures with youth.

Impressionistic evidence suggests that juvenile court also led boys to be institutionalized more frequently. The superintendent of the State Industrial School at Lansing, for one, blamed the juvenile court law for an increase in boys' committals to his facility, arguing that the reform school's population—733 boys in 1907—increased to 766 by the end of 1908 as a result of changed court procedures in Detroit. He maintained, "[W]e have received more boys from Wayne County in the last seven months than in any year in the history of the institution. . . . For a time we thought the new law would reduce the commitments to the School but this proved not to be the case, as we are receiving more boys [than] under the old law."[22] The superintendent in fact sensed a larger change. The reform school's new admissions increased by 20 percent in the decade following the creation of juvenile court, and a noticeably larger portion of the reform school's population came from Wayne County (24 percent between 1908 and 1918) than before (19 percent between 1898 and 1908).[23]

Public intervention in the lives of delinquent girls also increased following the creation of juvenile court, although perhaps not as obviously as in the lives of boys. As with boys, beginning in 1898, the truant squad investigated and documented all complaints involving girls under age eighteen. Their data indicate that the rate of arrest for girls between ages ten and seventeen increased raggedly during the first two decades of the twentieth century. That rate climbed from fewer than 5 arrests per 1,000 girls in 1899 and 1900 to a plateau around 7 in 1906 and 1907, spiked to 10 in 1913, dipped, and then plateaued again around 8 per 1,000 between 1918 and 1922 (see figures 4.3 and 4.4). Because police arrested far fewer girls than boys—in any given year between 1898 and 1922, the Detroit police reported no more than one-third as many arrests of girls as of boys—annual variations in arrest rates probably mean less than the overall trend. And the overall pattern was a gradual increase. Furthermore, in almost every year, status offenses or generically labeled charges of "juvenile delinquency" constituted the largest category of girls' arrests. Again, as with boys, the new interventionist ethic promulgated by the juvenile court movement seems to have driven the increase in girls' arrests.

**Figure 4.3**

Girls' Arrest Rates in Detroit, 1898–1922

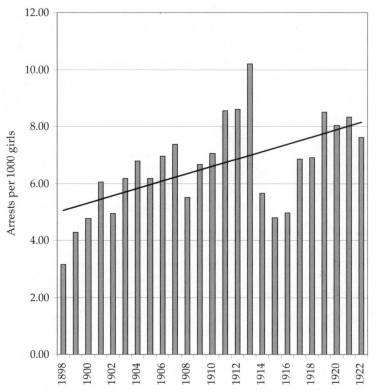

Sources: DPD, *Annual Reports* (1898–1922); U.S. Census Office, *11th Census: Population 1890,* 119; U.S. Bureau of the Census, *12th Census. Population,* 128; U.S. Bureau of the Census, *13th Census: Population 1910,* 453; U.S. Bureau of the Census, *14th Census, Population* (1920), 293; U.S. Bureau of the Census, *15th Census: 1930; Population,* vol. II, 729.
Note: For most years, arrests were reported and rates were calculated for girls between ages ten and seventeen. However, for 1898 and 1918, arrests were reported and rates were calculated for girls ages nine to sixteen; for 1904–7, 1912, and 1918, rates refer to girls ages ten to sixteen.

As was the case with boys, police typically petitioned girls whom they arrested to juvenile court. A court appearance represented a substantial departure from earlier methods of dealing with delinquent girls. Before the creation of juvenile court, parents, police, and the truant squad sought to keep girls out of the courts. Between 1898 and 1907, the truant squad sent only 23 percent of girls arrested to the criminal courts. Of the remainder, the

**Figure 4.4**

Girls' Arrest Rates in Detroit, 1898–1918, by Offense Category

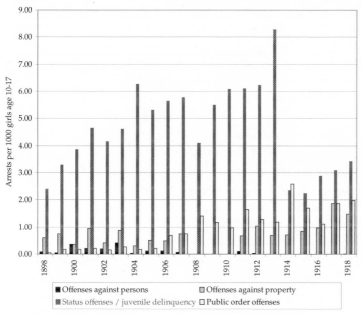

Sources: See figure 4.3.

Note: For most years, arrests were reported and rates were calculated for girls between ages ten and seventeen. However, for 1898 and 1918, arrests were reported and rates were calculated for girls ages nine to sixteen; for 1904–7, 1912, and 1918, rates refer to girls ages ten to sixteen.

police returned 38 percent to their parents, and directly committed 35 percent to the House of the Good Shepherd, a Catholic custodial home for "wayward" girls, or other comparable charitable agencies. By making unofficial dispositions to parents and to private agencies, the truant squad filtered many girls out of the criminal justice system prior to any contact with courts.[24] In contrast, between 1909 and 1918, police petitioned 61 percent of girls to juvenile court. They discharged 27 percent to their parents and sent only 11 percent directly to private custodial agencies.[25] This reversal suggests a fundamental change in how police dealt with delinquent girls. Rather than try to keep them out of court as they had before, now, with a new institution designed specifically to address the needs of young offenders, they sought to bring them in.

Of course, an alternative explanation for the increase in delinquency arrests and court hearings would be that kids were simply becoming worse. If that were the case, more severe behavior would be reflected in other measures. To a degree, it is. For one, the Detroit police paid increasing attention to juvenile felonies over time. Between 1898 and 1913, felonies never constituted more than 5 percent of total juvenile arrests in any given year. Between 1914 and 1918, during the World War I–era increase in juvenile arrests, the portion of felonies increased to between 7 and 10 percent in a given year.[26] Likewise, the boys committed to the reform school at Lansing seem to have been becoming more severe offenders. They averaged 1.15 prior arrests between 1908 and 1918, the decade following the creation of juvenile court, up from 0.85 between 1898 and 1908. In addition, the share committed for offenses against property increased to 58 percent between 1908 and 1918, up from 45 percent between 1898 and 1908.[27] Furthermore, arrests of girls also hint at more severe behavior. During World War I, for the first time, the Detroit police arrested more than one girl in a thousand for criminal offenses (see figure 4.4). Nonetheless, two points deserve note. First, the apparent increase in juvenile criminality is, at this time, small, and probably insufficient to explain the substantial increase in arrests and court hearings during these years. Second, a more interventionist justice system and increased juvenile crime are not incompatible. The increase in previous arrests among boys committed to Lansing could (and likely did) result from both increased criminal behavior and police more willing to arrest boys.

In short, in the decade following the creation of juvenile court, the police arrested more children and youth, and petitioned more of those arrested to the new juvenile justice system. The police used new legal mechanisms to send delinquent boys and girls to agencies that ostensibly were intended to help rather than punish them. In the eyes of its practitioners, the new juvenile justice represented the triumph of the progressive ideal of using state power to intervene on children's behalf—even if that meant increasingly arresting them to do them good.

## POLICE REFORM AND NET WIDENING

The net of juvenile justice became wider and stronger not only due to the creation of juvenile court but also due to police reform. While both occurred almost simultaneously, they emerged from different strains of the progressive reform impulse. Juvenile court and police reform combined, however, to pull children and youth more tightly into the net of juvenile justice.

The industrial transformation of many northern cities helped create the context for police reform. Again, Detroit exemplified this transformation. Detroit became an industrial metropolis between 1900 and 1920. It had already been a manufacturing center at the turn of the century, but the exceptional growth of the auto industry made it a giant. Furthermore, demands for industrial production generated by World War I accelerated this expansion. And the attraction of high-paying jobs in industry acted as a magnet to migrants. Detroit's population roughly doubled each decade between 1900 and 1920, making it the fourth-largest city in the United States.[28] This transformation contributed to an ongoing revolution in how city governments operated. Rather than passively trying to maintain order, as they had in much of the nineteenth century, cities increasingly had to act to provide a wide array of services for their residents, including water, sanitation, fire protection, and, in particular, more systematic policing.[29]

Early-twentieth-century changes in policing are often called "professionalization," but they are better understood as administrative reform or streamlining. At the turn of the twentieth century, both outside investigations and the main police professional organization, the International Association of Chiefs of Police (IACP), publicly maintained that urban police departments needed to do their jobs better. Most diagnosed the fundamental problem with police as administrative weakness. Cities denied tenure to their police chiefs and could replace them almost at will. Detroit, for example, had six police commissioners in sixteen years prior to appointing Couzens. In addition, most big city police departments exercised little centralized authority, so precinct captains could operate largely autonomously. Furthermore, officers in the field performed an erratic array of duties, recovering lost children one day and investigating serious crimes the next, and usually lacked training for either job. The public thus criticized urban police for being simultaneously incapable of maintaining order and undisciplined when they did choose to act. The Detroit police lacked the major scandals that plagued other departments of this era, but nonetheless had a reputation for inefficiency. Furthermore, with the advent of silent films, police were often portrayed as bumbling "keystone kops," an image they resented deeply. In response, the IACP under the leadership of District of Columbia Police Chief Richard Sylvester increasingly advocated the idea of "professionalism" to address these difficulties. What form professionalism should take, however, was open to debate. One option was to model "professional" policing on corporations and business; another was to apply the lessons of social reform movements to policing.[30]

A corporate model of police reform reflected the rationalizing spirit of the Progressive Era. Appalled at the apparent ineffectiveness of city governments managed via partisan politics, reformers associated with corporate interests sought to operate municipal administrations more efficiently. Changes such as supplementing elected mayors with appointed city managers and replacing ward-based city councils with councils elected at-large by the entire munici-pality were intended to separate government from the interference and inef-ficiency of partisan politics. In particular, America's upper middle and upper classes wanted more secure cities and so demanded more efficient policing. As historian Robert Fogelson argues, affluent urban "merchants, realtors, lawyers, bankers, investors, executives, industrialists, professors, ministers, and social workers" came together in civic organizations such as chambers of commerce, municipal leagues, and vice commissions to bankroll investigations of police and seek change.[31]

Advocates of a corporate model of reform sought explicitly to apply pio-neering management expert Frederick Winslow Taylor's principles of "scien-tific management" to municipal policing. The New York Bureau of Municipal Research, for example, advocated a business-like efficiency in police reform. Organized as a research agency for New York City in 1906, the bureau rapidly evolved into an independent consulting firm that, among its other activities, investigated police departments in at least seventeen major cities between 1913 and 1924. Unlike earlier police investigations, which had often been driven by partisan politics, these new inquiries were intended to be rational and objective. The ideal outcome, the bureau intended, was for police departments to operate like scientifically managed businesses. The bureau explicitly modeled its proposals on Taylor's principles; it even made Taylor's research papers required reading for its training programs. Its inves-tigations thus based their recommendations on Taylor's belief in replacing individual opinion about how to accomplish any task with precise analysis to determine the "one best way" to do things. Those police departments that adopted a corporate model of reform strove to implement the tenets of Taylor's scientific management into a new "scientific policing": job training, specialization, statistical analysis, and worker grading tied to incentives.[32]

No urban police department in the 1910s better exemplified the spirit of administrative streamlining than did Detroit's. With the doubling of its size in these years—from 732 officers in 1910 to 1,467 in 1917—training became critical to Detroit police work. Traditionally, as Chief Inspector William P. Rutledge wrote, "it was the custom of men entering the ranks . . . to have placed in their hands a revolver, a club, a pair of handcuffs and . . . they sallied forth to fulfill their oath of office to 'enforce the law.' . . . The only training they received was by accompanying an older patrolman two or three nights on his regular patrol duty and by occasional instructions from superior officers in 'rules and regulations.'" In the 1900s and 1910s, however, urban police departments acknowledged that this arrangement was no longer adequate and initiated more formal training programs. The Detroit Police Department established a training school for officers in 1911 "in keeping," explained Rutledge, "with other progressive innovations and for the purpose of elevating the standard of efficiency." In a one-month program, the training school instructed recruits in a dizzying array of fields. Not only did new officers learn the classification of crimes, when they had the power to make arrests, and what to do in court, they also received detailed instructions in street directions, first aid, and the use of their revolvers. How much of this instruction recruits retained may be uncertain, but the training school at least established consistent standards for police work.[33] Perhaps as important, the training school and an updated instruction manual sought to establish a new spirit for police work. The manual detailed specific duties, but it also articulated a concept of a proper officer as being engaged with his community. "The qualities most required in a policeman," the manual asserted, "are broad and intelligent kindliness, firmness, good judgment, good character, sympathy with his kind, and above all, a thorough knowledge of the laws and the people to whom he must apply them."[34]

Police reform achieved its height in Detroit during the administration of James Couzens between 1916 and 1918. Couzens represented the archetype of the police reformer in the late Progressive Era. Having already made his reputation and his fortune in the automobile business, he established a new career in politics. Resigning from Ford in 1915, he devoted his attention to public service. He believed that older, informal methods of law enforcement were no longer adequate for the modern city, arguing, "it is evident that the time has come in Detroit and elsewhere for a general change of methods in the administration of our institutions." To that end, he brought to public service not only his own experience, but also other administrators who believed that policing should be reorganized as a business. For example, Parker Sercombe, the head of the new statistical division, argued that "there is no more reason why police departments or other public bureaus should run their *business* in a haphazard manner . . . than there is for the Standard Oil Corporation or the Steel Corporation to run their affairs without a well organized statistical plan."[35] Administrators such as Couzens and Sercombe saw little difference between a police department and a large corporation.

As one manifestation of the new corporate model, the Detroit police embraced specialization in the 1910s. Dividing work duties into their component parts represented a key element of efficient management, one so basic that Taylor assumed it to be natural to any large organization. At first, specialization was something of a novelty for the police. In 1915, for example, an internal police department newsletter sought to explain the importance of specialization to the rank and file. The anonymous writer suggested the generalist policeman was a thing of the past, asserting that "now we want the patrolman to specialize." Officers on the beat should try to prevent crimes, "but when it is necessary to make investigations not directly connected with a crime in progress but for the purpose of obtaining evidence, that work should be left to the plain clothes investigators." Under Couzens, specialization accelerated markedly. During those years, the Detroit police department established or substantially expanded branches including an auto recovery bureau, a criminal identification bureau (using the latest scientific techniques such as fingerprinting), a traffic regulation squad, and a "clean-up" squad "to break up disorderly establishments and drive vice and immorality from the streets." Beat patrolmen continued to do yeoman labor for the Detroit police, but special divisions increasingly assumed investigative duties and regulatory jobs.[36]

Under Couzens, the Detroit police also adapted Taylor's principle of performance evaluation to beat cops. Detroit administrators judged officers on their success in "keep[ing] their beats in order, having the least crime, offenses and violations," rather than the most arrests (or "scalps"). In keeping with Taylor's principle of giving workers financial incentives, Couzens also created a "Merit System" to reward commanding officers for reducing crime in their precincts and individual officers for "maintaining order on their beats." He funded this bonus pool with $10,000 from his own pocket.[37]

Finally, the Detroit police embraced scientific methods of observation, evaluation, and prediction, popular among both sociologists and efficiency experts and in accord with Taylor's ideal of using scientific analysis of all tasks to establish the "one best system." Under Couzens, they established a "statistical division" directed by his associate, Parker Sercombe. This agency kept track of the work done by police, analyzed data to guide administrative decisions, and forecast crime trends for future years in order to develop better response plans.[38] In short, by the late 1910s, the Detroit police exemplified a new pattern of remaking urban law enforcement agencies so that they operated like well-managed, efficient businesses.

In contrast to this corporate model, police reforms that were directed toward improving social welfare reflected a more humane spirit of progressivism. Hiring policewomen to, in the words of historian Dorothy Moses Schulz, "undertake protective and preventive work among women and children" represents the most obvious example of social welfare–oriented police reform. Before the turn of the century, police officers had all been male. Lobbying from organizations such as the Women's Christian Temperance

Union and the Traveler's Aid Society, however, prompted big-city police departments to hire women. In 1905, at the insistence of these groups, Portland, Oregon, engaged Lola Baldwin as a policewoman to protect women and children from moral hazards arising from the Lewis and Clark Centennial Exposition. Similarly, during the brief tenure of a "good government" municipal administration in Los Angeles in 1910, social worker Alice Stebbins Wells convinced the Los Angeles Police Department to hire her to safeguard girls from the perceived threat of urban vice. Wells became the leader of a national movement for women police. She encouraged departments to hire female officers trained in social work, and she encouraged women to pursue this work in order to appropriate police authority to expose immorality, to regulate commercial amusements, and protect girls from seduction and prostitution. By 1917, at least thirty U.S. cities hired policewomen.[39]

The Detroit Police Department was slow to adopt this innovation, but in the 1920s, it too eventually engaged policewomen at the insistence of outside agencies. Detroit had employed matrons to supervise women and children in detention since 1897, but it only hired female officers and created a Women's Division in January 1921 after the Detroit Federation of Women's Clubs sponsored the ordinance in Common Council. As was the case elsewhere, the Detroit Women's Division sought to utilize investigation, probation, and external social agencies, rather than arrest, to help teenage girls who found themselves in trouble. Virginia Murray, director of the Women's Division, saw her agency as "an additional social organization . . . for the constructive treatment of the girl who has fallen into anti-social habits."[40]

Police departments also pursued a social welfare model of reform by creating or reshaping juvenile bureaus in the 1910s. Specialized agencies for young offenders—both girls and boys—sprang up in most urban police departments in these years. Here, Detroit was a leader, having operated a truant squad within the police department since 1882 and having used these officers to investigate all juvenile offenses since 1898. The function of the Detroit Police Department's truant squad changed substantially when the city's board of education took over enforcement of compulsory attendance laws in 1913, and the police department subsequently reorganized the unit into a "juvenile division." Having lost its longtime responsibility for controlling truancy, the new juvenile division increasingly focused on monitoring young offenders. Dressed in plain clothes, the members of the juvenile division quietly investigated all persons under seventeen who had been reported to be delinquent. In its early years, the juvenile division officers attempted to adjust neighborhood disputes personally and to dispose of minor offenses on their own.

Optimally, the officers would convince young offenders to return or pay for stolen property. The police even made them apologize to persons they had injured.[41]

These two models of police reform—one inspired by business, the other by social welfare—may seem contradictory. On the one hand, police sought to streamline their duties and accomplish them more efficiently; on the other hand, they adopted a much broader social reform agenda. However, these dual goals could sometimes complement one another. For administrators like Washington's Richard Sylvester, aiding children could also help make police more efficient. By "furnishing and protecting public playgrounds, protecting children against dissipated and criminal parents, . . . rescuing girls under age from evil resorts, [and] excluding youths from disreputable localities," Sylvester argued, the police could reduce the amount of delinquency at the same time as they rendered a "service to humanity." In Detroit, James Couzens may have felt similar sentiments, but expected more practical results. Couzens characterized his administrative reforms as a response to increased lawlessness and delinquency that seemed to accompany his city's growth in the 1910s. In such a situation, it only made sense for the police to establish programs to curtail juvenile crime and to coordinate their efforts with those of schools and social agencies. Nipping the problem in the bud, he implied, would better allow the police to minimize crime and maintain public order in the future.[42]

The New York City Police Department established one of the earliest programs to intervene with children and youth, describing it in rhetoric suggesting that even as they eliminated older duties, they should adopt new, social welfare–oriented functions. Henry Bruere, the City Chamberlain of New York, proposed that police should "be made the chief welfare workers of the city's government."[43] In 1914, newly elected Mayor John Purroy Mitchel appointed Arthur Woods (a former reporter and deputy police commissioner who had founded New York's first school for police officers) commissioner of the police in part to implement this idea.[44]

Woods believed that cities were poor environments for boys to become men. "If a boy has to depend on the street for his play," he argued, "that boy . . . is growing up under conditions full of temptation to crime." To address this problem, Woods assigned one officer in each district to work with juveniles and to provide recreation by closing some roads for a few hours each day, designating them as "play streets."[45] In addition, Woods's police tried to instill a sense of responsibility in children by recruiting them into a new squad of "junior police." Boys and girls under age fifteen who recited a pledge of good citizenship received suits, caps, badges, and manageable duties. They cleaned streets, cleared fire escapes, maintained garbage cans, and reported petty offenses by other kids such as shooting craps, building bonfires, and smoking cigarettes. Through these interactions, Woods hoped that boys who might have become burglars or criminals would instead become law-abiding "self-supporting citizens." In this way, a small investment of effort by the police to work with boys would generate long-term dividends in the form of reduced crime and disorder in future.[46]

As with the corporate model of reform, police reform oriented around social welfare (and especially child welfare) reached its height in Detroit during the administration of James Couzens between 1916 and 1918. In contrast to the "traditional feeling" that "a policeman is a natural enemy of the school child," Couzens asserted that during his tenure "children and policemen are on very cordial terms in Detroit." As he presented his thinking, Couzens argued that an educated public was the key to reducing crime. By this, he desired not necessarily a public deep in book learning but a public acculturated to urban life. To this end, Couzens and the Detroit Police Department presented their mammoth 1917 annual report as a textbook directed at teaching school children "how to live in large cities." As he argued, "it is only through more knowledge and the actual implanting of rational thought habits in the minds of children from infancy onward, that we may reach the maximum of safety from failure, crime, disease, and accidents."[47]

Under Couzens, the Detroit police maintained that establishing personal contacts with children and adolescents was critical to controlling crime and delinquency. This philosophy led the police to work closely with the Detroit school system, assigning officers to mundane duties such as helping assemble and dismiss students, transporting "crippled" children to and from schools, participating in traffic safety classes, and serving as crossing guards. As Couzens argued, "the first great effort [to reduce crime] must be made in the schools and that is where the earliest effect will be felt."[48] The Detroit police also sought to direct youths' minds "into lawful channels of thought and community cooperation during their early years." One proposed method was to interest boys in the work of the police by establishing a junior police force, akin to that in New York. No evidence indicates that the Detroit police followed through on this often-repeated proposal, but some boys did at least adopt duties akin to those of the police. Local Boy Scout troops, for instance, helped the police direct holiday pedestrian traffic in downtown Detroit. During the Christmas shopping rush, "cordons of the scouts held back the crowds by standing at the walks with locked arms while the holiday vehicular traffic streamed by in the opposite direction."[49] Cooperating with boys in this fashion, the Detroit police believed, would forge bonds between cops and kids that would help assimilate them into the urban community and dissuade them from committing future crimes.

## THE OUTCOMES OF REFORM

The axiomatic concept of "net widening" suggests that as justice systems become more efficient they often increase the proportion of people pulled into their nets. In early-twentieth-century Detroit, whatever the intent, both the corporate and social welfare models of reform contributed to a wider, stronger net of juvenile justice. While Couzens's goal in making his police more efficient may have been to reduce arrests, the outcome was to increase them. Furthermore, the closer bonds generated by what Couzens called "child-friendly policing" not only facilitated police contacts with children and youth, they also directed police attention to adolescents and fostered an ethos of intervening with young people. Cops largely abandoned their earlier goal of trying to find ways to keep kids out of police stations and courts. Instead, they adopted a new approach that brought in more kids.

These changes are evident in police operations. In Detroit, juvenile arrests increased sharply from roughly 31 per 1,000 boys in 1915, the last year before Couzens took over, to a peak of 49 per 1,000 in 1918, the final year of Couzens's tenure. Moreover, boys' arrest rates remained high even after Couzens left the police, remaining over 40 per 1,000 throughout the 1920s (see figure 4.1). As a result, the juvenile court and detention home for Detroit soon found themselves severely overburdened. Judge George M. Read asserted that the number of children held at the detention home at any time frequently exceeded 400, more than 125 over its intended capacity. The problem, according to a 1927 investigation, resulted from the police practice of rounding up and apprehending dozens of adolescents on a typical weekend on a range of charges and only investigating the cases afterward. The availability of mechanisms to deal with young offenders and an interventionist ethos apparently encouraged arrest and detention.[50]

Furthermore, the Detroit police implemented these new policies in the context of a rapidly changing city. Detroit's industrial maturation in the 1910s attracted massive migration, but the sources of migration changed from previous decades. World War I slowed the stream of migration from Europe to a trickle. Instead, employers in the U.S. urban North began to open their factories to black workers to fill their labor needs. Mainly in a one-year period between 1916 and 1917, a tremendous wave of African Americans from the rural South came to Detroit to find jobs in industry. As a result,

Detroit's black population increased from approximately 5,000 in 1910 to 40,000 in 1920, or from 1.2 percent of the total to 4 percent. This migration began a transformation of Detroit that would last for the better part of the century as the share of blacks in the city's population continued to increase to almost 8 percent in 1930, 9 percent in 1940, 16 percent in 1950, and 29 percent in 1960.[51] This "Great Migration" impacted all aspects of daily life, including police efforts to maintain public order. Casting a wider net of criminal justice made newly arriving African Americans—juvenile and adult—especially likely targets for police attention.

In contrast to the demographics of the city, the demographics of the Detroit police changed very little during this period. The police department continued to draw its recruits from working-class young men; compared to earlier decades, it became even more likely to hire native-born whites between 1910 and 1919. The police department had employed a few black officers since 1890, but these men mainly provided token representation intended to satisfy African American demands for political patronage. In fact, given African Americans' limited access to education and jobs, the police department's policy of raising standards for recruits in the 1910s may have made it increasingly difficult for blacks to join the force. The Detroit police reportedly also maintained a policy throughout the 1910s and 1920s that no more than 1 percent of the force should be African American; in 1926, only 14 "colored policemen" served.[52]

In their official publications of the late 1910s, the Detroit police remained astonishingly silent on the issue of race. In the 1917 annual report, written at the peak of the early Great Migration, Couzens expressed concern that Detroit police were battling an almost unprecedented crime wave. Citing statistics that arrests had more than doubled between 1915 and 1917, Couzens argued that "lawlessness in Detroit has been gathering momentum" due to the city's prosperity. At no point in the 340-page document, however, does either he or his associates suggest race as a factor in either increased crime or increased arrests. Furthermore, the data compiled by the truant squad and the juvenile division fail to distinguish juvenile arrestees by race or nativity at any point between 1898 and 1927. The silence on the question of race may indicate that it was not an important factor in the thinking of police administrators.[53]

Yet race nonetheless impacted police practice. For one thing, African Americans were disproportionately represented among total arrests (those of both adults and juveniles). In 1917, for example, at a time when blacks constituted less than 4 percent of Detroit's population, they constituted 12 percent of total arrests.[54] In addition, in the years following World War I, the

Detroit police utilized highly aggressive tactics at the urging of now-Mayor Couzens to respond to an apparent crime wave. Reporting that crime had reached "alarming proportions" by August of 1920, the Detroit police under Commissioner James W. Inches substantially increased its numbers of patrolmen and detailed them to intensive street patrols. By 1922, the police could claim that effective arrests and prosecutions had brought the problem under control.[55]

By all accounts, the weight of this crackdown on crime and vice fell most heavily upon the shoulders of African Americans. Throughout the 1920s, the Detroit branch of the National Association for the Advancement of Colored People considered police brutality to be one of its more pressing issues.[56] Moreover, the 1926 report of the Mayor's Committee on Race Relations was riddled with examples of police harassment and violence toward blacks. Most strikingly, the report demonstrated that, between January 1925 and June 1926, Detroit police officers killed twenty-five African Americans. In practice, during the 1920s, the Detroit police routinely used physical force to discipline the city's newly arrived black population.[57]

The Detroit police do not seem to have been as likely to use violence against younger black offenders, but they did apply their newly aggressive tactics and interventionist ethos to them. Although African Americans constituted only 3.3 percent of Detroit's 1920 population between ages ten and nineteen, they represented 12 percent of the youths whom police held in custody at the detention home between 1917 and 1928.[58] Moreover, juvenile court complaints against African American youths were filed at a rate more than twice that of white youths in 1926.[59] Examinations of black delinquency from the 1920s tend to emphasize how a perceived lack of family structure and the difficulty of the transition from the rural South to the urban North contributed to African American youth's misbehavior. Yet at the same time, it was newly assertive police tactics that pulled young blacks into the net of juvenile justice.

By the late 1910s and early 1920s, the Detroit police disproportionately targeted African Americans—both adults and juveniles—for intervention and arrest. This pattern emerged from the administrative reform movements of the 1910s that had sought to make police operations more efficient and to make individual officers more highly skilled and specialized. These goals reshaped the organization of police departments, but they may not have penetrated the daily work of rank-and-file patrolmen. What did seem to penetrate, however, was an aggressive interventionist ethos promoted by both police reformers and, to a lesser extent, social welfare advocates. In short, police reform created wider and stronger nets, more interventionist models of policing. And in the context of the Great Migration, wider and stronger nets helped generate discrimination.

# A Wider Net and Social Conflict in a Changing City

For modern observers, "net widening" has become an axiom of criminal justice reform. When criminal justice has sought to "get tough" on criminals, as in the 1980s and 1990s, wider and stronger nets were of course the intended outcomes. However, modern studies have also observed net widening as a result of reforms intended to divert offenders from the justice system or to offer treatment programs. The expansion of the juvenile and criminal justice systems' nets has been an almost unavoidable effect of change and reform.

The same phenomenon characterized the expansion of juvenile justice in the early years of the twentieth century. In a reversal of earlier law enforcement practices of diverting children and youth from judicial involvement, the police now pulled more juveniles into the justice system. This wider and stronger net had its origins in two very different sets of reforms.

First, the creation of juvenile courts was intended to widen the net of justice. Drawing on a progressive philosophy of social reform, juvenile court advocates argued that one of their fundamental purposes was to provide a new means of intervening with young offenders. Only through more extensive interactions with youth could they provide for their welfare. These reformers intended to replace the improvised juvenile justice system of the past with a more regular set of mechanisms and procedures for addressing the sources of juveniles' misbehaviors. In Detroit, this process did not take place overnight, but it was largely completed within a few years of the founding of juvenile court. In the 1910s, juvenile arrest rates increased sharply and the majority of children and youth arrested appeared in juvenile court.

Second, police reform also helped widen the net of juvenile justice. In this case, however, net widening was more of an unplanned side effect. Drawing on a different strain of progressive thinking, one that emphasized applying business-like efficiency to public administration, police reformers sought to do their jobs more effectively. To this end, police administrators in cities such as Detroit adopted specialization, officer training, and scientific management of their workers. They also incorporated social welfare into their duties by means of "child-friendly policing," justifying it as a means of reducing crime and disorder in the future and thereby consistent with their larger agenda. The result, again, was a wider net of juvenile justice. Although administrators such as James Couzens advocated an approach to policing based on *not* collecting "scalps," juvenile arrests again increased sharply during and after his administration. More kids were pulled into the net of juvenile justice, more than the system could accommodate by the 1920s.

Juvenile courts and their own administrative reform gave the police the means and the justification to intervene officially with adolescents more often than ever before. In the context of social change wrought by Detroit's industrial expansion, World War I, and the Great Migration, however, the resulting interventionist ethos in policing helped create the basis for conflict between law enforcement and the emerging African American community. Rather than seeing themselves as being aided by the wider net of juvenile policing, many youths—and black youths who were disproportionately targeted by it—might have seen themselves as being victimized. Thus, the idea that children had no reason to fear policemen proved to be ironic. At least in Detroit, progressive reforms promoted a significant extension of police authority over young people.

# ⁙5⁙

# Police in the Service of Chicago's "Court of Last Resort"

Like kids in Detroit, youths in Chicago also had occasions to fear the police, but for different reasons. In contrast to Detroit, Chicago police very rarely referred young offenders to juvenile court. In the 1920s, an Officer O'Connor, a "police probation officer" (the rough equivalent of a juvenile bureau officer elsewhere) told a sociology student that the police sought to decide most cases involving minor offenses on their own, particularly those involving first offenders. O'Connor explained that he did not petition boys to court for crimes such as petty thieving, window breaking, or running away "unless they had a previous record." He even released boys caught "auto thieving" if the car had just been stolen, was not damaged, and the owner was not anxious to prosecute.[1]

In light of these practices, some police officers chose to discipline young offenders themselves by using mild physical violence. The sociologist Everett Hughes reported that many officers did not bother to arrest young thieves, but instead gave them "a cuff on the ear, a stroke or two with a little switch . . . reprimanded [them] and let [them] go."[2] One park police officer named Gus Okon explained that when he caught a juvenile thief, he would typically reprimand him and give him a beating. Okon related a story that when one neighborhood boy was arrested for stealing:

> I went down and said, "Mike, did you take these things from that garage" And he knew I had the goods on him, so he admitted it. Then, bang, I socked him with my fist behind the ear. "What did you take them for" and bang, I socked him behind the other ear. I just kept on beating the stuffing out of him, then I said, "Mike, you know better than that. You got a good father and mother,

good Polish people. Don't let me catch you taking anything again; if you do, what you got now will be nothing to what you'll get then." Then I took him to the captain and said, "This boy has learned a good lesson." The captain let him go. The boy is a good boy now, and every time he sees me, he says, "Gus, I want to thank you for that trimming you gave me. It made a man out of me." That's my motto, scare 'em to death and knock hell out of them, and then let them go. I've set dozens of them right that way.[3]

For officers such as O'Connor and Okon, immediate intervention and, often, physical reprimands seemed to be more effective responses to minor juveniles' crimes than did arrests and petitions to juvenile court.

These examples may appear to be inconsistent with the way police were expected to handle young offenders by the 1920s, particularly in Chicago, home of the nation's first and most influential juvenile court. Founded in 1899, the Cook County Juvenile Court exemplified how progressive reformers sought to build institutions to rescue children from the crime and delinquency that seemed to result from urban-industrial life. According to Timothy Hurley, the court's first chief probation officer, and Julian Mack, an early juvenile court judge, it sought to embody the state's responsibility to act as a parent for every child. Juvenile court would do so by removing young offenders from the malignant influences of police, criminal courts, jails, and prisons, by investigating and resolving the social, familial, and psychological problems that led to delinquency, and by offering probation services that would rehabilitate the offender and transform the environment in which he or she lived. As Richard S. Tuthill, the first presiding judge, told his staff on the juvenile court's opening day of operations, "kindness and love for the children must be used in this work."[4]

In light of the ideals and influence of the Cook County Juvenile Court, the arbitrary and rough manner in which police officers treated young offenders in the 1920s—long after the court's creation—seems all the more surprising. However, early-twentieth-century Chicago and, in particular, the Chicago police enjoy a much less positive reputation than does the juvenile court. The city itself was associated strongly with crime and vice. Moreover, in the 1920s, Chicago earned notoriety as the most lawless city of the "lawless decade" by providing a home for massive bootlegging operations and organized crime. The Chicago police, in turn, reputedly were riddled with graft and corruption. Equally important, the Chicago police department did not undergo the same processes of reform that characterized departments elsewhere. To an extent, the problems with the Chicago police help explain why juvenile court advocates wanted to remove young offenders from their authority.[5]

In practice, however, the juvenile court and the police had no choice but to work closely on a daily basis. Both the large scale and the structure of the Cook County Juvenile Court led court officials to prefer to resolve children's problems informally. As Judge Tuthill also told his staff on the day the court opened, "the bringing of the child before court should be only as a last resort."[6] As a result, the Chicago juvenile court came to rely heavily on the police to investigate initial delinquency complaints and to determine which children should be petitioned to court. Officer O'Connor maintained that just "a very slight percentage of the complaints that came to the police station were ever brought into the Juvenile Court."[7] Hence, the police—an agency alien to the new juvenile justice system—fundamentally shaped the court's intake. Rather than restricting police power over juveniles, as reformers would have preferred, the creation of juvenile court in Chicago expanded the discretionary authority of the police. In many cases, the operations of juvenile justice in Chicago—more so than elsewhere—created opportunities for individual police officers to discipline young offenders as they saw fit.

Recent scholarship has emphasized the contested nature of the Chicago juvenile court, demonstrating that progressive juvenile justice did not represent one unitary goal that emerged naturally. Instead, the creation and evolution of juvenile justice was driven by the gender-based ideals of the court's largely white, middle-class, female founders, by the cooperation and resistance of its largely working-class clientele, by differing social scientific models of delinquency, and by public controversies about the legitimacy of the juvenile court itself.[8] Examining the interactions of the Cook County Juvenile Court and the Chicago police contributes to this ongoing reevaluation by bringing together the until-now separate stories of juvenile justice and policing in Chicago, and by placing the familiar story of the juvenile court in a broader perspective. If the court truly represented a "last resort," then police must have decided most delinquency cases themselves. Much of the real action took place not in courtrooms or reform schools but on the streets and in the station houses where officers such as O'Connor and Okon determined how best to correct young offenders.

## THE COOK COUNTY JUVENILE COURT IN OPERATION

In the eyes of its advocates, Cook County Juvenile Court represented a completely new approach to the problem of juvenile delinquency. Supported by a coalition of reformers including the Chicago Women's Club, Hull House, judges and lawyers from the Chicago Bar Association, and child welfare activists from Catholic and Protestant aid societies, the Illinois Juvenile Court Law went into effect in 1899. Rather than punishing children by sending them to a correctional institution (or ignoring their problems by releasing them, as was more often the case), the new juvenile court was intended to offer a flexible mechanism to rehabilitate young offenders. The object of the court, according to Hurley, was *not* "to punish the children brought before it," but to "inquire into his home surroundings" and either to "remove him entirely from the surroundings that make for vice" or to improve the home life of the child "through the agencies that the court might bring to bear."[9]

The Chicago juvenile court had jurisdiction over a wide range of youths: delinquents and dependents, boys and girls. Originally, it exercised authority only over boys under age sixteen and girls under seventeen, but a 1907 revision of the law extended its jurisdiction by one year to include boys under seventeen and girls under eighteen. In the fashion of progressive child saving, it defined "delinquency" broadly, not only as violations of state laws (crimes), but also as a child who "is incorrigible, or chooses evil associates; or is a runaway, or is growing up in idleness or crime; or frequents a house of ill-repute, gaming place, or dram shop; or idly roams the streets at night; or habitually trespasses on railway property; or is guilty of public profanity, or of indecency." "Dependency" was defined equally broadly, to cover homelessness, begging, parental neglect, or living in a home that might be deemed physically or morally unfit.[10] Operating with this broad definition in a huge city undergoing rapid growth, industrial development, and foreign immigration, the Chicago juvenile court could probably have exercised authority over as many cases as it wished. In practice, the court heard a median of 4,288 cases per year between 1904 and 1927. Of these, 1,833 per year were boys charged with delinquency (42 percent) and 581 per year were delinquent girls (13 percent); boy and girl dependents were the remainder.[11]

Sheer numbers suggest that boys—and particularly boy delinquents—constituted the primary concern of early juvenile courts. Recent historical works have emphasized the importance of female reformers in the founding and operation of juvenile court and their concern with female delinquents to such an extent that boys have been neglected. However, male reformers also played critical roles in the early years of juvenile justice, and they devoted much of their attention to male delinquents. As historian Robert Mennel has argued, "the preponderant figure of the first courts was the judge, and he was invariably a man who emphasized his masculinity in approaching delinquent children, especially boys."[12] Judge Morse Rohnert in Detroit certainly followed this model, balancing leniency and discipline in his dealings with boys.

Judge Tuthill in Chicago emphasized his almost paternal relationships, explaining that in court, "I talk with the boys, give him a good talk, just as I would my own boy." Most famously, Judge Ben Lindsey in Denver frequently described how his personal interactions with boys convinced them to do the right thing and bring other boys into juvenile court voluntarily to meet him.[13]

The children of immigrants also represented a major concern for early juvenile courts. Much of our knowledge about youths in the Chicago court comes from investigations by sociology students and faculty who employed the court as a social laboratory, and these investigations helped to reinforce an assumed environmental connection between immigration, poor living conditions, and delinquency. In one study of male delinquents brought before the juvenile court in 1905, University of Chicago doctoral candidate Mabel Carter Rhoades demonstrated that approximately 79 percent of these boys' parents were foreign-born; only 17 percent came from native-born white families and 4 percent were African American. Rhoades further connected delinquency with the absence or death of a parent, disrupted neighborhoods, and poverty—all problems likely to befall immigrants in early-twentieth-century Chicago.[14] Examining a much larger population, the social investigators Sophonisba Breckinridge and Edith Abbott also found virtually the same distribution of nativities among delinquents brought into court between 1899 and 1909. Like Rhoades, Breckinridge and Abbott linked delinquency to a range of social problems: immigration itself and cultural dislocations associated with it, poverty (again), parentlessness (again), and overcrowded and inadequate homes. These investigators concluded that the children of immigrants were most vulnerable to the social problems that contributed to delinquency.[15] In reality, the nativities of children petitioned to juvenile court in its early years were surprisingly consistent with Chicago's population at the time.[16] However, from the perspective of these studies—as well as early juvenile court advocates and officials—the purpose of the court was to resolve the social problems that they identified as being related to delinquency, so they assumed that the children of immigrants would be their natural clientele.

In its early years, the juvenile court had quite limited resources to accomplish its goals. Probation officers were to have been the key actors in the system, investigating initial court referrals, inquiring into children's home lives and backgrounds, devising plans for their rehabilitation, and monitoring their progress under court supervision. However, the initial Juvenile Court Act of 1899 did not allow Cook County to pay probation officers from public funds, nor did it make money available to the court for a detention home, transportation, or operating expenses. As a result, from its birth, the court depended on financial support and volunteer work from charitable agencies, especially the Juvenile Court Committee of the Chicago Women's Club (renamed the Juvenile Protective Association, or JPA, in 1907). Under the philanthropic leadership of Louise de Koven Bowen, the Juvenile Court Committee paid probation officers' salaries, ran a private detention home, and operated a bus to transport children from the detention home to the court (originally located more than two miles apart). The earliest probation officers were, for practical purposes, a handful of civic-minded volunteers. Only in 1905 did the Illinois legislature amend the original Juvenile Court Law to permit Cook County courts to hire their own professional probation officers. Even then, these officers supervised extremely large caseloads averaging 120 children in 1907, which prevented them from pursuing thorough investigations or maintaining close contact with individual delinquents.[17]

To help ameliorate these problems, the juvenile court used men from the Chicago Police Department as probation officers. With few resources at the court's disposal when it began operations, Judge Tuthill convinced Mayor Carter Harrison II to detail policemen to work as juvenile probation officers to supplement those supported by private funds. Tuthill reportedly argued, "while acting as probation officers, they would still be policemen looking after the welfare of the citizens of Chicago and their children, and that in effect they would still be doing police duty."[18] Following Harrison's approval, the police assigned roughly one officer per district to serve as "police probation officers," or PPOs. In the words of investigator Helen Jeter, "such officers met a very real need that could not have been met otherwise" by receiving complaints at the police station, investigating them, and appearing in court with children to present the case.[19] Before 1905, policemen constituted the large majority of probation officers. In 1904, the police assigned twenty-one men to probation duty, in comparison to four probation officers supported by philanthropies. After the county was permitted to hire its own probation officers, their number grew rapidly and by 1920 exceeded that of PPOs by 101 to 30. Nonetheless, the police remained central to court operations. Although county probation officers primarily supervised children following court hearings, PPOs continued to be responsible for most initial contacts with juveniles and performed many of the basic investigations prior to hearings.[20]

Advocates of the court were skeptical about hiring police officers for probation duties. One of the reformers' basic goals had been to remove children from the punitive control of the police. In the words of University of Chicago sociologist Charles R. Henderson, "their social function makes them agents of repression in relation to crime." In addition, because the police were reputed to receive and retain their jobs through political connections, using them as probation officers raised the distressing possibility that the court might also become politicized.[21] Nonetheless, court supporters eventually accepted the PPOs as part of the system, albeit grudgingly. One JPA investigator reported, "the general character of these officers is good. Care seems to have been exercised in their selection in order to get men who were especially intelligent and at the same time courteous and kind in their manner of dealing with children."[22] Chief Probation Officer John H. Witter likewise observed in 1909 that he had seen "few, if any, courts where police probation officers were entering into the spirit of juvenile work to the extent of that practiced in the Chicago Juvenile Court."[23]

The Cook County Juvenile Court strove for the ambitious goals of acting as a parent for delinquent and dependent children and transforming the social conditions that made for delinquency. However, due to its large caseload and its lack of necessary organizational mechanisms, it had to depend on police officers to operate. The structure of the juvenile court in Chicago put police officers in the position where they shaped the court's intake and work. In comparison to the reformers, activists, lawyers, and sociologists who created the juvenile court, however, the Chicago police were particularly unlikely participants in the new juvenile justice system.

## Unlikely Players

Both as individual officers and as an organization, the early-twentieth-century Chicago police exhibited little interest in the emerging juvenile justice system. In contrast to Detroit, where administrative reform had encouraged the police to engage in social welfare–oriented activity and child-friendly policing, reforms encountered greater obstacles in Chicago and experienced less success. As a result, working with children and youth did not become as important to the Chicago police as it did for the police in Detroit, and Chicago police rarely went out of their way to cooperate with the juvenile court or social reformers.

The case of Chicago highlights the divisions that sometimes emerged between civic reformers and the police. As historian Mark Haller has argued, reformers and police could cooperate when their goals coincided, such as when business leaders, lawyers, and the press demanded that police aggressively fight crimes against persons and property. However, when their goals differed, such as when reformers asked police to restrict drinking and gambling, the Chicago police proved less willing to help. Differing backgrounds represented one impediment to cooperation. Social reform advocates tended to be prosperous native-born Protestants, often court officials, settlement house residents, and probation workers. Police officers, in contrast, tended to come from working-class backgrounds and ethnic neighborhoods; the Chicago police demonstrated that there was a grain of truth in the stereotype of the Irish cop. Differing perspectives constituted a second impediment. While social reform advocates regarded drinking and gambling as moral hazards for children and youth, police officers tended to be sympathetic to these enterprises, regarding them as relatively harmless forms of leisure.[24]

Police probation officers—the men assigned to work with children and the juvenile court—were recruited from the ranks of patrolmen. Like the police department as a whole, they came from predominantly ethnic, and particularly Irish, backgrounds. In 1909, for example, 39 percent of PPOs had Irish surnames. Even in 1928, when Chicago's population had become more diversified, the Irish still constituted 31 percent of PPOs.[25] At least in appearance, PPOs distinguished themselves from the uniformed police force by wearing civilian clothes. In so doing, they sought to appear less intimidating to children and to eliminate uniformed police from the juvenile court system.[26] Wearing different clothes, however, could only partially disguise the fact that PPOs had a great deal in common with regular police. They were assigned to their jobs by the police department, and therefore subject to the same political pressures that affected all job designations. Sometimes juvenile duty represented, according to one investigation, "an easy assignment for a police officer whose usefulness to the Department was declining." The juvenile court could veto PPO appointments, thereby eliminating the worst candidates, but did not have an active authority to select officers it would have preferred. Furthermore, PPOs received no additional training; instead, they learned their jobs by experience and observation. Consequently, their abilities and approaches to their jobs varied widely. Some believed "a taste of an institution quite early" was the best means of preventing delinquency and therefore placed many youths in detention. Others saw detention or the juvenile court as only a last resort.[27] In short, as with Chicago policing more generally, a great deal of the work of a PPO depended on an individual officer's discretion.

Individual officers enjoyed so much autonomy partly due to the organization of the Chicago Police Department. The department was thoroughly decentralized, with each district operating almost autonomously. Furthermore, as late as the 1920s, new recruits received only nominal formal training. As a result, individual officers patrolling their beats became accustomed to independence and very limited supervision from their superiors.[28]

Officers were supervised, however, by larger political and commercial networks. The interconnection of partisan politics, organized vice, and policing often associated with turn-of-the-twentieth-century cities flourished in Chicago. Neighborhood political organizations substantially influenced police officers' hiring, assignments, and promotions. Alliances between political and commercial interests also deflected the police from regulating illicit businesses. In spite of reformers' frequent demands that they stamp out gambling, drinking, and prostitution, the police openly tolerated saloons and brothels in the Levee red light district. These policies came directly from the top of the political hierarchy. Carter Harrison II, the five-term mayor of Chicago first elected in 1897 (and the man who first authorized PPOs), maintained a hands-off policy toward organized vice as long as it remained segregated from the rest of the city. Individual officers, in turn, profited from widespread graft and payoffs; those who did not cooperate faced transfer. Furthermore, it was commonly reported that police officers avoided arresting anyone with connections to local politicians and accepted bribes to keep criminals out of jail. According to one investigator for reform-minded city alderman Charles Merriam, "Most of the policemen know that whenever [a person with ties to organized crime is arrested] there is always a piece of money in it for them."[29]

The powerful influences of politics and vice discouraged the Chicago police from adopting the professional practices that were becoming increasingly common in other cities. Even when they chose to, police leaders had limited power to change the conduct of patrolmen. For example, Chief LeRoy Steward, appointed in 1909 to clean up the scandals of a previous administration, sought to transfer the officers responsible for graft and corruption in the Levee out of that district but his efforts were frustrated. "I could never place my hand on the patrolman, detectives, or officers who were responsible," Steward later said. "Those who did the fixing were so thoroughly entrenched that it was impossible to find out who they were."[30] More fundamentally, frequent turnover also limited the power of leaders. Between 1897 and 1927, the Chicago police went through twelve chiefs with an average term of two and a half years.[31] Furthermore, according to social reformers such as Graham Taylor, founder of the Chicago Commons settlement house, these ongoing problems discouraged those officers who did want to be honest.[32]

This endemic graft and constant change in leadership focused the attention of police reformers on the issues of preventing corruption and controlling vice, not on systemic change. The story of the Chicago police in the 1910s and 1920s is a frustrating cycle of efforts to stamp out vice and corruption followed by renewed problems. In 1912, the state attorney's office and vigorous action by the police department's vice squad closed the Levee, but in so doing unintentionally encouraged drinking, gambling, and prostitution to spread throughout the city and increased the importance of organized crime. Furthermore, the 1915 mayoral election of William Hale ("Big Bill") Thompson marked a return to "wide open" official toleration of vice. Even the efforts of Mayor William Dever and Police Chief Morgan Collins to shut down the illegal liquor industry between 1923 and 1927 could not overcome unofficial cooperation between police officers and bootleggers. As late as 1929, the Illinois Crime Survey argued that uprooting corruption was the first step necessary for police reform.[33] In contrast to Detroit, administrative reform and operational efficiency were secondary concerns.

This pervasive corruption and lack of discipline impacted the policing of children in a negative way, at least according to child welfare reformers. Many specifically criticized the Chicago police for failing to protect children from vice. For example, although JPA agents investigated hotels, saloons, roadhouses, and dance halls for evidence that they served alcohol to juveniles or provided places of assignation, the police rarely acted on the violations discovered. JPA president Louise de Koven Bowen complained in 1920, "the Juvenile Protective Association is obliged to depend largely upon the help of the police in its work for children; it believes that it has a right to expect that when it reports to the police department violations of law that endanger childhood, the police will take immediate action. Yet in hundreds of instances during the past year where the welfare of children was involved, the service rendered by the police has been inadequate or entirely negligible." In spite of a law barring juveniles under age eighteen from pool halls, agents of the JPA managed to find boys playing pool, gambling, and even drinking in at least sixty. The JPA forwarded a report of each instance to the police, yet the police claimed they could confirm only seven violations.[34] The police of course had little incentive to exclude juveniles from pool halls or any other establishment if doing so would undermine the business of their financial partners. In these instances, child welfare reformers both expressed legitimate frustration and called attention to the fact that corruption discouraged the police from protecting young people from what reformers regarded as moral hazards.

Policewomen—usually assigned to supervise public behavior in dance halls and places of commercial amusement where youths and especially adolescent girls might congregate—offered only a limited response to these problems. Chicago first hired policewomen in 1913 and soon maintained one of the largest contingents in the country, with twenty-one officers in 1915, twenty-eight in 1920, and thirty in 1930. Policewomen, however, were distributed across the city's districts rather than centralized in a single bureau (as was most often the case in other cities), and did "whatever their respective commanding officers may prescribe. In some districts they supervise taxi dance halls, investigate houses of prostitution, and look for potential sources of crime. In others, they do practically nothing."[35]

The police department's disinterest in the JPA's complaints and in regulating vice reflected a more general pattern of inaction. Child saving was not a high organizational priority for the police. Their links to politics, vice, and organized crime created a disincentive to participate in moral reform campaigns aimed at cleansing the urban environment. Moreover, their tradition of operating very independently discouraged them from cooperating with juvenile court advocates. The antiprofessional culture of the Chicago police worked against their willing participation in the new system of juvenile justice.

# THE WORK OF POLICE PROBATION OFFICERS

Regardless of the problems that plagued Chicago law enforcement, assigning policemen to act as probation officers created an explicit link between the police department and the juvenile court. And these policemen made several key decisions in the early stages of the juvenile justice process.

The primary duty of PPOs was to investigate complaints involving delinquent boys prior to a court hearing.[36] In the juvenile court's early years, any concerned citizen could file a petition against a child, and the court would hear the case. The sheer number of cases, however, soon made this system unwieldy. Judge Julian Mack solved this problem around 1907 by encouraging the public to register complaints with probation officers or the police, who then investigated the case, determined if it was substantial enough to warrant the court's attention, and decided whether to file formal petitions.[37] PPOs conducted these preliminary investigations. In the usual flow of delinquency cases, it made perfect sense to assign an officer in each district to be in charge of juveniles. As Chief Probation Officer Joel D. Hunter acknowledged in 1915, "the natural place for a citizen to complain when an offense has been committed is the nearest police station."[38] Likewise, when patrol officers apprehended delinquents, they turned them over to their districts' PPO instead of taking them before a lower court, as they had traditionally done. At that point, PPOs determined how to proceed, largely on the basis of their experience and discretion. As one investigator noted, "there are no rules governing the process of investigation, and each officer is free to carry on the

Table 5.1

Complaints against Juveniles Investigated by Chicago Probation Officers,
1918–30

| Year | Number of Complaints Investigated | Rate of Complaints per 1,000 Juveniles between Ages 10 and 17 |
|---|---|---|
| 1918 | 19,019 | 60.31 |
| 1919 | 16,995 | 53.26 |
| 1920 | 16,488 | 51.07 |
| 1921 | 15,611 | 46.85 |
| 1922 | 16,110 | 46.89 |
| 1923 | 16,004 | 45.21 |
| 1924 | 16,640 | 45.67 |
| 1925 | 17,785 | 47.46 |
| 1926 | 19,566 | 50.81 |
| 1927 | 19,987 | 50.54 |
| 1928 | 18,141 | 44.70 |
| 1929 | 17,865 | 42.92 |
| 1930 | 16,908 | 39.63 |
| Median | 16,995 | |

Sources: Chicago Police Department, *Annual Reports,* 1918–1930; U.S. Bureau of the
Census, *13th Census, Population 1910,* 439; U.S. Bureau of the Census, *14th Population
Census, Population, 1920,* 291; U.S. Bureau of the Census, *15th Census, Population
1930,* 743.

investigation of each case as he sees fit." They could visit boys' homes or call
them to the police station, but in either case the primary issue was "ascer-
taining the truth or falsity of the complaint." On the basis of their findings,
they determined if the juvenile court should proceed with the case.[39]

In this manner, PPOs brought to juvenile court "by far the greater number of delinquent boys' cases." Available historical data do not indicate how
many cases PPOs actually handled in the first two decades of the century, but
beginning in 1918, the police tabulated and published detailed statistics on
their work with juveniles (see table 5.1). From that information, it is apparent that between 1918 and 1926, PPOs filed 82 percent of all delinquency
petitions to juvenile court. Delinquency represented 47 percent of the juvenile court's total caseload; dependency and mothers' pension cases constituted the rest. In all, police referrals accounted for 38 percent of the juvenile
court's caseload.[40]

Measuring delinquency in Chicago from the perspective of the PPOs gen-
erates a very different picture than from the perspective of the juvenile court.

As shown earlier, the Cook County Juvenile Court heard a median of 2,414 delinquency cases per year between 1904 and 1927 (1,833 boys, 581 girls). By contrast, as table 5.1 shows, the PPOs investigated a median of 16,995 complaints between 1918 and 1930. Controlling for Chicago's rapidly growing population, they investigated complaints against kids at a rate of between 40 and 60 per 1,000 juveniles between ages ten and seventeen each year.[41] These delinquency rates for Chicago are sharply higher than are those for Detroit in the same period, in part because the two police departments measured different things—the Detroit police counted arrests of juveniles, while the Chicago police counted all investigations and official contacts between cops and kids. Thus, Chicago's delinquency rates are virtually impossible to compare with other cities. They represent, however, the broadest possible measure of delinquency short of a "dark figure" encompassing all juvenile crimes and misbehavior.

The Chicago police also labeled delinquent behavior in very general ways, which suggests that they understood "delinquency" to encompass a broad and often arbitrary range of misbehaviors. For example, the police characterized 23 percent of juvenile offenses between 1919 and 1930 as "miscellaneous." Their figures vaguely describe another 45 percent of investigations as involving "immorality," "incorrigibility," "malicious mischief," and running away. In contrast, the police recorded criminal offenses with more precision, presumably both because these offenses were more serious and because there were fewer of them. Crimes against property such as burglary, larceny, and auto theft constituted 29 percent of juvenile offenses, while crimes against persons including robbery, assault, and weapons violations constituted just 4 percent.[42] These findings suggest that most of the juvenile complaints that PPOs investigated in the 1920s involved kid stuff—vague status offenses and minor misconduct—far more often than serious crimes.

Regardless of the offense, the police determined whether a child should be petitioned to court or if his case should be adjusted informally. Individual officers disposed of the vast majority of complaints against children on their own, without involving the juvenile court. Between 1918 and 1930, PPOs adjusted unofficially an average of 89 percent of the cases they investigated, petitioning only 11 percent to juvenile court. The police informally resolved a median of 15,141 cases per year between 1918 and 1930 and filed petitions to juvenile court on only 1,855 per year.[43]

Disposing of cases on their own initiative sometimes exposed the police to criticism from assiduous child welfare advocates. As one JPA investigator wrote, "it usually happened that the Captain or the Judge had never even seen or heard of these cases . . . a large number of children brought in are sent home after being questioned by the police probation officer, but the officer thought the record sheet would look better if it showed that the Judge or the Captain did the sending home."[44] This investigator, however, missed the point that PPOs were *supposed* to send boys and girls home without bothering higher authorities. It was widely understood that PPOs implemented the court's stated intention "to correct conditions in the home without bringing the child into Juvenile Court and thereby causing a public record to [be] made against him."[45] Court officials instructed PPOs to "take the place of a court of first jurisdiction in a large majority of cases of delinquency." They depended "upon the judgment of the police probation officers whether or not a case shall appear in court."[46] As Judge Victor Arnold told a gathering of police officials, "we believe that if we can satisfactorily and effectively and in a very constructive manner adjust a case without making a court record against your son or my son, if the case is not too serious, it will be better."[47] By this standard, the PPOs were highly effective. Chief Probation Officer John H. Witter asserted in 1910, "the very large percentage of cases settled out of court is evidence of the high order of work done."[48] Thus, the juvenile court truly represented a "last resort" for the disposition of delinquency cases. The Chicago juvenile court pursued an intake policy very different from the court in Detroit, which sought to pull children into its net. Instead, the Chicago court tried to keep them out, and in fact followed an intake policy reminiscent of the pre-juvenile court, diversion-based system in Detroit.

Not sending juveniles to court, however, does not mean that police did not have any means of control over them. PPOs determined whether boys should be held in custody during an investigation, and thus used detention as a very effective mechanism for disciplining young offenders.

As a rule, the police were discouraged from detaining juveniles, in part because Cook County had only limited facilities to hold them. Under the Illinois Juvenile Court Law, juveniles could not be jailed or transported with adult suspects, and children under age twelve could never be placed in jails or lockups at all, so initially police could detain them only in a house maintained voluntarily by the Juvenile Court Committee. In 1907, a county-managed Juvenile Detention Home (part of a new juvenile court building) replaced the earlier haphazard facility.[49] Even this new accommodation proved inadequate, and by the late 1910s, overcrowding at the Detention Home had become severe. Wards designed to accommodate sixty boys often held seventy, and some boys had to sleep on mattresses on the floor. More disturbingly, the Juvenile Detention Home began to refuse admission because of overcrowding, so the police had no choice but to hold youngsters in lockups condemned as "unfit . . . for prisoners or policemen."[50] Finally, an expanded

Juvenile Detention Home was opened in 1923 as part of a newer and larger juvenile court complex.[51]

Nonetheless, the police officers who controlled admissions to the Juvenile Detention Home still used it as if it were a jail, holding youth there for the equivalent of a brief sentence and then releasing them, hopefully chastened by the experience. Most boys who were detained were discharged following an investigation and never appeared in juvenile court. In 1926, for example, the Cook County Detention Home admitted 7,115 alleged delinquents, but the juvenile court only heard 2,265 delinquency cases. Moreover, 43 percent of all children detained (boys and girls, delinquent and dependent) were released within two days. The police essentially used the Juvenile Detention Home as a short-term punishment while they decided whether a judicial proceeding was warranted. As Harrison A. Dobbs, superintendent of the Detention Home, explained, "The Police Department assignment to the Juvenile Court has cooperated excellently well in the removal of children [from the Detention Home, but] the great difficulty appears to be in the regulation of intake. . . . Certainly it is a dangerous technique . . . which places the child in one or two days of detention and then offers a release without thorough study and investigation."[52]

In addition, boys whose "life histories" were recorded in the 1920s by sociologists affiliated with the Illinois Institute for Juvenile Research claimed that police occasionally held them at station houses rather than at the Detention Home with the apparent intention of scaring them straight. "Sidney," the narrator of sociologist Clifford R. Shaw's *The Natural History of a Delinquent Career,* reported that police detained him in a station lockup when he was only seven years old.[53] Another boy, *Frank Bono,*[54] reported that when he and his friends were arrested for robbing their school, the police "put [them] down in the cell with nothing to eat for three meals. Then the next day they brought us to the detention home." Likewise, when the police caught *Anthony Piazza* stealing candy from a truck, they booked him at the station and detained him in a holding cell for three hours until his father came. Anthony "was really worried . . . because this was the first time I was in a regular police station."[55] The police intended this type of treatment to frighten boys enough to deter them from future crime.

Police dispositions turn out to be the biggest factor shaping the outcomes of delinquency cases in early-twentieth-century Chicago. Relatively few nominal delinquents ever made it to juvenile court, so formal court dispositions remained a small component of juvenile justice. Among the total cases investigated by Chicago PPOs between 1918 and 1930, fewer than 5 percent were placed on probation, and fewer than 4 percent were sent to institutions.[56]

Even at the height of its national influence, the Chicago juvenile court was only a last resort. Instead, police investigators made the key decisions about what to do with juveniles in the streets, in the station houses, and in the Juvenile Detention Home.

## THE CONTOURS OF POLICE DECISION MAKING

This process gave the police an extraordinary amount of freedom to determine delinquents' fates. But on what basis did they decide how to correct particular offenders? What differentiated the minority of juveniles petitioned to court from the vast majority whose cases the police adjusted informally? Anecdotal evidence suggests that, for the most part, the police attempted to decide cases involving minor offenses on their own, particularly those involving first offenders, and to reserve juvenile court for more serious or repeat delinquents. According to Officer O'Connor (described at the beginning of this chapter), he and other PPOs rarely petitioned boys to court for offenses such as larceny or mischief unless complainants insisted or the boy had been in trouble before. Officers' ability to keep track of who had been in trouble before, however, was limited by their casual record keeping. Although officers were supposed to document every complaint they handled, investigators found that they rarely did so, nor did they often consult juvenile court records. They could encounter a boy already on probation and not even know it. As a result of this arrangement, according to one critic, most boys had "no case history except in the minds of the officers."[57] Thus, the decision whether to petition a delinquent to juvenile court seems to have been made quite often on the basis of little more than an individual officer's memory and discretion.

The context of particular neighborhoods offers some further clues as to the tendencies of police decisions. PPOs did not dispose of juvenile cases uniformly across the city. While the percentage of cases petitioned to juvenile court varied little year by year, it did vary geographically by police district. On average, between 1928 and 1930, the police referred 10.2 percent of cases to juvenile court, but this average varied within a range between 2.4 and 19.8 percent in different parts of the city.[58]

For example, the Near West Side was characterized in the 1920s as "Chicago's most extensive slum area" and the embodiment of the city's problems with crime and delinquency. Containing the Maxwell Street police district (No. 22), the neighborhood featured, according to sociologist Clifford Shaw, the "marked physical deterioration of its buildings and the presence of large accumulations of debris in the streets and alleys," extremely low rents, and tenement housing that attracted only "the lowest economic class." This area exemplified the social changes Chicago experienced in the early twentieth century. On the one hand, it was the home of a rapidly changing ethnic population of recent immigrants (particularly Italians, Jews, and African Americans who had newly migrated from the South) trying to adapt to urban life. On the other hand, it was also the home of Jane Addams's Hull House, the physical and intellectual center of the social reform movement in Chicago, which offered a myriad of programs to assist its neighbors. Furthermore, by the 1920s, the Near West Side sponsored organized criminal gangs that were variously involved in bootlegging liquor, "dope-peddling," protection rackets, and distributing stolen merchandise.[59]

In high-crime, high-tension neighborhoods such as the Near West Side, the police were most likely to take juvenile crime seriously and petition youths to juvenile court. Between 1928 and 1930, PPOs in District 22 petitioned an unusually large 19.2 percent of juvenile cases to court, the second highest percentage of any district in Chicago.[60] In these years, police there investigated delinquency complaints at a rate of 73 per 1,000 juveniles per year, among the highest rates for any neighborhood in Chicago and well above the delinquency rate for the city as a whole (only 42 per 1,000). In addition, 40 percent of these investigations involved crimes against property, as compared to just 30 percent for the city as a whole.[61]

These findings come as no surprise; the local setting in the Maxwell Street district offered adult criminals for role models and encouraged teenagers to commit frequent and relatively serious offenses. For example, connections with organized crime syndicates operating in Chicago in the 1920s allowed boys in the Near West Side's notorious "42" gang to "fence" stolen goods and thereby transition from stealing from coin-operated vending machines as younger boys to committing burglary and armed robbery when they became older. These boys also developed an almost contemptuous attitude toward the law, often treating encounters with police as a sport. After police arrested two teenagers from the "42" gang for carrying bags stuffed with candy and cigarettes late at night, the boys made a game of it, seeing how long it would take the officers to figure out they had taken their booty from the local A&P grocery store. First they said "we took it off some kids," but the police said that story "wouldn't stick." Then they claimed they took it from a store in Cicero (the notoriously crime-dominated suburb outside of Chicago police jurisdiction). The officers didn't believe that either but still did not guess the truth. By this point, the boys thought "it was pretty funny because all of the cigarettes were marked A&P on them, but the coppers didn't even look." Only when the officers were taking the boys to the station and happened to pass the store that had been robbed did they realize that the boys in custody were responsible. These sorts of difficult offenders were of the type that police would detain and then petition to court.[62]

Between 1928 and 1930, police in the Wabash Avenue police district (No. 5) petitioned an even larger share of juveniles to court: 19.8 percent.[63] The Wabash Avenue district was in the heart of Chicago's "Black Belt" in the 1920s. Beginning during World War I, Chicago's African American population had grown explosively due to the Great Migration, more than doubling each decade from 44,103 in 1920 to 109,458 in 1920 to 233,903 in 1930. Many (if not most) of these migrants found lodging in and around Chicago's traditional African American neighborhood on the South Side surrounding Grand Boulevard and State Street.[64] This area had long been the cultural and economic center of Chicago's black community, but during the 1920s it also experienced a demographic transition from being the home of people of a mix of ethnicities to being virtually all black. As the Great Migration brought African Americans into the community, older immigrant groups moved out; blacks increased from 32 percent of the district's population in 1920 to 94 percent in 1930.[65] High rates of delinquency (80 complaints per 1,000 juveniles between 1928 and 1930) accompanied this transition. Police did not investigate juveniles from the Wabash Avenue district for particularly severe crimes, however. Thirty-three percent were alleged to have committed offenses against property (only slightly above the 30 percent that characterized the city as a whole), and 4 percent were investigated for offenses against persons (the same as Chicago's total). Otherwise, police investigated kids in the Black Belt for the same sorts of kid stuff as they investigated kids for anywhere else.[66]

Nonetheless, police sent more black kids to juvenile court. Not only did the Wabash Avenue district petition a larger portion of delinquency cases to court than did any other district in Chicago, African Americans comprised a disproportionate share of boys in juvenile court, and had since its inception. In 1903, when African Americans constituted 1.8 percent of Chicago's population, black males represented 2.6 percent of total delinquents; by 1930, when Chicago's population was 6.9 percent African American, they comprised 21.3 percent of boys in juvenile court.[67]

Why were African American youths so disproportionately represented in juvenile court? The conventional wisdom of the time, as articulated by another University of Chicago–trained sociologist, Earl R. Moses, was that the combined experiences of migrating north, transitioning to urban life, and encountering economic dislocation in the city all contributed to unusual amounts of African American delinquency. According to Moses, these experiences exacerbated the socially disorganized environments that so many early juvenile court advocates and later Chicago sociologists believed led to delinquency.[68] More contemporary thinking about the continued racial disparities in juvenile justice has contributed an additional factor to this analysis, suggesting that systemic biases also play a role. While not denying racial discrepancies in delinquent behavior, modern studies have also found that subtle biases also affect decision making by police and other players in the juvenile justice system. Compounded together, small inequities in different stages of the decision-making process can add up to large disparities in outcomes.[69] Bluntly, racial biases by the police and unusually frequent (if not severe) delinquency by African American youth at least begin to explain why Wabash Avenue district PPOs petitioned so many black kids to juvenile court.

Regardless of race and even of offense, however, the large majority of boys did *not* end up in juvenile court. Far more typical was a pattern of warning and releasing youths accused of minor delinquencies. This pattern characterized not only PPOs, but also police officers and any sort of official with law enforcement authority. The store detective at Goldblatt's Department Store, for example, reported that he caught about 100 shoplifters per month, mostly boys from neighborhood schools. After he made them sign a confession, the detective usually released shoplifters with a warning not to be seen in the store again.[70] Likewise, police officers tried to intimidate younger boys to teach them a lesson not to commit crimes. After twelve-year-old *Frederick Donald* and a friend stole a fan from an abandoned house, the police brought them to the local station to see the captain. The captain "asked us several questions and kept us sitting in silence while he stared at us for nearly half an hour without saying a word. I think this was more frightening that any loud talk or blustering could possibly have been." He then released the chastened boys.[71] Sometimes the police discouraged young boys from delinquency just by talking to them on the street. For example, one officer confronted young *William Contencsik* while he was collecting scrap iron to sell to a junkman. When the cop asked what he was doing, Contencsik told the truth. The cop laughed, patted him on the shoulder, and walked away, but the encounter had a great impact on the boy: "There and then I decided I wasn't going to steal any more."[72]

These cases illustrate a more general pattern in the exercise of police discretion to dispose of complaints against juveniles. Although they caught boys in the act of committing delinquency and had the opportunity to take official action against them, these officers chose not to, instead releasing boys with reprimands that they hoped would discourage future crime. Likewise,

most PPOs adjusted nearly all officially reported delinquency cases themselves. Only in districts experiencing unusually severe crime problems, such
as Maxwell Street, or sharp social changes, such as Wabash Avenue, did this
pattern vary significantly. Even then, PPOs decided the great majority of
cases on their own. In practice, PPOs petitioned delinquents to juvenile court
only as a last resort.

## POLICING TEENAGERS ON CHICAGO'S STREETS

In the 1920s and 1930s, the day-to-day policing of juveniles in Chicago
seems like a throwback to an earlier era, before the creation of the Cook
County Juvenile Court. The court did little to curtail the enormous discretion that policemen enjoyed when dealing with juveniles. In fact, the indis-
pensable role that police officers played in determining juvenile court intake
expanded their discretionary authority and enhanced the informal power
they exercised over youth. Moreover, the court's continued reliance on the
police gave Chicago cops—beat officers as well as PPOs—license to adjudi-
cate offenses routinely on their own. Their often-rough methods of disciplining youths reflected officers' continuing belief that delinquency
constituted a natural behavior best addressed by immediate correction. The
primary interest of police officers on the streets lay in controlling juvenile
misbehavior and maintaining public order, so they acted as if they saw kids
as potential criminals. This police perspective allowed little room for sympathy or accommodation with young offenders, so it often generated hostile
interactions between cops and kids.

Standard operating procedure for Chicago cops was to discipline boys
informally, regardless of whether or not they had committed a particular
offense. Officers regularly hassled groups of youth they happened to meet on
the streets. One "street worker" affiliated with the Chicago Area Project, an
innovative grassroots social agency aimed at community improvement and
delinquency prevention organized by sociologist Clifford Shaw in the early
1930s, reported that the police regularly admonished boys not to lounge on
street corners. To him, these encounters were "marked on every occasion by
arbitrariness and sometimes even by brutality. On many occasions the activities of the squads were quite obviously motivated either by a desire to show
their authority or sometimes even by mere venal impulses."[73]

The police also hassled and preemptively arrested boys who had done little wrong. *Dick Tebrio,* the younger brother of two members of the "42" gang
who never participated in his siblings' crimes, encountered the police almost

as often as they did. Dick related that, at the age of twelve, he had gone to the police to report that his new shoes had been stolen while he was swimming at the Oak Street Beach. Rather than recording his complaint, however, the police arrested him on the spot because they associated him with some boys suspected of purse snatching. Dick and the other boys were taken to the East Chicago Police Station and "locked up in the Juvenile Home." On another occasion, the police arrested Dick when he was with a group having an argument about baseball on a street corner near a church. The church watchman had reported the boys for disturbing the peace. Only after they had been detained at the station did the police lieutenant let the boys go with a warning not to be spotted near the church again. Dick got into trouble once more when he was caught sneaking into a movie theater without paying. The theater manager called the police and signed complaints against the boys. Dick claimed that the police held him in the Juvenile Detention Home for nine days before discharging him.[74] Dick's relative innocence mattered little to the police; as with many boys, they were less interested in punishing him for a particular offense than in teaching him a general lesson. Detention or a good scare now, this practice suggested, would help prevent future misbehavior.

Intimidation, arrest, and detention were not the only methods at the disposal of the police. Patrolmen regularly used violence to regulate juvenile behavior. It was not unusual for officers to slap boys or to threaten them with being sent to jail, even when they had no intention of carrying out their threats. Gus Okon, a park police officer described earlier, explained that when he caught one boy masturbating, he dealt with the problem in a truly frightening fashion: "I brought him into the director's office. . . . I says to the head attendant, 'John, go out and get that knife.' And he went out real solemn like and came back with a big butcher knife. Then I says to the boy, 'Take it out.' And the kid started to cry, and I yelled at him again, 'Take it out!' He did and then I started to whet up the knife and talk to the attendant about what to do with the blood and whether we ought to have a doctor there to take care of the boy. The kid was scared he was about to faint, then I said to him, 'Well, if you promise not to do that again, we won't cut it off this time. But if you get caught again, off it comes sure. Now, beat it.' Then we had a big laugh."[75]

In addition, the police rarely hesitated to abuse suspects in custody, even if they were young. In 1931, the President's National Commission on Law Observance and Enforcement (or, the Wickersham Commission), formed two years earlier to investigate Prohibition-era lawlessness, found police violence to be rampant across the country. The police often gave suspects the "third degree," beating them to extort confessions and the names of accomplices. In particular, the commission reported that the third degree was so "thoroughly at home in Chicago" that it was a rare occasion when prisoners were not abused.[76] Even for juveniles, violence seems to have been a routine component of interrogation. When one boy refused to answer questions following arrest, he reported that the police "started to hit me and they wanted to know where I was at and what I did for a living and the rest of that crap." Only when he told them that he was sixteen did they transfer him to the Juvenile Detention Home.[77]

The police also regularly used firearms to apprehend fleeing criminals, rarely distinguishing between juvenile and adult offenders. In the 1920s, Chicago's police faced well-armed gangsters, and they developed the habit of drawing their guns even when dealing with delinquents. Cops almost routinely apprehended boys by pulling out their weapons and commanding suspects to stop or else they would shoot.[78] Some boys reported that police even fired warning shots to discourage them from stealing coal from railroad yards. Eleven-year-old Junior claimed, "Da coppers shoot at your feet or in de air to scare you."[79] The potential use of firearms, of course, constituted a very effective threat. When *Donald Franklin* and his accomplices were caught shoplifting in a department store, the policeman asked the manager what he wanted done to the boys. The manager "winked at him and said shoot them so they won't steal anymore." Both knew that the officer would not shoot juveniles for shoplifting, but they also knew that the police used their guns often enough in everyday crime fighting that the suggestion might effectively scare the boys and deter them from future crime.[80]

By their actions, the Chicago police expressed their own implicit program for dealing with delinquents. Although they could refer boys to probation officers and ultimately to juvenile court, they seemed to prefer to handle cases on their own terms, in their own ways, often by harassing suspicious boys, detaining them on a seemingly arbitrary basis, and using physical force (or its threat). Daily contact with delinquents and their neighborhood conditions encouraged police officers to believe that they had their own kind of expertise and understood how to discipline boys better than did court officials. In contrast to the police in Detroit, the police in Chicago did not offer their hands in friendship or seek to bring delinquents into the juvenile court. Instead, they sought to regulate and punish juvenile misbehavior quickly and tangibly in order to teach them the limits of acceptable conduct.

Parents' reactions to these methods of disciplining their children were decidedly mixed. Many times, parents and police loosely cooperated to correct delinquents. Some parents turned to the police for help if it suited their purposes. When young "Sidney" rode a bicycle around his block and ignored his mother's calls to come home, she informed a passing policeman that the bike was stolen. The officer stopped "Sidney," took the bicycle from him, and sent him back to his mother, thus doing exactly as she wished.[81] Police, in turn, sometimes turned to parents for aid in disciplining youth. Once, when the police arrested an eleven-year-old for purse snatching, the officers required the boy's father to beat him in the officer's presence.[82] Parents' approach to delinquency also sometimes paralleled the rough practices of the police. When *Anthony Piazza's* father picked him up following his first arrest, he took the boy home and, according to Anthony, "as soon as I put my first step into the house my father started to hit me." Anthony's father apparently also believed that physical punishment would curb his misbehavior.[83]

In contrast, parents sometimes disapproved of the seemingly arbitrary authority that police exercised over their children. Some parents simply encouraged delinquency. "Stanley," the narrator of another of Shaw's published "life histories," *The Jack-Roller,* reported that his stepmother sent him to steal food from nearby markets when he was only seven years old.[84] Other parents interfered with police operations. *Arthur Menzie's* father, for example, lied to an officer who tracked Arthur to his home, telling him that no boy fitting Arthur's description lived there. He then warned Arthur to stay away from police, saying, "next time play dice in a basement or some place where the squad can't see you guys."[85] Still others actively opposed the police. The father of the group of brothers in the "42" gang, for example, once gave his oldest son $10 to pay a bribe to get out of jail. When the police came the next day to arrest the boy on different charges, he would not let the officers into his house without a warrant. They entered anyway, so the father "jumped on them and started in fighting" as his son tried to escape.[86] Such fathers saw the police as little better than thugs trying to shake down their children.

Boys expressed greater and more open antagonism toward the police than did their parents. While teenage defiance of any authority figure may partially explain this animosity, the informal methods of discipline often used by the police deepened their natural hostility. Many slum-dwelling boys in Chicago believed that police officers arbitrarily harassed, arrested, and abused them. As one boy asserted, "I didn't like the police because whatever happened they would always blame me and always pick me up and take me to the police station and question me but later let me go because they couldn't prove anything against me."[87]

Boys also viewed the police as fundamentally dishonest. One claimed, "the majority of them are incompetent and corrupted. Take the Chicago Police department there is hardly an officer in this department that will not accept a bribe of some sort or other[;] their word is no good."[88] Boys' experiences led them to believe that, for many officers, payoffs were more important than enforcing the law. When a pair of Chicago police officers apprehended a boy who had committed a long string of assaults and robberies, they did not arrest him but instead demanded $75 to let him go.[89] Finally, boys linked police corruption to the arbitrary patterns of law enforcement that they regularly experienced. One boy connected graft to rough corrections, asserting, "they are a bunch of crooks worster [*sic*] than us, because we keep to one line of business and they don't. There are cops in the daytime and crooks at night. They want you to give the money if you got it and they'll be your friends. If you're broke they beat you . . . and throw you in jail." He concluded, "We don't think much of coppers. . . . We only hate them for not leaving us alone when we ain't doing anything."[90] The rough manner in which Chicago's police exercised authority over boys generated deep antagonisms between cops and kids—the kinds of antagonism that a modern juvenile justice system had been designed to supplant and eliminate.

# How Typical Was Chicago?

Although Chicago was in the forefront of child welfare reform in general and the juvenile court movement in particular, its often-corrupt police force remained central to the operations of the new system of juvenile justice. The Cook County Juvenile Court relied on the cooperation of external agents, and none more so than the police, to function. The police heavily influenced the intake of juvenile courts by adjusting the vast majority of cases themselves, deciding which youth should be petitioned, and maintaining informal supervision over the great majority of delinquents. Although police and reformers in Chicago were often portrayed as antagonists, in fact the police did exactly what court officials desired, utilizing juvenile court only as a last resort. The police had to screen out the large number of minor complaints so that juvenile court could devote its limited time and resources to handling persistent and more severely criminal offenders. In practice, however, police officers often exercised a discretionary and arbitrary style of correcting juveniles. For some delinquent youth, the police deemed a casual warning sufficient to dissuade them from future misbehavior. For others, the police readily resorted to violent "treatment" to discourage them from criminal conduct. They often regarded corporal punishment as a more effective response to minor crimes than formal arrest and probationary supervision. The resulting interactions contributed to an increasingly antagonistic relationship between police and juveniles in the 1920s and 1930s.

Examining early twentieth-century Chicago suggests that the overall operations of juvenile justice depended in large part on the place of the juvenile court within the larger criminal justice community. In Chicago, juvenile court was utilized only as a last resort, whereas in Detroit, it was utilized first in a much larger portion of cases. Why? The Chicago court had only limited resources—only one judge and never enough probation officers—and struggled in its early years to establish its own legitimacy. Simultaneously, Chicago faced almost unique issues of scale. It was the second-largest city in the United States, and had arguably the largest problem with delinquency. Thus, it required either much greater resources than it had, or a mechanism to screen out minor complaints that were not worth its time. This situation created its dependence upon the police. The development of Chicago's police, however, followed a different trajectory than did police elsewhere. Rather than experiencing administrative reform during the Progressive Era, the Chicago police remained tied to politics, and became perhaps even more deeply involved in graft and corruption by the 1920s. In short, unique characteristics of both the juvenile court and the police in Chicago encouraged the police to retain an informal discretionary style of disciplining youth even as this approach was becoming anachronistic elsewhere. Chicago, a model for juvenile justice in the United States, may also have been an anomaly.

# ⊰6⊱
# The Rise of Police Crime
# Prevention, 1919–40

I
n 1919, August Vollmer, chief of the Berkeley (CA) Police Department, spoke before the annual meeting of the International Association of Chiefs of Police (IACP) in New Orleans and articulated a new vision of policing. The policeman, he suggested to the assembled leaders, should function "as a social worker." Traditionally, according to Vollmer, policemen had been mainly concerned with catching offenders and putting them behind bars. These officers were honest and well intentioned, but they did little to address the sources of crime and delinquency. A modern policeman, however, had much greater obligations and much greater potential. "If he would serve his community by reducing crime," Vollmer argued, "he must go up the stream a little further and dam it up at its source, and not wait until it is a rushing torrent, uncontrollable and relentless." No public official, in his view, had more flexibility to work with other helping agencies or more opportunities to act for good in their community than the "intelligent, sympathetic, and trained policeman." And central to Vollmer's vision were systematic efforts to intervene with children and to prevent delinquency. "By close cooperation with schools and public welfare agencies," Vollmer suggested, "[the policeman] will soon learn who the potential delinquents and dependents are, and can do much to assist in preventing them from becoming social failures. Boy gangs may be transformed into juvenile police and taught to be friendly helpers, or they may be helped to join boy scouts or similar boys' organizations, and through these agencies become helpful members of the community."[1]

Vollmer's vision was profoundly influential. By the late 1910s, Vollmer had become the most prominent advocate of police reform in the United States. As in other areas of police administration, he did not necessarily gen-

126

erate new ideas for preventing crime himself, but he did consolidate, articulate, and attempt to implement an array of innovations that had been, until that time, somewhat formless and disparate.[2] In this case, Vollmer's vision of the policeman as a social worker organized a set of newly emerging concepts about what the function of the police in the community should be. In particular, he began to establish a new role for police in dealing with children and youth. One goal of the "child-saving" movement had been to minimize the influence of law enforcement officials over young offenders, marginalizing the police. Although courts depended on cops, court advocates had suggested that the police had little legitimate role in juvenile justice and sought to push them out of the system. In his 1919 speech, Vollmer articulated how the police could be brought back in.

Between the 1890s and the 1910s, juvenile courts had unquestionably been the key public innovations in dealing with troubled teenagers. As the primary institutions for addressing delinquent and dependent children, juvenile courts redefined how the state sought to discipline and help youth. In the 1920s and 1930s, however, the sources of innovation shifted from courts to the communities. Schools, child guidance clinics, neighborhood-organizing groups, and character-building agencies all assumed new importance in fighting delinquency.[3]

And in particular, many U.S. police departments sought to create new methods to deal with youth. As advocates of this new approach presented it, police strove not only to catch and punish criminals but to prevent crime as well. They would intervene early with potential delinquents by organizing recreation programs, befriending and monitoring young people, and resolving minor cases without referrals to court. They intended these activities to redirect boys away from antisocial activities and to minimize crime they might commit in the future. Vollmer and his ideal of making social workers of policemen helped inspire this movement, but other factors shaped it as well. Growing disenchantment with juvenile courts in the 1920s and 1930s also invited new approaches to handling delinquency. In particular, new psychiatric understandings of delinquency suggested that early intervention and individualized treatment had greater impacts on youths than did juvenile court. And new popular understandings of delinquents as potential criminals further encouraged communities to develop crime prevention programs. Together, these influences led many police departments to address delinquency more systematically than they had in the past. Beginning in the late 1920s and accelerating in the 1930s, police departments across the country inaugurated new efforts to prevent juvenile crime.

# A MODEL FOR "CRIME PREVENTION": VOLLMER'S BERKELEY

The Berkeley Police Department under August Vollmer established a key precedent for subsequent police "crime prevention." Preventing juvenile crime by making social workers of policemen, however, was not Vollmer's highest priority. Instead, it was one component of a larger campaign to professionalize policing more generally.

Vollmer became the most prominent police official of his time by developing new methods to maintain public order and fight crime effectively. Elected Berkeley's town marshal in 1905 at the age of twenty-nine, Vollmer immediately set out to modernize his tiny department. He hired additional deputies, placed officers on bicycles to make them more mobile, and established a signal system that allowed patrolmen and dispatchers to communicate. He also adopted innovations such as finger printing and forensic science to identify criminals, and maintained systematic records to keep track of them. Vollmer's administration coincided with tremendous growth for his town. In 1906, the San Francisco earthquake brought thousands of refugees across the bay into Berkeley, fostering a permanent jump in both population and commerce. The expansion of the main campus of the University of California also fueled the town's growth. In 1909, Berkeley incorporated as a city and appointed Vollmer as police chief, a position he retained until he retired in 1932. In an era when big-city police chiefs were lucky to retain their positions for even a few years, Vollmer's long term in office, his comfortable base in a small city, and the support of a relatively progressive municipal administration all allowed him to build the police department he envisioned. Plus, he publicized his innovations widely through vigorous writing and through his positions as president of California Police Chiefs Association and, later, the IACP.[4]

Vollmer sought to set a higher standard for police work. Observers first noticed the technological innovations. By the late 1910s, Berkeley police officers responded to radio calls from a central headquarters and drove automobiles to reach crime scenes quickly. When they apprehended offenders, they collected fingerprints, handwriting samples, and physical measurements, identified them by cross-referencing detailed records, and interrogated them using a newly invented lie-detector machine. Such technical innovations quickly became standard operating procedures for police in other cities by the 1920s.[5]

Vollmer, however, placed greater importance on improving the quality of officers. In principle, he argued that police departments needed to attract better-qualified recruits and provide more systematic training. In practice, Vollmer implemented these goals in three ways. First, he established rigorous standards for job applicants, eventually using intelligence testing to screen them. Second, he actively recruited undergraduate and graduate students from the University of California to serve as police officers. These "college cops" became one of Vollmer's best-known innovations. Third, he established a permanent training program in 1908, one of the first in the United States. While the few police schools elsewhere trained recruits primarily in military drill and firearms, Berkeley's school taught the principles of public service and scientific crime detection. Vollmer's ultimate goal was to transform policing from a low-status occupation filled with ill-educated working-class men into a profession filled with college-educated public servants armed with the latest techniques to detect and prevent crime. He went a step beyond other police leaders who sought administrative reform and instead sought a more professional model of policing.[6]

Beginning in the late 1910s, Vollmer devoted increased attention to questions of what caused crime and how to prevent it, particularly among juveniles. In this, he was influenced heavily by psychiatric thinking and adopted ideas from the new field of child psychology. In the early years of the twentieth century, sociological models focusing on troubled social environments had dominated scholarly understandings of delinquency. But at the turn of the century, psychiatry was also emerging as its own discipline, focusing particularly on questions related to children's development. The widely accepted environmental model of delinquency gradually evolved into a multicausal model influenced heavily by psychiatry. This new interpretation provided a more complete explanation of delinquency, but it did not provide an immediate prescription of what to do about it. Thus, reformers were increasingly willing to experiment.

In Chicago, the same reform coalition that originally had sponsored the juvenile court looked to psychiatry to supplement the court's work. In 1909, at the initiative of philanthropist Ethel Sturges Dummer, the Juvenile Protective Association (JPA) established a Juvenile Psychopathic Institute to investigate boys and girls petitioned to the Chicago juvenile court. They hired Dr. William Healy to direct the institute, perform mental examinations on children referred by the court, treat them, and use them as a basis for research on psychological factors contributing to misbehavior. In his initial findings, first published in 1915, Healy challenged most accepted thinking about delinquency. Finding neither purely social nor purely biological explanations consistent with the children he had studied, Healy instead suggested that much delinquency resulted from the interaction of social circumstances, psychological maladjustment, and minor mental disorders. Healy's arguments provided an intellectual justification for establishing new institutional mechanisms across the country to address delinquency, particularly psychiatric clinics affiliated with juvenile courts and, later, "child guidance" clinics to screen younger children.[7]

Vollmer embraced Healy's perspective, particularly his conclusion that public officials should facilitate expert intervention into the lives of "predelinquent" youngsters. Moreover, in 1919, Vollmer conducted his own study (in collaboration with psychiatrist Dr. Jau Don Ball) of the personality characteristics of 220 students at Berkeley's Hawthorne Elementary School. They found that as many as 10 percent of students tested deviated substantially enough from the norms to be considered "problem children" requiring close supervision. From this study, Vollmer concluded that "predelinquent" traits could be detected in children, and potentially treated.[8]

Thus was born Vollmer's argument that the policeman should act as a social worker. In the early twentieth century, "social work" had evolved from a general term for any activism or voluntary charity into a more concrete profession. Driven by a largely female group of academics and activists who pioneered social scientific research as well as the "case work" method of delving deeply into clients' lives and experiences, social work developed substantial professional cachet by the late 1910s.[9] For Vollmer, the new social work provided a model for both diagnosing and treating predelinquency. Somewhat oversimplifying the results of Healy's work and of his own Hawthorne School study, Vollmer concluded that "it is possible to detect in children of predelinquent age the mental peculiarities" found by other researchers in teenage delinquents and adult criminals. Scientists, he suggested, had confirmed what policemen had long believed, that the "habitual offender's criminalistic tendencies were displayed by non-conformity to regulations at a very tender age." Building on this logic, Vollmer asked fellow police administrators, "does it not seem reasonable that our efforts to check crime should begin before the habits are so firmly fixed that it is too late to correct evil inclinations that forever blight a child's chances of making good in this world? Is it not better to devote a few hours toward guiding him along the paths of rectitude that he may acquire essentials of character . . . than to spend days attempting to unravel a murder, robbery, or other vicious act which may follow our neglect of preventive police work?" As usual, Vollmer had suggestions how police could accomplish this. First, officers should build relationships with schools and teachers so that they could learn which children could become problems. Next, the police should record this information (Vollmer suggested maps with a system of color-coded pins so they could see which children with what problems lived where). Finally, the police should turn to experts for analysis and instruction, and potentially to refer predelinquent children for treatment.[10]

Vollmer's public pronouncements on crime prevention consolidated and systematized existing thinking about the role of police in dealing with young offenders. His most original insight was giving the old notion that police could intervene early with young offenders a new psychiatric twist. In so doing, he created both a practical justification for police crime prevention work that was consistent with what many police leaders and rank-and-file officers already believed, and an intellectual justification that could help ensure the cooperation he needed from the educational, psychiatric, and social welfare communities. Importantly, juvenile courts did not play a major role in his vision.

Vollmer put his ideas into practice almost from the beginning of his tenure as Berkeley's police chief. As early as 1909, policemen placed potential delinquents on "voluntary police probation," requiring them to report to officers on the beat. In 1925, Berkeley established an official Crime Prevention Division headed by psychiatric social worker Elizabeth Lossing. Like similar police bureaus elsewhere, the Crime Prevention Division investigated girls and young boys suspected of delinquency and attempted to resolve their problems before they reached the police station. Unlike other juvenile bureaus, however, officers educated in psychiatry and social work were trained to diagnose a child's potential for delinquency, evaluate his or her home and community life, and coordinate with other social agencies.[11] Vollmer also encouraged all of his patrolmen to conceptualize their work as "preventing trouble." This meant not only admonishing boys they viewed as being at risk for delinquency, but also directing them to Berkeley's wide array of social or psychiatric services. Patrolman George Brereton explained, "I try to know the youngsters on my beat, make friends with them, and if I see tendencies that may lead to trouble, steer them toward the right help. A policeman ought to know the welfare agencies and how to use them."[12]

Cooperation between all social agencies dealing with children was essential to make this system work. Beginning in 1919, informal lunchtime meetings between Vollmer and Dr. Virgil Dickson, director of the Berkeley Public Schools' Bureau of Research and Guidance, gradually began to include the heads of other social agencies and to function as a "Coordinating Council." This voluntary organization, formally incorporated in 1924, linked the efforts of Berkeley's police, schools, recreational bureaus, and public and private welfare agencies to detect and treat signs of delinquency. The group had no official powers, but they discussed individual cases and collectively agreed which agency could best intervene with each youth. By working together, they avoided duplicating their efforts and treated children more systematically than was possible for any one agency.[13]

Vollmer provided other leaders with a model for establishing a more professional and efficient method of policing. In particular, Vollmer's concept of the policeman as a social worker, rooting out predelinquency, became the key idea in a wave of police crime prevention programs established in subsequent decades. By adapting cutting-edge psychiatric insights about delinquency to make them useful for police work, Vollmer established an intellectual justification for police to engage in crime prevention. Whether or not they fully embraced his model, Vollmer's Berkeley became the precedent that police reformers elsewhere looked to throughout the 1920s and 1930s.

## BEYOND THE JUVENILE COURT

Vollmer developed his ideas at a time when popular concerns about crime and delinquency were rising and when professional enthusiasm for juvenile courts was fading. In the early 1900s, juvenile court advocates had presented them as panaceas for delinquency, and even for more general problems related to children and youth. But by the early 1920s, these problems remained and seemed to be worsening. Many scholars, child welfare workers, and members of the public became disenchanted with the juvenile court and began to look for new ways to deal with young offenders.

Delinquency became a particularly pressing public concern in the 1920s as America seemed to experience a national crime wave. The conclusion of the First World War late in 1918 brought a rapid military demobilization, labor unrest, and an apparent breakdown in morals. In addition, beginning in 1920, the prohibition of alcohol spawned widespread violations by otherwise law-abiding citizens. Gangsters such as Al Capone became popular icons by performing the public service of supplying liquor. Moreover, the existing institutions of criminal justice—police, courts, and jails—were widely viewed as ineffective. As local, state, and ultimately national crime commissions reported, the justice system failed to prosecute and punish more than a small minority of criminals.[14]

The apparent crisis of adult crime was widely believed to contribute to juvenile delinquency as well. Both in social work journals such as *The Survey* and in general interest magazines such as *Collier's,* writers fretted that gangsters were becoming role models for youth and guiding them into delinquency. And in Chicago, juvenile court officials associated increased delinquency with the larger social changes of the 1920s. A short-term increase in delinquency complaints resulted, Chief Probation Officer Joseph Moss argued, from "the restlessness and the new freedom to which youth has not yet adjusted itself, and also the breaking down of respect for law on the part of the youth and adult."[15]

Almost simultaneously, the high hopes that had been associated with the juvenile court began to fade among a growing number of social workers, law enforcement officials, and academics. Investigations conducted under the auspices of the U.S. Children's Bureau found the results of the juvenile court movement to be disappointing. A national survey showed that, as of 1920, while juvenile courts had been established in all cities with populations over 100,000, they were less common in smaller towns and virtually unknown in rural areas. More disturbingly, courts hearing children's cases often lacked many key mechanisms, with fewer than half offering probation services and only 7 percent conducting mental examinations. In short, big-city courts were likely to offer diagnosis and treatment, while rural courts hearing children's cases were not. A 1925 examination of ten urban courts found much to criticize as well. Many courts only sporadically maintained separate detention facilities for children, few offered well-developed probation services, and psychiatric treatment was even scarcer. In short, investigators found that the "resources at the disposal of the court seemed to have been developed in a haphazard manner and did not fit together to form a complete community program for the care of delinquent and dependent children."[16]

These studies were meant to provide constructive criticism, but they also reflected a growing disenchantment with juvenile courts. As the twenty-fifth anniversary of the first juvenile court approached, many of its original advocates became increasingly dissatisfied with the results of their movement. Papers presented in January 1925 at a conference organized in Chicago to commemorate this anniversary evidence their uneasiness. Henry S. Hulbert, the long-time judge of the Wayne County (Detroit) Juvenile Court and current president of the National Probation Association, expressed concern about the use of probation. He suggested that, although the public had accepted probation as a remedial tool, many who worked in juvenile justice felt "a queer current of dissatisfaction with the quality of our work." Too often, judges granted probation in cases when it was not appropriate, when children were not amenable or circumstances prevented close supervision.[17] Likewise, Louise de Koven Bowen, the former president of the Chicago Juvenile Protective Association, lamented the state of the Chicago Detention Home. By the mid-1920s, Bowen claimed, the Detention Home had "every appearance of being a jail, with its barred windows and locked doors," the attendants knew little about the psychology of childhood, and children were harmed rather than helped by their experiences.[18]

The implied solution seemed to lie in integrating mental examinations and psychiatric treatment into investigations and probation work. Discussions of the personality of the child and the operation of psychiatric clinics dominated the 1925 conference. In particular, William Healy argued that the key to treating delinquency was analyzing the psychology of individual youths, understanding how multiple social and personal traits contributed to misbehavior, and considering how contact with the juvenile justice system impacted the child.[19] Psychiatric clinics, however, never had as much impact as their advocates hoped. Clinics associated with courts required extensive resources and expensive personnel and did not spread widely; they remained concentrated in only a handful of the largest cities. Instead, by the late 1920s, "child guidance" clinics became common. These aimed at offering psychiatric services to younger children with milder behavioral problems long before they ran into trouble with the law. At most, psychiatric clinics remained a supplement to already-existing court mechanisms.[20]

Harvard criminologists Sheldon and Eleanor Glueck further crystallized these debates with their 1934 publication of *One Thousand Juvenile Delinquents,* one of the first efforts to evaluate systematically the effectiveness of juvenile courts and psychiatric clinics. The Gluecks conducted a longitudinal study of one thousand boys handled by the Boston Juvenile Court and its psychiatric clinic, the Judge Baker Foundation, between 1917 and 1922 (during which time Healy served as the clinic's director). They found that a stunning 88 percent of boys continued to commit delinquencies in the five years following their treatment. Apparently, neither the court nor the highly touted clinics reformed offenders. Consequently, the Gluecks urged greater cooperation between court and clinic, and proposed that social agencies more actively try to prevent delinquency before it became serious enough to reach the courts.[21] Other commentators, such as Richard C. Cabot, a professor of social ethics at Harvard, interpreted the Gluecks' research differently. In a review of their work in *The Survey,* he rejected entirely the juvenile court and its preventive mission. Cabot argued instead that the court was "an appallingly complete and costly failure, a stupendous waste of time, money and effort in an attempt to check delinquency."[22]

Cabot's interpretation (as much as the actual study) provoked furious responses from social work professionals and juvenile court administrators. In particular, Judge Harry L. Eastman of the Cuyahoga County (Cleveland) Juvenile Court questioned both Cabot's and the Gluecks' understanding of the court. Eastman dismissed Cabot by arguing that he "has gone far afield and out of his way to register his own preconceived prejudices . . . without foundation in fact." While Eastman took the Gluecks more seriously, he defended juvenile courts by defining their functions very narrowly. The Gluecks, he argued, "fail to discriminate between the proper function of the court and those of other community agencies." In his view, "The juvenile court was never designed to prevent delinquency. It was planned as a better method of combating delinquency after its occurrence." To uphold the legitimacy of juvenile courts as judicial institutions, Eastman rejected the idea that they had ever been meant to prevent crime.[23]

These debates suggest that the intended purpose of juvenile courts underwent a subtle yet important shift in the 1920s and 1930s. Early advocates had envisioned juvenile courts as institutions to diagnose the sources of delinquency, treat its manifestations, and prevent its recurrences. By the 1920s and 1930s, however, decades of experience and evaluations of courts' results had undermined even professional child welfare workers' faith in their efficacy. Less and less often did observers and court officials believe that juvenile courts, probation, and institutionalization could treat delinquency and stop recidivism. Instead, they began to look more and more toward preventive approaches. For example, Grace Abbott, former head of the U.S. Children's Bureau, argued that as "treatment agencies," juvenile courts faced "fundamental difficulties" and proposed that new community agencies should be created as an alternative.[24]

This disenchantment with juvenile courts in the scholarly and social welfare communities paralleled a growing concern about juvenile crime among the public. By 1930, it was not uncommon to see the supposed failures of a kind-hearted juvenile court presented as the source of delinquency. In one *Collier's* article, an unnamed (and possibly fictional) female probation officer in Philadelphia exemplified the problem. She reportedly handled delinquent boys under her supervision by inviting them into her home on Friday nights and asking if they had been good during the previous week. While she interviewed one boy, others would rob the houses on either side of hers. According to Philadelphia District Attorney Charles Edwin Fox, this type of "stupid and sentimental" probation told first-time offenders that their actions had no repercussions and encouraged them to commit further crimes.[25]

More generally, during the apparent surge in crime that accompanied the Great Depression, the national press repeatedly articulated a popular view that boys who committed minor offenses as juveniles would grow up to commit more serious crimes as adults. Article after article suggested that, without proper adult guidance, boys could be lured easily into gangs and crime. For example, journalist Howard McLellan used an account of one boy, Red, to encapsulate what he believed to be a much more common problem. After losing a father figure at age twelve, Red found friendship and structure in a local street-corner gang. He then committed petty offenses as a teenager, was arrested and released repeatedly, committed murder at age eighteen, and was executed finally at twenty-one. Geneva (NY) Police Chief R. W. Morris summarized a common public perception in the 1930s when he wrote "the juvenile delinquent of today is tomorrow's criminal."[26]

In addition, the gangster films of the era—notably *Little Caesar* (1931), *The Public Enemy* (1931), and *Scarface* (1932)—reinforced this narrative trope that young offenders would mature into serious criminals. They showed boys committing petty thefts and vandalism in their early teens, advancing into more serious crimes as they grew up, and becoming leaders in organized crime as adults. These movies were particularly disturbing not only because they captured a common public understanding of how criminals developed, but also because they romanticized gangsters. Although James Cagney's character in *The Public Enemy,* Tom Powers, died in the end, while he lived he enjoyed power, authority, and the finest luxuries that money could buy. Some child psychologists feared that movies (and gangster films in particular) encouraged youths to commit crimes. Studies sponsored by the Payne Fund and published between 1929 and 1933 argued that movies portrayed criminals sympathetically and as potential role models, demonstrated criminal techniques for children to emulate, and stimulated unattainable material desires among the over 20 million juveniles who attended them at least once a week.[27]

Both declining faith in the juvenile court and the increased popular concern about young offenders fostered a range of new programs to prevent delinquency. "About fifty public-spirited citizens" organized the Boys' Club of Detroit in 1926, for example. Housed in its own four-story building that had once been used as a cigar factory, the club offered games and "wholesome sports," classes in trades such as carpentry and auto mechanics, and medical and dental clinics. Rather than investigate potential delinquents on a case-by-case basis, as a psychiatric approach would have suggested, interested citizens sought to prevent delinquency via a collective approach that was intended to build character in urban boys and give them something to do other than commit crimes.[28]

Organized recreation became a particularly popular tool. Throughout the 1920s, child welfare workers had implicitly assumed a connection between a lack of recreational opportunities and delinquency, and had thus haphazardly organized programs such as boy scouting for urban youth.[29] In the 1930s, as the Great Depression closed job opportunities for working-class youth and forced them to delay careers and marriage, recreation became a more serious issue. Social workers and social scientists looked to recreation to redirect young peoples' energies and build character. Their studies also provided greater scientific validity for the use of recreation to prevent delinquency. For example, M. L. Pettit, a South Bend (IN) probation officer, believed that the large majority of cases of "maladjustment among boys" resulted from inadequate recreation or "antisocial companionship." He conducted an informal experiment, attempting to determine the recreation needs of boys, and to fulfill them by providing athletics through cooperation with the YMCA and outdoor activities through the Boy Scouts. Organized recreation, he claimed, helped rehabilitate about 60 percent of boys in the study.[30] Likewise, sociologist Frederic Thrasher argued on the basis on his work with Chicago gang youth, "It is the unwise use of leisure by boys and young men . . . which . . . is responsible for the development of delinquency and crime." Lacking worthwhile activities in their homes or communities, urban lower-class boys gravitated to an often-delinquent peer group in the streets. Thrasher proposed that communities financially support existing programs for boys and establish additional opportunities for "wholesome recreation." "Here is the fruitful field for crime prevention," he argued, "the virile and intelligent control of the leisure time of boys and young men."[31]

Perhaps no organization carried these ideas further than the Chicago Area Project (CAP), founded by sociologist Clifford Shaw in 1931 and incorporated in 1934. Drawing on his experience as a Chicago probation officer and graduate student at the University of Chicago, Shaw came to understand delinquency as a product of deteriorating neighborhoods in modern industrial cities, and sought to create a new sort of community organization in response. Like other agencies, neighborhood organizing committees affiliated with CAP sponsored recreation programs, operating boys' clubs and athletic leagues, but they also sought to elicit as much grassroots engagement in the process as possible. Shaw envisioned delinquency prevention as being fundamentally about rebuilding communities. To do so, CAP sought vigorously to incorporate neighborhood leaders, to cooperate with existing institutions such as churches and schools, and to let local people determine what form community renewal should take. Furthermore, CAP used young "street workers" to shadow each community's principal juvenile gangs, trying to gain gang members' trust and to provide "curbstone counseling" that would help them see that the values of conventional society were more desirable than lives of low-level delinquency.[32]

By the early 1930s a certain public consensus emerged in favor of working with boys to prevent delinquency, and these programs slowly became more systematic. In 1936 Sheldon and Eleanor Glueck followed through on their call for greater preventive efforts by organizing a symposium on various agencies' programs for youth. They paralleled their efforts to those of a modern fire department to prevent fires but argued that, "in relation to the control of delinquency and crime, . . . society has not progressed much beyond the stage of putting out the flames. It has waited for violations of law and then bent its efforts to pursuing, arresting, prosecuting, and punishing offenders without giving much thought to the elimination of the forces that produced them." That, they argued, had to change. Based on the best current practices of neighborhood groups, schools, boys' clubs, recreation agencies, child guidance clinics, and the police, the Gluecks and their collaborators promoted a range of experimental crime prevention programs built around existing community agencies. And while they sought to segregate children from official contacts with police stations, criminal courts, and jails, they nonetheless agreed that crime prevention programs organized by police had "certain unique values."[33]

The Gluecks' symposium represented a turning point. No longer did leading thinkers and activists consider juvenile courts the primary institutions for fighting delinquency. Rather than bring children into the juvenile justice system, social workers, teachers, law enforcement officials, and others working with children all sought to address the sources of delinquency before kids reached court. To be sure, not all of their ideas were terribly original; the notion of using recreation to prevent delinquency had been around for decades. But these ideas did signal a fundamental shift in how the problem of delinquency was to be approached. The focus of attention had moved beyond the juvenile courts and toward community-based crime prevention programs. And urban police departments found themselves involved deeply once again.

## OPERATIONS OF POLICE CRIME PREVENTION

Police officials certainly talked about preventing crime in the 1920s, but they did not initially agree about what this meant. From the origins of municipal police departments in the nineteenth century, the primary purpose of conducting patrols had been to discourage crime. This perspective continued into the early 1920s, when police often used the phrase "crime prevention" to describe tough law enforcement based on deterrence. For example, hard-line Detroit Police Commissioner James Inches attributed his department's success in reducing crime to "intensive work on crime prevention," which he characterized by "the increased number of men which the Police Department has been able to detail for street patrol."[34] In contrast, policewomen in the 1910s and 1920s also used the language of "crime prevention" to explain their goals. By performing social work with girls and young boys and by policing their behavior, pioneer policewomen expected to prevent crime and immorality in the future.[35]

For the most part, police officials continued to see delinquency as boys' normal response to the opportunities of an urban environment. But, by the late 1920s, they also began to share the public's worry that today's delinquent would become tomorrow's criminal, and increasingly regarded salvaging potentially delinquent youth as a logical extension of normal policing. In so doing, they often ignored policewomen, demonstrating more interest in boys who might commit crimes against property and persons than in status offenders or in girls who might slip into "immoral" behavior. Police reformer Raymond B. Fosdick led the way in his seminal 1920 guide to police practice. Highlighting the seriousness of juvenile crime, Fosdick reported that in 1916, of seven persons awaiting execution in Sing Sing prison in New York, five were "boys" under age twenty-one. "Statistics such as these," Fosdick argued, "furnish indisputable evidence that criminals are recruited from the ranks of childhood. The rollicking, mischievous boy of today, uncontrolled and out of hand, becomes the hardened offender of tomorrow. In their efforts to prevent crime, therefore, the police have no more fruitful field of work than is presented by the boys and girls of our cities." He endorsed all existing crime prevention programs of his day—junior police, assigning uniformed police to talk to school children, creating special squads of juvenile officers—and urged greater efforts. Police departments were slow to follow this particular bit of Fosdick's advice but did so eventually. In its 1929 annual report, the New York City Police Department used his precise language to justify its provisional creation of a Crime Prevention Bureau. The premise of stopping delinquents from growing up to become criminals emerged as the one concept that most police leaders could agree upon.[36]

Just what form police crime prevention programs should take, however, remained a subject of debate. On one hand, leaders such as William Rutledge of the Detroit Police Department, speaking at the 1927 meeting of the IACP, presented crime prevention in medical terms, comparing police efforts to prevent crime among youth to physicians' efforts to prevent disease. Police, according to Rutledge, should form "Protective Divisions" to investigate complaints against boys and girls and to work closely with "treatment agencies" in the community.[37] Others suggested how this disease prevention model could be implemented. Dr. Bradford Murphey advocated close cooperation between police and child guidance clinics, while Gillmore Bush suggested that it would suffice for police to act as big brothers to youth.[38] On the other hand, other police leaders presented crime prevention as an old-fashioned effort to deter crime among youth. James Broughton, police chief in Portsmouth, Virginia, explained that he had carried out "an educational campaign against crime" by placing "a series of large hand-painted pictures (6' by 40') at a central location in the City, depicting the progress of the wrong-doers from the first transgression on through various stages until the inevitable consequences of prison or death." His point, Broughton asserted, was to teach young people that "crime never pays."[39] A 1927 survey asking municipal police "what does your department do or recommend to prevent crime?" revealed the variety of work that police officials considered crime prevention. Most described new social programs aimed at reducing delinquency, but quite a few simply suggested that more efficient investigations and faster court hearings would make punishment more certain and thereby discourage crime.[40]

In spite of this debate, a consensus in favor of some sort of police crime prevention work involving friendly interactions with boys emerged gradually in the late 1920s and early 1930s. Even police leaders who ridiculed scientific study of delinquency—for example, San Francisco's Captain Duncan Matheson derided "so-called crime experts" as "bunkologists"—nonetheless urged close cooperation with boys' clubs, parent-teacher associations, and Sunday schools as the best means of preventing juvenile crime.[41] And in 1931, the federal government's Wickersham Commission strongly endorsed crime prevention. Writing for the commission, Earle W. Garrett (a former research assistant for Vollmer), argued, "The youngster . . . is just starting out in life, has long to live, and is a greater potential threat to society if allowed to fall into criminal way. The young are plastic, impressionable, yielding, and can usually be influenced to go along in productive paths if taken in hand early enough."[42]

The resulting police crime prevention programs assumed a variety of forms. The Chicago Police Department, for example, opened an Unemployed Boys Bureau in 1927. While the Chicago police did not necessarily consider social work a legitimate element of policing, they nonetheless believed that that "if boys are regularly employed when they leave school there will be less chance of their getting into mischief and later, crime."[43] To this end, the Unemployed Boys Bureau aimed to match boys between ages fourteen and twenty with jobs. It collected applications from boys in each district, matched them with a parallel citywide file of available positions, and wrote introduction slips to help boys meet potential employers. The bureau was quite successful in its early years. As of the end of 1929, it reported that it had found jobs for 87 percent of the over 27,000 boys who had applied. Ironically, while the Great Depression encouraged crime prevention programs elsewhere, it contributed to the demise of the Unemployed Boys Bureau. When adult male breadwinners were out of work, employment programs for teenagers seemed extravagant and inappropriate. Critics of the police also maintained that finding jobs for teens wasted scarce resources. In 1931, the Citizen's Police Committee asserted, "the Police Department clearly should not support an official employment agency catering to all classes of boys without some evidence that it performs a service in preventing delinquency" and recommended that it be abolished. Subsequent investigations of the police and departmental annual reports never referred to the program again; apparently it had been abandoned.[44]

More typically, police departments sought to prevent delinquency by establishing friendly contacts with boys before they accumulated a criminal record. The New York City Police Department, for example, devoted little attention to "boys' work" in the 1920s, but it revived many programs in response to a 1928 investigation by the New York State Crime Commission's Sub-Committee on Crime Causes. Drawing on the environmental thinking of Chicago sociologists, the commission argued that "improper parental supervision, bad housing, and a poverty-stricken environment" contributed to juvenile misbehavior and, ultimately, to adult crime. "The street," the commission suggested, "is found to have supplanted the home . . . and to have fostered gangs, and gang ethics appalling to older people."[45] In response to the commission's recommendation that police should actively supervise potential offenders, the NYPD established an experimental "Crime Prevention Bureau" in 1930. Police officials justified this new program not on theoretical grounds suggested by the Crime Commission, but on a very practical basis consistent with public thinking about delinquency. In 1931, Police Commissioner Edward P. Mulrooney reminded his listeners, "the child who is playing in the street today . . . is the gangster and gunman of tomorrow. And the work of this Crime Prevention Bureau . . . is the best method we have yet found for diverting these youngsters from evil paths."[46]

The NYPD Crime Prevention Bureau sought initially to combine the social work approach characteristic of probation officers and policewomen with the law enforcement ethos of more traditional policing. Between its founding and 1934, it was led by social worker Henrietta Additon, whose status as deputy police commissioner made her the highest-ranking woman in the NYPD.[47] In 1931, the Crime Prevention Bureau personnel also mixed a substantial number of women with backgrounds in social work (twenty-five female crime prevention investigators and forty-four policewomen) and a majority of men drawn from the police force (130 lieutenants, sergeants, and patrolmen).[48] The bureau's main functions were controlling conditions that fostered delinquency and intervening with potential offenders. It sent officers to supervise poolrooms where boys encountered alcohol, gambling, or narcotics, to monitor movie theaters where young boys and girls engaged in "immorality" in darkened balconies, to visit dance halls or cabarets where children encountered a range of vices, and to keep an eye on candy stores and penny arcades where gangs congregated.[49]

The NYPD Crime Prevention Bureau achieved its broadest impact not through these planned efforts, but by supporting individual initiatives sponsored by officers in daily contact with children. Organized recreation activities administered through the Police Athletic League (PAL, founded in 1932) quickly became the centerpiece of NYPD crime prevention. The creation of PAL is attributed to Lieutenant Edward W. Flynn, a patrolman in the Bronx. In 1931, Flynn confronted a gang of boys between ages fourteen and sixteen who had been robbing and vandalizing local shops. He thought the boys "weren't basically mean, but they were hell-bent for total delinquency." Flynn asked what they wanted and they responded that they wanted to be a baseball team. Rather than allow boys to gather in poolrooms or on street corners and cause trouble for lack of opportunities to play, Flynn volunteered to provide uniforms and equipment and to arrange games. He also approached local businesses and churches (including victims of theft and vandalism) to sponsor the teams, suggesting that the neighborhood would benefit in the long run. As Flynn gradually organized a baseball league, the boys reportedly "no longer had the time, energy or inclination for destructive activity."[50] By 1932, when the program was formally established, the police had organized almost 5,000 boys into PAL baseball teams that played 2,500 games.[51]

PAL's promoters portrayed it as a means of reducing juvenile crime. One 1932 account describes "Shorty," a seventeen-year-old who turned to crime for want of places to play. Because the local playground was always crowded, he and his "gang" played at being cops and robbers, then committed real burglaries, and then ended up in prison. By contrast, other boys exposed to organized baseball reportedly stopped giving their teachers trouble and threw themselves into sports. The message here is clear: without recreation, boys would likely drift into delinquency and crime, but with games organized under the benevolent supervision of the police, they would find more productive uses for their time and energies.[52]

Beginning in 1934, NYPD crime prevention programs focused more on recreation and less on investigation and supervision. Following the election of Mayor Fiorello LaGuardia, the NYPD's newly appointed leadership questioned if the Crime Prevention Bureau's annual $600,000 budget might be spent in ways that produced more immediate returns. Additon resigned in September, publicly declaring that LaGuardia had little knowledge of or sympathy for crime prevention work. The NYPD subsequently reorganized the Crime Prevention Bureau under the new name of the Juvenile Aid Bureau, appointed a male commissioner, Byrnes MacDonald, to succeed Additon, and focused on recreation as its primary method of intervention and treatment.[53] PAL expanded accordingly, peaking at a membership of over 74,000 children in 1937, plus establishing a series of youth centers around the city that provided organized recreation and after-school activities.[54]

While the NYPD had initially sought to combine social work with policing, its approach to crime prevention quickly shifted to one that emphasized interactions on the ball field. The theoretical principles derived from psychiatry and sociology that justified crime prevention do not seem to have penetrated deeply or to have lasted long. Instead, the vague goal of discouraging young offenders from growing up to become criminals seems to have been at the root of the NYPD's efforts. This is not to say that PAL did not do good work; it provided large numbers of New York teenagers with all that sports entailed—discipline, character building, and male bonding. At the same time, it was not as successful at transforming police officers into community-organizing agents as early crime prevention advocates such as Vollmer might have desired.

The police in Detroit also considered the degree to which juvenile officers should act like social workers. The Detroit Police Department's Juvenile Division ultimately settled on a solution of engaging vigorously with potential delinquents but also setting limits on their involvement. The issue of boys' work first emerged with the appointment of James K. Watkins as police commissioner in 1931. An attorney, Watkins had no prior experience in law enforcement, but did have a background in social work; in 1910 he had served the Wayne County Juvenile Court as a probation officer for boys.[55] As a probation officer, he had found the police "not very helpful," but as commissioner, Watkins brought a new orientation to policing. He encouraged his juvenile division officers to adjust as many cases as possible without sending youths to court. Instead, they were to investigate children's offenses and encourage their parents to supervise them more closely. He sold these changes to the public on the basis of the efficiency they brought to police work and the "advantages" they offered. According to Watkins, delinquency prevention would rescue potential offenders themselves, relieve city residents from becoming victims of crime, and generate "financial savings to the public treasury" by reducing the expenses of courts and prisons.[56]

Watkins saw the police as part of a larger social service network, but not as social workers themselves. On the one hand, he dismissed a position that "police should leave the problem almost entirely alone and should not attempt protective work with young people." On the other hand, he did not embrace the notion that police should engage in "treatment work with the individual." Instead, Watkins believed "that the proper function of the police lies between those two extremes." Believing that police officers were unsuited to diagnose boys' behavioral problems, Watkins urged his officers to refer juveniles to specialists who would decide whether informal disposition, social or psychological treatment, or juvenile court was necessary. "The police officer cannot be a case worker," he stated, "but he can be a feeder to case workers and he likewise can be instrumental in bringing to the attention of proper agencies conditions and situations which need attention."[57] When juvenile officers and policewomen investigated minor complaints involving loitering, disorderly conduct, and petty theft by preadolescent boys, they often referred the problems to local social workers instead of making arrests.[58] The most direct contact Detroit police had with local youth was as leaders of Boy Scout troops. Beginning with a single troop in 1934, the Detroit police organized sixteen troops by 1937.[59]

Police crime prevention programs akin to those in New York and Detroit spread widely in the 1930s. Major cities such as Washington, D.C., and San Francisco established multifaceted programs, while in smaller towns like Bridgeport, Connecticut, and Freeport, Illinois, police organized Boy Scout troops or supervised afternoon play in the interest of crime prevention.[60] At least thirty-six cities, large and small, began operating police crime prevention programs before 1940.[61] The emergence of these programs marks a fundamental transition in the workings of juvenile justice. In the early twentieth century, social agencies had done all they could to keep children away from police, and in turn police had often been reluctant to cooperate with social agencies or juvenile courts. By the 1930s, however, both sides began to meet halfway. By establishing crime prevention programs, police also reestablished legitimate roles for themselves in handling young offenders. Social agencies in turn came to accept the police, in the words of probation officer Helen Pigeon, as the "first line of defense" against crime and delinquency.[62] After juvenile courts had pushed police out of an official role in juvenile justice, crime prevention brought them back in.

# The Appeal of Police Crime Prevention

In the 1920s and 1930s, many police departments assumed active roles in delinquency prevention. As the effectiveness of existing correctional agencies such as juvenile courts increasingly fell into question, new proposals that crime could be prevented, rather than punished or treated after the fact, extended the job of prevention to all community agencies. Following Vollmer's ideal that policemen could act as social workers and the example of Vollmer's experimental programs in Berkeley, police were among the most prominent agencies to engage in "crime prevention." Not only did they cooperate with existing social agencies; police also supported programs such as scouting and Boys Clubs and often implemented their own programs to reach troublesome youths. More and more often, diversion to social agencies, to organized recreation, and to character-building programs became standard methods of handling young offenders.

In practice, however, police programs drew only indirectly on the new psychiatric and social scientific approaches to delinquency prevention. The reality of their efforts paralleled older efforts to deal with young offenders. Some police departments—such as New York's—initially sought to balance policing and social work but quickly fell back into offering large-scale recreation in the general hope of giving boys something to do other than crime. Other departments—such as Detroit's—were reluctant to extend the function of the police. They relied instead upon diverting some young offenders into social programs or organized recreation that might offer boys some guidance. Police crime prevention programs helped to reestablish legitimate roles for the police as intermediaries between young offenders and the juvenile justice system, and represent an important step forward in terms of organizational sophistication. They did not, however, entail the fundamental change in the function of the police that Vollmer had envisioned. Nor did these programs approach the community renewal model of delinquency prevention suggested by the Chicago Area Project. Nor did they represent a substantial change in police thinking about delinquency. Police leaders and rank-and-file officers adopted the new perspective in broad strokes because it seemed to support what many had already believed, that undirected youth would drift naturally toward misbehavior unless something was done to prevent it. And public fears that today's delinquent would become tomorrow's criminal gave this idea greater urgency. Most police officers had relatively modest goals other than discouraging boys from committing crimes. They saw informal dispositions, friendly personal contacts, and organized recreation as means of enabling boys to become law-abiding adults. And nowhere was this more the case than in Los Angeles, where innovative delinquency prevention programs coexisted with repressive campaigns to control crime.

# ᵇ7ᵇ

# Shifting Priorities:

## TARGETING SERIOUS CRIME AND MINORITY YOUTH IN INTERWAR LOS ANGELES

U pon his appointment as chief of the Los Angeles Police Department for the second time in 1933, James E. Davis proclaimed three objectives. First, under his leadership, the LAPD sought to "eliminate all gangsters"; second, they would "decrease burglaries . . . [and] robberies to the lowest point in the history of the city"; and third, he intended to "utilize every member of the department to the utmost in actual police duty."[1] One year later, in 1934, Davis claimed success. In spite of strains placed on his department by "economic stress" and "gangster terrorism," the LAPD had prevented gang murders for the previous ten months, helped solve a widely publicized kidnapping, and barred known criminals from entering the city. In addition, the LAPD also claimed credit for a 15 percent decrease in burglary, a 16 percent drop in robbery, and a 23 percent decline in auto theft in the previous year.[2]

In short, according to Davis, the LAPD was waging and winning a war against crime. Although Davis's rhetoric may have been exaggerated to appeal to a public concerned about law and order in the face of Prohibition and Depression Era fears of crime, he also pointed out a very real shift in police priorities. Rather than focus on maintaining public order, as urban police departments had done in the late nineteenth and early twentieth centuries, police departments came to prioritize fighting crime in the 1920s and 1930s. Rather than see their primary functions as providing general services and arresting ne'er-do-wells for disorderly conduct, police came to define their purpose more narrowly as investigating and preventing crimes against persons and property, and apprehending and punishing criminals.[3]

If August Vollmer represented a leader who could help professionalize policing and make officers more like social workers, then James Davis represented an ideal leader in a war on crime. Born in northern Texas in 1889, Davis had arrived in Los Angeles in 1911 after being discharged from the U.S. Army with little education and $150 to his name. He soon found a job as a patrolman for the LAPD and worked his way up through the ranks. In contrast to leaders such as James Couzens in Detroit who made careers in other fields and entered policing laterally as chiefs, Davis began his career as a rank-and-file patrolman and shared the values of many officers on the beat. Davis came to prominence working in the LAPD's vice squad, where he developed political connections with Mayor George Cryer and political boss Kent Kane Parrot in the 1920s, and rapidly ascended into the LAPD's leadership. Davis found himself appointed chief in 1926 (at the youthful age of thirty-seven), was forced to accept a demotion in 1929 in a political scandal, and was reappointed chief in 1933. In all, Davis served nine years as chief, the longest tenure for any LAPD leader until then. During that time, Davis constructed a public image of himself as a fearless crime fighter. He made bold declarations against criminals and gangsters, arranged frequent demonstrations of his prowess as a marksman and of the renowned skill of the LAPD pistol team, and displayed the power of the police through their daily approach to crime control.[4]

Davis encouraged his officers to fight crime using repression and violence. Under Davis, according to historian Gerald Woods, the LAPD "reached the lowest depths of its dreary history."[5] During his first term, Davis developed the highly visible tactic of the dragnet, in which officers commandeered major street intersections, stopped and searched all passing vehicles, and interrogated anyone deemed suspicious. Citizens complained, but Davis countered that only criminals had anything to worry about. In addition, Davis condoned brutality among his men, brushing aside protests about police violence. Davis also encouraged officers to utilize their heavily promoted skills with firearms to apprehend serious criminals, stating that he would just as soon see them brought in dead as alive. And in 1933, Davis fulfilled his promise to fight gangsterism by convincing the city to implement a "criminal registration ordinance" that required persons convicted of felonies within the past ten years to register with the LAPD within forty-eight hours of their arrival in Los Angeles. These men and women would be the usual suspects apprehended first when persons unknown committed major crimes. Davis did not believe that constitutional niceties should interfere with effective policing.[6]

And yet in the 1920s and 1930s, the LAPD also participated vigorously in juvenile crime prevention programs as extensive as those in any city in the country. It worked closely with community-coordinating agencies and sponsored Boy Scout troops, summer camps, and organized recreation for children at risk. How could the same agency engage both in this lawless law enforcement and in child-friendly efforts intended to save potentially delinquent youth?

The LAPD's approach to policing youth in these years encapsulates a change in how U.S. law enforcement agencies handled young offenders, a change built on larger changes in American society during the Great Depression and New Deal. Between 1926 and 1940, the LAPD broke from older informal models of intervention with youth and sought more aggressively to control juvenile crime. In doing so, they engaged in and benefited from crime prevention programs that diverted many minor juvenile offenders to child welfare agencies prior to or in place of arrest. This change helped to free the LAPD to concentrate on more serious youthful offenses. As a result, by the end of the 1930s, the LAPD arrested very different sorts of juveniles than police had in previous decades—these youths were older, more often drawn from targeted minority communities, and more often accused of felony crimes. And this resulted almost inevitably in the LAPD petitioning to juvenile court a larger percentage of serious criminal offenders. By remaking the clientele for juvenile court, the police helped remake the juvenile justice system, forcing it to address the new problem of controlling crime as much as the older goal of saving delinquent youth.

# The LAPD in the 1920s and 1930s

In the first decades of twentieth century, the LAPD embodied many of the problems endemic to big-city police nationwide. Almost from its origins in 1876, the LAPD had been closely associated with both machine politics and organized crime. Municipal reformers continually demanded changes in both the police and the larger city administration, only to vote their candidates into office and see them make compromises with criminal networks inside and outside of government. As a result, like departments in many other urban centers, Los Angeles policing was marked continually by scandal and turbulence. In the 1920s and the 1930s, however, police practices changed dramatically, both nationwide and in Los Angeles, as departments gradually severed their ties to political machines and remade themselves into more professional law enforcers.[7] The LAPD thus serves as a focal point both for viewing national trends in law enforcement and for examining more closely how the distinctive features of Los Angeles shaped its policing, particularly of juveniles.

In the early twentieth century, the LAPD dealt with issues of growth comparable to those faced in Detroit and Chicago a few decades earlier. The population of Los Angeles more than doubled each decade for forty years, increasing from roughly 50,000 persons in 1890 to 1.24 million in 1930. Los Angeles went from being the fifty-seventh largest city in the United States in 1890 (just behind Evansville, Indiana) to the fifth largest in 1940, with a population of over 1.5 million (just shy of Detroit's). Los Angeles achieved some of that growth by annexing surrounding municipalities—the area of the city increased from 101 square miles in 1910 to 442 square miles in 1930—but it also grew through migration. Los Angeles offered both a desirable climate and an often-forgotten but thriving industrial sector built around oil and shipping. Thus it attracted wave after wave of migrants, both members of the white Protestant middle class mainly from the U.S. Midwest, and working people of a variety of ethnicities from the entire United States and Mexico. The result, as in other places that experienced growth earlier, was a boom for the city but a complicated job for the police.[8]

During the 1920s and 1930s, the ideal of professionalism also established new expectations for policing. Much as other fields such as medicine and the law had used access to specialized knowledge and services as the basis for establishing a clearly delineated and independent occupational status for their practitioners, police, too, sought to craft their own professional autonomy. Advocates of police professionalization in the 1920s such as Vollmer and the International Association of Chiefs of Police (IACP) argued that police officers had developed expert knowledge and skills in controlling and preventing crime, and therefore deserved professional status. A series of investigations by independent crime commissions—beginning in Cleveland in 1922, then in Missouri in 1926 and in Chicago in 1929, and culminating with the federal Wickersham Commission in 1931—reinforced this argument. Discovering that ties to local political parties and civic administrations undercut police effectiveness, these commissions advocated greater autonomy for municipal police. By the end of the 1920s, police departments strove for new independence from political interference, more centralized administrative authority, and higher standards of education and training for police personnel. In some cases, departments brought in outsiders to enact changes. Los Angeles, for example, convinced Vollmer to take a leave from Berkeley and serve as chief of the LAPD for one year between August 1923 and August 1924. During that time, he reorganized the department so that the chief had central command over all its branches, improved its standards for selecting officers, established a training school, systematized record keeping, and introduced the principles of scientific crime detection.[9]

Technology also reshaped policing in the 1920s. The police patrol car, in the words of Samuel Walker, "had been a novelty prior to World War I [but] had become an inescapable necessity by the 1920s." Patrol officers gradually abandoned their walking beats and adopted automobiles in order to cope with the expanding geographic sizes of cities, to respond to criminals who were already motorized, and to address complaints received via another new technology—the telephone. With the spread of telephones, citizens increasingly called the police to report problems, rather than contacting them in person. And police utilized a third new technology—the two-way radio—to dispatch officers to investigate and to maintain contact between patrolmen and supervisors. The LAPD, assigned to cover the geographic sprawl of Los Angeles, eagerly embraced the technology. In just one year, Vollmer's administration purchased sixty-three patrol cars and sixty motorcycles. The new technology, however, changed the relationship between the police and the public. On the one hand, it increased public demands. The new technology encouraged citizens to phone in complaints and ask the police to address an increasingly wide range of disturbances. On the other hand, it also separated the police from the public under any other circumstances. Isolated in their patrol cars, officers could easier see themselves as distinct from the public they monitored.[10]

These changes were gradual. In Los Angeles, Vollmer failed to achieve the level of professionalism that he sought, at least in the short term. He could not penetrate the LAPD's existing culture of corruption and its ties to the business community and organized illegal enterprises. He returned to Berkeley after one year with his most fundamental goals frustrated. Vollmer was succeeded first by one former commander of the central vice squad and then, in 1926, by another, James Davis.[11]

Davis's position at the time of his appointment illustrates the difficulties faced by police administrators in the 1920s. The LAPD had begun taking steps toward more professional policing, but still lacked autonomy; Davis served a variety of interests. He owed his job to Mayor Cryer, and indirectly to the political machine that supported Cryer. That machine derived much of its income and power from organized vice, so the police had to ignore operations that had the machine's approval. Davis also had to satisfy the vocal and influential moral reform community in Los Angeles, led by Protestant ministers such as the Reverend Robert Schuler, by demonstrating enthusiasm for fighting crime. And Davis had to satisfy the business interests that dominated Los Angeles, led by *Los Angeles Times* publisher Harry Chandler. These interests wanted crime suppressed to a level where it did not interfere with business, and expected the LAPD's help in keeping organized labor out of Los Angeles.[12]

Davis balanced the competing interests exerting pressure on the LAPD by turning his police loose on criminals, transients, minorities, and vice operators not enjoying the protection of the machine. The LAPD took advantage of its centralized command, tighter organizational structure, and improved efficiency to get tough on crime and suspected criminals. Violence against suspects both during arrests and in custody was routine and tacitly permitted by administrators. In addition, the LAPD regularly stretched the boundaries of legally permissible methods of investigation. Beginning in 1922, California courts accepted evidence obtained through unauthorized searches and seizures and thereby encouraged the LAPD to raid suspected criminals. In 1931, the Wickersham Commission reported that "arresting and holding men on suspicion is considered legal by the police." The courts allowed them to detain suspects for forty-eight hours without bringing charges against them, and the LAPD often extended this grace period to as much as a week.[13]

In the 1930s, the Great Depression strained police departments' resources, as they had to meet the threat of an apparent increase in crime with diminishing budgets and personnel numbers. They sought to address these difficulties by increasing their efficiency, conducting scientific studies of the best ways to allocate their forces and concentrating on the most visible public problems.[14] The LAPD was no exception. Even as Los Angeles grew in population and area, the number of LAPD officers remained virtually constant from the middle of the 1920s until World War II. The department employed as many as 2,364 officers in the 1924–25 fiscal year, but its growth ceased thereafter; its numbers remained virtually the same through 1940. Thus, the ratio of police to the public declined steadily from a peak of 2.61 per 1,000 residents in the 1924–25 fiscal year to 1.54 in 1940. In addition, salaries remained flat. In 1926, the city council set a starting patrolman's salary at $170 per month and, again, kept it at that level until the war years. Policing may have offered a steady paycheck during the Depression, but that paycheck did not go as far in the late 1930s as it did in the 1920s.[15]

Davis met these challenges in part by shifting officers out of desk jobs or specialized duties and into patrol. In 1926–27, his first year as chief, only 66 percent of sworn LAPD officers worked as patrolmen, down from a more typical range between 70 and 78 percent in the previous decade. Davis immediately put men on the streets; 82 percent of officers served as patrolmen each year throughout the rest of the 1920s and 1930s.[16]

"Efficiency" became a constant buzzword of Davis's reports. In 1933, he

proclaimed his intention to "energize the department as a whole into a force-
ful, active, and efficient group of police officers" and returned to this theme
again and again. As the decade progressed, his reports to the city highlighted
his department's efficiency in contrast to its limited resources. In 1936, for
example, Davis advertised the LAPD's "increasing effectiveness in the protection of life and property. . . . This was accomplished without any increase
in the number of sworn police. It is evidence of the energetic performance of
conscientious men and women connected with this Department and the
splendid personnel direction under which they have functioned." And in
1937, he argued that the LAPD's successes reflected "a high standard of efficiency and morale in the Department despite the physical handicap of insufficient manpower."[17]

Police in the 1930s associated professionalism and efficiency with fighting
serious crime. These connections derive in part from the influence of Federal
Bureau of Investigation Director J. Edgar Hoover, who made a public spec-
tacle of the FBI's efforts to catch kidnappers, bandits, and bank robbers in the
early 1930s. Furthermore, Hoover associated his "war on crime" with the latest investigative techniques such as fingerprinting and a style of cool bureau-
cratic detachment that proved very appealing both to the public and to police
striving for professionalism. Hoover thus helped to establish crime fighting as
the special area of expertise that would allow police at both the federal and
local levels to achieve professional status.[18] Just as much as Hoover did, local
law enforcement officials such as Davis also engaged in a war on crime in the
1930s. Working on a local rather than a national scale, however, allowed
organizations such as the LAPD to operate differently than the FBI. First, they
concentrated as much on preventing crime as investigating and pursuing it.
Second, confident in the support of the local powers-that-be, they could exercise repression on anyone they deemed potential criminals.

The weight of Davis's war on crime fell disproportionately on communities lacking political power or long-term residency in Los Angeles. For example, in 1936, Davis famously established a border patrol (a "bum blockade")
to prevent transients from entering California. During the Great Depression,
as millions of workers lost their jobs and hundreds of thousands of farm families on the Great Plains were forced off their land, many of the dispossessed
took to the road or the rails and traveled the country looking for work. To
them, California represented an attractive destination. To Californians, however, these Depression Era transients represented potential sources of crime.
Davis argued that dust bowl refugees were responsible for "crimes of all types"
and the LAPD claimed that an annual 20 percent winter increase in crime
could be attributed to transients. In response, Davis sent LAPD officers far

outside of their jurisdiction to the borders of California to prevent transients from entering the state via major highways or railroads. They arrested transients on charges such as vagrancy or evading railroad fares, gave many "their choice of returning to the place from whence they came or appearing before the local magistrate," and convinced the majority (of those they caught) to leave California. Hampered by negative publicity and court injunctions, the LAPD gave up the bum blockade after a few months, but applied its principles to vagrants and transients within Los Angeles, vigorously targeting for arrest anyone without visible means of support throughout the 1930s. These exercises, in the eyes of Davis and the eyes of the LAPD, divided respectable Los Angeles residents from the less respectable and protected the city from crime.[19]

The weight of the LAPD's tactics also fell heavily upon the city's Mexican American community. The largest minority group in Los Angeles in the 1930s, Latinos faced pervasive discrimination in employment, housing, and education.[20] In particular, Latinos faced discrimination and ill treatment from the LAPD. Mexican American informants recalled verbal abuse from the police, arbitrary interrogations in public, sexual harassment of women, and mass arrest of Latino youths. For Mexican teenagers, according to historian Eduardo Obregon Pagan, "repeated confrontations with the LAPD simply become one of the strands woven into their adolescent experience."[21] These practices resulted not so much from the conscious policies of Davis but from the confrontational stance that the LAPD took against any group of outsiders. They saw working-class Mexican Americans as sources of disorder and treated them as such.

In short, in the 1920s and 1930s, police in general and the LAPD in particular placed an increased emphasis on controlling serious crime, in part because doing so helped increase their own professional status. Furthermore, improved management and technology allowed them to fight crime more efficiently even with limited personnel. Their methods, however, went beyond responding effectively and investigating thoroughly. They also sought to maintain order and prevent crime by targeting communities such as transients and Latinos whom they perceived to be potential criminals.

## JUVENILE CRIME PREVENTION IN LOS ANGELES

Leaders like James Davis did not pay much attention to juvenile delinquency except to the extent that it contributed to crime more generally. Nonetheless, the LAPD established one of the most widely publicized,

extensive crime prevention programs of the 1930s. Like police crime prevention in other cities, they justified their efforts in terms of social scientific approaches to delinquency, yet the reality of their programs paralleled
older efforts to deal with young offenders. In practice, they relied mainly on
cooperation with community agencies, organized recreation, and one-on-
one interactions with kids. Davis, we can imagine, tolerated crime prevention programs because they allowed the LAPD to appear sophisticated and
professional, and because diverting run-of-the-mill delinquents to community correctional agencies allowed the LAPD to concentrate on more serious
juvenile offenses.

Los Angeles was, in the early twentieth century, a surprising source of
innovative child welfare reform. Although California established juvenile
courts for major cities (including Los Angeles) in 1903, it was not a leader in
juvenile justice. California's main early innovations in the field lay in work
with female offenders. First in 1916, the state established a separate correctional facility for female delinquents in Ventura (noted for its extensive educational programs and clinical treatment). Then in 1919, the Los Angeles
County Probation Department, under the leadership of juvenile court refer-
ee Miriam Van Waters, opened its own experimental reform school for girls,
El Retiro. With the close supervision of Van Waters, a pioneering leader in
girls' corrections, El Retiro became a model institution by eliminating corporal punishments and prison-like elements such as uniforms and barred windows, and offering schooling, recreation, vocational training, and some
self-government.[22] The LAPD was an even less likely source of child welfare
innovation. Nonetheless, the police made a number of steps toward protecting children and youth during the Progressive Era. It assigned a special officer to handle juvenile cases in 1909, hired social worker Alice Stebbins Wells
as its first policewoman in 1910, and established an official Juvenile Bureau
in 1913. The Juvenile Bureau also worked closely with the City Mother's
Bureau, a parallel agency established in 1914 and entirely staffed by policewomen that primarily guarded girls from seduction and prostitution.[23]

The main function of the LAPD Juvenile Bureau was investigating and
adjusting delinquency cases. Between the 1910s and 1930s, when patrolmen
arrested persons age seventeen or younger, they immediately transferred them
to the Juvenile Bureau. There, officers were to investigate each case and
design a plan intended both to benefit the child and to safeguard society from
harm. They maintained children's records of arrests, recommended whether
detention was appropriate, and made preliminary dispositions, seeking to
adjust cases without taking children to court. When youths were first-time
offenders, the police usually lectured them, released them with a "promise of

good behavior" if their parents were cooperative, and kept track of them through "voluntary" probation. Only when informal treatment turned out to be insufficient did they petition youths to juvenile court.[24]

The Juvenile Bureau did not, however, devote much attention to preventing delinquency for the better part of the 1910s and 1920s. Nor did it sponsor child-friendly initiatives akin to those in New York or Detroit. Even Vollmer, in his one-year stint with the LAPD, did little to bring a social work perspective to policing. Frustrated with the scale of problems in Los Angeles, Vollmer sponsored only narrowly administrative reforms such as consolidating an array of services into a single Crime Prevention Division (CPD).[25]

In the late 1920s, however, the CPD joined the national crime prevention bandwagon, advocating proactive work with predelinquent youth. These programs actually began when Davis was out of office in 1929, but continued and expanded after his return in 1933. During this time, CPD spokespersons adopted current psychiatric rhetoric to explain their new approach to delinquency. It was essential, they argued, to reconceptualize the juvenile delinquent not "as a criminal who must be punished" but "as a socially mal-adjusted individual who needs correction and guidance."[26] They further argued that new psychiatric diagnoses and treatments of delinquents represented better long-term solutions to crime than did detecting and apprehending criminals. "Crime prevention," asserted the CPD, was "the salvation of this era in which crime is so prevalent."[27]

What did the police bring to crime prevention that other agencies did not? According to CPD spokespersons, the police were in the unique position of being "the first agency that comes in contact with the juvenile delinquent." They made a virtue of the LAPD's aggressive approach to crime and disorder. In particular, the CPD claimed that it could provide around-the-clock emergency service, conduct investigations of criminal cases involving children, discover and eliminate many community-based causes of delinquency, detect children at risk for trouble, and coordinate with other agencies interested in child welfare and crime prevention.[28]

This last point was key. The LAPD put crime prevention into practice mainly through cooperation with the Los Angeles County Coordinating Council (LACCC). In January 1932, Los Angeles Juvenile Court Judge Samuel R. Blake and Probation Officer Kenyon Scudder brought together "representatives of case-working agencies that deal with children"—court officials, educators, social workers, and police officers—to form a Coordinating Council to oversee all "delinquency prevention" work in Los Angeles. The LACCC was explicitly modeled on the pioneering coordinating committee initiated by Vollmer in Berkeley in 1919. Like the Berkeley committee, it gathered officials from all agencies that dealt with children in order to address both the social problems that contributed to delinquency and specific issues regarding particular juveniles.[29] It also maintained that work with potential delinquents should extend beyond the aegis of the by-now traditional juvenile court. Judge Blake "decided that inasmuch as the Juvenile Court procedure had proved so successful after delinquency, why could not the same principles be applied in the field of prevention, before the child reached the Court?"[30]

The context of the Great Depression and the New Deal help explain why the LACCC emerged when it did. For Judge Blake, during economic hard times, reducing the cost of juvenile court represented a major concern. Preventing delinquency was a welcome goal not only because it promised to accomplish good in society but also because it promised to reduce the number of expensive investigations, hearings, and treatments conducted by juvenile court. By the end of 1933, Judge Blake claimed that new crime prevention initiatives had already saved Los Angeles County over $500,000.[31] And funding for the new programs came from state and federal programs, not local taxpayers. Initially maintained through volunteer work and then funded modestly by the Civil Works Administration, the LACCC soon acquired extensive financial support from the California State Emergency Relief Administration (SERA), and the federal Works Progress Administration. Through relief programs, the LACCC hired over eighty previously unemployed men and women—reportedly including teachers, lawyers, ministers, and filmmakers—to serve as local youth workers.[32] The convergence of Depression Era concerns about juvenile delinquency, the need to reduce the costs of government, and New Deal support for experimental social programs made large-scale crime prevention possible.

The LACCC performed three major types of work. One committee sought to improve the social environment that contributed to delinquency. It addressed concerns such as juvenile access to pornography and alcohol (especially worrisome with the repeal of Prohibition in 1933).[33] A second "character-building" committee sought to link "unattached" youths with organizations such as the Boy Scouts, the YMCA, churches, and playgrounds that would provide them with structured recreation and group activities designed to discourage delinquency.[34]

A third committee sought to adjust delinquency cases without formal police or court action. When children "on the verge of trouble" came to the attention of any agency affiliated with the LACCC, the Adjustment Committee could intervene and refer them to social services or recreation programs. The LAPD played a key role in the referral process by directing minor delinquents with whom they had had contact to the LACCC.[35] These referrals allowed the police to divert many adolescents who might previously have been arrested, and to release them ("kick them loose") to neighborhood adjustment committees that offered a variety of programs to keep them out of future trouble. This continued the earlier practice of "voluntary" probation but passed responsibility to the LACCC. Not only did this policy relieve the police of one duty; it also provided social benefits. As James Davis and LAPD Captain E. M. Slaughter wrote, the LACCC helped establish a "united front for law enforcement," serving as "an outlet for cases of delinquency not serious enough to demand Court action," and creating "a close and constant contact between the Police and the community."[36]

Cooperation with the LACCC helped the LAPD establish organized recreation programs. Police in Los Angeles maintained that "supervised recreational pastimes" would not only discourage crime and delinquency but also promote "better citizenship."[37] In addition to sponsoring baseball leagues and a citywide softball tournament, the CPD instituted continuing programs such as a summer camp (Camp Valyermo) ninety miles from Los Angeles for "underprivileged" children. In 1936, 1,400 boys between ages nine and sixteen and 400 girls between twelve and sixteen went to the camp (200 at a time) for six days of swimming, hiking, games, and entertainment.[38] The LAPD also sponsored Boy Scout troops for slightly younger boys. Beginning with one troop organized by the 77th Street Division in January 1935, the program grew to eighteen troops (and one Girl Scout troop led by policewomen) that used Camp Valyermo during the school year in 1938.[39]

In addition, police often utilized sports such as boxing to make crucial initial connections with youngsters. For example, in the mid-1930s, the LAPD and the LACCC became very concerned about boys—mostly Latino—stealing produce from the East Side Wholesale Market. Dealers claimed that the boys stole between $20,000 and $40,000 in fruit and vegetables each year, and whenever police tried to catch them, they would scatter and run away. The police and coordinating council tried a new tactic: they recruited Bert Colima, a prominent local Mexican American prizefighter, to come and talk to the boys. Colima reportedly told the boys that the police were coming to arrest them, but if they ceased committing minor crimes they could be referred to a community center and given boxing lessons. Colima's standing within the Latino community helped create a point of entry for police and social workers to recruit troublesome boys into crime prevention programs. His approach also exemplified a characteristic crime prevention tactic of balancing the threat of arrest with the opportunity to participate in recreation.[40]

Similarly, police recreation programs often evolved from the LAPD's efforts to divert youths from arrest. In one widely publicized 1934 example, police officers from the Hollenbeck Heights division sponsored a seven-mile hike and overnight camping trip for neighborhood boys as a reward for completing an organized recreation program. As a result of the outing, "the attitude of children and parents toward the Police has changed remarkably." The LAPD asserted, "friendly cooperation [had] replaced suspicious distrust." This effort originated not from casual encounters or parental requests, however, but from nighttime patrols that were intended to stop a flurry of vandalism and petty theft. Through "constant surveillance of streets, parks, and alleys at night," the police apprehended over 900 boys, contacted each boy's home, declared that subsequent encounters would result in arrests, and insisted that, as an alternative, the children be enrolled in recreation programs sponsored by the LACCC and the police.[41]

The LAPD justified recreation programs by arguing that they reduced delinquency. One CPD officer claimed that these efforts slashed juvenile crime as much as 35 percent during children's summer vacation from school. He explained this sharp drop by suggesting that, because only youth with clean records were allowed to attend the camp, juveniles tried to stay out of trouble.[42] The CPD primarily sought to reduce delinquency, however, by constructing recreation programs that would attract boys (girls were an afterthought at best) and introduce them to guidance from male role models such as police officers. The summer camp, as well as activities like baseball and scouting, "create[d] a bond of friendship between the potential delinquent and the law enforcement officer which tends to forever protect the child from a life of crime."[43]

Police also sought to use individual encounters to form personal connections with boys. Los Angeles probation officer Kenyon Scudder recounted one incident in which a policeman found two boys, ages fifteen and twelve, out after midnight in an alley behind a small grocery store that they apparently planned to rob. The officer—writing up the boys for violating curfew but ignoring the intended burglary—happened to wave his flashlight at the grocery store and mused about what a "good old guy" the owner was. Shaming the boys about their planned heist without explicitly acknowledging it, the officer, according to Scudder, "supplant[ed] youthful lust for adventurous plunder with respect for a good old guy whose property it is an honor to defend." The officer ultimately convinced the boys to participate in one of the LAPD's night baseball programs. At least in this instance, the patrolman dealt with the boys in a manner similar to that of a Chicago Area Project street worker. Through simple exchanges like this one, crime prevention officers believed that they could teach boys to respect rather than to prey upon their communities.[44]

The LAPD may have used psychiatric rhetoric occasionally to explain its crime prevention programs, but these programs were built largely on the common sense notion that boys would naturally drift into delinquency without adult male guidance. The LAPD's methods of dealing with juveniles were very different from those of dealing with other potential offenders, but the fundamental assumptions were strikingly similar. Via early and sometimes coercive intervention, they could prevent crime. LAPD officers used the threat of arrest to push boys into crime prevention and recreation programs, hoping that they could discourage them from delinquency.

James Davis was forced to retire as chief of the LAPD in 1938 under pressure from another scandal. At least for juveniles, however, the change in administrations made little difference. Davis's successor, Arthur H. Hohmann, urged the CPD to maintain a balanced approach to young offenders, avoiding "any tendency toward retrogression into the field of penal treatment of juvenile delinquents or a progress into the particular field of social welfare work."[45] Police crime prevention work persisted into the 1940s and later in large part because diverting large numbers of minor delinquents to preventive programs allowed the LAPD to devote greater attention to fighting serious juvenile crime.

## Juvenile Arrests in Los Angeles

The LAPD's arrest patterns reflect how its approach to controlling juveniles changed and how it sought to get tough on juvenile crime. Beginning in the mid-1920s, the LAPD published extensive tabulated records of arrests of juveniles, separate from arrests of adults. As with tables published by the Detroit Police Department, these data do not allow the detailed analysis that individual arrest records would make possible. However, they do distinguish arrests by sex, age, race, charge, and initial dispositions, making it possible to reconstruct general patterns and to chart change over time.

The arrest data reveal a startling trend: controlling for population, juvenile rates of arrests increased somewhat between the middle of 1920s and the early 1930s and then dropped by roughly half between the early 1930s and 1940. Among boys between ages ten and seventeen, the arrest rate fell from a high of over 65 arrests per 1,000 in the 1931–32 fiscal year to 38 per 1,000 in 1940 (see figure 7.1). Among girls between ten and seventeen, it fell from over 19 arrests per 1,000 in 1929–30 to 9 per 1,000 in 1940 (see figure 7.2).[46] In addition, arrests decreased for all categories of offense even though their distribution remained fairly even. Among boys, for example, between

**Figure 7.1**

Boys' arrest rates in Los Angeles, 1925–26 to 1940

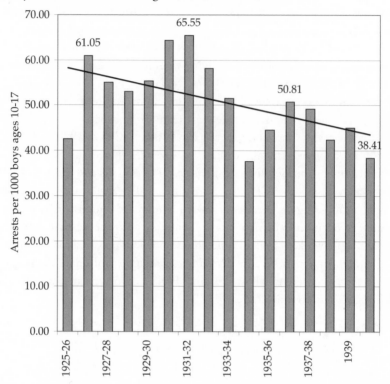

Sources: LAPD, *Annual Reports* (1925–26 to 1940); U.S. Bureau of the Census, *14th Census, Vol. II: Population, 1920,* 294; U.S. Bureau of the Census, *15th Census, Vol. II: Population, 1930,* 730, 744; U.S. Bureau of the Census, *16th Census, Vol. II: Population, 1940,* 629; U.S. Bureau of the Census, *16th Census, Vol. IV: Population; Characteristics by Age, Part 2, 1940,* 172.

1926 and 1940, offenses against property constituted 59 percent of all arrests; for any given year, they constituted between 57 and 62 percent; yet the rate of arrests for property crimes fell sharply from roughly 37 per 1,000 boys in 1930–31 to 22 in 1940. Likewise, throughout the period, the share of status offenses constituted 22 percent of boys' arrests, public order offenses 11 percent, offenses against persons 6 percent, and other categories 3 percent, all with little variation from year to year; yet in each case, rates of arrests per population dropped sharply.

Do the declining arrest rates mean that juvenile crime diminished substantially during the Great Depression? Probably not, if we consider the

**Figure 7.2**

Girls' arrest rates in Los Angeles, 1925–26 to 1940

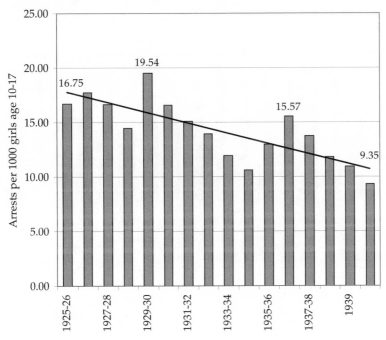

Sources: See figure 7.1.

degree of the offenses for which the LAPD arrested boys.[47] While boys' over-all arrest rate declined throughout the 1930s, arrests for offenses labeled felonies remained fairly steady, slipping only from 22 per 1,000 in 1931–32 to 19 per 1,000 in 1940. By contrast, the arrest rate for misdemeanors fell from almost 31 per 1,000 in 1931–32 to less than 8 per 1,000 in 1940 (see figure 7.3). In other words, the police continued to arrest boys almost as often for felonies in 1940 as in 1930, but far less often for misdemeanors. Whereas in 1930–31, misdemeanors accounted for 46 percent and felonies for 35 percent of all boys' arrests, in 1940 felonies accounted for 51 percent and misdemeanors for only 21 percent of boys' arrests. Felonies came to constitute the bulk of boys' arrests.

Why the change? With limited personnel and an increasing priority of fighting serious crime, the LAPD delegated some of its traditional responsibilities in curbing delinquency to the LACCC and its affiliated agencies. By 1940, the police increasingly reserved arrests, court hearings, and correctional

**Figure 7.3**

Boys' Arrest Rates in Los Angeles, 1925–26 to 1940, by Degree of Offense

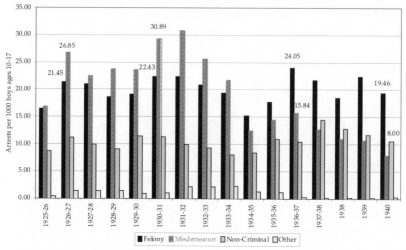

Sources: See figure 7.1.

treatment for youths who had committed felonious offenses, not the status offenses and misdemeanors that had occupied much of their attention earlier.

Similar changes can be detected in other cities as well. In Chicago, the overall rate of complaints against juveniles investigated by PPOs decreased from approximately 40 per 1,000 in 1930 to 29 per 1,000 in 1940.[48] And in Detroit, boys' arrest rates remained flat between 1933 and 1940, averaging just over 40 per 1,000 boys between ages ten and sixteen, but police charged a noticeably larger share of boys with felonies than in the past. Whereas between 1898 and 1907, felonies had constituted only 1 percent of boys' arrests, and between 1908 and 1918 they had constituted 6 percent, between 1933 and 1940, felonies constituted 21 percent of boys' arrests.[49] Los Angeles may encapsulate the new approach to policing youth, but its transition was not unique.

The LAPD's new focus on serious juvenile crimes also contributed to changes in the demographic profile of kids it arrested. The ages of boys who were arrested shifted upward. Boys' average age rose from 14.2 in 1930–31 to 14.7 in 1940.[50] The rate of arrest for boys between fifteen and seventeen in 1940 (64 arrests per 1,000) more than tripled that of boys between ten and fourteen (20 per 1,000).[51]

The LAPD also arrested minority youth in disproportionate and increas-

**Figure 7.4**

LAPD Arrests of Boys by Race, 1925–26 to 1940

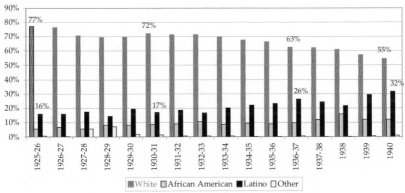

Sources: LAPD, *Annual Reports* (1925–26 to 1940).

ing shares between 1930 and 1940. Latinos, the largest non-Caucasian eth-
nic group in the city, constituted approximately 8 percent of the total population but 17 percent of the boys arrested in 1930 (see figure 7.4).[52] African
Americans represented 3 percent of the population (and 3 percent of Los
Angeles males between ages 10 and 17) but 9 percent of the boys arrested.[53]
These racial disparities grew over the course of the decade, most dramatically for Latinos. By 1940, Latinos constituted 32 percent and African
Americans 12 percent of all boys arrested by the LAPD (versus 8 percent and
4 percent of the population, respectively).[54] In comparison, the share of
whites decreased from 72 percent of boys arrested in 1930–31 to 55 percent
in 1940.

In contrast to boys, the LAPD arrested the vast majority of girls—85 percent between 1925–26 and 1940—for non-criminal offenses such as dependency and sexual delinquency.[55] The decline in girls' rate of arrest on these
charges—from over 15 per 1,000 in 1929–30 to less than 9 per 1,000 in
1940—accounts for the decline in girls' overall arrest rate in these years (see
figure 7.5). Minorities were disproportionately represented, but not to the
same degree as among boys. Nor did their ratios change substantially over
time. Latinas, who constituted 17 percent of girls arrested in 1929–30,
increased to 22 percent in 1940. Blacks remained at approximately 8 percent

**Figure 7.5**

Girls' Arrest Rates in Los Angeles, 1925–26 to 1940, by Degree of Offense

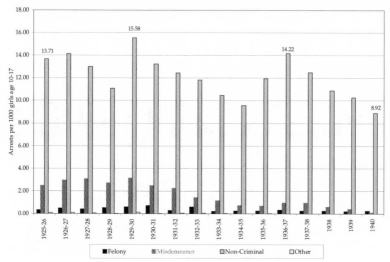

Sources: See figure 7.1.

between 1930 and 1940 while whites declined from 74 to 69 percent (see figure 7.6). Girls' average ages remained in a roughly constant range between 13.7 and 14.0.[56]

In essence, the LAPD continued to arrest similar types of girls for the same reasons throughout the 1930s, but it arrested fewer of them. By 1940, coordinating councils and other social welfare agencies represented new institutional actors capable of protecting girls. They could intervene before girls encountered the police or before police contacts escalated to the point where an arrest became necessary. With limited resources at their disposal, the police in turn demonstrated little interest in arresting girls on charges that did not immediately threaten public safety or order. Because girls committed few criminal offenses, they were of less concern to a Depression Era police department that was increasingly channeling its resources toward crime control.

The LAPD's changing arrest practices also substantially impacted the juvenile court and the larger juvenile justice system. Following arrest, officers from the Crime Prevention Division investigated each case and determined whether it could be resolved informally or whether it should be petitioned to court. And, as the LAPD concentrated increasingly on serious juvenile offenders, CPD officers determined that more and more cases required for-

**Figure 7.6**
LAPD Arrests of Girls by Race, 1925–26 to 1940

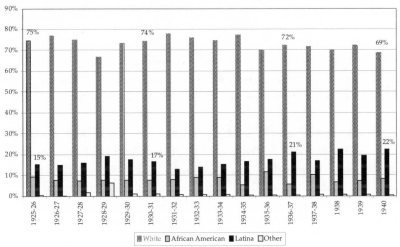

Sources: LAPD, *Annual Reports* (1925–26 to 1940).

mal adjudication. The share of boys petitioned to court by the CPD increased from 29 percent in 1930–31 to 48 percent in 1940.[57] Predictably, the felons whom the police increasingly arrested more often required court supervision than did boys who committed minor offenses, thus increasing the court's burden. In addition, the LAPD became more likely to petition felons to court. In 1930–31, CPD officers referred 49 percent of boys arrested for felonies to court; in 1940, they referred 70 percent. As a result, felons came to account for an increasing share of the juvenile court's workload. In 1930–31, felons represented 58 percent of boys' cases petitioned by the LAPD; in 1940, they represented 73 percent.

When processing girls during the Depression decade, the CPD continued to rely on juvenile court, but they also became increasingly likely to send them to outside agencies. Throughout the 1930s, the share of girls' arrests petitioned to court remained fairly flat, generally ranging between 40 and 45 percent. However, the proportion of girls sent to other law enforcement or correctional agencies—probation officers, most often—increased noticeably from 9 to 19 percent between 1930–31 and 1940. Likewise, the share of girls referred to the Los Angeles Federation of Charities rose sharply from 6 percent to a high of 18 percent in 1938. These increases resulted in a reduction in the percentage of girls who were released; 33 percent of girls arrested in 1929–30 had their cases dismissed or suspended by the police, but only 18 percent were so fortunate in 1940.[58] Girls were arrested overwhelmingly on non-criminal charges throughout this period, so these shifts cannot be attributed to changing offense patterns. Instead, they reflected a shift in police procedure. Over time the police released a smaller portion of girls and instead increasingly chose to send them to agencies inside or outside of the formal juvenile justice system that would provide some form of guidance or treatment.

In sum, the purpose of the LAPD's juvenile arrests narrowed considerably in the 1930s to focus on crime control. At the end of the decade, officers arrested boys and girls for lesser offenses at much lower rates than they had at the beginning. The LAPD ceased to use arrest as a catchall method for handling any sort of delinquency, minor or major. Instead, it increasingly reserved arrest for mid-teenage boys who had committed felonies and who were disproportionately members of racial minorities. Juveniles arrested in Los Angeles were becoming older, darker, and more criminal. Furthermore, by 1940, the LAPD petitioned more and more juvenile offenders to juvenile court. For adolescent offenders, release after arrest was becoming a thing of the past. Instead court adjudication increasingly became the routine outcome of an arrest. Thus, the LAPD's concentration on felony arrests not only impacted the youths apprehended and the communities targeted, but also contributed to a substantial remaking of the intake and operations of juvenile court.

## CRIME PREVENTION TO FACILITATE CRIME CONTROL

No one would accuse James E. Davis of worrying too much about juvenile offenders or of adopting a "child-friendly" approach to policing youth. Yet between his appointment as chief in 1926 and his final resignation in 1938, the LAPD contributed substantially to a transformation of juvenile justice. The LAPD under Davis's watch prioritized crime control. Their methods—centralizing organization, utilizing automotive patrols and communications technologies, targeting seemingly disreputable elements of the community for harassment and arrest, and often ignoring suspects' constitutional rights—may have been extreme, but they also paralleled a general trend toward more hard-boiled policing in the 1930s. Yet at the same time, the LAPD also participated vigorously in delinquency prevention programs by organizing sports teams, conducting camping trips, and cooperating with community-based social agencies. The LAPD apparently engaged in crime prevention because doing so fit its larger institutional agenda and interests in two ways. First, if they assumed that today's delinquent naturally became tomorrow's criminal, then redirecting present-day young offenders would make future crime control more manageable. And second, diverting predelinquent and moderately delinquent youth to social service programs allowed the LAPD to focus its attention on adolescent offenders who had committed more severe crimes. Their new priority of fighting more serious juvenile crime would, in turn, also remake the juvenile court.

# ❧8❧

# Saving Young Offenders or Getting Tough on Juvenile Crime?
## POLICE AND THE EXPANDING NETWORK
## OF JUVENILE JUSTICE

A t about one o'clock on a Thursday afternoon in August 1940, Los Angeles Police Officers Brady and Willis saw a Latino teenager, *Paul "Halloween" Silva*, trying unsuccessfully to start a 1939 Buick.[1] When they confronted him, Silva could not produce any proof of ownership but claimed that the car belonged to his father. The two officers took him to where he said his father lived, but when they got out of the police car, the boy ran into a nearby house. As Brady and Willis pursued him, Silva fled into a second home. When Silva continued to run even after one of the officers commanded him to stop, the officer fired a single shot that struck him in the leg.

After apprehending Silva and finding that he had been hit, the patrolmen took him to a hospital. There they discovered that he was just sixteen years old and that, as they had suspected, he had stolen the car three days earlier. They then referred the case to the LAPD's Crime Prevention Division (CPD); the CPD eventually referred him to juvenile court. In spite of an allegation that Silva was involved with gang activity and his mother's acknowledgment that she had trouble controlling him, the court initially placed him on probation. Perhaps his willingness to admit his offense after he had been caught contributed to the court's decision. Silva, however, did not change his ways. The police arrested him again a few months later (for stealing from lockers at the All Nations Boys Club), and this time the court decided to remove him from his home and place him in a forestry camp outside of Los Angeles for more intensive supervision. The court appeared to make this decision as much because his mother could not manage him and because his father refused to make him go to school as because he had committed a string of crimes.[2]

Silva's case reflected new patterns that came to characterize young offenders, policing, and juvenile justice immediately before World War II. Silva himself fit the profile of boys whom the police increasingly targeted for arrest. He was, at sixteen, older than the typical juvenile offender had been thirty or forty years earlier, a Latino, and twice arrested for felony crimes. The LAPD arrested him on its own initiative. The juvenile court gave him one chance to redeem himself, but when he persisted in committing crimes, institutionalized him.

On the eve of World War II, the day-to-day operation of juvenile justice was changing. The rise of crime prevention programs to divert a large share of predelinquents to community-based youth agencies and the new crime control orientation of the police together impacted both the experiences of young offenders and the operations of juvenile court. By 1940, the typical characteristics of juveniles in the justice system had shifted significantly to include more boys in their mid- to late teens, more accused of felonies, and disproportionately more racial minorities. These changes also impacted juvenile courts. Although they sought to maintain their Progressive Era commitment to rehabilitating juveniles by nonpunitive means, courts also had to adapt to youths' more serious offenses by developing graduated levels of formal, custodial supervision and treatment. The juvenile justice system sought simultaneously to save young offenders and get tough on juvenile crime.

The LAPD contributed heavily to this reshaping of juvenile justice. Police initiative resulted in the arrest of more serious offenders and brought tougher kids into the juvenile court. And the police concentration on serious and repeat juvenile offenders helped foster an expansion of the court's mechanisms for institutional treatment. In short, without conscious plan or intent, police practices subtly redirected the juvenile justice system so that it balanced its own rehabilitative mission with the LAPD's new mission of crime control.

## OFFENDERS IN JUVENILE COURT

To see how juvenile justice was changing by 1940, we need to return first to fundamental questions about delinquency. Who were the children and youth in juvenile court? What had they done wrong? How did they get there? On the eve of World War II, the problem of juvenile delinquency was discussed widely. Even then, commentators thought the delinquents of their time to be far worse than those of earlier years. Delinquents were perceived as becoming increasingly organized in gangs, increasingly violent, and increasingly likely to commit serious crime. And in Los Angeles, outsiders considered the emerging but socially isolated Mexican American community a breeding ground for crime and violence.[3] How real were these concerns?

These questions may be explored in considerable detail via analysis of individual case records from Los Angeles County Juvenile Court. In addition, focusing on cases petitioned to juvenile court by the LAPD reveals how police efforts to fight juvenile crime contributed to the larger juvenile justice system. The court records confirm what police arrest data already indicated: by 1940, the LAPD predominantly referred boys to juvenile court for felonies (66 percent), not misdemeanors or status offenses. In addition, the profile of boys in court paralleled that of boys arrested. Boys' average age was 14.97; 33 percent were between ages ten and fourteen, and 67 percent were between fifteen and seventeen. Sixty percent were white, 29 percent were Latino, and 11 percent were black.[4]

Boys may have been petitioned to juvenile court for felonies, but when examined in terms of the offenses they actually committed, their crimes seem less severe. The LAPD typically petitioned boys accused of property offenses. Motor vehicle theft (a felony) represented the leading crime at 32 percent, followed by burglary (another felony) at 22 percent, and petty theft (a misdemeanor) at 18 percent. Robbery, assault, and other violent offenses against persons constituted 9 percent, and rape or sexual assault accounted for 6 percent of petitions. Only 9 percent of boys were petitioned for status offenses.[5]

So many boys were charged with felonies in part because they stole property worth large amounts of money. The median value of theft by boys in 1940 may seem low at first glance—only $50—but, when adjusted for inflation, would represent the equivalent of over $600 in 2002 (see table 8.1). The predominance of auto theft with a median value of $400 in 1940 (or almost $5,000 in 2002 dollars) obviously inflates this figure, but other offenses also involved property of substantial value. Burglaries typically netted goods or cash worth the equivalent of over $300, and petty theft netted a median of $170. Robberies from persons—the most confrontational form of theft—actually gained the least, a median of just under $150 in today's money (or less than $12 in 1940).

The charges that led police to petition boys to court varied by age. Younger boys primarily stuck to small-scale thefts and occasional break-ins; they rarely stole the most valuable property or confronted their victims in per-

**Table 8.1**

Value of Offenses Petitioned to Los Angeles Juvenile Court, 1940

| Offense Category | Median Value | Median Value (2002 Dollars) | |
|---|---|---|---|
| All thefts by boys | $50.00 | $623.22 | N = 174 |
| Robbery (from person) | $11.86 | $147.85 | N = 14 |
| Petty theft | $13.65 | $170.17 | N = 40 |
| Burglary | $26.30 | $327.87 | N = 58 |
| Auto theft | $400.00 | $4,986.59 | N = 66 |
| All thefts by girls | $122.50 | $1,527.14 | N = 6 |

Source: Los Angeles Juvenile Court 1940 database. Results were translated to 2002 dollars using "The Inflation Calculator," an online conversion tool utilizing data from the Consumer Price Index published by the U.S. Bureau of Labor Statistics located at <http://www.westegg.com/inflation/> (June 21, 2004).

son. Between the ages of ten and fourteen, boys were significantly more often charged with burglary (34 percent) and with petty theft (26 percent) than were boys between fifteen and seventeen (16 percent and 14 percent, respectively).[6] In contrast, boys between ages fifteen and seventeen were much more often petitioned to court for auto theft (39 percent, vs. 17 percent of ten- to fourteen-year-olds).

In spite of the amount of crime boys committed, their offenses were rarely predatory. They usually committed crimes against strangers (only 16 percent knew their victims), but in spite of that, boys rarely used violence (10 percent), possessed weapons (8 percent), or were labeled as being involved in gangs (9 percent). Alcohol and drug use were even less common (6 percent). A small minority of young offenders in juvenile court fell into a number of the categories above and did in fact engage in the gang-related violent crime that observers worried about at the time, but the large majority did not.

Instead, youthful pastimes like aimlessly hanging out on street corners with friends often escalated into delinquency and triggered encounters with the police. Most boys committed criminal offenses in groups: 58 percent had one or two accomplices and 15 percent had three or more; only 28 percent acted alone. On average, boys acted with 1.37 accomplices. In addition, many boys had prior histories of informal or formal contact with the police before they were initially petitioned to court. Boys averaged 1.1 arrests or official warnings from the police before their first court appearance.

In short, boys petitioned to juvenile court in 1940 by the LAPD seem to have engaged in juvenile delinquency not so very different from that of boys decades earlier. Yes, a small percentage committed violence, used weapons, and participated in nascent gangs. Most, however, hung out with their friends, stole when opportunities arose, and were arrested when police caught them. To kids, the biggest difference from earlier decades may have been the availability of more exciting and more expensive items to steal, such as automobiles. That said, the world of 1940 was very different from that of 1900, and those differences generated a more aggressive law enforcement response.

## COMPLAINTS, POLICE INITIATIVE, AND A CHANGING APPROACH TO JUVENILE CRIME

The day-to-day policing of juveniles in 1940 Los Angeles revealed a curious mix of continuity and change. On the one hand, the general nature of offenses committed by youth displayed strong continuities with earlier forms of delinquency. And the general fashion in which offenses came to the attention of police and law enforcement displayed continuities as well. But the larger social context had changed substantially.

Sociological analyses of policing—which often tend to assume historical constancy—help explain how police operated. As Arthur Stinchcombe has argued, police have more latitude to observe and to regulate behavior in public than to regulate private actions. To discover offenses committed behind closed doors, they usually depend on complainants to report the offense and invite them in, whereas with offenses committed in public they can intervene on their own. Thus the interests of citizens and particularly of crime victims shape how police handle certain types of offenses—those committed in private—whereas the agenda of the police contribute more heavily to their handling of other sorts of misbehaviors—typically those committed in public.[7] Empirical studies support this premise. When investigators have acted as participant-observers, riding along with police officers and watching them do their jobs, they have discovered that whether police encounters with youth were initiated by complainants or by police represented a key situational variable in deciding the outcome. When citizens report offenses, their complaints substantially determine which transgressions the police must address and influence whether the police make an arrest. However, when the police observe what they regard as a violation of the law, they can exercise greater discretion, deciding entirely on their own whether to act and, if so, how to respond to the offense.[8]

Within this sociological framework, historical context also matters. Los Angeles in 1940 experienced particular conditions that shaped the policing of youth and the way in which officers exercised discretion. First, the rapid growth of an autonomous Latino community seemed to pose a threat that the LAPD sought to control. Second, the LAPD's Depression Era policies of targeting apparent transients and vagrants as a means of preventing crime also shaped its interactions with youth. And third, the increasingly widespread availability of automobiles and their popularity as items to steal accounted for the most frequent source of documented encounters between cops and kids.

Complaints by the public initiated most contacts between the police and male juvenile delinquents in 1940 Los Angeles. The LAPD arrested 47 percent of the boys they petitioned to juvenile court after crime victims had reported a specific offense to them. In addition, they arrested substantial shares of boys following reports of illegal activities by witnesses (10 percent) and by culprits' own parents or relatives (4 percent). In these cases, members of the public provided the initial information about offenses that triggered formal police intervention and implicitly shaped the LAPD's actions.[9]

How did this work in practice? When victims filed a formal complaint or witnesses reported an offense, the LAPD sent officers to investigate. If complainants simply reported a crime, regular patrolmen or detectives performed the initial investigation. When they arrested suspects younger than age eighteen (who were therefore under juvenile court jurisdiction), the LAPD transferred them to its Crime Prevention Division (CPD) for further inquiry. In approximately half of the complaints, suspects were known to be juveniles from the outset, so their cases were handled entirely by the CPD. While it is impossible to know how many complaints were never resolved, the process was surprisingly rapid when it did lead to an arrest. A median of just one day passed between reported offenses and arrests of suspected juveniles.

Complainants were particularly important in offenses against property. A police officer could rarely be present to observe a boy commit petty theft and catch him in the act, even if the boy stole something in broad daylight. Instead, 57 percent of boys' cases that the LAPD petitioned to juvenile court for petty theft—bicycle theft, theft from autos, and shoplifting—resulted from victims' complaints, and another 13 percent were initiated by witnesses.[10]

Victims sometimes resolved petty thefts by identifying their stolen property and pointing it out to the police. A boy named Richard Johns, for example, reported that his bicycle had been stolen from outside a movie theater on a Thursday evening in July. The following night, Johns saw another boy working on a bike at a gas station near the theater and recognized the handlebars as his own. Johns fetched a police officer, who arrested the boy. Upon questioning, fourteen-year-old *David Burbank* admitted that he had stolen three bicycles in the previous few days and was stripping parts from them to assemble another bike that would be unrecognizable. Without Johns, it seems unlikely that the police would have been able to track down and arrest Burbank.[11]

Although burglary—breaking into a home or business to steal property—was a felony and therefore considered a more serious offense than petty theft, police officers could not do much to stop burglary unless they witnessed boys in the act. Instead, the LAPD depended on complainants to initiate burglary cases; 63 percent resulted from complaints by the victims. Another 14 percent originated from reports by witnesses or from the perpetrators' families (who discovered that their sons had brought home stolen property).[12] In isolated cases, victims apprehended boys themselves and handed them over to the police. For example, seventeen-year-old *Chester Bailey* and his friend, *George Silver,* broke into the house of Silver's uncle, Police Officer N. E. Manning. They stole two Colt revolvers, as well as six packs of cigarettes and ninety-eight pennies. Unfortunately for the boys, Manning suspected that they were responsible. That evening, he called Silver's mother and had her confiscate the guns, then contacted the CPD and accompanied a juvenile officer to Silver's home to arrest the boys.[13]

Complaints by the public also drove most police investigations of sexual offenses—public indecency, sexual abuse, and statutory rape. These offenses constituted only a small share of total delinquency—6 percent of cases that the LAPD petitioned to juvenile court in 1940. However, a majority—twelve of eighteen—were initiated by victims, victims' families, or other witnesses. Sexual offense cases illustrate how the public could influence police and court actions even though (almost by definition) the offenses occurred out of sight of the police and (by their actions) the LAPD does not seem to have regarded them as a high priority.

A number of boys appeared in court for coercing younger children, both girls and boys, to engage in sexual experimentation with them. For example, sixteen-year-old *Frank Williams* enticed a six-year-old girl into a car parked in his garage "by showing her funny papers." There, he removed her pants and "fondled her private parts." Four days later, he lured her into his house, where he tried unsuccessfully to have sexual intercourse with her. In a similar case, fourteen-year-old *Seth Jamison* was charged with enticing a six-year-old neighborhood boy into his garage to perform oral sex on him. Jamison gave the boy a wooden toy gun in exchange. In each case, the victims eventually told their parents what had happened and the parents promptly informed the police. CPD officers arrested each boy and started investigations.[14]

Neither the perpetrators nor the police viewed these as particularly serious offenses. Both boys admitted the behavior; Jamison even explained that he had "gained knowledge of sex perversion by listening to boys at school" and had become curious. The police in turn did not pursue the cases vigorously. They allowed Jamison, the younger of the two boys, to be released to his home rather than placing him in detention. In both cases, the police suggested that the boys required medical attention rather than punishment. The investigator in charge of Williams's case asserted, "this trouble could be remedied if the boy is handled properly," while Jamison's investigator characterized him as merely being "over sexed" and recommended a psychiatric examination. Although the victims' families made the police and court initiate proceedings against the teenage abusers that could result in therapy and supervision, in neither case did their actions make officials take punitive action against the boys. Both were ultimately placed on probation by the juvenile court.

In contrast, the LAPD did police Latino youth very aggressively. In the late 1930s and early 1940s, Los Angeles experienced what has been labeled "zoot suit hysteria," a widespread panic that Mexican American youth were responsible for rampant crime. The largest and fastest-growing ethnic group in Southern California on the eve of World War II, Latinos also experienced overt discrimination in housing and jobs and found themselves clustered in crowded barrios. Some Mexican American teenagers and young men and women responded by developing an autonomous youth culture characterized by dancing, drinking, using drugs, and, for some, expressing hostility toward white society. They demonstrated this posture most visibly by wearing "zoot suits," baggy pants and oversized, almost knee-length coats with wide lapels and shoulder pads that defied conventional values of neatness and respectability. On the one hand, their self-enclosed ethnic communities encouraged boys to associate in tight-knit neighborhood groups, to behave in confrontational manners, and to commit violence largely against other Latino youths. On the other hand, this youth culture's manifestly antagonistic stance generated public fears that its violence was directed outward toward the city as a whole. And in the early 1940s, the LAPD contributed to this panic by feeding the press stories of criminal depredations by "Zoot-Suit Gangsters."[15]

Latino boys were in fact significantly more often charged with violent offenses than were whites or African Americans. The LAPD petitioned 17 percent of Latino youth to juvenile court for robberies and assaults, as compared to just 6 percent of the other two groups combined.[16] Put differently, over half—54 percent—of all boys accused of offenses against persons were Latinos.[17]

Group activities and an emergent gang culture among Latino youth contributed to these differences. In general, juveniles tend to commit offenses together with other juveniles, but this pattern was exaggerated among Mexican American teens whom police petitioned to juvenile court in 1940. Latino boys averaged 1.94 accomplices, compared to 1.14 for whites and African Americans.[18] Latino boys committed 88 percent of offenses with at least one accomplice (and sometimes quite a few more) versus 66 percent for other groups. According to the LAPD, moreover, 18 percent of Latino offenders were involved in gangs versus 5 percent of whites and African Americans.[19]

For Mexican American boys, group associations and gang involvement were a recipe for interpersonal violence. For example, *Albert Del Grande,* thirteen, *Rick Cordova,* sixteen, and a rotating groups of nine other Latino boys in the "Dog Town Gang" got into a series of fights, apparently to maintain territorial authority against other boys both Latino and not. In July 1940, they assaulted three Italian boys who were sitting in front of a grocery on Lemar Street in their Lincoln Heights neighborhood. A few days later, they confronted another group as they left a Boys Club meeting at a nearby Catholic Church. Two of the victims escaped, but the "Dog Town" boys caught three others and beat them with their fists. In each case, Del Grande, Cordova, and their friends claimed to be protecting local territory from implicit challenges by other boys.[20]

The LAPD could do little to regulate these sorts of violent altercations as long as they remained within the Mexican American community. The police intervened only when complainants (or witnesses such as medical personnel who treated victims) asked them to. An assault against eighteen-year-old Mark Tejada, for example, came to police attention only after he was admitted to a hospital. The investigating officers discovered that two seventeen-year-old Latino boys (both drunk and apparent gang members), *Lee Reynoso* and *Javier Veras,* had "called out" Tejada from a party to which they had not been invited. When Tejada emerged, Veras attacked him, beating him with his fists and kicking him when he was down. Tejada somehow reached his car, but the attackers had already slashed his tires, so he could not escape. Reynoso and Veras stopped the car by throwing rocks and bricks at it, then pulled Tejada out of the vehicle and beat him further with a brick, opening a deep laceration on his head. The LAPD only arrested Reynoso and Veras six days later, after receiving a report from the admitting hospital and compiling statements from witnesses.[21]

That said, the LAPD was alert to wrongdoing by Latino youth, particularly if it threatened to spread outside of their community. Seeing Latino teenagers gathered in street-corner groups sent a message to the police that the boys were ready to cause trouble. Clusters of Latino boys thus became easy targets for police harassment. Latino boys had an average of 1.5 contacts with police prior to their first court appearances versus 0.9 for boys of other ethnicities; 64 percent of Latinos had at least one prior official encounter with the police versus 47 percent of other groups. By the early 1940s, the LAPD frequently rounded up Mexican American youths gathering in public and charged them with unlawful assembly. On one occasion in October 1942, they arrested twenty-four juvenile boys, six juvenile girls, and forty-seven adults milling around a dance hall on a Saturday evening, charging them with unlawful assembly, and petitioning those youths with previous records to juvenile court. Via this general sort of harassment, they sought to keep the lid on any particular crimes that might be committed by Mexican American youths. Before the term was invented, the LAPD engaged in a prototypical form of racial profiling.[22]

In addition, the LAPD targeted particular types of juvenile misbehaviors for intervention, regardless of the ethnicity of the perpetrators. Among boys' delinquency cases they petitioned to juvenile court in 1940, they initiated 34 percent on their own, most often when they actually saw the boys commit a crime or act in a suspicious manner.[23] And encounters initiated by the police tended to be concentrated in certain types of offenses, particularly transience and automobile theft. Although encounters initiated by the police were rarer than those initiated by complainants, these encounters reflect more clearly police decision-making practices unmediated by the preferences of others. To some extent, the practical factor that kids engaged in transience or committed auto theft in public where they could be observed determined when police could intervene on their own. Yet these offenses also reveal the priorities of the LAPD. Police policies of the late 1930s and early 1940s encouraged officers to crack down on vagrant youth lacking means of support. During this time also auto theft represented one of the most rampant criminal problems in Los Angeles, a problem that a police department intent on getting tough on crime needed to address.

The LAPD demonstrated its institutional concern with boys who had become runaways, transients, or vagrants by initiating the majority (56 percent) of arrests on these charges.[24] These transgressions loosely fit the definition of status offenses: violations contingent on youths' age and status as juveniles rather than on a particular crime. In practice, the working definition of "status offense" had become narrower than in earlier decades when it also included many cases of truancy and incorrigibility. Instead, by 1940, the LAPD charged boys with status offenses when they arrested them for a more specific array of misbehaviors that seemed in their eyes to be portents of more serious problems in the future.

The LAPD especially targeted transient boys, youths who had wandered to Los Angeles from all over the country. Among the hundreds of thousands of displaced workers and farmers traveling the country looking for work during the Great Depression were as many as 250,000 teenagers. Local communities tended to regard these transient youth "riding the rails" as, at best, drains on their resources and, more often, sources of crime. Cities and towns rarely welcomed these travelers, and Los Angeles exemplified this attitude. Even after the end of James Davis's 1936 "bum blockade," Los Angeles allowed vagrants to stay in town for only one night before sending them on their way. The LAPD, like police departments elsewhere, enforced this policy by monitoring train stations and freight yards for the arrival of transients. As late as 1940, they still sometimes utilized the mechanisms of juvenile court to remove unwanted young vagrants. Two officers, for example, arrested fifteen-year-old *Charles Guzman* as soon as he disembarked from a freight train in Los Angeles. The day before, Guzman and two friends, *Taylor Donaldson* and *Bill Shaw,* both also fifteen, had climbed aboard the train in Phoenix, Arizona, "to see the country." Guzman, as it turned out, was exactly the kind of boy that the police did not want in Los Angeles. In Arizona, he had been arrested twice, once for purse snatching and once for bicycle theft, and had been placed in a reform school for his second offense. The LAPD responded to his arrival by putting him on a train back to Arizona to be supervised by his brother.[25]

The LAPD similarly targeted young vagrants who lived on the streets and traded sex with older men for money, food, or lodging. They did so by monitoring public parks where gay men frequently met. For example, two police officers arrested sixteen-year-old *Alan Garson* after observing him lingering in Pershing Square, near a neighborhood with a relatively well-known gay community. Garson, who had been traveling the country since the death of his parents three years earlier, "told the arresting officers that he had been making a practice of submitting his person to acts of degeneracy by perverts who loiter around Pershing Square and on these occasions received small sums of money and lodging for the night in some adjacent hotel."[26] It is difficult to determine how many boys were involved in this street culture, but anonymous homosexual encounters accounted for 27 percent of the status offense cases that the LAPD petitioned to juvenile court and 2 percent of the total male cases.[27]

Furthermore, the police were so concerned with the matter that vice officers sometimes entrapped boys in homosexual offenses. After observing *Carl Reynolds,* age fifteen, emerging from a men's toilet at Exposition Park with "his clothing disarranged and the front part of his pants open," officers followed him back into the toilet and struck up a conversation. "Subject stated to Officer Wynn that he had been queer for several years, and asked the officer if he was waiting for anyone in particular, officer Wynn told him he was [not], and subject then asked the officer if he had a car and . . . suggested that they go and sit in same, and at this point subject asked officer Wynn to allow him to commit an act of 288-A-PC [oral sex] upon the officer and which time officer Wynn placed subject under arrest." The officers in charge of these cases seemed to regard boys' homosexuality as a sad outcome of running away and transience, but also as a threat to the larger society. Investigating officer W. J. Sims recommended institutionalization for Reynolds "for the protection of not only his own welfare but also the welfare of others."[28] For the police, homosexuality was not only morally objectionable, but also linked to the larger problem of rootlessness. Individual officers might be sympathetic to individual offenders, acting to protect their welfare, but as an organization the LAPD sought to remove such potentially corrupting elements from the community.

The LAPD also devoted tremendous efforts to fighting motor vehicle theft, especially by juveniles. Auto theft represented a major problem in Southern California in part because automobile ownership was tremendously common, much more so than in the rest of the country. In 1940, one automobile was registered in Los Angeles for every 1.4 residents, as compared to one car for every 4.8 people in the nation as a whole. In addition, the geographic spread of Los Angeles and surrounding communities made automobiles a virtual necessity for many residents to get from one place to another.[29] And the amount of auto theft in Los Angeles in the 1920s and 1930s was striking as well. The number of stolen automobiles reported to the LAPD increased sharply from 1,520 in the 1915–16 fiscal year to a peak of 11,461 in 1926–27. Although auto theft declined somewhat during the Depression decade, the LAPD continued to investigate a median of 8,351 stolen cars per year between 1930 and 1940.[30] Few offenses affected the Los Angeles public more than auto theft, so if the LAPD intended to battle crime vigorously, it represented an obvious target.

How much auto theft teenagers were responsible for cannot be known, but it was a substantial share. The LAPD arrested a median of 501 boys per year between 1930–31 and 1940 on charges of grand theft auto.[31] And auto theft accounted for roughly one-third of boys' delinquency cases the LAPD petitioned to juvenile court in 1940. Boys approached auto theft with the same casual disregard they displayed toward lesser criminal behaviors. They often just took vehicles that they found unattended, drove them around for an evening, and abandoned them when they were done. Not surprisingly, the

LAPD recovered 89 percent of cars stolen between 1930–31 and 1940, usually within a week or less.[32] Little malice seems to have been involved; only 2 percent of auto thieves in juvenile court knew their victims. Instead, boys stole cars with their friends as a form of group recreation and thrill-seeking; 79 percent acted with between one and three companions, the number that could ride together comfortably.[33] Fifteen-year-olds *John Richards* and *Joe Lincoln,* for example, took a 1938 Packard Coupe from the vicinity of 89th Street and Zamora Avenue and went joy-riding around the southern section of Los Angeles. Around 5:30 P.M. they stopped at Richards's house to get something to eat and went out again. Later, they stopped at another friend's house to pick him up. At about 10:15 they left the undamaged car near 78th and Hooper and went home with the naive sense that they really had not committed a serious crime because they had only borrowed the car for a while.[34]

Although boys stole cars with a surprisingly cavalier attitude, the LAPD took it very seriously indeed. From the police perspective, vehicle theft differed from other forms of stealing in three important ways. First, the property involved was substantially more expensive. The median value of property among vehicle thefts in juvenile court cases was $400, as compared to $50 among all thefts by boys. Second, juveniles driving stolen cars around greater Los Angeles threatened public safety. Probably not the best drivers to begin with and often too young to have a license, boys in stolen cars were likely to be nervous and excited and therefore hazards to other drivers. Third, auto theft was an unusually visible crime. Driving on public thoroughfares, boys could be spotted easily by patrolmen. Because these factors encouraged and enabled police to intervene, the LAPD initiated 52 percent of boys' 1940 arrests for vehicle theft on their own.[35]

How did police accomplish this? The LAPD targeted groups of boys out for joy rides. They routinely pulled over cars filled with adolescent boys cruising around the city. Often, the car turned out to be stolen. For example, *Jack Vasquez,* fifteen, *Ricardo Veras,* fourteen, *Adam DiFilice,* thirteen, and *Gilbert Velarde,* fourteen, together stole a 1935 Willys Coupe to go to a picnic in Pico Park. At the park, a highway patrol officer noted the concentration of very young boys driving a fairly recent car. Upon being questioned about the car's ownership, DiFilice claimed that it belonged to his uncle. The policeman allowed them to drive to the home of this supposed uncle, following on his motorcycle. At an intersection, the boys leapt from the car and ran away, abandoning it in the street. Three days later, all four boys stole another vehicle, a 1934 Oldsmobile. Again, a police officer noticed them driving through Compton and pulled them over. Without giving them the opportunity to talk their way out of the jam, LAPD Motor Officer Ray Wiley arrested the boys and arranged for them to be detained, first at the Compton police station and then in Juvenile Hall.[36]

In their day-to-day work in 1940, the LAPD seem to have policed boys' misbehavior in two different ways. On the one hand, they certainly did their jobs when citizens asked them to, taking action particularly in the routine property offenses that they usually only discovered after the fact. This approach to policing juveniles seems to represent a continuity from earlier practices, in which police largely acted in response to complaints from the public, and it seems consistent with sociological models that suggest that complainants substantially influence police decision making. On the other hand, the LAPD also targeted groups and behaviors regarded as particular problems: the threat of Latino youths, transience, vagrancy, and homosexuality among youths on their own, and auto theft. In these cases, LAPD officers acted more often on their initiative, not only because the visibility of many of these offenses allowed them to do so but also because their department's "get tough" stance encouraged it. This more aggressive approach to particular juvenile crimes represents a break from past, when complaints were the driving force behind many arrests, a break that reveals how historical context and the specific departmental policies affect police officers' decisions and behavior. By 1940, the LAPD was beginning to use the mechanisms of juvenile court and juvenile justice to enact its own "tough on crime" agenda.

## THE PROBLEM OF GIRLS

Girls' and young women's experiences with the LAPD and the juvenile court differed sharply from those of boys. To a degree, they represent exceptions that prove the rule. The police did not target girls aggressively for arrest or intervention in large part because their offenses fell outside the rubric of misbehaviors that the LAPD regarded as important problems on the eve of World War II. Girls were less often transient or vagrant in the obvious ways that some boys were, and they less often hung out on street corners, stole cars, or committed visible criminal offenses. Instead, most of their offenses involved behaviors considered immoral, or at least wildly inappropriate and risky for respectable young women. During the Progressive Era, police—especially policewomen—and courts would have acted vigorously to regulate their actions, but by 1940, these sorts of offenses had become less of a priority.

In 1940, the vast majority of girls in trouble with the law were accused of status offenses. Among girls whom the LAPD arrested and petitioned to juvenile court, 87 percent were charged with status offenses, usually labeled as having "no proper supervision" or being "in danger of leading an immoral life." All criminal offenses combined—offenses against persons, burglaries, petty thefts, and vehicle thefts—constituted only the remaining 13 percent. These girls tended to be older than the boys whom the LAPD petitioned to court. Their average age was 15.5; 78 percent were between fifteen and seventeen. In addition, the girls were more often white: 70 percent were white, 17 percent were Latina, 9 percent were African American, and 4 percent were Asian.[37]

The handful of girls in juvenile court on criminal charges, it should be noted, had committed fairly serious offenses. Thefts by girls had a median value of $122.50 (compared to a $50.00 median for boys' crimes). In addition, six of the nine girls accused of criminal offenses knew their victims, three used violence, and four possessed a weapon, all far higher shares than comparable measures for boys. Seventeen-year-old *Joan Beam*, for example, helped her boyfriend commit armed robbery. Soon after she ran away from Detroit, Joan took a job as a housekeeper. In that position, she stole her employer's guns, let her boyfriend into the home where she worked, assisted him as he stole property worth $415.00, and escaped with him through the back door.[38]

But more often, girls' offenses involved sexual and social precocity. Premarital sexual intercourse was the most obvious among many behaviors that could lead to public intervention, but these could also include running away from home, staying out late, associating with people of dubious character, and going to dance halls or other places of amusement without a chaperone. As a number of historians have demonstrated, Progressive Era child welfare reformers feared that modern urban society threatened adolescent girls with moral and social ruin. The temptations of the city would corrupt girls' natural innocence and lead to premarital sex, which carried with it the pervasive danger of sexually transmitted disease as well as pregnancy and (illegal) abortion. Around the turn of the century, child welfare and law enforcement agencies had sought to "protect" girls via careful investigations, juvenile court hearings, probation, and, not infrequently, placement in correctional institutions. The LAPD, as has already been noted, was among the leaders in this movement, staffing its Juvenile Bureau with policewomen as early as 1910 and establishing a City Mother's Bureau in 1914.[39]

For the most part, girls' cases in 1940 reflected this long-standing pattern of using juvenile court to regulate adolescent female sexuality. Seventy-one percent of girls petitioned to juvenile court had engaged in sexual activity (always heterosexual). Having a sexual relationship while under age eighteen (the legal age of consent) constituted all the evidence necessary to place a girl under formal supervision by public authorities. At the same time, by the 1930s, this sort of progressive enthusiasm for intervening in the lives of sexually precocious girls had diminished. In 1924, as part of Vollmer's reorganization, the LAPD brought policewomen and the City Mother's Bureau under administrative control of the Crime Prevention Division and subsequently reduced the autonomy of each. In addition, rather than maintaining a separate sphere of women's police work, newly hired policewomen in the 1930s were increasingly partnered with male CPD officers.[40] Furthermore, by the late 1930s, the LAPD less consistently segregated adolescent girls from male police officers and the larger system of law enforcement than it had in the past. While all girls' cases were still supposed to be investigated by policewomen, men from the CPD sometimes interviewed female suspects because of a shortage of personnel.[41]

In 1940, the LAPD did not aggressively target girls for investigation or arrest. The police initiated only 9 percent of girls' cases on their own. Instead, they relied on outsiders to bring cases to them. Parents and relatives introduced 56 percent of girls' cases to the police, and witnesses and concerned employees of schools and social agencies initiated another 26 percent.[42] In a typical scenario, parents used the police as a tool to establish greater control over their rebellious and sexually active daughters. The parents of fifteen-year-old *Gayle Rupert* reported her to the LAPD when they were unable to break up her "association" with a seventeen-year-old boy, *Houston Gallagher*. Gayle and Houston had been seeing one another for about nine months and had engaged in at least "four acts of sexual intercourse," the most recent in a local church. Perhaps because Gayle and Houston flouted social norms so obviously, her parents strongly disapproved of the relationship. At her parents' request, CPD officers arrested them both, holding Gayle for "sex delinquency" and Houston for statutory rape. Gayle was detained at Juvenile Hall for eleven days and then placed on probation in her parents' custody, so they evidently achieved their goal.[43]

Parents, however, sometimes struggled to convince police to intervene. Policewomen reportedly turned away many parental supplicants who came to them to ascertain how much legal authority they had over their daughters.[44] One father, *Alberto Rodriguez*, had to go to extraordinary efforts to get the police to take action when his fifteen-year-old daughter, *Virginia*, ran away with a former adult boarder in the Rodriguez home, *Jesus Batista*. After Virginia left home in April 1940, Rodriguez suspected that Batista was hiding his daughter, so he had the man arrested. The police, however, failed to discover any evidence against Batista and released him. Friends subsequently gave Rodriguez the address of Batista's hotel. They told Rodriguez, furthermore, that

Batista often bragged that he wanted to kill him and keep Virginia. Rodriguez again brought this information to the police but was told that they could do nothing unless he found out exactly where his daughter was staying. Rodriguez eventually went to Batista's hotel and identified his room, but hesitated to confront him on his own. Instead, he hailed a passing police car "and asked the officers to help which they were kind enough to do." Together, Rodriguez and the officers burst into the room and discovered Batista in bed with Virginia. The police arrested him for statutory rape and held Virginia as a sex delinquent. The court eventually committed her to the Convent of the Good Shepherd, a Catholic correctional home for wayward girls.[45]

Virginia's case illustrates how far some parents would go to involve the police in their efforts to control their daughters. It also illustrates one reason why parents went to the police. Rodriguez was afraid to confront Batista because "he could not go armed . . . and did not know what complications might arise." He saw the duty of the police as helping him to intervene and he expected them to lend him their authority. At the same time, the LAPD as an organization did not act strenuously in this case until Rodriguez cornered a pair of officers near the scene. Until then, the police could not make the earlier charges against Batista stick, nor would they try to confront Batista until Rodriguez had ferreted out his precise location.

More so than in earlier years, the LAPD tended to react to reports of girls' offenses rather than to act preemptively to stop them. Particularly in cases involving runaways and sexual delinquents, the police did not make concerted efforts to discover girls' misbehaviors, but instead waited until complainants made demands on them. In dealing with boys, the LAPD had subtly reshaped the intake of juvenile court to focus on their own concern with controlling crime, but with girls the LAPD in 1940 acted almost entirely as intermediaries. They picked up girls reported by parents or the public and then passed them along to juvenile court. The LAPD cooperated fully with parents and the court, but did not exercise much initiative in addressing the problems of female delinquents. The police had other priorities.

## DISPOSITIONS IN JUVENILE COURT

Once adolescents appeared in juvenile court, their cases were largely out of the hands of the police. Partly because the LAPD placed an increasingly high priority on detecting and punishing youthful offenses, however, the Los Angeles County Juvenile Court expanded its mechanisms for institutional treatment between 1930 and 1940 and applied them to a larger share of young offenders. Thus, although the court retained its historic commitment to saving young offenders, it also became noticeably "tougher" toward juvenile crime.

Juvenile court dispositions continued to emphasize treatment and, to outside observers, could seem quite lenient. In theory, the juvenile court operated on the assumption that all delinquencies were essentially the same, regardless of the category or degree of an offense, and should be understood as symptoms of more fundamental social, familial, or psychiatric problems that could be resolved via appropriate treatment. Following a petition, court probation officers conducted a "careful investigation . . . as to the causes of delinquency." This investigation could include physical and mental examinations, interviews with parents, witnesses, and victims, as well as the child him- or herself, and consultations with the child's school, community, and police. "The more we know about a child and the influences which have played upon his life," asserted Juvenile Court Judge Samuel R. Blake, "the better the Court will know how to prescribe." The probation officers, together with judges, the LAPD's Crime Prevention Division, and sometimes the parents, then used their findings to devise a plan of treatment that sought to eliminate the sources of delinquency.[46]

In practice, by 1940, treatment more and more often meant placing boys in custodial institutions. Juvenile justice experienced sharp changes during the Depression decade. First, the court itself had developed a range of increasingly specialized institutions, designed to implement the more sophisticated responses to delinquency developed in the 1920s and 1930s. Second, the problem of youth transience seemed to demand vigorous action, especially in the perceived destination of choice, Los Angeles. Third, the LAPD brought the juvenile court an increasingly criminal clientele, for whom the old solutions did not seem to apply. Together, the cumulative effect of these changes on juvenile court practices is striking. Forty percent of boys petitioned to juvenile court by the LAPD in 1940 were placed in some sort of institution—state reform schools, county institutions, or private custodial facilities—prior to the dismissal of their cases.[47] By contrast, the Los Angeles Juvenile Court placed only 16 percent of delinquent boys in custodial institutions in 1930.[48]

The Los Angeles Juvenile Court did not, however, characteristically institutionalize boys on their first petition. Instead, it used an escalating scale of response. Children petitioned to juvenile court were almost always found delinquent; their cases would be dismissed only after the child had demonstrated proper behavioral adjustment over the course of six months to a year. The court would dismiss a case at an initial hearing only if "the charge in the petition alleging delinquency ha[s] not been sustained."[49] The juvenile court's helping ideology, however, assumed that virtually any behavior suspicious or problematic enough to warrant a petition was a signal that the child needed the court's guidance, and that could only be given if the child was found delinquent. Petitions were therefore almost always sustained. The court dismissed only 4 percent of petitions involving boys and none involving girls in 1940; it forwarded almost every child to the probation staff and other agencies for treatment.

The Los Angeles Juvenile Court in 1940 placed most offenders—57 percent—on probation following their first petition. Juveniles on probation technically became "wards" of the court, but they were usually permitted to live with their parents or relatives. Probation officers maintained reasonably regular contact with these boys, trying to assist their guardians if possible and encouraging the boys to perform responsibly at school or at work and to get involved in character-building programs such as the Big Brothers, the YMCA, or the Boy Scouts. Although probation usually entailed only very loose supervision of a child at home, school, work, or recreation, it nonetheless required boys to follow court-mandated guidelines in order to be removed from probation at follow-up hearings, usually less than a year after the initial sentence.[50]

Court dispositions, however, varied significantly by boys' age groups. Younger boys stood a much better chance of being placed on probation than did older ones. Whereas 71 percent of boys between ten and fourteen were placed on probation, only 50 percent of boys between fifteen and seventeen were.

The Los Angeles Juvenile Court sent the bulk of older and more criminal offenders—its new clientele—to county-operated "forestry camps" located outside the city of Los Angeles that were first opened in the 1930s. These camps received 21 percent of delinquent boys adjudicated in juvenile court and 32 percent of boys between fifteen and seventeen, almost one-third of the older age group.[51] Technically, the court granted boys a stay of commitment from state-operated reform schools to work at the forestry camps, where they often labored "eight hours a day with pick and shovel building a motor highway."[52] The forestry camps gave the Los Angeles Juvenile Court a critical new option for dealing with older and tougher offenders such as Halloween Silva who did not respond to traditional mechanisms such as probation, but whose numbers were becoming so great that they could not be placed in long-term institutions either. The forestry camps represented a key component in the juvenile court's efforts to treat and punish more serious offenders in 1940. The court's ability to commit boys to the forestry camps largely accounted for the overall increase in institutionalization between 1930 and 1940.[53]

Los Angeles County had established its first forestry camp in 1932 as a means of dealing with juvenile transients who found their way to Southern California during the Depression. Traditionally, the county had shipped runaways who drifted into Los Angeles home at their parents' expense, but few parents could afford to pay for their sons' return in the mid-1930s. As an alternative, the county founded the camps, first in San Dimas Canyon and later outside the town of Newhall, where boys worked to earn enough money to buy their transportation home. As the transient problem abated by the end of the 1930s, the Los Angeles Juvenile Court began to use the forestry camps to treat local boys, first-time juvenile offenders, usually between the ages of fifteen and eighteen, who had committed criminal offenses and "have been in serious trouble."[54]

The Los Angeles Juvenile Court viewed forestry camp as integral to its philosophy of rehabilitation. Although they were custodial institutions, forestry camps exercised much more moderate control over boys than did reform schools. They were not fenced or locked, nor did they use corporal punishment or loss of food to discipline their inmates. In addition, a boy's average stay in forestry camps was four months, in comparison to over a year at reform school. Labor, not lengthy incarceration, was the key to forestry camps' mission. In a manner much like the contemporaneous Civilian Conservation Corps (CCC), Los Angeles probation officer K. J. Scudder hoped "open air, hard work, harder play, and decent treatment" would give boys the opportunity to make a proper adjustment and become more responsible men.[55] Still, in contrast to the voluntary CCC, forestry camps were fundamentally punitive institutions. The court used them to incarcerate and to discipline boys whom it had formally adjudicated guilty of serious delinquencies. If the boys misbehaved, the court could remove them from the camps and send them to more overtly penal juvenile reform schools.

The Los Angeles Juvenile Court also had a different, if less often used, set of dispositions available. It committed 5 percent of boys to smaller custodial facilities that removed them from their homes and sought to give them an opportunity to reform themselves before they got into more serious trouble. For example, the California Junior Republic in Chico (founded in 1907) offered boys at least nominal self-government in order to teach them to be more capable and honest adults.[56] In addition, state hospitals such as Pacific Colony offered treatment for juveniles adjudged "mentally deficient" according to the new psychiatric approaches to delinquency.[57] As a rule, the court reserved these institutions for younger boys, committing to them 10 percent of boys between ten and fourteen but only 3 percent of boys between fifteen and seventeen. The point of these intermediate institutions was (in the psychological language of the day) to help younger, salvageable boys "make an adjustment" *before* committal to reform school became necessary, not to punish them for their crimes.

While the court frequently removed boys from their homes, it reserved the state reform schools for the worst young offenders, those not amenable to treatment elsewhere. At this time, California operated two reform schools for boys. One, the Preston School of Industry, employed military training and a "cadet" system to instill discipline in boys ages fifteen and older. The other, the Whittier State Reform School, had earlier embodied "progressive" correctional ideals by trying to improve a somewhat younger group of boys through academic schooling, vocational training, and athletics. By 1940, both Preston and Whittier had become highly punitive, secure institutions that received the worst of California's young offenders.[58] In 1940, the Los Angeles Juvenile Court sent only 4 percent of boys to reform school following their first petition. As a rule, it did so only if they had committed a particularly heinous offense or a long string of crimes prior to being arrested. For example, a fifteen-year-old African American youth, *George Manchester,* was confined at Preston following his first petition because he, along with three other boys, had perpetrated five armed robberies of shops and liquor stores. In each case, they had held the clerks at gunpoint while they emptied the cash registers.[59]

Surprisingly the Los Angeles Juvenile Court's dispositions did not vary significantly by race. While the LAPD's arrest practices created a juvenile court clientele disproportionately composed of minorities, the court's treatment of Latinos and African Americans was similar to that of whites. For example, the juvenile court was no more likely to place whites on probation than other groups. Likewise, it was no more likely to send Latinos to Preston and Whittier on their first petition. The Los Angeles Juvenile Court ultimately institutionalized 44 percent of African American boys in correctional facilities prior to the dismissal of their cases (not just following their first petition), but it also institutionalized 42 percent of whites and 35 percent of Latinos.[60] If anything, the finding that Latinos were committed to institutions slightly less often than other groups suggests that the LAPD petitioned them to juvenile court more often than other groups on the basis of weak (or nonexistent) evidence that did not warrant serious treatment. The police may have been biased in determining how to enforce the law, but the court treated delinquents of all races with relative evenhandedness.

Dispositions did become more punitive, however, if boys' delinquencies continued after they were placed on probation. The Los Angeles Juvenile Court institutionalized boys much more regularly when they committed repeat offenses. And some boys committed crimes over and over and were arrested again and again. Twenty-two percent of boys whom the LAPD petitioned to juvenile court were subsequently rearrested and petitioned at least one more time on a new criminal offense.[61] Offenses by recidivists accounted for 43 percent of the total boys' cases that police petitioned to court.[62] Moreover, in cases of repeat offenders, an element of the LAPD's racialized pattern of arrests and petitions becomes evident. The police arrested and petitioned 44 percent of delinquent African American boys more than once, in contrast to 19 percent of Latino boys and 19 percent of whites. Thus, minority youth ended up in court more often. African American boys averaged 1.94 separate petitions to juvenile court, as compared to 1.47 for Latinos and 1.25 for whites. These patterns suggest that the Los Angeles Juvenile Court did not treat minority youth differently than whites once they ended up in court, but that the LAPD's arrest and petition practices sent minorities to juvenile court more often than whites.

Recidivism mattered tremendously in juvenile court dispositions. Boys making second, third, fourth, and later appearances in juvenile court received probation significantly less often (38 percent) than did first-time offenders (57 percent).[63] The court also sent fewer recidivists (9 percent) to forestry camp than it did first-timers (21 percent). If boys returned to court after an earlier arrest and custodial placement, they were generally considered too hardened to merit treatment in a facility that emphasized character building as a means of adjustment. Instead, the Los Angeles Juvenile Court committed 33 percent of boys appearing on repeat petitions to either Preston or Whittier (as compared to 4 percent of first-timers). If boys failed to change their delinquent ways after several chances, the court was likely to confine them at a reform school.

Repeat offenders typically committed a string of relatively similar crimes; rarely did they commit progressively more severe offenses as they became more experienced. Offenses committed by boys petitioned to juvenile court for a second, third, fourth, or subsequent time were essentially the same as those committed by boys making their first court appearance. In addition, repeat offenders were only marginally more likely to use violence in the commission of a crime (15 percent of repeaters vs. 10 percent of first-timers) or to employ weapons (11 percent vs. 8 percent).[64] Instead, boys just committed crimes over and over. Not surprisingly, repeat offenders averaged 3.9 prior arrests, while boys in court for the first time averaged only 1.1. Thus, these boys gained experience dealing with the police, and the police gained experience dealing with individual problem children.

*Sam Martin,* an African American boy, thirteen years old at the time of his first appearance in juvenile court, exemplifies both the patterns typical of repeat offenders and the ways that police and courts dealt with them. Already arrested three times in 1940 (each time for petty theft), the LAPD finally petitioned Martin to juvenile court in November for burglary after he was caught leaving a home where he had stolen six empty RC Cola bottles, worth six cents. Martin admitted to police that he prowled the rear yards of homes at night, burglarizing three or four houses every Friday night and stealing bottles that he could return to stores for money. Temporarily detained in Juvenile Hall and ultimately placed on probation, Martin was again arrested in June 1941 for burglarizing a print shop. Following another round of detention and a short stay in a boarding home, police again arrested and petitioned the fifteen-year-old Martin in November 1942 for another series of break-ins. Martin explained his actions as the result of "an uncontrollable desire to steal." The police, by contrast, at first cited standard factors such as "irresponsible parents" who "allowed him to roam the streets late at night" and "lack of supervision" to explain his delinquencies, but eventually just chalked it up to "recidivism." Having developed this view of Martin, the LAPD came to see him as a likely candidate whenever unsolved small-scale burglaries accumulated. Following a string of break-ins committed in a bungalow court near his home in 1942, local police officers suspected Martin immediately, took him to an alley behind the bungalows, and persuaded him to identify which homes he had robbed. In the eyes of the police, an initial court appearance transformed some boys (and perhaps particularly African Americans) into usual suspects who should be immediately questioned for all subsequent comparable crimes. And boys such as Martin did little to dispel this impression. Following his third court petition, the juvenile court finally committed him to Whittier, but he escaped less than two months later, committed another string of burglaries, and found himself again arrested, petitioned to juvenile court, and ultimately institutionalized in the reform school at Preston.[65]

The goals of supervision and treatment seemed to dominate the Los Angeles Juvenile Court's methods of handling girls. It placed 75 percent of them on probation at their first appearance, and girls were almost never petitioned to court again.[66] For girls, however, dispositions tended to be an either/or proposition with little middle ground. The court placed almost all of the girls to whom it did not grant probation in custodial institutions, sending 10 percent to the State Reform School at Ventura and 7 percent to Los Angeles County's experimental school for girls, El Retiro. The court also sent 7 percent of girls—mostly Latina—to a variety of other institutions including the private Convent of the Good Shepherd and the state hospital at

Pacific Colony. In addition, the Los Angeles Juvenile Court proved willing to institutionalize the small number of girls accused of criminal offenses substantially more often than those accused of status offenses.[67] For example, it sentenced Joan Beam, who helped her boyfriend commit armed robbery, to serve a term at Ventura.[68] For the most part, however, the court placed the first-time status offenders who constituted the bulk of its female clientele on probation. Apparently county officials regarded the process of arrest, detention, court hearing, and continued supervision as sufficient to reprimand most girls and guide them back to respectable behavior.

The Los Angeles Juvenile Court's sense of mission changed less overtly than did that of the police during the 1930s. Even when juveniles committed crimes, the court still viewed them much as it had viewed delinquents of earlier eras: as relatively immature children who perpetrated crimes mainly for the thrill of doing it, and who would respond positively to rehabilitative discipline designed to set them back on the right track. The overriding principle governing dispositions in the Los Angeles Juvenile Court in 1940 remained providing youths with supervision and treatment.

In practice, however, by 1940, the court increasingly sought to rehabilitate juveniles by institutionalizing them. Particularly in the preceding decade, it had developed a broader, more flexible array of institutions, including not only probation for the most amenable youths and reform schools for the most difficult, but also forestry camps, state hospitals, and a county school for girls for those in between. As the LAPD increasingly brought the juvenile court older, more serious offenders—boys such as Halloween Silva, boys who stole cars, boys who fled from the police, boys who might have been affiliated with gangs—these new institutions seemed to be the perfect mechanisms to discipline them. And the court still had the option of long-term institutionalization in reform schools for those who continuously failed to take advantage of second-, third-, and fourth-chance opportunities to forgo delinquent behavior. In practice if not in theory, the juvenile court's expansion of its means of saving young offenders paralleled and functioned in harmony with the LAPD's goal of getting tough on juvenile crime.

# THE EMERGING SHAPE OF JUVENILE JUSTICE

At the end of the Depression and on the eve of World War II, the interest of police in controlling crime—even crime by juveniles—contributed to the expansion of the juvenile justice system as it developed more intensive means of supervision and extensive mechanisms of control over young offenders. To be sure, other factors contributed to the changes in juvenile justice in the 1930s. In particular, the gradual development of new ideas about delinquency and new institutions for delinquents, the dual crises of the Great Depression and the perceived influx of youthful transients, and, in Los Angeles, a growing and seemingly foreign Latino population all made a difference in operations of juvenile court. And to be sure, the LAPD's ability to fight juvenile crime was limited by its inability to initiate arrests except in the public arena and by its dependence on citizens to report offenses before it could act. But nonetheless, the police had become key to the larger system of juvenile justice. The LAPD set in motion changes in the system. They made arrests on their own initiative that reflected their own priorities and they created a pool of criminal offenders that shaped the intake and operations of the juvenile court. By the 1930s, the LAPD learned to use the mechanisms of the rehabilitative juvenile justice system to pursue their own agenda of getting tough on juvenile crime. This new model, however, also contained the roots of ongoing conflict between law enforcement officials and the youths policed.

# Conclusion

The 1940s represent a turning point in the histories of both juvenile justice and juvenile delinquency. On the one hand, during the 1940s, the rehabilitative ideals that had driven the juvenile court movement continued to lose support. As juvenile crime seemed to increase during World War II, the general public increasingly regarded the treatment-oriented goals of juvenile court as inconsistent with the practical demands of maintaining public order. In addition, the legal profession began to criticize juvenile courts' loose procedures and rehabilitative goals as denying young people their due process rights. Juvenile courts also encountered practical impediments. After 1933, Chicago's pioneering juvenile court fell under the influence of that city's Democratic political machine and became a vehicle for the patronage appointments that its founders had dreaded. As historian Mara Dodge has shown, by the 1940s, leading child welfare advocates such as Juvenile Protective Association President Jesse Binford feared that the Chicago court had "become more like a Criminal than a Parental court."[1]

Any remaining enthusiasm for innovative juvenile justice reform seemed to have migrated west from Chicago to California, where the state established the California Youth Authority (CYA) in 1941. Created in response to both the negative stimulus of two inmate suicides at Whittier and the positive stimulus of widely publicized reform proposals advanced by the American Law Institute, the CYA acted as a coordinating agency for all juvenile courts and correctional facilities in the state. Previously, county-level courts had operated on their own, but the CYA placed them under state supervision. The CYA became a centralized agency to diagnose the state's young offenders, design plans of treatment, and coordinate sentences and parole. It also assumed control of the state's reform schools. In effect, the CYA acted as a super juvenile court, but it also transferred the center of authority from the county to the state level. While most states did not go as far as to establish equivalent agencies, the CYA nonetheless represented the new cutting edge in juvenile justice.[2]

On the other hand, the 1940s also saw increased public fears about juvenile delinquency. World War II was believed to have generated a sharp increase in juvenile crime. Although scholars have questioned whether delinquency did in fact increase during the war, there is no doubt that the public and the press perceived it to be on the rise.[3] Encouraged by sociologists and social workers concerned that wartime conditions would foster youthful misbehavior, in 1942 and 1943 newspapers, magazines, and newsreels were filled with reports of juvenile delinquency, bringing what historian James Gilbert has characterized as a "rather marginal issue to the center of public attention." Boys, with access to income from wartime jobs but reportedly lacking the paternal guidance of male role models away at war, were expected to engage in property crimes and violence. Girls, supposedly enamored of men in uniform, were feared to be at increased risk for sexual delinquency.[4] Much of the blame fell upon a perceived breakdown of the family. In a series of speeches and articles, for example, FBI Director J. Edgar Hoover attributed a sharp wartime increase in juvenile offenses to "adult delinquency"—the moral laxity of parents—and, in particular, mothers working outside of the home.[5]

Beginning in the early 1940s and continuing into the postwar years, urban gangs did in fact undergo qualitative changes. As Eric C. Schneider has demonstrated in his study of New York City, ongoing urban transformations—continued migration to the city, reduced job opportunities for young men with limited education, and pressures on neighborhood housing and facilities created by urban redevelopment—all encouraged working-class youth to band together as gangs. Furthermore, experience in the armed forces during the war allowed some older youth to return to their cities better trained and better armed. Thus, gang violence and homicide increased in the mid-1940s.[6]

This wartime increase and change in juvenile crime—both perceived and real—fostered increased conflict between police and youths in U.S. cities. In Los Angeles, the LAPD renewed its policy of conducting mass arrests and interrogations of suspicious youths, reserving its particular antipathy for Latinos. On the one hand, Los Angeles officials issued a number of policy papers in the early 1940s blaming Latino youths for a perceived crime wave, and the LAPD fed stories of Latino depredations to the local press. On the other hand, in 1942 and 1943, the nationally publicized Sleepy Lagoon murder case—in which the LAPD arrested hundreds of Latino youths for the death of one teenager, placed twenty-two on trial, and convicted seventeen on various charges—revealed the indiscriminate tactics that the LAPD routinely used to control juvenile crime. And the "Zoot Suit Riots" further highlighted the divide between police and urban youth. For eight nights in June 1943, white soldiers, sailors, and civilians stationed around Los Angeles attacked Latino youths while the LAPD did little to stop the upheaval other than arresting over six hundred Mexican American boys and young men, the victims of the riots. A race riot in Detroit just a few weeks later followed a similar pattern. White youths and workers attacked African Americans, and again the police intervened by arresting a disproportionate share of black youth.[7]

In reality, these wartime conflicts had less to do with juvenile delinquency than with changes in American society. At the time, many people believed that these conflicts illustrated the growing hazard of unrestrained youth. During World War II, delinquency seemed to be out of control. In retrospect, however, these conflicts suggest something different. The wartime fears of delinquency, the public response, and the urban riots all highlight a newly combative relationship between urban communities and the agencies designated to police them. Young African Americans and Latinos, finding their own ways to adapt to urban industrial life, frequently found themselves at odds with established law enforcement authorities. This clash between local populations and the police seems to be one of the dominant themes of urban history in the second half of the twentieth century, highlighted so much by race riots and accusations of police brutality and racial profiling. Yet the history of police and juvenile offenders suggests that all the pieces were set into place for this discord much earlier.

The emergence of professional policing and modern juvenile justice in the late nineteenth and early twentieth centuries laid the foundations for ongoing relations between kids, cops, and courts. Already at the turn of the twentieth century, reform-minded advocates of juvenile courts and law enforcement–minded police leaders maintained different concepts of delinquency. Reformers tended to regard delinquency as a symptom of the degrading effects of social change and urban industrial life, whereas police tended to regard delinquency as a more natural behavior. To cops, the key question was not the source of delinquency but how to minimize it. In Detroit, juveniles arrested at the turn of the century could fit either view. Young offenders paralleled the demographic profile of Detroit's adolescent population as a whole, and they were arrested mainly for opportunistic theft and for status offenses such as truancy, often as a result of complaints from victims or from the public. From the perspective of child welfare reformers, these misbehaviors might be signs of deeper problems, but from the perspective of policemen and law enforcement officials, they were more likely to have been regarded as kids' stuff; and at the turn of the century, Detroit police and courts largely treated delinquency as if it were kids' stuff. They rounded up and arrested young offenders but also found ways to protect them from the worst consequences of their own behavior, diverting them from the harsh penalties that they could face in courts, jails, and prisons intended for adults.

Following the turn-of-the-century establishment of juvenile courts, the new system of juvenile justice began to cast a wider and stronger net over young offenders. More children and youth were arrested than before the creation of juvenile courts, more faced official adjudication, and more spent increased time under official supervision or in correctional facilities. From the perspective of reformers and juvenile court advocates, this was precisely the purpose of the new institutions. They intended to bring more young offenders under supervision so that officials could help address the fundamental social and familial sources of their delinquency. Reformers also intended for juvenile courts to replace the discretionary authority of the police with the more expert decision making of judges, social workers, and psychologists. But police continued to exercise power within the new system, and, in particular, changes in policing also encouraged an expansion of juvenile justice. As police departments such as Detroit's sought to professionalize in the 1910s, they embraced new models of business-like efficiency and social welfare–minded friendliness to children. Both strategies brought them increasingly into contact with youths and encouraged them to bring more into the juvenile justice system.

The results of expanded juvenile justice could be problematic, however. As the Great Migration beginning in the 1910s relocated more and more African Americans to northern cities such as Detroit and Chicago, the expanded population of minority youths became disproportionately subject to arrest as well. And in cities like Chicago, where juvenile courts had limited resources and the police department did not undergo a process of professional reform, police officers assigned to deal with youth and even beat officers retained extraordinary discretionary power. In deciding on the streets and in the station houses whether to arrest a young offender or to discipline him informally, whether to petition him to juvenile court or to release him with a warning, the individual values of the police officer often superseded the institutional values of the juvenile court.

Police assumed more visible positions in the operations of juvenile justice in the 1920s and 1930s. As juvenile court innovations gradually lost public enthusiasm and intellectual support, outside crime prevention programs—especially those operated by police departments—became centers of innovation. These police programs often adopted the rhetoric of modern social science but continued to embrace older naturalistic thinking about delinquency. Popular concerns about crime—fueled first by Prohibition Era gangsters and then by Depression Era bandits—granted police programs added urgency as they argued that today's delinquent would become tomorrow's criminal. By the 1930s, police began to define a new model for regulating juvenile delinquency, exemplified by the Los Angeles Police Department. The LAPD established some of the most extensive "crime prevention" programs designed to intervene early with potential delinquents both because such programs added to their aura of professionalism and because they facilitated the LAPD's larger goal of getting tough on crime. Allowing the crime prevention division to handle minor offenders permitted police to concentrate more narrowly on fighting serious juvenile crime by arresting a greater share of young felons and by focusing its attention on policing minority communities.

By 1940, juvenile delinquency had not changed much from the turn of the century. Kids from immigrant backgrounds not too dissimilar from urban kids as a whole still committed opportunistic offenses. Complaints from the public still helped determine what offenses constituted delinquency and warranted police intervention. The world around these kids had changed, however. Because they were available, young offenders in 1940 stole cars more often than candy (or at least they were arrested for stealing cars more often). Police, in turn, took thefts of expensive property in public seriously, and targeted auto thieves for intervention and arrest. Urban growth and population in-migration, particularly by African Americans and Latinos, had also changed the social environment in which cops and kids coexisted. In Los Angeles, these changes fostered a Latino youth subculture both more violent than most other juveniles and more clearly targeted by the police. And finally, police get-tough policies had contributed to a toughening up of juvenile courts. The LAPD's arrest practices subtly altered the intake and operations of Los Angeles County Juvenile Court by requiring it to handle an increasing concentration of serious offenses. By 1940, juvenile courts still maintained a rehabilitative ethos, but dealt with an increasingly criminal clientele and dealt with them via increased use of institutional placement and supervision.

In essence, the means by which the police sought to regulate juvenile delinquency shifted from child protection to crime fighting. From the perspective of most histories of juvenile justice, this finding is counterintuitive. The juvenile court and subsequent community-based innovations in delinquency prevention had been expected to reduce the role of the police and to ameliorate police treatment of youth. Instead, the new institutions widened and strengthened the net of juvenile justice by encouraging the police to adopt a more interventionist and authoritative model of regulating delinquency. Furthermore, the police were able, at least in part, to reshape the juvenile justice system to reflect their priorities. In practice, the everyday control of juvenile delinquency revolved around the police.

This study suggests that the policing of juvenile delinquency in U.S.

cities—and the public regulation of behavior more generally—can best be understood by examining actions as close to the source as possible. Looking at decisions made on the streets and in police stations, rather than in the more removed setting of juvenile court, helps to develop a clearer picture of how juvenile behavior was typically managed on an everyday level. More broadly, focusing on cops and kids also provides a historical window for seeing how social change affected the regulation of behavior in the late nineteenth and early twentieth centuries. Larger dynamics including social welfare reform, police professionalization, the explosive growth of U.S. cities, and a partial rethinking of the nature of youth all combined to transform the means used to maintain order in urban environments. And finally, a police-centered approach to juvenile justice helps reveal some of the precedents for conflicts between law enforcers and communities policed that have characterized much of the subsequent decades. The roots of today's problems can be found in the interactions between cops and kids between the Progressive Era and the New Deal.

# NOTES

## NOTES TO INTRODUCTION

1. *West Side Story* (Mirisch/Seven Arts, 1961). On cultural imaginings of delinquency (and the song "Gee Officer Krupke"), see James Gilbert, *A Cycle of Outrage: America's Reaction to the Juvenile Delinquent in the 1950s* (New York: Oxford University Press, 1986), esp. 193–95.

2. For a useful introduction to the history of juvenile justice, see Robert M. Mennel, *Thorns and Thistles: Juvenile Delinquents in the United States, 1825–1940* (Hanover, NH: University Press of New England, 1973). On ongoing debates about public policy toward juvenile offenders, see Barry C. Feld, *Bad Kids: Race and the Transformation of the Juvenile Court* (New York: Oxford University Press, 1999).

3. Historical treatments of juvenile courts often have evaluated them in the same terms as they evaluate other social reform movements that flourished in the early twentieth century, contrasting their lofty rhetoric with an often-ineffective reality. See, as examples, Thomas J. Bernard, *The Cycle of Juvenile Justice* (New York: Oxford University Press, 1992); Mennel, *Thorns and Thistles;* David J. Rothman, *Conscience and Convenience: The Asylum and its Alternatives in Progressive America* (Boston: Little, Brown, 1980); Ellen Ryerson, *The Best-Laid Plans: America's Juvenile Court Experiment* (New York: Wang and Hill, 1978). The subject has sometimes been overwhelmed by a relatively unproductive debate over whether the "child savers" were primarily motivated by a desire to exercise "social control" over the youth and families they purported to help. For example, see Anthony M. Platt, *The Child Savers: The Invention of Delinquency,* 2d ed. (1969; Chicago: University of Chicago, 1977). The best works in this vein address the operations of the resulting institutions, analyzing how juvenile courts functioned in practice. On the one hand, the protective goals of the juvenile court movement justified a cycle of expanded institutional intervention into children's lives. On the other hand, operational constraints and the divergent interests of the very people they were trying to help often prevented juvenile justice institutions from having a substantial impact. See, in particular, Steven L. Schlossman, *Love and the American Delinquent: The Theory and Practice of "Progressive" Juvenile Justice, 1825–1920* (Chicago: University of Chicago Press, 1977); Eric C. Schneider, *In the Web of Class: Delinquents and Reformers in Boston, 1810s–1930s* (New York: New York University Press, 1992); Mary E. Odem, *Delinquent Daughters: Protecting and Policing Adolescent Female Sexuality in the United States, 1885–1920* (Chapel Hill: University of North Carolina Press, 1995). Recent works on the early history of juvenile justice have begun to address a new set of issues, showing how private activists and charitable agencies participated in state formation by establishing reform organizations on their own and then encouraging public officials to take over, emphasizing the gender component of social reform by showing how female professionals engaged in politics to accomplish their goals, and demonstrating the role of expert knowledge in reform by showing how new social scientific analysis contributed to the emergence

of institutions for the protection of children. For examples of these new trends, see Elizabeth J. Clapp, *Mothers of All Children: Women Reformers and the Rise of Juvenile Courts in Progressive Era America* (University Park: Pennsylvania State University Press, 1998); Victoria Getis, *The Juvenile Court and the Progressives* (Urbana: University of Illinois Press, 2000); Anne Meis Knupfer, *Reform and Resistance: Gender, Delinquency, and America's First Juvenile Court* (New York: Routledge, 2001). Perhaps most importantly, historians have begun to rethink the tendency to see juvenile courts as inevitable forward-thinking institutions, emphasizing instead the courts' ongoing struggles to establish their legitimacy. See L. Mara Dodge, "'Our Juvenile Court Has Become More Like a Criminal Court': A Century of Reform at the Cook County (Chicago) Juvenile Court," *Michigan Historical Review* 26 (Fall 2000): 51–89; David S. Tanenhaus, *Juvenile Justice in the Making* (New York: Oxford University Press, 2004).

4. Lawrence M. Friedman and Robert V. Percival, *The Roots of Justice: Crime and Punishment in Alameda County, California, 1870–1910* (Chapel Hill: University of North Carolina Press, 1981). See also Samuel Walker, *Sense and Nonsense about Crime and Drugs: A Policy Guide*, 3d ed. (Belmont, CA: Wadsworth, 1994), 29–36; David Wolcott, "'The Cop Will Get You': The Police and Discretionary Juvenile Justice, 1890–1940," *Journal of Social History* 35 (Winter 2001): 349–72.

5. Alexander Von Hoffman, "An Officer of the Neighborhood: A Boston Patrolman on the Beat in 1895," *Journal of Social History* 26 (Winter 1992): 309–30.

6. Historical works on the operations of police discretion include Mark H. Haller, "Historical Roots of Police Behavior: Chicago, 1890–1925," *Law and Society Review* 10 (1976): 303–23; Wilbur R. Miller, *Cops and Bobbies: Police Authority in New York and London, 1830–1870*, 2d ed. (1973; Columbus: The Ohio State University Press, 1997).

7. Useful examinations of police professionalization include Robert Fogelson, *Big City Police* (Cambridge, MA: Harvard University Press, 1977), and Samuel Walker, *A Critical History of Police Reform* (Lexington, MA: D.C. Heath, 1977). On the larger urban transformation, see Howard P. Chudacoff and Judith E. Smith, *The Evolution of Urban Society*, 5th ed. (Upper Saddle River, NJ: Prentice Hall, 2000), and Eric H. Monkkonen, *America Becomes Urban: The Development of U.S. Cities and Town, 1780–1980* (Berkeley: University of California Press, 1988).

8. On migration and resulting social changes, see Chudacoff and Smith, *Evolution of Urban Society*, esp. 118–29, 212–17, 229–36; James R. Grossman, *Land of Hope: Chicago, Black Southerners, and the Great Migration* (Chicago: University of Chicago Press, 1991; George J. Sanchez, *Becoming Mexican American: Ethnicity, Culture, and Identity in Chicano Los Angeles, 1900–1945* (New York: Oxford University Press, 1993).

9. Thomas Hine, *The Rise and Fall of the American Teenager: A New History of the American Adolescent Experience* (New York: Harper, 1999), 138–76; Joseph F. Kett, *Rites of Passage: Adolescence in America, 1790 to the Present* (New York: Basic Books, 1977); David I. Macleod, *The Age of the Child: Children in America, 1890–1920* (New York: Twayne Publishers, 1998).

# NOTES TO CHAPTER 1

1. David J. Talbot Reminiscences, 20–21, 28, Chicago Historical Society. In 1957, David J. Talbot recorded his childhood memories of his father's—Edward Talbot's—

experiences as a police officer in turn-of-the-century Chicago. This particular incident was recounted to the younger Talbot by Judge Tuthill.

2. Talbot Reminiscences, research note, 22–23, 26, 35–36, 48.

3. Ibid., 22, 27.

4. Ibid., 42, 47.

5. On the background of juvenile court advocates, see Platt, *Child Savers;* Clapp, *Mothers of All Children;* Tanenhaus, *Juvenile Justice in the Making.*

6. On the Chicago police, see Mark H. Haller, "Civic Reformers and Police Leadership: Chicago, 1905–1935," in *Police in Urban Society,* ed. Harlan Hahn (Beverly Hills, CA: Sage Publications, 1971), 39–56; Richard C. Lindberg, *To Serve and Collect: Chicago Politics and Police Corruption from the Lager Beer Riot to the Summerdale Scandal, 1855–1960* (1991; Carbondale: Southern Illinois University Press, 1998). On the working-class backgrounds of police, see Rebecca Reed, "Regulating the Regulators: Ideology and Practice in the Policing of Detroit, 1880–1920" (Ph.D. diss., University of Michigan, 1992); Joanne Marie Klein, "Invisible Working-Class Men: Police Constables in Manchester, Birmingham, and Liverpool, 1900–1939" (Ph. D. diss., Rice University, 1992).

7. Clapp, *Mothers of All Children;* Knupfer, *Reform and Resistance.*

8. Talbot Reminiscences, 27, 42.

9. This tendency is exemplified by legal scholar Thomas Bernard's *Cycle of Juvenile Justice.* Looking at informed opinion about delinquency at three widely separated points in time—the 1820s, the 1890s, and the 1960s—Bernard shows how changing ideas of delinquency drove cyclical changes in juvenile justice policy. However, Bernard's work assumes that only one prevailing idea at a time shaped public and institutional responses to delinquency; it does not provide room for other competing ideas to exercise influence simultaneously.

10. Getis, *Juvenile Court and the Progressives.* See also Clapp, *Mothers of All Children;* Knupfer, *Reform and Resistance;* Tanenhaus, *Juvenile Justice in the Making.*

11. Hine, *Rise and Fall of the American Teenager,* 95–137; Harvey J. Graff, *Conflicting Paths: Growing Up in America* (Cambridge, MA: Harvard University Press, 1995).

12. Macleod, *Age of the Child,* xi–xii.

13. Ibid., 139–45; Kett, *Rites of Passage,* 215–44; Hine, *Rise and Fall of the American Teenager,* 158–76; Peter C. Baldwin, "'Nocturnal Habits and Dark Wisdom': The American Response to Children in the Streets at Night, 1880–1930," *Journal of Social History* 35 (Spring 2002): 593–611.

14. Mornay Williams, "The Street Boy—Who He Is, and What to Do with Him," in *Proceedings of the National Conference of Charities and Correction,* ed. Isabel C. Barrows (Fred. J. Herr, 1903), 238–41; quote from 239 [hereafter cited as "NCCC"].

15. Elbridge T. Gerry, "Causes of Delinquency in New York City, 1892," in *Juvenile Offenders for a Thousand Years: Selected Readings from Anglo-Saxon Times to 1900,* ed. Wiley Britton Sanders (Chapel Hill: University of North Carolina Press, 1970), 437.

16. G. W. Goler, "The Juvenile Delinquent," in *Proceedings of the NCCC,* ed. Isabel C. Barrows (Boston: Geo. H. Ellis, 1896), 355.

17. Myron E. Adams, "Municipal Regulation of Street Trades," in *Proceedings of the NCCC* (Fred J. Herr, 1904), 297.

18. Williams, "Street Boy," 240–41.

19. Platt, *Child Savers,* 37; Thomas Lee Philpott, *The Slum and the Ghetto:*

*Immigrants, Black, and Reformers in Chicago, 1880–1930* (1978; Belmont, CA: Wadsworth, 1991), 5–41; Donald L. Miller, *City of the Century: The Epic of Chicago and the Making of America* (New York: Simon and Schuster, 1996), esp. 417–32, 455–58.

20. Platt, *Child Savers*, 75–100; Julia C. Lathrop, "The Background of the Juvenile Court in Illinois," in *The Child, the Clinic, and the Court*, ed. Jane Addams (New York: New Republic, 1925), 290–97; Gwen Hoerr McNamee, "The Origin of the Cook County Juvenile Court," in *A Noble Social Experiment? The First 100 Years of the Cook County Juvenile Court, 1899–1999*, ed. Gwen Hoerr McNamee (Chicago: Chicago Bar Association, 1999), 14–23.

21. Paul Boyer, *Urban Masses and Moral Order, 1820–1920* (Cambridge, MA: Harvard University Press, 1978), 1–21, 94–107, quotation from 1. See also Bernard, *Cycle of Juvenile Justice*, 58–67; Clay Gish, "Rescuing the 'Waifs and Strays' of the City: The Western Emigration Programs of the Children's Aid Society," *Journal of Social History* 33 (Fall 1999): 121–42; Mennel, *Thorns and Thistles*, 3–15, 32–77; Schlossman, *Love and the American Delinquent*, 18–49; Steven Schlossman, "Delinquent Children: The Juvenile Reform School," in *The Oxford History of the Prison: The Practice of Punishment in Western Society*, ed. Norval Morris and David J. Rothman (New York: Oxford University Press, 1995), 329–32; Schneider, *In the Web of Class*, 17–71.

22. Getis, *Juvenile Court and the Progressives*, esp. 18–27. For contrary views that emphasize a social control model, see Platt, *Child Savers*.

23. Lathrop, "Background of the Juvenile Court," 290.

24. Jane Addams, *The Spirit of Youth and the City Streets* (New York: Macmillan, 1920).

25. Timothy D. Hurley, *Origin of the Illinois Juvenile Court Law*, 3d ed. (1907; New York: AMS Press, 1977), 56.

26. Sophonisba P. Breckinridge and Edith Abbott, *The Delinquent Child and the Home* (1912; New York: Arno Press, 1970), 45–47.

27. Clarence Lexow, *Report and Proceedings of the Senate Committee Appointed to Investigate the Police Department of the City of New York* (1895; New York: Arno Press, 1971); Alexander R. Piper, "Report of an Investigation of the Discipline and Administration of the Police Department of the City of Chicago, 1904," in *Chicago Police Investigations: Three Reports* (1904; New York: Arno Press, 1971).

28. John Peter Altgeld, *Live Questions; including Our Penal Machinery and Its Victims*, 3d ed. (1884; Chicago: Donohue and Henneberry, 1890), 182–83, 186–87. On Altgeld, see Platt, *Child Savers*, 124–26.

29. Ben B. Lindsey, "The Boy and the Court," *Charities* 13 (January 7, 1905): 350.

30. On limited numbers of reform schools, see Schlossman, "Delinquent Children," 333–34. Forty-seven reform schools operating nationwide in 1890 are listed in Homer Folks, *The Care of Destitute, Neglected, and Delinquent Children* (Albany: J. B. Lyon Co., 1900), 125–26; fifty-eight are listed in U.S.Department of the Interior, Census Office, *Report on Crime, Pauperism, and Benevolence in the United States at the Eleventh Census: 1890; Part II: General Tables* (Washington, DC: Government Printing Office, 1895), 519.

31. Calculated from U.S. Census Office, *Report on Crime: 1890*, 299–300, 516.

32. Hon. Richard S. Tuthill, "History of the Children's Court in Chicago," in *Children's Courts in the United States: Their Origin, Development, and Results*, ed. Samuel J. Barrows (Washington, DC: Government Printing Office, 1904), 1; Hurley, *Origin of the Illinois Juvenile Court Law*, 9–10, 11.

33. Platt, *Child Savers,* 117–34; Hurley, *Origin of the Illinois Juvenile Court Law,* 12–15.

34. Helen R. Jeter, *The Chicago Juvenile Court,* U.S. Children's Bureau Publication No. 104 (Washington, DC: Government Printing Office, 1922), 2; Hurley, *Origin of the Illinois Juvenile Court Law,* 11–12, 20; McNamee, "Origin of the Cook County Juvenile Court," 17. Flower is quoted in *Chicago Tribune* (December 12, 1899), 8.

35. The best recent accounts of the origin of the Cook County Juvenile Court are Getis, *Juvenile Court and the Progressives,* 28–52; Tanenhaus, *Juvenile Justice in the Making,* 3–22.

36. This distinction is articulated in Franklin E. Zimring, "The Common Thread: Diversion in the Jurisprudence of Juvenile Courts," in *A Century of Juvenile Justice,* ed. Margaret K. Rosenheim, Franklin E. Zimring, David S. Tanenhaus, and Bernadine Dohrn (Chicago: University of Chicago Press, 2002), 142–57.

37. Schlossman, *Love and the American Delinquent,* 55–62.

38. Hurley, *Origin of the Illinois Juvenile Court Law,* 60; Julia Lathrop, "The Development of the Probation System in a Large City," *Charities* 13 (January 7, 1905): 344–49; Frederic Almy, "The Economics of the Juvenile Court," *Charities* 13 (January 7, 1905): 337.

39. Hurley, *Origin of the Illinois Juvenile Court Law,* 56; Julian W. Mack, "The Juvenile Court," *Harvard Law Review* 23 (December 1909–10): 107; Lindsey, "The Boy and the Court." On affectional discipline, see Schlossman, *Love and the American Delinquent,* 55–62, 124–27.

40. Roger Lane, *Policing the City: Boston, 1822–1885* (Cambridge, MA: Harvard University Press, 1967); James F. Richardson, *The New York Police: Colonial Times to 1901* (New York: Oxford University Press, 1970); Lindberg, *To Serve and Collect;* John C. Schneider, *Detroit and the Problem of Order, 1830–1880: A Geography of Crime, Riot, and Policing* (Lincoln: University of Nebraska Press, 1980).

41. In addition to the works cited in the previous note, see Fogelson, *Big City Police;* Haller, "Historical Roots of Police Behavior"; Sidney R. Harring, *Policing a Class Society: The Experience of American Cities, 1865–1915* (New Brunswick, NJ: Rutgers University Press, 1983); David R. Johnson, *Policing the Urban Underworld: The Impact of Crime on the Development of the American Police, 1800–1887* (Philadelphia: Temple University Press, 1979); David R. Johnson, *American Law Enforcement: A History* (St. Louis: Forum Press, 1981); Miller, *Cops and Bobbies;* Eric H. Monkkonen, *Police in Urban America, 1860–1920* (Cambridge: Cambridge University Press, 1981); Von Hoffman, "An Officer of the Neighborhood"; Walker, *Critical History of Police Reform.*

42. Horatio Alger, *Ragged Dick, or Street Life in New York with the Boot-Blacks* (1868; New York: NAL, 1990).

43. *Detroit Free Press* (July 8, 1900) [hereafter cited as *DFP*].

44. Mrs. E. E. Williamson, "The Street Arab," in *Proceedings of the NCCC* (1898), 358–61.

45. Talbot Reminiscences, 40, 46–47, 50.

46. Ibid., 52–54; McNamee, "Origin of the Cook County Juvenile Court," 20; *Chicago Tribune* (December 11, 1899), 1.

47. Jerome E. Richards, "Juvenile Offenders," in *Proceedings of the Seventh Annual Convention of the International Association of Chiefs of Police* (1900; New York: Arno Press, 1971), 24–25 [hereafter cited as "IACP"]; Thomas F. Farnan, "Is Crime a Disease?" in

*Proceedings of the 15th Annual Convention of the IACP* (1908), 86. On biological and hereditary theories of crime, see Nicole Hahn Rafter, *Creating Born Criminals* (Urbana: University of Illinois Press, 1997), esp. 36–39, 110–23.

48. Benjamin Murphy, "Prevent Crime—The Principal Duty of the Police," in *Proceedings of the 8th Annual Convention of the IACP* (1901), 13.

49. W. H. H. Rodenbaugh, "Juvenile Reformation," in *IACP, 9th Annual Session* (1902), 59–60.

50. Joshua B. Gray, "Probation Laws and Their Workings," in *Proceedings of the 18th Annual Convention of the IACP* (1911), 129–30.

51. James M. Buckley, "The Present Epidemic of Crime," *The Century Magazine* 67 (November 1903): 151; Henry D. Cowles, "Probation," in *Proceedings of the 18th Annual Convention of the IACP* (1911), 113–18.

52. *Proceedings of the 18th Annual Convention of the IACP* (1911), 118–25.

53. William Moore, "The Boy and the Policeman," in *IACP, 9th Annual Session* (1902), 46–47.

54. William Desmond, "The Juvenile Court," in *IACP, 10th Annual Session* (1903), 72, 74.

55. J. N. Tillard, "The Child, the Home, and the State," in *IACP, 14th Annual Session* (1907), 38–41.

56. J. N. Tillard, "The Juvenile Criminal," in *IACP, Proceedings 23rd Convention* (1916), 30–34.

# Notes to Chapter 2

1. *DFP* (January 3, 1907); *DFP* (January 4, 1907).

2. *DFP* (January 4, 1907); *DFP* (January 5, 1907); *DFP* (January 6, 1907). The character A. J. Raffles was featured in at least three collections by author E. W. Horning: *The Amateur Cracksman* (1899), *The Black Mask* (1901), and *A Thief in the Night* (1905). See Ian Ousby, *The Cambridge Guide to Literature in English* (Cambridge: Cambridge University Press, 1993), 452.

3. *DFP* (January 3, 1907); *DFP* (January 26, 1908).

4. This is less true of studies addressing the more recent period from World War II to the present, which benefit from better sociological data and oral interviews with former juvenile offenders and which emphasize the contested nature of "delinquency" itself. See Eric C. Schneider, *Vampires, Dragons, and Egyptian Kings: Youth Gangs in Post-War New York* (Princeton, NJ: Princeton University Press, 1999); Andrew Diamond, "Rethinking Culture on the Streets: Agency, Masculinity, and Style in the American City," *Journal of Urban History* 27 (July 2001): 669–85; Eduardo Obregon Pagan, *Murder at the Sleepy Lagoon: Zoot Suits, Race, and Riot in Wartime LA* (Chapel Hill: University of North Carolina Press, 2003).

5. Platt, *Child Savers;* Mennel, *Thorns and Thistles;* Bernard, *Cycle of Juvenile Justice;* Joseph M. Hawes, *Children in Urban Society: Juvenile Delinquency in Nineteenth-Century America* (New York: Oxford University Press, 1971).

6. Schlossman, *Love and the American Delinquent;* Steven L. Schlossman and Alexander W. Pisciotta, "Identifying and Treating Serious Juvenile Offenders: The View from California and New York in the 1920s," in *Intervention Strategies for Chronic Juvenile*

*Offenders: Some New Perspectives*, ed. Peter W. Greenwood (Westport, CT: Greenwood Press, 1986); Steven Schlossman and Susan Turner, "Status Offenders, Criminal Offenders, and Children 'At Risk' in Early Twentieth-Century Juvenile Court," in *Children at Risk in America: History, Concepts, and Public Policy*, ed. Roberta Wollons (Albany: State University of New York Press, 1993); Schneider, *In the Web of Class*, esp. 45–50, 164–68.

7. Odem, *Delinquent Daughters;* Knupfer, *Reform and Resistance;* Ruth Alexander, *The "Girl Problem": Female Sexual Delinquency in New York, 1900–1930* (Ithaca, NY: Cornell University Press, 1995); Tamara Myers and Joan Sangster, "Retorts, Runaways, and Riot: Patterns of Resistance in Canadian Reform Schools for Girls, 1930–60," *Journal of Social History* 34 (Spring 2001): 669–98.

8. Olivier Zunz, *The Changing Face of Inequality: Urbanization, Industrial Development, and Immigrants in Detroit, 1880–1920* (Chicago: University of Chicago Press, 1982), 1–7, 17–20, 97–99.

9. On the late origin of a juvenile court for Detroit, see William T. Downs, *Michigan Juvenile Court: Law and Practice* (Ann Arbor, MI: Institute of Continuing Legal Education, 1963), esp. 45–47.

10. See, as examples, Schlossman and Pisciotta, "Identifying and Treating Serious Juvenile Offenders"; Schneider, *In the Web of Class*, 45–50; Alexander, *The "Girl Problem";* Myers and Sangster, "Retorts, Runaways, and Riot."

11. See, as examples, Schlossman, *Love and the American Delinquent;* Schneider, *In the Web of Class*, 164–68; Schlossman and Turner, "Status Offenders, Criminal Offenders"; Odem, *Delinquent Daughters.*

12. Philip J. Cook and John H. Laub, "The Unprecedented Epidemic in Youth Violence," in *Crime and Justice: An Annual Review of Research*, vol. 24, *Youth Violence*, ed. Michael Tonry and Mark H. Moore (Chicago: University of Chicago Press, 1998), 27–64; Howard N. Snyder, "Juvenile Arrests 2001," *Juvenile Justice Bulletin* (December 2003); National Research Council and Institute of Medicine, *Juvenile Crime, Juvenile Justice*, ed. Joan McCord, Cathy Spatz Widon, and Nancy A. Crowell (Washington, DC: National Academy Press, 2001), 26–31.

13. Detroit Police Department, "Record of Arrests," Vols. 16–18, 20–21, 23–24, 27, 30, and 33, located in Police Department Collection, Detroit City Archives, Burton Historical Collection, Detroit Public Library [hereafter cited as PDC, BHC]. I selected these particular years in order to capture the operation of justice for juveniles immediately prior to the creation of Detroit's juvenile court. Taking a 20 percent sample of boys between eight and sixteen yielded 790 cases for my Detroit juvenile arrest database: 367 for the three years in the 1890s and 423 for the three years in the 1900s. The arrest records were organized chronologically; they did not separate offenders by age, sex, race, crime, or outcome of the case. That is, each day each police precinct simply listed all of its arrests for that day. In my sample, I selected every fifth arrest involving a boy between ages eight and sixteen. This age range was chosen for two reasons. First, the Detroit police arrested virtually no boys younger than eight. Second, these age groups parallel those later used by the Detroit police after they began separately recording juvenile arrests in 1898, and by the Wayne County Juvenile Court following its creation in 1907. See Detroit Police Department, *Thirty-Third Annual Report of the Board of Commissioners of the Metropolitan Police to the Common Council of the City of Detroit, 1898* (Detroit: Raynor and Taylor, 1899), 52; State of Michigan, *Laws Relating to Juvenile Courts and County Agents* (Lansing, MI: Industrial School Press, 1910), 5.

14. Collecting data on every girl arrested yielded 330 cases in my Detroit juvenile arrest database. Age groupings for girls were determined in essentially the same way as for boys but are slightly different because police and courts treated girls differently. The Detroit police arrested virtually no girls younger than ten, but unlike boys, they did include girls up to age seventeen under juvenile procedures and place them under the jurisdiction of the Wayne County Juvenile Court after 1907. See DPD, *33rd Annual Report* (1899), 52, and Michigan, *Laws Relating to Juvenile Courts*, 5.

15. Monkkonen, *Police in Urban America, 1860–1920;* Eugene J. Watts, "Police Response to Crime and Disorder in Twentieth-Century St. Louis," *Journal of American History* 70 (June 1983): 340–58.

16. The Detroit Metropolitan Police Force was established by state law in 1865 and remained under a state-appointed board of four commissioners until 1891. Even after the city assumed administrative control, the police continued to operate under the commissioner system until 1901, when a single commissioner was granted sole executive authority. On Detroit policing, see Schneider, *Detroit and the Problem of Order;* Reed, "Regulating the Regulators."

17. Reed, "Regulating the Regulators," 30–35.

18. Ibid., 97–98. On policewomen, see DPD, *56th Annual Report* (1922), 9. On black police, see W. Marvin Dulaney, *Black Police in America* (Bloomington: Indiana University Press, 1996).

19. *DFP* (October 7, 1900); Reed, "Regulating the Regulators," 99–112; U.S. Department of the Interior, Census Office, *Twelfth Census of the United States, Taken in the Year 1900; Volume II: Population* (Washington, DC: Government Printing Office, 1902), 128.

20. DPD, *Manual of the Metropolitan Police Force,* 1905, PDC, BHC; Reed, "Regulating the Regulators," 122–23; Haller, "Historical Roots of Police Behavior"; Von Hoffman, "An Officer of the Neighborhood."

21. Examples of police aid for injured children may be found in "Incidental Events," February 14, 1889; March 23, 1889; April 2, 1889; October 24, 1899; October 25, 1899; November 10, 1899; November 25, 1899; December 4, 1899; December 7, 1899; December 19, 1899; December 30, 1899, all located in PDC, BHC.

22. On lost children, see "Incidental Events," May 8, 1889; October 21, 1899; *DFP* (June 9, 1907); *DFP* (April 27, 1908); *DFP* (May 25, 1908). For foundlings, see "Incidental Events," March 28, 1889; May 13, 1889; January 9, 1900. See also Monkkonen, *Police in Urban America,* 109–28.

23. *DFP* (January 12, 1908); *DFP* (May 22, 1908); *DFP* (May 25, 1908; *DFP* (December 13, 1908).

24. For boys, 790 arrests (from my Detroit juvenile arrest database) were multiplied by five (to compensate for 20 percent sample), then divided by 45,743 total male arrests derived from tabulated aggregate figures in DPD *Annual Reports* for corresponding years. For girls, 330 arrests were divided by 6,736 total female arrests. My discussions of arrest patterns for the total Detroit population are derived from different sources than are my calculations regarding juvenile arrests. While all discussion of juvenile arrest patterns is based on my arrest database, discussion of total arrests is based on aggregate data tabulated and published by the DPD in its *Annual Reports* for the years 1891, 1894, 1896, 1901, 1904, and 1907. The 1897 *Annual Report* (covering 1896) is unavailable, so data from the previous year was substituted.

25. Throughout the book, rates of arrest were calculated by taking the total number of arrests (here, from my Detroit juvenile arrest database), if necessary multiplying by a constant (five, in this case) to compensate for any sampling, dividing by the age-appropriate population for the years in question, and multiplying by 1,000 to achieve rates per 1,000. Populations interpolated from U.S. Department of the Interior, Census Office, *Report of the Population of the United States at the Eleventh Census: 1890; Part II* (Washington, DC: Government Printing Office, 1897), 119; U.S. Census Office, *Twelfth Census; 1900 Population,* 128; and U.S. Department of Commerce and Labor, Bureau of the Census, *Thirteenth Census of the United States Taken in the Year 1910; Volume I: Population 1910: General Reports and Analysis* (Washington, DC: Government Printing Office, 1913), 453.

26. Zunz, *Changing Face of Inequality,* 3, 94–105, 139; U.S. Census Office, *Twelfth Census; 1900 Population,* 128. It is important to note that Detroit was not yet divided by race, as it would become later in the century. Although blacks had settled there for decades, still only 4,114 blacks lived in Detroit in 1900. Unlike other ethnic groups, no geographic cluster of blacks had emerged by 1900, mainly because their numbers were so small. Detroit's black population began to grow in the mid-1910s, with the Great Migration of blacks out of the South and the wartime demand for labor in the industrial North. By 1920, 40,828 blacks lived in Detroit, a more noticeable 4 percent of the total. See Thomas J. Sugrue, *The Origins of the Urban Crisis: Race and Inequality in Postwar Detroit* (Princeton, NJ: Princeton University Press, 1996); Richard W. Thomas, *Life For Us Is What We Make It: Building Black Community in Detroit, 1915–1945* (Bloomington: Indiana University Press, 1992).

27. Robert Conot, *American Odyssey* (1974; Detroit: Wayne State University Press, 1986), 139.

28. Calculated from data in U.S. Census Office, *12th Census; 1900 Population,* 128; U.S. Census Bureau, *13th Census; Population 1910,* 453; U.S. Department of Commerce, Bureau of the Census, *Fourteenth Census of the United States Taken in the Year 1920; Volume II: Population 1920: General Report and Analytical Tables* (Washington, DC: Government Printing Office, 1922), 293. On the nationwide decline in the ratio of young people to adults in the nineteenth century, see Macleod, *Age of the Child,* 3–4.

29. Calculated from data in U.S. Census Office, *12th Census; 1900 Population,* 128.

30. Clifford R. Shaw, with Frederick M. Zorbaugh, Henry D. McKay, and Leonard S. Cottrell, *Delinquency Areas: A Study of the Geographic Distribution of School Truants, Juvenile Delinquents, and Adult Offenders in Chicago* (Chicago: University of Chicago Press, 1929); Earl R. Moses, *The Negro Delinquent in Chicago* (Washington, 1932). See also Donald J. Shoemaker, *Theories of Delinquency: An Examination of Explanations of Delinquent Behavior,* 2nd ed. (New York: Oxford University Press, 1990), 79–113.

31. Travis Hirschi and Michael Gottredson, "Age and the Explanation of Crime," *American Journal of Sociology* 89 (November 1983): 552–84. In fact, criminologists have disagreed with this assumption on two fronts. First, different offenses tend to peak at different ages. High-risk, low-yield crimes such as robbery peak at younger ages, while other offenses such as embezzlement peak at later ages and decline more slowly. Second, the age crime curve better reflects the prevalence of offending–the proportion of people committing crimes–than it does the incidence of offending–when in their lives individual offenders commit crime. Persistent individual offenders have much more extended criminal careers. See Darrell J. Steffensmeier, Emilie Andersen Allan, Miles D. Harer, and Cathy

Streifel, "Age and the Distribution of Crime," *American Journal of Sociology* 94 (January 1989): 803–31, and David P. Farrington, "Age and Crime," in *Crime and Justice: An Annual Review of Research,* vol. 7, ed. Norval Morris and Michael Tonry (Chicago: University of Chicago Press, 1986), 189–250.

32. Limited historical evidence also suggests that the age-crime curve may not apply to the period before the modern experience of adolescence. Eric H. Monkkonen has shown that the age distribution of homicides in nineteenth-century New York was much more even than the modern age-crime curve would suggest. Children, he suggests, left school and home early in life, started working early in life, became more like adults early in life, and therefore committed murder earlier. See Monkkonen, *Murder in New York City* (Berkeley: University of California Press, 2001), 80–93.

33. On patterns of schooling and work, see Hine, *Rise and Fall of the American Teenager,* 120–57; Kett, *Rites of Passage,* 126–32, 144–72; Macleod, *Age of the Child,* 74–77, 101–17.

34. U.S. Census Office, *12th Census; 1900 Population,* 386.

35. Zunz, *Changing Face of Inequality,* 227–35; figures calculated from data in U.S. Bureau of the Census, *Special Reports: Occupations at the Twelfth Census* (Washington, DC: Government Printing Office, 1904), 544–49. On the transition to adulthood, see John Modell, *Into One's Own: From Youth to Adulthood in the United States, 1920–1975* (Berkeley: University of California Press, 1989).

36. On female occupations and domestic service, see Alice Kessler-Harris, *Out to Work: A History of Wage-Earning Women in the United States* (New York: Oxford University Press, 1982), 103, 127–28. On new social opportunities and the risks associated with them, see Kathy Peiss, *Cheap Amusements: Working Women and Leisure in Turn-of-the-Century New York* (Philadelphia: Temple University Press, 1986); Joanne J. Meyerowitz, *Women Adrift: Independent Wage Earners in Chicago, 1880–1930* (Chicago: University of Chicago Press, 1988).

37. On the decline of prostitution, see Timothy J. Gilfoyle, *City of Eros: New York City, Prostitution, and the Commercialization of Sex, 1790–1920* (New York: W. W. Norton, 1992), 298–315. The experience of turn-of-the-century working girls has generated an extensive historical literature, including Peiss, *Cheap Amusements;* Meyerowitz, *Women Adrift;* Odem, *Delinquent Daughters;* Alexander, *The "Girl Problem."*

38. Donald J. Black and Albert J. Reiss, Jr., "Police Control of Juveniles," *American Sociological Review* 35 (1970): 63–77; Donald J. Black, *The Manners and Customs of the Police* (New York: Academic Press, 1980); Richard M. Brede, "Complainants and Kids: The Role of Citizen Complainants in the Social Production of Juvenile Cases," in *Law and Order in American Society,* ed. Joseph M. Hawes (Port Washington, NY: Kennikat Press, 1979), 77–100; Robert J. Lundman, Richard E. Sykes, and John P. Clark, "Police Control of Juveniles: A Replication," *Journal of Research in Crime and Delinquency* 18 (January 1979): 74–91; Douglas A. Smith and Christy A. Visher, "Street-Level Justice: Situational Determinants of Police Arrest Decisions," *Social Problems* 29 (December 1981): 167–77.

39. In Oakland, California, between 1875 and 1910, 64 percent of arrests were for public order offenses. Similarly, public order charges comprised over half of all urban arrests (in a nationwide sample) between 1860 and 1920. See Friedman and Percival, *Roots of Justice,* 67–113; Monkkonen, *Police in Urban America,* 64–85.

40. Each difference among juveniles arrested discussed in this chapter meets conventional standards of statistical significance of at least the $p < 0.05$ level.

41. *DFP* (November 6, 1907); *DFP* (February 10, 1907); *DFP* (March 25, 1907); *DFP* (June 8, 1908); *DFP* (July 5, 1908).

42. *DFP* (January 3, 1907); *DFP* (January 4, 1907); *DFP* (January 5, 1907); *DFP* (January 6, 1907).

43. *DFP* (April 10, 1907).

44. *DFP* (January 11, 1907); *DFP* (January 13, 1907).

45. As example, see "Complaints," May 25, 1896; June 1, 1896; July 6, 1896; December 22, 1897; May 14, 1898; June 24, 1898; June 21, 1903; January 24, 1908, located in PDC, BHC.

46. *DFP* (January 17, 1907); *DFP* (July 19, 1907).

47. "Complaints, Vol. 1," June 1, 1896, 30.

48. "Complaints, Vol. 3," December 24, 1897, 79. For similar examples, see "Complaints, Vol. 1," June 16, 1896, 55; "Complaints, Vol. 3," May 24, 1898, 355; "Complaints, Vol. 3," June 23, 1898, 417.

49. "Complaints, Vol. 3," May 7, 1898, 316.

50. "Complaints, Vol. 3," December 18, 1897, 60. For other examples of burglaries, see "Complaints, Vol. 1," May 18, 1896, 11; June 11, 1896, 45; June 22, 1896, 64; July 3, 1896, 83; July 4, 1896, 84. "Complaints, Vol. 2," April 24, 1898, 304; May 7, 1898, 316; June 10, 1898, 387.

51. *DFP* (February 12, 1907); *DFP* (April 1, 1907); *DFP* (May 13, 1907); *DFP* (June 10, 1907); *DFP* (August 4, 1907); *DFP* (October 28, 1907).

52. *DFP* (March 31, 1907); *DFP* (July 7, 1907).

53. As earlier, discussion of total arrests is based on aggregate data tabulated and published by the DPD in its *Annual Reports* for 1890, 1893, 1895, 1900, 1903, and 1906; data on homicide arrests from all DPD *Annual Reports,* 1890–1906.

54. "Complaints, Vol. 3," May 18, 1898, 341; "Complaints, Vol. 3," June 13, 1898.

55. "Complaints, Vol. 1," May 9, 1896, 1.

56. Here, "armed" means that the police indicated boys possessed something that could be construed as a weapon at the time of arrest. However, most of these boys were listed as carrying a "knife" and the records do not indicate when this refers to a simple pocketknife or to something more dangerous. $N = 790$.

57. Assault arrests—51 of 64 involving boys—were attributed to the "police court" rather than to a specific precinct and were listed as taking place at 10:00 AM. These arrests reflect formal complaints after the fact rather than arrests at the time of the offense. Likewise, the same pattern applies to all twenty-seven assault arrests involving girls.

58. "Incidental Events," Oct. 28, 1899.

59. Ibid., March 1, 1903.

60. *DFP* (January 30, 1907).

61. "Juvenile disorderly persons" were defined under the 1895 compulsory education law as persons between ages seven and sixteen who were habitually truant from school, children who were "turbulent, disobedient, or insubordinate" in school, or children who "are not attending any school and who habitually frequent streets and other public places, having no lawful business, employment, or occupation." See Richard A. Bolt, *Juvenile Offenders in the City of Detroit, With Suggestions for the Establishment of a Juvenile Court and Probation System* (Ann Arbor, MI: Richmond and Backus, 1903), 8.

62. Ibid., 53. This source does not provide boys' full names.

63. Conot, *American Odyssey,* 140.

64. *N* = 71.

65. Bolt, *Juvenile Offenders*, 53.

66. *N* = 89.

67. *DFP* (July 15, 1907). On the use of status offenses to regulate girls' sexuality, see Odem, *Delinquent Daughters;* Steven L. Schlossman and Stephanie Wallach, "The Crime of Precocious Sexuality: Female Juvenile Delinquency in the Progressive Era," *Harvard Education Review* 48 (February 1978): 65–93.

68. *DFP* (March 2, 1907); *DFP* (March 30, 1908).

69. *DFP* (January 7, 1907); *DFP* (March 30, 1908); *DFP* (February 4, 1909). On the white slavery scare, see Odem, *Delinquent Daughters,* 97–99; Gilfoyle, *City of Eros,* 207–74.

70. *DFP* (March 6, 1907); *DFP* (March 7, 1907).

# NOTES TO CHAPTER 3

1. "Street Urchins Play Their Way to Liberty," *DFP* (May 12, 1907).

2. DPD, General and Special Orders (May 10, 1898), PDC, BHC; DPD, *33rd Annual Report* (1899), 52; DPD, *39th Annual Report* (1904), 71.

3. See Altgeld, *Live Questions,* 182–83, 186–87; Lindsey, "The Boy and the Court," 350–57; Tuthill, "History of the Children's Court in Chicago," 1; Hurley, *Origin of the Illinois Juvenile Court Law,* 9–11.

4. National Probation Association, "Pinched for Stealing," solicitation pamphlet, circa. 1925, located in clipping file "Juvenile Court," Burton Historical Collection, Detroit Public Library (hereafter abbreviated as "NPA").

5. Platt, *Child Savers;* Hawes, *Children in Urban Society;* Ryerson, *Best-Laid Plans.* Other histories of juvenile justice portray the creation of juvenile court as the culmination of earlier efforts to protect children, yet also an important break from past practice. See, as examples, Mennel, *Thorns and Thistles;* Schlossman, *Love and the American Delinquent;* Schneider, *In the Web of Class.*

6. Bernard, *Cycle of Juvenile Justice,* esp. 70–73, 86–87; Henry S. Hulbert, "Detroit's Juvenile Court and Its Functions in the Community," *Detroit Saturday Night* (December 18, 1909): 22–23.

7. Bolt, *Juvenile Offenders;* Lindsey, "The Boy and The Court"; Helen Page Bates, "Digest of Statutes Relating to Juvenile Courts and Probation Systems," *Charities* 13 (January 7, 1905): 329–37; Downs, *Michigan Juvenile Court;* Getis, *Juvenile Court and the Progressives,* 50.

8. Michigan Industrial School for Boys, *Biennial Report of the Board of Trustees of the Industrial School for Boys of Michigan* (Lansing, 1894), 5, 14–19; Downs, *Michigan Juvenile Court,* 42–43.

9. Downs, *Michigan Juvenile Court,* 43–44; Bolt, *Juvenile Offenders,* 35; Michigan, *Laws Relating to Juvenile Courts,* 7–9. Quote from Mrs. Mildred E. Bennett, "New Dynamics and Philosophy in Detention Home Care" (M.S.W. Thesis, Wayne University, 1946), 9. For a more positive assessment of county agents, see Lorna F. Hurl and David J. Tucker, "The Michigan County Agents and the Development of Juvenile Probation, 1873–1900," *Journal of Social History* 30 (Summer 1997): 905–36.

10. Michigan's compulsory education laws are quoted in Bolt, *Juvenile Offenders,* 8–9,

27–28, and in Michigan State Reform School, *Report of the Superintendent of the State Reform School at Lansing Michigan, to the State Board of Inspectors for the Biennial Period Ending June 30, 1892* (Lansing, 1892), xvi–xvii.

11. Detroit Police Department, *Story of the Detroit Police Department, 1916–17; Fifty-Second Annual Report of Commissioner of Metropolitan Police for the Twelve Months Ending June 30, 1917* (Detroit, 1917), 75.

12. The number of official cases varied widely from a low of 412 in 1892 to a high of 720 in 1895. Data from DPD, *Annual Reports,* 1890–96.

13. Bolt, *Juvenile Offenders,* 28; DPD, *26th Annual Report* (1891), 50; DPD, *29th Annual Report* (1894), 41.

14. *DFP* (December 12, 1907); David Tyack and Michael Berkowitz, "The Man Nobody Liked: Toward a Social History of the Truant Officer, 1840–1940," *American Quarterly* 29 (Spring 1977): 31–54.

15. This analysis relies on my Detroit juvenile arrest database, which is more fully described in chapter 2, notes 13 and 14.

16. $N = 782$.

17. By comparison, 25 percent of total arrestees were discharged and 29 percent were given suspended sentences; thus, 54 percent never penetrated past the courts. Discussion of total arrests is based on aggregate data tabulated and published by the DPD. Unfortunately, the DPD's tabulated data on dispositions did not distinguish offenders by sex, so these findings include dispositions of both male and female offenders. See DPD, *26th Annual Report* (1891), 73–74; DPD, *29th Annual Report* (1894), 60–61; DPD, *31st Annual Report* (1896), 62–63; DPD, *36th Annual Report* (1901), 70–71; DPD, *39th Annual Report* (1904), 100–101; DPD, *42nd Annual Report* (1907), 78–79.

18. Also unfortunately, the information available in my Detroit juvenile arrest database does not indicate whether boys actually paid their fines or served their time in jail. However, the DPD's tabulated data on dispositions helps to answer this question. Among total arrestees given the choice of a fine or jail, only about 2 percent paid their fines. It seems safe to assume that most boy offenders served time.

19. $N = 326$.

20. The remaining almost 4 percent were usually returned to law enforcement officials in nearby towns. The percentages do not total 100 due to rounding.

21. Herbert Harley, "Detroit's New Model Criminal Court," *Journal of Criminal Law and Criminology* 11 (November 1920): 398–418; Raymond R. Fragnoli, *The Transformation of Detroit: Progressivism in Detroit—And After, 1912–1933* (New York: Garland Publishing, 1982), 193–94; Friedman and Percival, *Roots of Justice,* 134.

22. On modern diversion, see John P. Kenney and Dan G. Pursuit, *Police Work with Juveniles and the Administration of Juvenile Justice,* 5th ed. (1954; Springfield, IL: Charles C. Thomas, 1975); Edwin M. Lemert, "Diversion in Juvenile Justice: What Hath Been Wrought," *Journal of Research in Crime and Delinquency* 18 (January 1981): 34–45.

23. Again, the DPD's tabulated data on dispositions did not distinguish offenders by sex, so these findings include dispositions of both male and female offenders.

24. $N = 37$. For a more detailed discussion of these findings, see David Wolcott, "Juvenile Justice before Juvenile Court: Cops, Courts, and Kids in Turn-of-the-Century Detroit," *Social Science History* 27 (Spring 2003): 109–38.

25. Detroit Police Department, "Record of Arrests," vol. 20 (Sept. 20, 1893), PDC, BHC.

26. *N* = 37.

27. Bolt, *Juvenile Offenders;* Arthur B. Moehlmann, *Public Education in Detroit* (Bloomington, IN: Public School Publishing Company, 1925), 122.

28. DPD, *27th Annual Report* (1892), 42.

29. *N* = 46.

30. "Complaints," Vol. 3, May 8, 1898; "Complaints," Vol. 1, May 15, 1896; located in PDC, BHC.

31. "Complaints," Vol. 3, December 22, 1897, PDC, BHC.

32. *N* = 55.

33. *N* = 55.

34. State of Michigan, *Laws Relating to Board of Corrections and Charities, Juvenile Courts, and County Agents* (Lansing, MI: Industrial School Press, 1911), 61. See also Mary Bigger, "A Study of the Factors Underlying the Behavior of Twenty Delinquent Girls in the House of the Good Shepherd," (M.S.W. Thesis, Wayne University, 1944), 4–7.

35. Peiss, *Cheap Amusements;* Odem, *Delinquent Daughters;* Janis Appier, *Policing Women: The Sexual Politics of Law Enforcement and the LAPD* (Philadelphia: Temple University Press, 1998).

36. *DFP* (September 21, 1907); *DFP* (September 22, 1907).

37. Bolt, *Juvenile Offenders;* Michigan, *Laws Relating to Juvenile Courts;* DPD, *Story of the Detroit Police,* 290.

38. *N* = 251.

39. This difference does *not* achieve conventional standards of statistical significance; chi-square (1) = 1.49; $p$ = 0.22.

40. This and all subsequent differences achieve conventional standards of statistical significance of at least the $p < 0.05$ level.

41. *DFP* (January 15, 1907); also *DFP* (May 10, 1908).

42. *DFP* (February 26, 1907).

43. *DFP* (March 30, 1907).

44. *N* = 251.

45. A $5.00 fine and a thirty-day sentence are both the medians in these categories. Fines ranged between $1.00 and $30.00, with an average of $7.78. Sentences to the House of Correction ranged between one day and ninety days, with an average of thirty-two.

46. Quoted in Helene Freud Siegel, "A History of the Detroit House of Correction" (M.S.W. Thesis, Wayne University, 1940), 73–74.

47. Detroit House of Correction, *Twentieth Annual Report of the Officers of the Detroit House of Correction to the Common Council of the City of Detroit for the Year 1881* (Detroit: Post and Tribune Job Co., City Printers, 1882), 18–19, 25; Detroit House of Correction, *47th Annual Report for the Year 1908* (1909), 18, 24; Siegel, "History of Detroit House of Correction," 72–73.

48. Michigan State Reform School, *Report for 1892,* x, 235, 315; Michigan Industrial School for Boys, *Biennial Report* (Lansing, 1896), 18

49. Because the police courts heard many more criminal cases involving kids than just those accused of status offenses, the majority—52 percent—of boys they ultimately committed to Lansing were criminal offenders; 44 percent were status offenders. These findings are similar to the population of Lansing as a whole in the 1890s. See Michigan State Reform School, *Biennial Report* (Lansing, 1890), 12; Michigan State Reform School,

*Biennial Report* (1892), 234; Michigan Industrial School for Boys, *Biennial Report* (1894), 18; Michigan Industrial School for Boys, *Biennial Report* (1896), 17.

50. Bolt, *Juvenile Offenders,* 49–55.

51. *DFP* (January 22, 1907); *DFP* (January 24, 1907).

52. For boys sent to the Lansing reform school by recorder's court, $n = 7/27$; for status offenders sent to Lansing by recorder's court, $n = 5/11$. For James Roberts, see *DFP* (January 22, 1907); *DFP* (January 24, 1907).

53. $N = 102$. I have interpreted the police and recorder's courts as one entity in discussions of girls' cases. Only five girls were referred to the recorder's court in the 1890s sample, and the courts performed similar functions, so it makes sense to analyze them together.

54. Forty-five percent of girls accused of criminal offenses were discharged; 34 percent had sentences suspended. $N = 47$.

55. $N = 28$.

56. *DFP* (May 3, 1907).

57. DPD, General and Special Orders (May 10, 1898), PDC, BHC; DPD, *33rd Annual Report* (1898), 52; DPD, *36th Annual Report* (1901), 47–48; DPD, *42nd Annual Report* (1907), 62.

58. DPD, *39th Annual Report* (1904), 71; *DFP* (July 12, 1908); *DFP* (May 12, 1907).

59. All discussion of arrests between 1890 and 1896 is derived from analysis of arrests in 1890, 1893, and 1896 in my Detroit juvenile arrest database, while discussions of arrests between 1900 and 1906 is based on arrests in 1900, 1903, and 1906. Juvenile populations interpolated from U.S. Census Office, *Population at the 11th Census: 1890,* 119; U.S. Census Office, *12th Census; 1900 Population,* 128; and U.S. Census Bureau, *13th Census; Population 1910,* 453.

60. Total male arrest rates were calculated from data published in DPD, *Annual Reports* (1891–96, 1898–1907). In her analysis of the Detroit police between 1880 and 1918, Reed similarly found a sharp decline in total arrest rates from a peak in the late 1880s to a low point in the early 1900s. See Reed, "Regulating the Regulators," 205–16.

61. Calculated from my Detroit juvenile arrest database.

62. Ibid.

63. DPD, *40th Annual Report* (1905), 51; DPD, *41st Annual Report* (1906), 48; DPD, *42nd Annual Report* (1907), 62.

64. Michigan, *Laws Relating to Board of Corrections,* 41–42; Bolt, *Juvenile Offenders,* 35–37.

65. As with girls' cases throughout this analysis, these two courts have been treated as one for boys' cases between 1900 and 1906. They performed similar functions, plus only nine boys' cases were referred to recorder's court in these years.

66. The police and recorder's courts together discharged 27 percent of boys between 1900 and 1906, as compared to 26 percent between 1890 and 1896. They sentenced 25 percent to a fine or jail between 1900 and 1906, 22 percent between 1890 and 1896. They committed 11 percent to reform school between 1900 and 1906, 12 percent between 1890 and 1896.

67. The police and recorder's courts together discharged 31 percent of girls between 1900 and 1906, as compared to 32 percent between 1890 and 1896. They suspended 25 percent of girls' sentences in the 1900s, as compared to 28 percent between 1890 and 1896.

68. The increase in committals to reform schools occurred in exchange for a decrease

in fines or jail sentences for girls, which fell from 24 percent of dispositions in the 1890s to 15 percent in the 1900s.

69. Between 1890 and 1896, 73 of 169 boys between ages eight and fourteen whose cases were heard by police courts and the recorder's court were granted suspended sentences. Between 1900 and 1906, 54 of 166 were granted suspended sentences.

70. The use of probation was concentrated later in the period. All fifteen probation dispositions were in 1906. Probation in fact accounted for 31 percent (*n* = 14/45) of court dispositions of eight- to fourteen-year-olds in that year. Probation was also mainly confined to boys. The Detroit juvenile arrest database includes only three girls who were placed on probation, all in 1906.

71. *DFP* (March 17, 1907); see also *DFP* (March 8, 1907).

72. *DFP* (February 13, 1908).

73. *DFP* (March 17, 1907); *DFP* (September 20, 1908).

# Notes to Chapter 4

1. DPD, *Story of the Detroit Police*, 41.

2. On Couzens, see Harry Barnard, *Independent Man: The Life of Senator James Couzens* (New York: Charles Scribner's Sons, 1958), esp. 107–12; Robert Lacey, *Ford: The Men and the Machine* (Boston: Little, Brown, 1986), esp. 68–79, 115–26. On Couzens's approach to policing, see DPD, *Story of the Detroit Police*.

3. Walker, *Critical History of Police Reform*, 53–78; quote from 53; Fogelson, *Big-City Police*, 40–91; Johnson, *American Law Enforcement*, 64–71, 115–17. On urban progressivism more generally, see Samuel P. Hays, "The Politics of Reform in Municipal Government in the Progressive Era," *Pacific Northwest Quarterly* 55 (1964): 157–69; Arthur S. Link and Richard L. McCormick, *Progressivism* (Arlington Heights, IL: Harlan Davidson, 1983), esp. 47–50.

4. On the social reform side of progressivism, see Link and McCormick, *Progressivism*, 67–104; Linda Gordon, *Heroes of Their Own Lives: The Politics and History of Family Violence, Boston 1880–1960* (New York: Viking, 1988), esp. 59–81; Michael McGerr, *A Fierce Discontent: The Rise and Fall of the Progressive Movement in America, 1870–1920* (New York: Free Press, 2003).

5. James Austin and Barry Krisberg, "Wider, Stronger, and Different Nets: The Dialectics of Criminal Justice Reform," *Journal of Research in Crime and Delinquency* 18 (January 1981): 165–96, quote from 169; Walker, *Sense and Nonsense about Crime and Drugs*, 213–14.

6. Bolt, *Juvenile Offenders*, 36–37.

7. *DFP* (December 15, 1900); *DFP* (January 16, 1907); *DFP* (January 20, 1907); Downs, *Michigan Juvenile Court*, 45–46.

8. H. A. Gilmartin, "Court for Juveniles," *DFP* (March 20, 1907); *DFP* (April 18, 1907); *DFP* (May 16, 1907); *DFP* (May 21, 1907).

9. *DFP* (June 30, 1907); *DFP* (July 25, 1907). The comparative ease of passing juvenile court legislation in Michigan in 1907 stands out in contrast to the earlier difficulty of enacting a juvenile court law in Illinois. See Getis, *Juvenile Court and the Progressives*, 28–52; Tanenhaus, *Juvenile Justice in the Making*, 3–22.

10. Michigan, *Laws Relating to Juvenile Courts,* 5–14. DPD, *Story of the Detroit Police,* 291–92.

11. "In the Juvenile Court," *DFP* (October 27, 1907); *DFP* (December 20, 1908); Bertha V. O'Brien, "Boys Who 'Made Good' Are Now Graduated," *DFP* (January 5, 1909). On Judge Lindsey's approach, see Judge Ben B. Lindsey, "The Juvenile Court of Denver," in *Children's Courts in the United States: Their Origins, Development, and Results,* ed. Samuel J. Barrows (Washington, DC: Government Printing Office, 1904), 28–46; Lindsey, "The Boy and The Court."

12. "In the Juvenile Court," *DFP* (October 27, 1907). See also *DFP* (December 8, 1907); *DFP* (December 15, 1907); *DFP* (April 19, 1908); *DFP* (May 24, 1908); *DFP* (June 10, 1908); *DFP* (June 27, 1907).

13. "In the Juvenile Court," *DFP* (October 27, 1907); *DFP* (March 22, 1908); *DFP* (May 3, 1908).

14. *DFP* (June 1, 1908).

15. *DFP* (August 18, 1908); *DFP* (September 13, 1908); *DFP* (November 8, 1908); *DFP* (December 9, 1908).

16. *DFP* (December 6, 1908); *DFP* (December 11, 1908). On Hudson, see "Hudson, Joseph Lowthian," in *The National Cyclopaedia of American Biography,* vol. 47 (New York: James T. White, 1965), 221–22.

17. *DFP* (November 22, 1908); *DFP* (November 23, 1908); *DFP* (December 5, 1908); *DFP* (January 11, 1909).

18. "Children's Court Enters New Home," *Detroit News* (March 29, 1916); DPD, *Story of the Detroit Police,* 290–91.

19. Hulbert, "Detroit's Juvenile Court," 22–23.

20. DPD, *43rd Annual Report* (1908), 53; Michigan, *Laws Relating to Juvenile Courts,* 12.

21. Calculated from DPD, *Annual Reports,* 1909–18, 1920–28, 1930–40.

22. Michigan Industrial School for Boys, *Biennial Report* (Lansing, 1908), 7.

23. Calculated from Michigan Industrial School for Boys, *Biennial Reports,* 1900–1918.

24. $N = 1,116$. Percentages do not total 100 due to rounding and a small number of miscellaneous dispositions. Calculated from DPD, *Annual Reports,* 1898–1907.

25. $N = 2,657$. Calculated from DPD, *Annual Reports,* 1909–18.

26. Calculated from DPD, *Annual Reports,* 1898–1918.

27. Calculated from Michigan Industrial School for Boys, *Biennial Reports,* 1900–18.

28. Zunz, *Changing Face of Inequality,* 286–87; Thomas, *Life for Us Is What We Make It,* 24–26.

29. On the rise of the "service city," see Monkkonen, *America Becomes Urban.*

30. Walker, *Critical History of Police Reform,* 56–61; Fogelson, *Big-City Police,* 49–66; Johnson, *American Law Enforcement,* 64–71. On Detroit commissioners, see DPD, *69th Annual Report* (1935), 9.

31. Walker, *Critical History of Police Reform,* 59–61; Fogelson, *Big-City Police,* 44–45, 53. On municipal reform more generally, see Raymond H. Mohl, *The New City: Urban America in the Industrial Age, 1860–1920* (Arlington Heights, IL: Harlan Davidson, 1985), 108–37; Chudacoff and Smith, *Evolution of American Urban Society,* 174–80, 202–5.

32. Jane S. Dahlberg, *The New York Bureau of Municipal Research: Pioneer in*

*Government Administration* (New York: New York University Press, 1966), 39–43, 47–48; Frederick Winslow Taylor, *The Principles of Scientific Management* (1911; New York: W. W. Norton, 1967).

33. DPD, *Story of the Detroit Police,* 55, 91, 92; Reed, "Regulating the Regulators," 121–31.

34. DPD, *Training School for Police Service,* revised ed. (1911; Detroit: Police Department, 1921), 2. On the new model Detroit policeman, see also DPD, *Story of the Detroit Police,* 68–70; Reed, "Regulating the Regulators," 61–79.

35. DPD, *Story of the Detroit Police,* 13, 239; Lacey, *Ford,* 166–67.

36. "Patrolmen Specializing Too," *Detroit Police News* 2 (February 1915): 5; DPD, *Story of the Detroit Police,* 80–83, 86–88, 99–109. For Taylor's views on specialization and division of duties, see *Principles of Scientific Management,* esp. 89–90, 98–99, 125–28.

37. DPD, *Story of the Detroit Police,* 10, 13, 19–20; *New York Times* (October 7, 1916) [hereafter cited as *NYT*]; Taylor, *Principles of Scientific Management,* 44–48, 74–77, 119–22.

38. DPD, *Story of the Detroit Police,* 238–41, 44–48; Taylor, *Principles of Scientific Management,* 25–26 and passim. On the scientific method in sociology, see Getis, *Juvenile Court and the Progressives,* 20–21, 80–82.

39. Dorothy Moses Schulz, *From Social Worker to Crime Fighter: Women in United States Municipal Policing* (Westport, CT: Praeger, 1995), 1–6, 21–36; quote from 23. See also Appier, *Policing Women,* esp. 22–33; Walker, *Critical History of Police Reform,* 84–94.

40. DPD, *56th Annual Report* (1922), 9; "Morals Squad Urged for City," *Detroit News* (February 18, 1920); Virginia M. Murray, "Policewomen in Detroit," *The American City* 25 (August 1921): 209–10. On police matrons, see Bennett, "New Dynamics and Philosophy in Detention Home Care," 97.

41. DPD, *48th Annual Report* (1914), 7–8; DPD, *Story of the Detroit Police,* 75–76. See also Ethel M. Westcott, "The Wayne County Juvenile Court" (M.A. thesis, Wayne University, 1936), 7.

42. Richard Sylvester, "Principles of Police Administration," *Journal of Criminal Law and Criminology* 1 (September 1910): 411; DPD, *Story of the Detroit Police,* 14–17; Walker, *Critical History of Police Reform,* 53–54.

43. Henry Bruere, "The Police as Social Workers," *American City* 10 (March 1914): 282; "The Police as Social Workers," *The Outlook* 108 (December 16, 1914): 861.

44. Woods, an associate of one-time Police Commissioner Theodore Roosevelt and William Howard Taft, had covered the police as a reporter for the *New York Evening Sun* in the 1900s and served as a deputy police commissioner between 1907 and 1909. After leaving the NYPD in 1918, Woods subsequently served in the federal government under both Democratic and Republican administrations, concluding his career as the chair of the Depression-era President's Committee for Employment between 1929 and 1931. See "Arthur Woods, 72, Is Dead in Capital," *NYT* (May 13, 1942); "Woods, Arthur," in *The Encyclopedia of New York City,* ed. Kenneth T. Jackson (New Haven, CT: Yale University Press, 1995), 1273.

45. Arthur Woods, *Crime Prevention* (Princeton, NJ: Princeton University Press, 1918), 105, 109–11, 118–20; "The New York City Junior Police," *The Outlook* 113 (July 12, 1916): 588.

46. Woods, *Crime Prevention,* 106–9, 112; "New York City Junior Police," 588; "The Kid Cops," *Literary Digest* 50 (February 20, 1915): 396–97; Alfred J. Kahn, *Police and*

*Children: A Study of the Juvenile Aid Bureau of the New York City Police Department* (New York: Citizens' Committee on Children, 1951), 12. "The City Child, Playgrounds, and the Police," *The Outlook* 113 (May 3, 1916).

47. DPD, *Story of the Detroit Police*, 230, 17, 5, 7.

48. Ibid., 230–31, 17.

49. Ibid., 322–23, 8; Detroit *Tribune* (December 19, 1915); Detroit *Tribune* (December 22, 1915); Detroit *News* (December 15, 1915).

50. Sherman C. Kingsley, *A Study of the Juvenile Court and Detention Home of Wayne County, Michigan* (1928; Glen Rock, NJ: Microfilming Corporation of America, 1976; microfiche), 1, 7–8, 10, 22–24.

51. Thomas, *Life for Us Is What We Make It,* 20–35; Zunz, *Changing Face of Inequality,* 318–22, 374–98; Sugrue, *Origins of the Urban Crisis,* 23.

52. Reed, "Regulating the Regulators," 96–109; Dulaney, *Black Police in America,* 20–26; Mayor's Inter-Racial Committee, *The Negro in Detroit,* Part IX: *Crime* (Detroit Bureau of Governmental Research, 1926), 38.

53. DPD, *Story of the Detroit Police,* 7, 14.

54. $N = 37{,}764$. Ibid., 59.

55. DPD, *55th Annual Report* (1921), 1–2; James W. Inches, "Increased Police Force Checks Crime," *The American City* 24 (June 1921): 589–90; Arch Mandel, "Why Crime Decreased in Detroit," *The American City* 27 (August 1922): 149–52.

56. "Detroit Negroes Facing Acute Police Situation" (January 21, 1927); "Detroit Policeman Charged with Wanton Killing of Negro" (April 29, 1927); Walter White to Dr. Robert L. Bradby, Jan. 25, 1927; all in the National Association for the Advancement of Colored People Papers, Part 12, Series C, Reel 12, Frames 313–16 (Washington, DC: Library of Congress, microfilm).

57. Mayor's Inter-Racial Committee, *Negro in Detroit,* Part IX: *Crime,* 25–37. See also Walter White, "Negro Segregation Comes North," *The Nation* 121 (October 21, 1925): 458–60. Historical studies of Detroit's African American community in the 1920s also emphasize police brutality; see Thomas, *Life for Us Is What We Make It,* 164–66; David Allen Levine, *Internal Combustion: The Races in Detroit, 1915–1926* (Westport, CT: Greenwood Press, 1976), esp. 63–64; Victoria W. Wolcott, *Remaking Respectability: African American Women in Interwar Detroit* (Chapel Hill: University of North Carolina Press, 2001), 111–12.

58. Calculated from data in Kingsley, *Juvenile Court and Detention Home,* 33–34.

59. Mayor's Inter-Racial Committee, *The Negro in Detroit,* Part IX: *Crime,* 44.

# NOTES TO CHAPTER 5

1. "A short interview with Officer O'Connor," 1926, Ernest W. Burgess Papers, box 37, folder 2, Special Collections, Joseph Regenstein Library, University of Chicago.

2. Everett Hughes, "The Person Policeman as a Person," typescript, 1925, in Burgess Papers, box 131, folder 4.

3. Hughes, "Policeman as a Person." See also Haller, "Historical Roots of Police Behavior."

4. Hurley, *Origin of the Illinois Juvenile Court Law,* 23–24, 33–34, 56, 60–61; Mack, "The Juvenile Court," 104–22. Tuthill is quoted in "New Court Begins Work," *Chicago*

*Tribune* (July 4, 1899). The continued rehabilitative ideals of juvenile court today are evident in works such as William Ayers, *A Kind and Just Parent: The Children of Juvenile Court* (Boston: Beacon Press, 1997).

5. Carl Schurz Lowden, "Chicago, the Nation's Crime Centre," *Current History* 28 (September 1928): 892–98; David E. Ruth, *Inventing the Public Enemy: The Gangster in American Culture, 1918–1934* (Chicago: University of Chicago Press, 1996), 120–43. On Chicago policing, see Haller, "Civic Reformers and Police Leadership"; Lindberg, *To Serve and Collect.*

6. "New Court Begins Work," *Chicago Tribune* (July 4, 1899).

7. "A short interview with Officer O'Connor," 1926, Ernest W. Burgess Papers.

8. Tanenhaus, *Juvenile Justice in the Making;* Clapp, *Mothers of All Children;* Getis, *Juvenile Court and the Progressives;* Dodge, "'Our Juvenile Court Has Become More Like a Criminal Court'"; Knupfer, *Reform and Resistance.*

9. Hurley, *Origin of the Juvenile Court Law,* 9–26, 60.

10. Tuthill, "History of the Children's Court in Chicago," 1; Hastings H. Hart, ed., *Juvenile Court Laws in the United States* (New York: Russell Sage Foundation, 1910), 26–27.

11. Calculated from data compiled from the Cook County Juvenile Court *Annual Reports* by Anne Meis Knupfer. See Knupfer, *Reform and Resistance,* 182–83, 186–87.

12. Mennel, *Thorns and Thistles,* 135. For alternative views emphasizing female reformers and delinquents, see Clapp, *Mothers of All Children,* and Knupfer, *Reform and Resistance.*

13. "In the Juvenile Court," *DFP* (October 27, 1907); Tuthill quoted in Mennel, *Thorns and Thistles,* 135; Lindsey, "Juvenile Court of Denver," 28–46.

14. Mabel Carter Rhoades, "A Case Study of Delinquent Boys in the Juvenile Court of Chicago" (Ph.D. diss., University of Chicago, 1907), 6. On sociological studies of juvenile court, see Getis, *Juvenile Court and the Progressives,* 53–64; Knupfer, *Reform and Resistance,* 18–34.

15. Breckinridge and Abbott, *Delinquent Child and the Home,* esp. 45–47, 60–61.

16. In 1910, foreign-born whites and whites with foreign-born parents constituted 78 percent of Chicago's population, and 75 percent of the population under age twenty. African Americans, by contrast, were brought to court more often than their small share of the population would predict. Roughly 4 percent of boys in juvenile court, blacks constituted 2 percent of Chicago's population in 1910, and 1.2 percent of the population under age twenty. Populations calculated from data in U.S. Census Bureau, *13th Census; Population 1910,* 439.

17. Charles R. Henderson, "Juvenile Courts: Problems of Administration," *Charities* 13 (January 7, 1905): 342; Lathrop, "Development of the Probation System," 345; Cook County Juvenile Court and Juvenile Detention Home, *Annual Report for 1907* (Chicago: 1908), 111 [hereafter cited as "CCJC, *Annual Reports*"]. On the early operations of juvenile court, see Tanenhaus, *Juvenile Justice in the Making,* 23–54.

18. "Testimony of Judge Merritt W. Pinckney," in Breckinridge and Abbott, *Delinquent Child and the Home,* 240–41. See also Henderson, "Juvenile Courts," 342; Lathrop, "Development of the Probation System," 345; Hurley, *Origin of the Juvenile Court Law,* 17.

19. Jeter, *Chicago Juvenile Court,* 32–33.

20. CCJC, *Annual Reports for 1909,* 15; CCJC, *Annual Reports for 1923,* 21.

21. Henderson, "Juvenile Courts," 342.

22. Gertrude Howe Britten to Harry E. Smoot, July 14, 1909, Juvenile Protective Association Papers, Folder 16, located at the University of Illinois at Chicago Special Collections (hereafter cited as JPA Papers).

23. CCJC, *Annual Report for 1909,* 6.

24. Haller, "Civic Reformers and Police Leadership: Chicago, 1905–1935"; Haller, "Historical Roots of Police Behavior." On reformers' social origins, see also Fogelson, *Big-City Police,* 40–65.

25. In 1909, twelve of thirty-one PPOs had Irish surnames; in 1928, this was the case for nine of twenty-nine. PPOs in 1909 listed in Britten to Smoot, JPA Papers; PPOs in 1928 listed in Chicago Police Department, *Annual Report* (1928), 57, and ethnic extraction of names derived from Patrick Harris and Flavia Hodge, *A Dictionary of Surnames* (Oxford: Oxford University Press, 1988).

26. Jeter, *Chicago Juvenile Court,* 32–33; CCJC, *Annual Reports for 1915,* 10; CCJC, *Annual Reports for 1917,* 7.

27. Citizens' Police Committee, *Chicago Police Problems* (Chicago: University of Chicago Press, 1931), 169–71; quotes from 170.

28. Citizens' Police Committee, *Chicago Police Problems,* 89–93.

29. Reports of Merriam's investigators located in the Charles E. Merriam Papers, Box 87, Special Collections, Joseph Regenstein Library, University of Chicago; quotation from folder 4, Informant B, July 29, 1914. See also Haller, "Civic Reformers and Police Leadership," 39–56; Mark H. Haller, "Urban Crime and Criminal Justice: The Chicago Case," *Journal of American History* 57 (December 1970): 619–35; and Lindberg, *To Serve and Collect,* 126–29.

30. Graham Taylor, "The Police and Vice in Chicago," *The Survey* 23 (November 26, 1909): 60–65; H. M. Campbell, John M. Flynn, and Elton Lower, "The Chicago Police: Report of the Chicago Civil Service Commission, *"Journal of Criminal Law and Criminology* 3 (May 1912): 62–84. Steward is quoted in Lindberg, *To Serve and Collect,* 128.

31. Chicago Police Department, *Annual Report, Year Ending December 31st, 1928* (Chicago, 1929), 59. See also Haller, "Civic Reformers and Police Leadership," 40.

32. "Disciplining Chicago's Police," *The Survey* 23 (February 12, 1910): 695; Graham Taylor, "Police Efficiency the First Effect of Vice Inquiries," *The Survey* 28 (April 22, 1912): 136–41.

33. Haller, "Civic Reformers and Police Leadership"; Haller, "Urban Crime and Criminal Justice," 630–32; Lindberg, *To Serve and Collect,* 137–84; August Vollmer, "The Police (in Chicago)," in *The Illinois Crime Survey,* ed. Illinois Association for Criminal Justice (1929; Montclair, NJ: Patterson Smith, 1968), 358–65.

34. Mrs. Joseph T. Bowen, "The Policeman with a Wink: His Menace to Youth as Shown in the Present Chicago Administration," *The Survey* 43 (January 24, 1920): 458–59. These investigations are documented in the JPA Papers, especially folders 73 and 104.

35. Citizens' Police Committee, *Chicago Police Problems,* 174–76; "Chicago's Policewomen," *The Outlook* 104 (August 30, 1913); Schulz, *From Social Worker to Crime Fighter,* 27–28, 68–69, 88.

36. Jeter, *Chicago Juvenile Court,* 32–33, 40–41. PPOs were to investigate only boys, not girls. The Chicago police were specifically instructed, "a wayward girl shall be reported

to the commanding officer to be referred to a patrolwoman or the appropriate juvenile authority." See Chicago Police Department, *Rules and Regulations of the Police Department of the City of Chicago* (Chicago, 1933), 111.

37. Tanenhaus, *Juvenile Justice in the Making*, 47–49.

38. CCJC, *Annual Reports for 1915*, 9.

39. Jeter, *Chicago Juvenile Court*, 32–33, 36–41; quotes from 40. See also CCJC, *Annual Reports for 1918*, 15; "Testimony of Judge Merritt W. Pinckney," 206–7, 240–41.

40. Jeter, *Chicago Juvenile Court*, 36. Police probation officers filed 18,640 of 22,609 delinquency petitions between 1918 and 1926. In these years, the juvenile court received a total of 48,605 petitions. Calculated from data in Chicago Police Department, *Annual Reports* (1918–26); CCJC, *Annual Reports for 1923*, 22; and CCJC, *Annual Reports for 1926*, 16.

41. The Chicago police did not differentiate complaints against boys and girls, so both sexes are included in this calculation. Because recorded delinquency tends to be far more common among boys than among girls, we should assume that the delinquency rate was substantially higher for boys and lower for girls.

42. Calculated from data in Chicago Police Department, *Annual Reports*, 1919–30. The *Annual Report* for 1918 does not specify juvenile offenses.

43. Calculated from data in ibid., 1918–30. The lowest proportion for any year was 85 percent, while the highest share was 92 percent. The frequency with which police adjusted complaints against juveniles was also noted in Jeter, *Chicago Juvenile Court*, 40–41; Clifford R. Shaw and Earl D. Myers, "The Juvenile Delinquent," in *The Illinois Crime Survey*, ed. Illinois Association for Criminal Justice (1929; Montclair, NJ: Patterson-Smith, 1967), 678; and Citizens' Police Committee, *Chicago Police Problems*, 172–73.

44. Britten to Smoot, July 14, 1909, 4–5.

45. CCJC, *Annual Reports for 1909*, 5. The police probation officers' duty to adjust cases is explained in Chicago Police Department, *Rules and Regulations* (1933), 94.

46. CCJC, *Report of the Juvenile Court of the fiscal year ending November 13, 1913* (Chicago, 1914), 99.

47. Victor Arnold, "The Juvenile Court," in *Proceedings of the 33rd Annual Convention of the IACP* (1926), 191.

48. CCJC, *Annual Reports for 1910*, 11.

49. Chicago Police Department, *Book of Rules and Regulations of the Department of Police of the City of Chicago* (Chicago, 1905), 59; Hart, *Juvenile Court Laws*, 28–29; Jeter, *Chicago Juvenile Court*, 9, 49–51; CCJC, *Annual Reports for 1919*, 19. On Chicago Detention Homes, see also Knupfer, *Reform and Resistance*, 99–118.

50. CCJC, *Annual Reports for 1918*, 10–11; Jeter, *Chicago Juvenile Court*, 51–52

51. CCJC, *Annual Reports for 1923*, 16.

52. Shaw and Myers, "Juvenile Delinquent," 680–81; CCJC, *Annual Reports for 1926*, 64–77; quote from 77. See also Florence M. Warner, *Juvenile Detention in the United States: Report of a Field Survey of the NPA* (Chicago: University of Chicago Press, 1933).

53. Clifford R. Shaw with Maurice E. Moore, *The Natural History of a Delinquent Career* (1931; New York: Greenwood Press, 1968), 67. In the late 1920s and early 1930s, University of Chicago sociology graduate student Clifford R. Shaw, via his affiliation with the Illinois Institute for Juvenile Research, secured the "life histories" of over 100 delinquents. Publications based on the "life histories" include Shaw, *Natural History*; Clifford R. Shaw, *The Jack-Roller: A Delinquent Boy's Own Story* (1930; Chicago: University of

Chicago Press, 1966); and Clifford R. Shaw with Henry D. McKay and James F. McDonald, *Brothers in Crime* (Chicago: University of Chicago Press, 1938). Approximately 130 additional unpublished "life histories" are currently located at the Chicago Historical Society. In creating these accounts, boys responded to standard questions, wrote individual autobiographies, and participated in interviews with Shaw or his associates, usually either at the IJR offices on Chicago's Near West Side or in juvenile correctional facilities. The "authors" were almost all white males; only one was identifiable as being African American and two were female. The "life histories" are also undated and usually omit important data such as the boys' ages. Some of this information, however, has been inferred from context. In particular, my sense that all the events described in this chapter took place in the 1920s is derived from internal evidence, the initial funding of the life history project by the Social Science Research Council in 1927, and the publication of works derived from the project in the 1930s. On the IJR and the origins of the "life histories," see Getis, *Juvenile Court and the Progressives,* esp. 101–2, and James Bennett, *Oral History and Delinquency: The Rhetoric of Criminology* (Chicago: University of Chicago Press, 1981), 277–82.

54. Here, and throughout this book, I have replaced names from confidential records with pseudonyms in order to protect subjects' anonymity. I indicate this by placing the first mention of these names in italics.

55. Illinois Institute for Juvenile Research Life Histories (hereafter cited as IJR Life Histories), box 3, folder 7, located at the Chicago Historical Society; IJR Life Histories, box 10, folder 4.

56. Calculated from Chicago Police Department, *Annual Report* (1918–30).

57. Britten to Smoot, July 14, 1909, 4. See also Jeter, *Chicago Juvenile Court,* 41; Citizens' Police Committee, *Chicago Police Problems,* 172–74.

58. Calculated from data in Chicago Police Department, *Annual Reports,* 1928–30. Frequent changes in district boundaries prevent a comparison of petitions for earlier years. The Chicago Police Department established a consistent system of forty districts that I have been able to identify only beginning in the 1928 fiscal year. For district boundaries, see Citizens' Police Committee, *Chicago Police Problems,* 91, 261–65.

59. The neighborhood is described in Shaw, *Natural History,* 13–25; quotations from 13 and 14. See also Jane Addams, *Twenty Years at Hull-House* (1910; New York: N A L, 1999). The Maxwell Street police district (No. 22) was bounded on the north by Harrison Street, on the south by 16th Street, on the east by the Chicago River, and on the west by Ashland Avenue. See Citizens' Police Committee, *Chicago Police Problems,* 263.

60. Calculated from data in Chicago Police Department, *Annual Reports,* 1928–30.

61. Rates of complaints investigated were calculated from data on complaints investigated, tabulated by district, in Chicago Police Department, *Annual Reports* (1928–30). The juvenile populations in each police district were determined by matching the 935 census tracts reported in 1930 with the forty extant police districts, then tabulating the population of all juveniles (boys and girls) between ten and seventeen in each district. Population data from Ernest W. Burgess and Charles Newcomb, eds., *Census Data of the City of Chicago, 1930* (Chicago: University of Chicago Press, 1933).

62. IJR Life Histories, box 13, folder 3, 19–20. See also IJR Life Histories, box 15, folder 14 and box 16, folder 4, which both describe this incident. The "42" gang was studied extensively by the IJR, which operated in the same neighborhood. See in particular IJR Life Histories, box 3, folder 8; box 3, folder 9; box 4, folder 4; box 8, folder 8; box 10,

folder 4; box 10, folder 6; box 4, folder 7; box 13, folder 3; box 13, folder 6; box 16, folder 4, and John Landesco, "Member of the 42 Gang," *Journal of Criminal Law and Criminology* 23 (March 1933): 964–98. In the 1920s, Chicago was widely noted as the home of hundreds of youth gangs, which also became objects of study for University of Chicago sociologists. See Frederic M. Thrasher, *The Gang: A Study of 1,313 Gangs in Chicago* (Chicago: University of Chicago Press, 1927).

63. The Wabash Avenue police district (No. 5) was bounded on the north by 39th Street, on the south by 60th Street, on the east by Cottage Grove Ave., and on the west by the Chicago Rock Island and the Penn Central Railroads. See Citizens' Police Committee, *Chicago Police Problems*, 261.

64. Grossman, *Land of Hope;* U.S. Bureau of the Census, *Fifteenth Census of the United States: 1930; Population,* vol. II: *General Report Statistics by Subjects* (Washington, DC: Government Printing Office, 1933), 726.

65. Grossman, *Land of Hope;* Glen E. Holt and Dominic A. Pacyga, *Chicago: A Historical Guide to the Neighborhoods: The Loop and the South Side* (Chicago: Chicago Historical Society, 1979), 88–91. This rather astonishing change in the racial composition of District No. 5's population is confirmed by data from Burgess and Newcomb, eds., *Census Data of Chicago, 1930,* 618.

66. Calculated from data in Chicago Police Department, *Annual Reports,* 1928–30, and Burgess and Newcomb, eds., *Census Data of Chicago, 1930.*

67. Moses, *Negro Delinquent in Chicago,* 13–19.

68. Ibid., 12–19, 112–16.

69. For an introduction to this literature, see National Research Council, *Juvenile Crime, Juvenile Justice,* 228–60.

70. "Interview with Goldblatt's Detective," April 13, 1934, in Mary E. McDowell Papers, folder 10, Chicago Historical Society.

71. IJR Life Histories, box 15, folder 13, 10–11.

72. Ibid., box 4, folder 1, 4.

73. MacMurray, "Introduction," unpublished manuscript, circa. 1935, Chicago Area Project Records (hereafter cited as CAP Records), box 95, folder 12, 28, located at the Chicago Historical Society. On the Chicago Area Project itself, see Ernest W. Burgess, Joseph D. Lohman, and Clifford R. Shaw, "The Chicago Area Project," in *Coping with Crime: Yearbook of the NPA,* ed. Marjorie Bell (New York, 1937), 8–28; Solomon Kobrin, "The Chicago Area Project—A 25-Year Assessment," *Annals of the American Academy of Political and Social Sciences* 322 (March 1959): 19–29. On the operation of CAP in the 1930s, see Harold Finestone, *Victims of Change: Juvenile Delinquents in American Society* (Westport, CT: Greenwood Press, 1976), 116–50; Steven L. Schlossman and Michael Sedlak, "The Chicago Area Project Revisited," *Crime and Delinquency* 26 (July 1983): 398–462; Dominic A. Pacyga, "The Russell Square Community Committee: An Ethnic Response to Urban Problems," *Journal of Urban History* 15 (February 1989): 159–84.

74. IJR Life Histories, box 13, folder 5.

75. Hughes, "Policeman as a Person."

76. National Commission on Law Observance and Enforcement [Wickersham Commission]. *Report No. 11: Lawlessness in Law Enforcement* (1931; Montclair, NJ: Patterson Smith, 1968), 125. See also Marilynn S. Johnson, *Street Justice: A History of Police Violence in New York City* (Boston: Beacon Press, 2003), esp. 122–42.

77. IJR Life Histories, box 5, folder 2, p. 58. Other examples may be seen in IJR Life

Histories, box 3, folder 13, p. 5; box 15, folder 12, p. 21; box 7, folder 2, p. 7; box 3, folder 5, p. 14.

78. For example, see IJR Life Histories, box 4, folder 4. Police used their firearms so often that the press occasionally criticized them for accidentally shooting innocent civilians. Critics perceived guns as a crutch used by inefficient police officers. See "Stop Reckless Shooting," *The Outlook* 149 (May 23, 1928): 141. The police, in turn, regarded firearms as tools to fight an outbreak of robbery-homicides in the early twentieth century. In Chicago alone, police officers shot and killed seventy-six "hold-up men" between 1900 and 1920. See Jeffrey S. Adler, "'On the Borders of Snakeland': Evolutionary Psychology and Plebian Violence in Industrial Chicago, 1875–1920," *Journal of Social History* 36 (Spring 2003): 551; Roger Lane, *Murder in America: A History* (Columbus: The Ohio State University Press, 1997), 331.

79. John L. Brown, "Diary of the Area Representative" (1938), CAP Records, box 108, folder 12, 24. Further examples of police using firearms against juveniles may be found in IJR Life Histories, box 3, folder 3, p. 24; box 3, folder 8, p. 15; box 4, folder18; box 4, folder 23; box 5, folder 15; p. 19; box 13, folder 3; box 16, folder 4; "The Ways of Cops," box 16, folder 6, p. 5.

80. IJR Life Histories, box 5, folder 15.

81. Shaw, *Natural History,* 89.

82. IJR Life Histories, box 12, folder 11.

83. Ibid., box 10, folder 4.

84. Shaw, *Jack-Roller,* 51–55.

85. IJR Life Histories, box 8, folder 5, 19.

86. Ibid., box 13, folder 3. See also box 13, folder 5.

87. Ibid., box 15, folder 3.

88. Ibid., box 3, folder 13.

89. Ibid., box 9, folder 8, 54–60.

90. "The Ways of Cops," IJR Life Histories, box 16, folder 6.

## NOTES TO CHAPTER 6

1. August Vollmer, "The Policeman as a Social Worker," in *IACP, Proceedings 26th Convention* (1919), 32–38.

2. On Vollmer, see Gene E. Carte and Elaine H. Carte, *Police Reform in the United States: The Era of August Vollmer, 1905–1932* (Berkeley: University of California Press, 1975); Julia Liss and Steven Schlossman, "The Contours of Crime Prevention in August Vollmer's Berkeley," *Research in Law, Deviance, and Social Control* 6 (1984): 79–107.

3. Many prominent delinquency prevention programs are discussed in Sheldon Glueck and Eleanor Glueck, eds., *Preventing Crime: A Symposium* (New York: McGraw-Hill, 1936).

4. Carte and Carte, *Police Reform,* esp. 17–30; Liss and Schlossman, "Contours of Crime Prevention"; Walker, *Critical History of Police Reform,* 72–73.

5. Anne Roller, "Vollmer and his College Cops," *The Survey* 62 (1929): 304–7; Carte and Carte, *Police Reform,* esp. 40–50; Walker, *Critical History of Police Reform,* 72–73, 136–37.

6. August Vollmer, "Aims and Ideals of the Police," in *Journal of the American*

*Institute of Law and Criminology: Selected Articles* (1922; New York: Arno Press, 1971), 251–57; Roller, "Vollmer and his College Cops," 304–7; Carte and Carte, *Police Reform,* esp. 40–50; Liss and Schlossman, "Contours of Crime Prevention," 81–89.

7. Getis, *Juvenile Court and the Progressives,* 64–78; Margo Horn, *Before It's Too Late: The Child Guidance Movement in the United States, 1922–1945* (Philadelphia: Temple University Press, 1989); Schneider, *In the Web of Class,* 170–80; Tanenhaus, *Juvenile Justice in the Making,* 111–37. William Healy articulated his findings in *The Individual Delinquent* (1915; Montclair, NJ: Patterson Smith, 1969).

8. August Vollmer, "Predelinquency," *Journal of Criminal Law and Criminology* 14 (August 1923): 279–283; August Vollmer, *The Police in Modern Society* (Berkeley: University of California Press, 1936), 198–99; Elizabeth Lossing, "The Crime Prevention Work of the Berkeley Police Department," in *Preventing Crime,* ed. Glueck and Glueck, 240–41; Liss and Schlossman, "Contours of Crime Prevention," 89–93.

9. Getis, *Juvenile Court and the Progressives,* 106–16.

10. Vollmer, "Predelinquency," 280–81, 282.

11. Lossing, "Crime Prevention Work," 239, 244–47, 249. Lossing was a graduate of Mills College with psychiatric training at the University of California and the New York School of Social Work. See Roller, "Vollmer and his College Cops," 304.

12. Roller, "Vollmer and his College Cops," 305–7; Brereton quoted on 306. Brereton exemplified Vollmer's "college cop" initiative by combining beat patrol work with study for his Ph.D. He later joined the faculty at San Jose State College. See Carte and Carte, *Police Reform,* 43; "Cop Colleges," *The Survey* 66 (June 15, 1931): 318.

13. Lossing, "Crime Prevention Work," 242–43; Liss and Schlossman, "Contours of Crime Prevention," 97–101.

14. On the perceived "crime wave," see Ruth, *Inventing the Public Enemy,* 11–36; Samuel Walker, *Popular Justice: A History of American Criminal Justice,* 2d ed. (New York: Oxford University Press, 1998); Claire Bond Potter, *War on Crime: Bandits, G-Men, and the Politics of Mass Culture* (New Brunswick, NJ: Rutgers University Press, 1998).

15. On the influence of gangsters, see William Bolitho, "The Gangster Traumatism," *The Survey* 63 (March 1, 1930): 661–65; William G. Shepherd, "How to Make a Gangster," *Collier's* 92 (September 2, 1933), 12–13. On Chicago, see CCJC, *Annual Reports for 1924,* 5.

16. Evelina Belden, *Courts in the United States Hearing Children's Cases: A Summary of Juvenile-Court Legislation in the United States,* U.S. Children's Bureau Publication No. 65 (Washington, DC: Government Printing Office, 1920); Katherine F. Lenroot and Emma O. Lundberg, *Juvenile Courts at Work: A Study of the Organization and Methods of Ten Courts,* U.S. Children's Bureau Publication No. 141 (1925; New York: AMS Press, 1975); quote from 160. See also Horn, *Before It's Too Late;* Tanenhaus, *Juvenile Justice in the Making,* esp. 128–29.

17. Henry S. Hulbert, "Probation," in *The Child, the Clinic, and the Court,* ed. Jane Addams (New York: New Republic, 1925), 238–45.

18. Mrs. Joseph T. Bowen, "The Early Days of the Juvenile Court," in *The Child, the Clinic, and the Court,* ed. Addams, 309.

19. William Healy, "The Psychology of the Situation: A Fundamental for Understanding and Treatment of Delinquency and Crime," in *The Child, the Clinic, and the Court,* ed. Addams, 37–52

20. Schneider, *In the Web of Class,* 170–81; Horn, *Before It's Too Late.*

21. Sheldon Glueck and Eleanor T. Glueck, *One Thousand Juvenile Delinquents* (Cambridge, MA: Harvard University Press, 1934). See also Sheldon Glueck, "A Thousand Juvenile Delinquents," in *Yearbook of the NPA* (1934), 63–75.

22. Richard C. Cabot, "1000 Delinquent Boys," *The Survey* 70 (February, 1934), 38.

23. Harry L. Eastman, "The Juvenile Court Today," in *Yearbook of the NPA* (1934), 76, 79, 80.

24. Grace Abbott, "The Juvenile Courts," *The Survey* 72 (May 1936): 131–33.

25. Walter Davenport, "The Making of a Gunman," *Collier's* 85 (June 7, 1930): 12–13.

26. Howard McLellan, "Boys, Gangs, and Crime," *Review of Reviews* 79 (March 1929), 54–59; R. W. Morris, "Tomorrow's Criminals," *The Rotarian* 44 (April 1934): 29–30.

27. *Little Caesar* (Warner Brothers, 1931); *The Public Enemy* (Warner Brothers, 1931); *Scarface* (Howard Hughes, 1932). The findings of the Payne Fund studies are summarized in Henry James Forman, *Our Movie-Made Children* (New York: Macmillan, 1933). See also John Springhall, "Censoring Hollywood: Youth, Moral Panic and Crime / Gangster Movies of the 1930s," *Journal of Popular Culture* 32 (Winter 1998): 135–54.

28. A. P. Pilides, "Detroit, Where Boys Went Bad," *Review of Reviews* 79 (June 1929), 69–71.

29. See, as examples, Paul L. Benjamin, "The Pirates' Den," *The Survey* 48 (May 20, 1922): 277; Orange E. McMeans, "Boy Scouts from Boy Gangs," *The Survey* 64 (July 1, 1930): 308–10.

30. M. L. Pettit, "An Experiment in the Use of Recreation in Treating Delinquents," in *The Yearbook 1931: Probation, Juvenile Courts, Domestic Relations Court, Crime Prevention* (New York: NPA, 1931), 61–68. See also Alice Hinkley, "Venturing for Idle Boys and Girls," *The Survey* 69 (May 1933): 190–91; Karl G. Johanboeke, "Waging War on Juvenile Delinquency," *Recreation* 27 (November 1933), 382–85; Glen O. Grant, "Recreation as Crime Prevention," in *The Offender in the Community: Yearbook, NPA,* (1938), 256–72. These programs extended an earlier ideology of using organized recreation to assimilate immigrants and inculcate appropriate American values. See Dominick Cavallo, *Muscles and Morals: Organized Playgrounds and Urban Reform, 1880–1920* (Philadelphia: University of Pennsylvania Press, 1981).

31. Frederic M. Thrasher, "The Problem of Crime Prevention," in *Yearbook of the NPA* (1934), 9, 12.

32. On CAP's influence, see in particular Kobrin, "Chicago Area Project"; Schlossman and Sedlak, "Chicago Area Project Revisited"; Tanenhaus, *Juvenile Justice in the Making,* 138–50.

33. Glueck and Glueck, *Preventing Crime,* 1, 5–13. For a sense of the range of crime prevention programs, see Julian Montgomery, "Boys Don't Want to Be Criminals," *The Rotarian* 47 (December 1935), 38–40; Roland Hall Sharp, "Checking Crime at the Source," *Christian Science Monitor Weekly Magazine* (July 3, 1937), 4.

34. Inches, "Increased Police Force Checks Crime," 589–90.

35. Appier, *Policing Women,* esp. 46–61.

36. Raymond B. Fosdick, *American Police Systems* (1920; Montclair, NJ: Patterson Smith, 1972), 367; 367–73; New York City Police Department, *Annual Report for the Year 1929* (New York, 1930), 54 [hereafter cited as NYPD, *Annual Report*].

37. William P. Rutledge, "Police as a Preventive Agency in Juvenile Delinquency," in *Proceedings of the 34th Annual Convention of the IACP* (1927), 133–37.

38. Bradford J. Murphey, "Delinquency," in *Proceedings of the 35th Annual Convention of the IACP* (1928), 87–92; Gillmore O. Bush, "Juvenile Delinquency," in *Proceedings of the 35th Annual Convention of the IACP* (1928), 111–12.

39. James M. Broughton, "Crime Prevention," in *Proceedings of the 35th Annual Convention of the IACP* (1928), 151–53.

40. "Crime Prevention Work by American Police Departments," *American City* 36 (March 1927): 387–89.

41. Duncan Matheson, "Character Building and Crime Prevention," in *Proceedings of the 34th Annual Convention of the IACP* (1927), 119–21.

42. National Commission on Law Observance and Enforcement [Wickersham Commission], *Report No. 14: Police* (1931; Montclair, NJ: Patterson Smith, 1968), 113.

43. "Cooperative Cops," *The Survey* 63 (December 15, 1929): 343

44. Citizens' Police Committee, *Chicago Police Problems,* 176–79, quotation from 179; Chicago Police Department, *Annual Report* (Chicago, 1928), 55; Chicago Police Department, *Annual Report* (Chicago, 1929), 16; Chicago Police Department, *Annual Report* (Chicago, 1930), 20.

45. "Juvenile Crime Study Reveals Urgent Need for More Recreation," *American City* 39 (July 1928), 157. See also McLellan, "Boys, Gangs, and Crime," 56.

46. NYPD, *Annual Report 1929,* 55; NYPD, *Annual Report 1930,* 18; NYPD, *Annual Report 1931,* 89; "Preventive Policemanship," *The Survey* 65 (October 15, 1930), 92; Henrietta Additon, "The Crime Prevention Bureau of the New York City Police Department," in *Preventing Crime,* ed. Glueck and Glueck, 216–17; Kahn, *Police and Children,* 12–13. Mulrooney is quoted in *NYT* (May 30, 1931).

47. Additon earned a master's degree in social work from the University of Pennsylvania and, prior to her work with the NYPD, had served as assistant director of the U.S. War Department's Committee on Protective Work for Girls (assigned during World War I to discourage young women from fraternizing with soldiers at training camps) and subsequently as the chief probation officer for the Philadelphia Juvenile Court. See *NYT* (October 12, 1930); *NYT* (June 23, 1931); *NYT* (July 12, 1931); "Miss Deputy Commissioner Additon," *The Survey* 66 (July 15, 1931), 379; Additon, "Crime Prevention Bureau," 215–18.

48. NYPD, *Annual Report 1931,* 89; Additon, "Crime Prevention Bureau," 218.

49. NYPD, *Annual Report 1929,* 59; NYPD, *Annual Report 1930,* 27–28; Diana Rice, "The Crime Bureau's Aid for Young Delinquents," *NYT* (April 10, 1932).

50. Alan Hynd, "PALS—Cops and Kids," *Collier's* 126 (November 11, 1950): 20–21. See also Flynn's obituary in *NYT* (January 4, 1938); Additon, "Crime Prevention Bureau," 229; Kahn, *Police and Children,* 14; and George L. Kelling, "Juveniles and the Police: The End of the Nightstick," in *From Children to Citizens, Volume II: The Role of the Juvenile Court,* ed. F. X. Hartman (New York: Springer-Verlag, 1987), 203–18.

51. NYPD, *Annual Report 1932,* 78.

52. "Stealing Bases to Stop Theft," *Literary Digest* 113 (May 21, 1932): 18–19; see also "Gangs without Gangsters," *Literary Digest* 115 (April 8, 1933), 14.

53. *NYT* (September 28, 1934); *NYT* (September 29, 1934); *NYT* (December 14, 1934); *NYT* (December 23, 1935); *NYT* (December 6, 1936); NYPD, *Annual Report 1934,* 438; NYPD, *Annual Report 1940,* 9; Byrnes MacDonald, "The Juvenile Aid Bureau," in *Police Yearbook; Proceedings of the 43rd Annual Convention of the IACP* (1937), 191–96.

54. Kahn, *Police and Children,* 15; NYPD, *Annual Report* 1937, 41; *NYT* (December 23, 1935); *NYT* (December 6, 1936).

55. On Watkins, see "Police Commissioner Watkins and His Tough Job," *Detroit Sunday News* (January 17, 1931); "The New Police Commissioner," *Detroit Tribune* (January 21, 1931); "Watkins, James Keir," in *The National Cyclopaedia of American Biography,* Vol. J, 1960–63 (New York: James T. White and Co., 1964), 354.

56. James K. Watkins, "The Police and the Prevention of Delinquency," in *Yearbook of the NPA* (1933), 42–49; DPD, *Annual Report* (1931), 14.

57. Watkins, "The Police and the Prevention of Delinquency," 43, 46–48. See also James K. Watkins, "The Function of a Police Department in a Community Social Welfare Program," in *Proceedings of the NCSW, 60th Annual Session* (1933), 109.

58. Policewomen Zelma Arney and Madeline Fales often referred these cases to local community-organizing programs. See memos in Lewis Larkin Papers, box 6, folders 4, 5, and 6, University Archives, Wayne State University.

59. DPD, *Annual Report* (1934), 30; DPD, *Annual Report* (1937), 18; DPD, *Annual Report* (1935), 5.

60. Major Ernest W. Brown, "Cutting to the Core of Crime," in *Yearbook of the IACP, 44th Annual Convention* (1937–38), 153–54; William J. Quinn, "The San Francisco Police Department Big Brother Bureau," in *Yearbook of the IACP, 43rd Annual Convention* (1936–37), 196–204; Charles A. Wheeler, "A Boy Scout Program as an Aid in the Police Juvenile Problem," in *Yearbook of the IACP, 44th Annual Convention* (1938–39), 209–12; A. J. Wilkby, "Crime Prevention in Cities Under 25,000," in *Yearbook of the IACP, 46th Annual Convention* (1939–40), 135–38. See also "Police Departments Install Crime Prevention Programs," *American City* 52 (December 1937), 103–5.

61. James J. Brennan, "The Prevention and Control of Juvenile Delinquency by Police Departments: A Critical Study of Programs in Urban Police Departments" (Ph.D. diss., New York University, 1952), 20–25.

62. Helen D. Pigeon, "The Role of the Police in Crime Prevention," in *Trends in Crime Treatment: 1939 Yearbook, NPA* (1939), 1.

# Notes to Chapter 7

1. Los Angeles Police Department, *Annual Report of the Police Department, Fiscal Year 1932–33* (Los Angeles, 1932–33), 5 [hereafter cited as LAPD, *Annual Report*]. Until 1939, the LAPD published annual reports for a fiscal year from July to June.

2. LAPD, *Annual Report* (1933–34), 4.

3. This "social control to crime control" argument has become central to the historical literature on law enforcement, both explicitly and implicitly. Eric Monkkonen, its foremost advocate, dates the transition as early as the 1890s. See Monkkonen, *Police in Urban America, 1860–1920.* Others date the transition as late as the 1940s. See Eugene J. Watts, "Police Priorities in Twentieth Century St. Louis," *Journal of Social History* 14 (Summer 1981): 649–73; Watts, "Police Response to Crime and Disorder," 340–58. Still others do not address explicitly this thesis, but do argue implicitly that police professionalization was tied closely to efficiently repressing and scientifically solving crimes. See Walker, *Critical History of Police Reform;* Potter, *War on Crime.*

4. Joe Domanick, *To Protect and To Serve: The LAPD's Century of War in the City of*

*Dreams* (New York: Pocket Books, 1994), 21–28, 40–58; Gerald Woods, *The Police in Los Angeles: Reform and Professionalization* (New York: Garland, 1993), 110–11, 117–21.

5. Woods, *Police in Los Angeles,* 103.

6. Domanick, *To Protect and To Serve,* 53–54, 59–68; Woods, *Police in Los Angeles,* 117–19, 124–28, 163–69; LAPD, *Annual Report* (1933–34), 4.

7. Woods, *Police in Los Angeles,* 11–70; Domanick, *To Protect and To Serve.*

8. Robert M. Fogelson, *The Fragmented Metropolis: Los Angeles, 1850–1930* (1967; Berkeley: University of California Press, 1993), 63–84, 108–34, 226–27; U.S. Bureau of the Census, *Sixteenth Census of the United States: 1940, Population; Volume II: Characteristics of the Population* (Washington, DC: Government Printing Office, 1943), 629.

9. Carte and Carte, *Police Reform,* 58–62; Fogelson, *Big-City Police;* Walker, *Critical History of Police Reform,* 125–37; Woods, *Police in Los Angeles,* esp. 3–9, 71–97. On Vollmer's year in LA, see *Law Enforcement in Los Angeles: Los Angeles Police Department (August Vollmer, Chief) Annual Report 1924* (1924; New York: Arno Press, 1974).

10. Walker, *Critical History of Police Reform,* 136–37; Domanick, *To Protect and To Serve,* 48–49.

11. Carte and Carte, *Police Reform,* 58–62; Woods, *Police in Los Angeles.*

12. Domanick, *To Protect and To Serve,* 50–58.

13. Woods, *Police in Los Angeles,* 103–59; Domanick, *To Protect and To Serve,* 53–55, 59–68; Wickersham Commission, *Report No. 11: Lawlessness in Law Enforcement,* 143. See also Kevin Starr, *Material Dreams: Southern California Through the 1920s* (New York: Oxford University Press, 1990), 169–72.

14. Walker, *Critical History of Police Reform,* 139–46.

15. Calculated from LAPD, *Annual Reports* (1924–25 to 1940).

16. Ibid., (1916–17 to 1940).

17. LAPD, *Annual Report* (1932–33), 5; LAPD, *Annual Report* (1935–36), 4; LAPD, *Annual Report* (1936–37), 4.

18. Potter, *War on Crime;* Richard Gid Powers, *Secrecy and Power: The Life of J. Edgar Hoover* (New York: Free Press, 1987), esp. 179–228; Walker, *Critical History of Police Reform,* 151–59.

19. LAPD, *Annual Report* (1935–36), 4, 40–41, 49. See also *NYT* (February 5, 1936); *NYT* (February 9, 1936); Domanick, *To Protect and To Serve,* 59–68; Kevin Starr, *Endangered Dreams: The Great Depression in California* (New York: Oxford University Press, 1996), 177–79; Errol Lincoln Uys, *Riding the Rails: Teenagers on the Move During the Great Depression* (New York: TV Books, 1999), esp. 34–37; Woods, *Police in Los Angeles,* 168–69.

20. Edward J. Escobar, *Race, Police, and the Making of a Political Identity: Mexican Americans and the Los Angeles Police Department, 1900–1945* (Berkeley: University of California Press, 1999), 166–72. The number of Mexican Americans or Latinos in Los Angeles is uncertain, mainly because the U.S. Census Bureau seldom distinguished Latinos in its published tabulations prior to 1950, and when it did, it reached this figure based on language, not ethnicity or place of origin. In 1930, the census did report a Latino population of 97,116 in the city of Los Angeles. For 1940, Escobar uses local sources to estimate a Mexican American population of roughly 133,000, or 8 percent of the total population of Los Angeles. On LA's Latino population, see also U.S. Department of Commerce, Bureau of the Census, *Abstract of the Fifteenth Census of the United States: 1930* (Washington, DC: Government Printing Office, 1933), 98; Fogelson, *Fragmented Metropolis,* 77; Sanchez, *Becoming Mexican American,* 90, 292.

21. Escobar, *Race, Police, and the Making of a Political Identity,* 172–85; Pagan, *Murder at the Sleepy Lagoon,* 59. See also Janis Appier, "Juvenile Crime Control: Los Angeles Law Enforcement and the Zoot-Suit Riots," *Criminal Justice History* 11 (1990): 147–70; Edward J. Escobar, "Zoot-Suiters and Cops: Chicano Youth and the Los Angeles Police Department during World War II," in *The War in American Culture: Society and Consciousness During World War II,* ed. Lewis A. Erenberg and Susan E. Hirsch (Chicago: University of Chicago Press, 1996), 284–312.

22. Steven Schlossman, *The California Experience in American Juvenile Justice: Some Historical Perspectives* (Sacramento: California Bureau of Criminal Statistics, 1989), 4–5; Mary Odem, "City Mothers and Delinquent Daughters: Female Juvenile Justice Reform in Early Twentieth-Century Los Angeles," in *California Progressivism Revisited,* ed. William Deverell and Tom Sitton (Berkeley: University of California Press, 1994), 175–99; Odem, *Delinquent Daughters,* 133–34, 147–49. On Van Waters, see Estelle B. Freedman, *Maternal Justice: Miriam Van Waters and the Female Reform Tradition* (Chicago: University of Chicago Press, 1996).

23. A brief history of the LAPD Crime Prevention Division appears in LAPD, *Annual Report* (1935–36), 35. On Los Angeles policewomen, see Appier, *Policing Women;* Schulz, *From Social Worker to Crime Fighter;* Walker, *Critical History of Police Reform,* 84–94; Odem, "City Mothers and Delinquent Daughters."

24. LAPD, *Annual Report* (1916–17), 22; LAPD, *Annual Report* (1927–28), 31; LAPD, *Annual Report* (1929–30), 37; LAPD, *Annual Report* (1932–33), 21. See also see Lenroot and Lundberg, *Juvenile Courts at Work,* 42–43.

25. Carte and Carte, *Police Reform,* 58–62; *Law Enforcement in Los Angeles.*

26. LAPD, *Annual Report* (1927–28), 31; LAPD, *Annual Report* (1929–30), 37. Quotation from LAPD, *Annual Report* (1930–31), 38.

27. Ibid., (1932–33), 21.

28. Ibid., (1935–36), 36.

29. Kenyon J. Scudder, "The Los Angeles County Coordinating Council Plan," in *Preventing Crime,* ed. Glueck and Glueck, 28; Kenyon J. Scudder and Kenneth S. Beam, *Who Is Delinquent?* (Los Angeles: Rotary Club of Los Angeles, 1934), 13. See also Judge Samuel R. Blake, *Report on Conditions and Progress of the Juvenile Court of Los Angeles,* 1930–33 (Los Angeles: Rotary Club of Los Angeles, 1934); Martin H. Neumeyer, "The Los Angeles County Plan of Co-Ordinating Councils," *Sociology and Social Research* 19 (May-June 1935): 460–71; Katherine Glover, "Project I-E4-I5, Los Angeles," *The Survey* 71 (November 1935): 362–63.

30. California State Emergency Relief Administration, Bureau of Research, *Project 1-E4–15: A Juvenile Delinquency Prevention Program* (1934), 2; see also Scudder and Beam, *Who Is Delinquent?,* 3.

31. Blake, *Report on the Juvenile Court of Los Angeles,* 6, 74–80.

32. See Glover, "Project I-E4-I5, Los Angeles," 362–63; SERA Bureau of Research, *Project 1-E4–15,* 7–8; Scudder and Beam, *Who Is Delinquent?,* 17; Neumeyer, "Los Angeles County Plan," 464; Kenneth S. Beam, "The Coordinating Council Movement," in *Yearbook of the NPA* (1935), 207–8.

33. K. J. Scudder, "Drunken Children," *Juvenile Research Bulletin* 2 (July-August 1934): 1–4; K. J. Scudder, "Perverted Children," *Coordinating Council Bulletin* 3 (July 1935): 3; Scudder and Beam, *Who Is Delinquent?,* 41–47.

34. Scudder and Beam, *Who Is Delinquent?,* 36–40. See also Beam, "The Coordinating Council Movement," 208–9.

35. Scudder and Beam, *Who Is Delinquent?,* 30–35; Scudder, "Los Angeles County Coordinating Council Plan," 31–32; SERA Bureau of Research, *Project 1-E4–15,* 5.

36. James E. Davis and E. M. Slaughter, "Council Participation Recommended by Captain," *Coordinating Council Bulletin* 5 (April 1937), 4.

37. LAPD, *Annual Report* (1934–35), 29; LAPD, *Annual Report* (1935–36), 35.

38. LAPD, *Annual Report* (1935–36), 35–36; LAPD, *Annual Report* (1936–37), 30; LAPD, *Annual Report* (1937–38), 39; William Davis, "Summer Recreation Camps Reducing Delinquency," *Coordinating Council Bulletin* 4 (August 1936): 3; Will Davis, "L.A. Police Summer Camp Reduces Delinquency," *Coordinating Council Bulletin* 4 (September 1936): 3; "Los Angeles Police Open Boys Camp at Valyermo," *Coordinating Council Bulletin* 5 (July 1937): 2.

39. LAPD, *Annual Report* (1937–38), 39.

40. Glover, "Project I-E4-I5," 362; "Busting Gangs as They Blossom," *Literary Digest* 123 (May 29, 1937), 19.

41. LAPD, *Annual Report* (1934–35), 29–30; quote from 29; SERA Bureau of Research, *Project 1-E4–15,* 40–49; "An Over Night Hike for 570 Boys," *Juvenile Research Bulletin* 2 (September-October 1934): 2.

42. Davis, "Summer Recreation Camps Reducing Delinquency," 3; Davis, "L.A. Police Summer Camp Reduces Delinquency," 2.

43. LAPD, *Annual Report* (1936–37), 30. Likewise, police departments in Detroit, San Francisco, and Washington, D.C., also attributed declining juvenile arrests to their crime prevention programs in the 1930s. See DPD, *Annual Report* (1932), 18; Quinn, "Big Brother Bureau," 203–4; Brown, "Cutting to the Core of Crime," 153–54.

44. K. J. Scudder, "Coordinating to Beat the Devil," *Rotarian* 51 (September 1937): 21–23.

45. LAPD, *Annual Report* (1939), 7. On Davis's ouster and Hohmann's succession, see Woods, *Police in Los Angeles,* 182–86, 191–99.

46. Arrest rates were calculated from data on juvenile arrests in LAPD, *Annual Reports* (1925–26 to 1940). Population data is from U.S. Census Bureau, *14th Census; Population, 1920,* 294; U.S. Census Bureau, *15th Census: 1930; Population,* 730, 744; U.S. Census Bureau, *16th Census: 1940, Population; Vol. II,* 629; U.S. Bureau of the Census, *Sixteenth Census of the United States: 1940, Population; Volume IV Characteristics by Age, Part 2: Alabama–Louisiana* (Washington, DC: Government Printing Office, 1943), 172. In 1939, when the LAPD shifted to annual reports based on the calendar year, the annual report included separate tables of arrest data for both the 1939 calendar year and the period from July to December of 1938 not covered by the annual report for 1937–38. All arrest rates for the period labeled "1938" cover only the final six months of the year; I have multiplied the rates for 1938 by two in order to compare them with rates based on a full year.

47. The LAPD's tabulated arrest data placed each charge in one of five degrees: felonies (such as auto theft, burglary, assault), misdemeanors (such as petty theft, battery), noncriminal offenses (such as dependency, sexual delinquency), violations of municipal ordinances, and federal offenses. Because the number of arrests in the last two categories was extremely low, I have combined them into a single group labeled "Other."

48. Calculated from Chicago Police Department, *Annual Reports* (1930 to 1940); U.S. Census Bureau, *15th Census, Population,* 726, 743; U.S. Bureau of the Census, *16th Census: 1940, Population Characteristics by Age, Part 2,* 610.

49. DPD, *Annual Reports* (1898–1918, 1933–40); U.S. Census Bureau, *15th Census,*

*Population,* 728, 743; U.S. Bureau of the Census, *Sixteenth Census of the United States: 1940, Population; Volume IV Characteristics by Age, Part 3: Maine–North Dakota* (Washington, DC: Government Printing Office, 1943), 184. The Detroit *Annual Reports* do not include data on boys' specific offenses between 1919 and 1932.

50. Calculated from LAPD, *Annual Report* (1930–31), 44–45; LAPD, *Annual Report* (1940), 68–71. Using a single-factor ANOVA test, this difference is statistically significant; $p < 0.01$.

51. Calculated from LAPD, *Annual Report* (1940), 68–71; U.S. Census Bureau, *16th Census: 1940, Population; Vol. II,* 629.

52. The LAPD actually classified juveniles by color, not by race. "Red" denoted Mexicans, Mexican Americans, and Native Americans; however, the LAPD arrested very few Native Americans, so "Red" primarily meant people of Latin descent. "Brown" denoted Filipinos and "Yellow" denoted Asians and Asian Americans; for the purpose of this study, these groups have been classified as "Other." The percentage of boys arrested by race was calculated from LAPD, *Annual Report* (1930–31), 46–47. Population data was taken from U.S. Census Bureau, *15th Census, Population,* 730, and U.S. Bureau of the Census, *Abstract of the 15th Census,* 98. Because the Census Bureau offers only rudimentary data on the Latino population of Los Angeles in 1930, it is impossible to determine how large a share of the age-relevant population (people between ages ten and seventeen) Latinos constituted.

53. African American populations calculated from U.S. Census Bureau, *15th Census, Population,* 730, 744.

54. The Latino population was derived from Escobar's figure of 133,000. See Escobar, *Race, Police, and the Making of a Political Identity,* 166. African Americans also constituted 4 percent of Los Angeles males between ages ten and seventeen in 1940. See U.S. Census Bureau, *16th Census: 1940, Population; Vol. II,* 629; U.S. Bureau of the Census, *16th Census: 1940, Population Characteristics by Age, Part 2,* 172.

55. LAPD, *Annual Reports* (1925–26 to 1940).

56. LAPD, *Annual Reports* (1929–30 to 1940).

57. LAPD, *Annual Reports* (1927–28 to 1940). The LAPD was the largest single source of petitions for the Los Angeles County Juvenile Court, but it was not the only one. Juvenile court also received petitions from other police departments in Los Angeles County, the LA County Sheriff's Office, the LA County Probation Department, schools, social agencies, parents, and concerned citizens.

58. LAPD, *Annual Reports* (1927–28 to 1940).

# NOTES TO CHAPTER 8

1. Again, I have replaced names from confidential records with pseudonyms in order to protect subjects' anonymity. I indicate this by placing these names in italics at first mention.

2. Los Angeles County Juvenile Court Case No. 91592. The analyses of juvenile court cases in chapter 8 are based on case files from the Los Angeles County Juvenile Court. The original case files are part of a much larger set of records resulting from all new petitions filed in 1903, 1910, 1920, 1930, 1940, 1950, and approximately two-thirds of the petitions filed in 1960, altogether totaling over 25,000 cases. The records are in the possession of Steven L. Schlossman and used with his permission.

I have analyzed a 10 percent systematic sample of delinquency cases petitioned by the LAPD from 1940. I have not included cases petitioned by other agencies, such as the county sheriff's office or probation department, nor have I included dependency cases—that is, those in which children were taken to juvenile court as a result of neglect or abandonment by parents. The resulting sample yielded 300 boys and sixty-eight girls. Not all of the records contain full information on each case, and in some instances I have performed calculations based on subsets of the total sample. In these instances, I have indicated the number of case records (N) that I used to make that particular calculation.

Published studies using data from the larger body of Los Angeles County Juvenile Court case files include Mary E. Odem and Steven Schlossman, "Guardians of Virtue: The Juvenile Court and Female Delinquency in Early 20th-Century Los Angeles," *Crime and Delinquency* 37 (April 1991): 186–203; Mary E. Odem, "Single Mothers, Delinquent Daughters, and the Juvenile Court in Early 20th Century Los Angeles," *Journal of Social History* 25 (Fall 1991): 27–43; Schlossman and Turner, "Status Offenders, Criminal Offenders"; Steven Schlossman and Susan Turner, *Race and Delinquency in Los Angeles Juvenile Court, 1950* (Sacramento: California Bureau of Criminal Statistics, 1990); Odem, *Delinquent Daughters;* Wolcott, "'Cop Will Get You.'"

3. Gilbert, *A Cycle of Outrage,* esp. 24–41; Schneider, *Vampires, Dragons, and Egyptian Kings,* esp. 3–26, 51–77. On Los Angeles, see Appier, "Juvenile Crime Control"; Escobar, *Race, Police, and the Making of a Political Identity;* Pagan, *Murder at the Sleepy Lagoon;* Joan W. Moore, *Homeboys: Gangs, Drugs, and Prison in the Barrios of Los Angeles* (Philadelphia: Temple University Press, 1978).

4. Calculated from Los Angeles Juvenile Court database; *n* = 300. The results of LAPD arrest data are discussed in chapter 7. None of these findings—the percentage of felonies, boys' average age, or their racial composition—precisely matches those of boys who were arrested in 1940 but the differences are so small in each case that they can all probably be attributed to random chance.

5. Calculated from Los Angeles Juvenile Court database; *n* = 300. The remaining 4 percent were petitioned for public order offenses or violations of city ordinances. For a more detailed discussion of the quantitative findings discussed in this chapter, see David Bryan Wolcott, "Cops and Kids: The Police and Juvenile Delinquency in Three American Cities, 1890–1940" (Ph.D. diss., Carnegie Mellon University, 2000), 209–82, 301–9.

6. Each difference among juveniles in juvenile court discussed in this chapter was checked using a chi-square test and found to meet a conventional standard of statistical significance of at least the *p* < 0.05 level.

7. Arthur L. Stinchcombe, "Institutions of Privacy in the Determination of Police Administrative Practice," *American Journal of Sociology* 69 (1963): 150–60.

8. See Black and Reiss, "Police Control of Juveniles"; Black, *Manners and Customs of the Police;* Lundman, Sykes, and Clark, "Police Control of Juveniles: A Replication"; Brede, "Complainants and Kids"; Smith and Visher, "Street-Level Justice."

9. *N* = 289.

10. *N* = 54.

11. Los Angeles Case No. 91769.

12. *N* = 64.

13. Los Angeles Case No. 93629.

14. Los Angeles Case Nos. 93879 and 91730.

15. Escobar, *Race, Police, and the Making of a Political Identity,* 166–72, 178–85,

197–202; Pagan, *Murder at the Sleepy Lagoon,* esp. 45–59. The scholarly literature on youth and masculine subcultures and the uses of violence within those cultures has become enormous. For historians, useful starting points are Schneider, *Vampires, Dragons, and Egyptian Kings;* and Joan Jacobs Brumberg, *Kansas Charley: The Story of a Nineteenth-Century Boy Murderer* (New York: Viking, 2003).

16. The difference between Latinos, on the one hand, and whites and African Americans, on the other, achieves a conventional standard of statistical significance; chi-square (1) = 8.75; $p$ <0.01. Whites and African Americans are treated as a single group in order to isolate Latinos as the independent variable.

17. $N$ = 28.

18. All differences between averages were checked using a single-factor ANOVA tests and found to achieve conventional standards of statistical significance of at least the $p$ < 0.05 level.

19. Put differently, Latinos accounted for sixteen of the twenty-six boys (62 percent) whom the LAPD reported as belonging to gangs. However, during an era of emerging public fear of violent youth gangs, the police and the press frequently misperceived Latinos and Latinas who were parts of the same social circles to be more highly organized "gangs" than they really were. See Pagan, *Murder at the Sleepy Lagoon,* esp. 82, 131–33.

20. Los Angeles Case Nos. 92548 and 92525.

21. Los Angeles Case No. 92000.

22. Los Angeles Case No. 94192. See also Escobar, *Race, Police, and the Making of a Political Identity,* 172–77.

23. $N$ = 289.

24. $N$ = 26.

25. Los Angeles Case No. 93284. Transients constituted 38 percent of boys whom the police petitioned to juvenile court for status offenses ($n$ = 26). On youth transiency, see Thomas Minehan, *Boy and Girl Tramps of America* (1937; Seattle: University of Washington Press, 1976); K. J. Scudder, "How California Anchors Drifting Boys," *The Survey* 69 (March 1933): 101–2; Uys, *Riding the Rails,* esp. 11, 32–38.

26. Los Angeles Case No. 91219. Similar examples may also be seen in Los Angeles Case Nos. 91260 and 93450. On Pershing Square, see Pagan, *Murder at the Sleepy Lagoon,* 160. On sexual assignations in public, see George Chauncey, *Gay New York: Gender, Urban Culture, and the Making of the Gay Male World, 1890–1940* (New York: Basic Books, 1994), esp. 179–206.

27. For gay sexual encounters in public among status offense charges, $n$ = 7/26; among total cases the LAPD petitioned to juvenile court, $n$ = 7/300.

28. Los Angeles Case No. 90852.

29. Scott L. Bottles, *Los Angeles and the Automobile: The Making of the Modern City* (Berkeley: University of California Press, 1987), 92–94; James J. Flink, *The Automobile Age* (Cambridge, MA: The MIT Press, 1988), 140–45, 159–60.

30. Calculated from LAPD, *Annual Reports* (1915–16 to 1940).

31. Ibid., (1930–31 to 1940).

32. Ibid., (1930–31 to 1940).

33. $N$ = 96

34. Los Angeles Case No. 91528.

35. $N$ = 91.

36. Los Angeles Case No. 92168.

37. *N* = 68. As with boys, these findings——the offenses that brought girls to juvenile court, their average age, and their racial composition—do not precisely match those of girls whom the LAPD arrested in 1940, but the differences are so small that they can be attributed to random chance.

38. Los Angeles Case No. 92338.

39. Alexander, *The "Girl Problem"*; Appier, *Policing Women*; Odem, "City Mothers and Delinquent Daughters"; Odem, *Delinquent Daughters*; Odem and Schlossman, "Guardians of Virtue"; Schlossman and Wallach, "Crime of Precocious Sexuality"; Schlossman and Turner, "Status Offenders, Criminal Offenders."

40. Appier, *Policing Women*, 155–58. On the age of consent, see Odem, *Delinquent Daughters*, 14–15, 63–81; Stephen Robertson, "Age of Consent Law and the Making of Modern Childhood in New York City, 1886–1921," *Journal of Social History* 35 (Summer 2002): 781–98.

41. Margaret Saunders, "A Study of the Work of the City Mother's Bureau of the City of Los Angeles" (M.S.W. thesis, University of Southern California, 1939), 45, 60. See also Appier, *Policing Women*, 155–66; Odem, "City Mothers and Delinquent Daughters," esp. 192–93.

42. *N* = 66. Crime victims filing complaints in criminal cases account for the remaining 9 percent.

43. Los Angeles Case No. 90778.

44. Saunders, "City Mother's Bureau," 57–58.

45. Los Angeles Case No. 92938. On the Convent of the Good Shepherd, see Odem, *Delinquent Daughters*, 148.

46. Blake, *Report on the Juvenile Court* (1930–33), 15.

47. *N* = 298. This figure, it must be emphasized, refers to boys who were *ever* institutionalized, not boys who were institutionalized on their first petition to court. Many boys were referred to juvenile court on a number of occasions and were only institutionalized after repeat appearances.

48. The 1930 statistic derives from ongoing research being conducted by Steven L. Schlossman using the larger set of Los Angeles County Juvenile Court case files described in note 1. I thank him for the use of his preliminary findings.

49. Blake, *Report on the Juvenile Court* (1930–33), 17.

50. *N* = 300. See Blake, *Report on the Juvenile Court* (1930–33), 15–16.

51. For fifteen- to seventeen-year-olds, *n* = 201. In contrast, only one percent of boys between ten and fourteen were sent to forestry camp (*n* = 99).

52. K. J. Scudder, *Life Anew: Annual Report, Los Angeles County Probation Department, for the Year Ending December 31st, 1935* (Los Angeles, 1936), 28.

53. In 1940, the juvenile court placed a total of 23 percent (*n* = 298) of boys petitioned by the LAPD in forestry camps, following either their first hearing or subsequent ones. In contrast, Schlossman's analysis found that the court sent no boys to county-operated facilities (forestry camps) in 1930. This difference roughly accounts for the sharp increase between 1930 and 1940 in the share of boys institutionalized.

54. Description from Blake, *Report on the Juvenile Court* (1930–33), 22–27; Scudder, "How California Anchors Drifting Boys," 101–2; Scudder, *Life Anew*, 28–30. Los Angeles also established parallel forestry camps for boys between twelve and fifteen in 1941. See John M. Zuck, "The Junior Probation Camps of Los Angeles County," in *Current Approaches to Delinquency, 1949 NPA Yearbook* (1949), 76–89.

55. Scudder, "How California Anchors," 102. On the CCC and the shared philosophy of using hard to work to help youths adjust to responsible adulthood, see Jeffrey Ryan Suzik, "'Building Better Men': The CCC Boy and the Changing Social Ideal of Manliness," in *Boys and Their Toys? Masculinity, Technology, and Class in America*, ed. Roger Horowitz (London: Routledge, 2001), 111–38.

56. On the California Junior Republic, see Jack M. Holl, *Juvenile Reform in the Progressive Era: William R. George and the Junior Republic Movement* (Ithaca, NY: Cornell University Press, 1971), 150, 156–57.

57. Blake, *Report on the Juvenile Court* (1930–33), 19. On institutions for "mentally deficient youth," see Rafter, *Creating Born Criminals*, 188–235.

58. On reform schools, see Schlossman and Pisciotta, "Identifying and Treating Serious Juvenile Offenders," 3–5; Schlossman, "Delinquent Children," 379–82.

59. Los Angeles Case No. 92278.

60. For African Americans, $n = 32$; for whites, $n = 178$; for Latinos, $n = 88$.

61. $N = 300$.

62. $N = 413$.

63. For boys making later appearances in juvenile court, $n = 113$.

64. Neither of these differences achieves statistical significance at a $p < 0.05$ level.

65. Los Angeles Case No. 93799.

66. $N = 68$. Only two of these girls were petitioned to juvenile court more than once, so I have not included female repeat offenders in this analysis.

67. The court committed to institutions 55 percent of girls accused of criminal offenses ($n = 5/9$), as compared to 20 percent of girls accused of status offenses ($n = 12/59$). In spite of the small number of cases, this difference meets conventional standards of statistical significance; chi-square $(1) = 5.16$; $p < 0.05$.

68. Los Angeles Case No. 92338.

## Notes to Conclusion

1. Dodge, "'Our Juvenile Court Has Become More Like a Criminal Court'"; Christopher P. Manfredi, *The Supreme Court and Juvenile Justice* (Lawrence: University Press of Kansas, 1998), 32–45.

2. Schlossman, *California Experience in Juvenile Justice*, 6–10.

3. Gilbert, *A Cycle of Outrage*, 24–41; Manfredi, *The Supreme Court and Juvenile Justice*, 33–36; Edwin D. Sutherland, "Crime," in *American Society in Wartime*, ed. William Fielding Ogburn (Chicago: University of Chicago Press, 1943), 185–206.

4. Gilbert, *A Cycle of Outrage*, 32; Ernest W. Burgess, "Delinquency or Recreation," in *Delinquency and the Community in Wartime; Yearbook, NPA* (1943), 138–49; Elsa Castendyck, "Helping to Prevent Sex Delinquency," in *Proceedings of the NCSW, Seventieth Annual Meeting* (1943), 104–47; Camille Kelley, "Solving the Problem of Juvenile Delinquency," in *The Police Yearbook, 1944; Proceedings of the 46th Annual Conference of the IACP* (1944), 110–15; Anna W. M. Wolf and Irma Simonton Black, "What Happened to the Young People," in *While You Were Gone: A Report on Wartime Life in the United States*, ed. Jack Goodman (New York: Simon and Schuster, 1946), 64–88.

5. J. Edgar Hoover, "Criminals Are Home Grown" *The Rotarian* 56 (April 1940): 16–18; J. Edgar Hoover, "Mothers . . . Our Only Hope," *Woman's Home Companion*

(January 1944), 20, reprinted in *Women's Magazines 1940–1960: Gender Roles and the Popular Press,* ed. Nancy A. Walker (Boston: Bedford / St. Martin's, 1998), 45; J. Edgar Hoover, "Wild Children," *American Magazine* 136 (July 1943): 40.

6. Schneider, *Vampires, Dragons, and Egyptian Kings,* 27–77.

7. Appier, "Juvenile Crime Control"; Escobar, *Race, Police, and the Making of a Political Identity,* esp. 203–53; Pagan, *Murder at the Sleepy Lagoon.* On Detroit, see Dominic J. Capeci, Jr. and Martha Wilkerson, *Layered Violence: The Detroit Rioters of 1943* (Jackson: University Press of Mississippi, 1991).

# BIBLIOGRAPHY

## ARCHIVAL SOURCES

Bubacz, Stephen S. Papers. Department of Special Collections, University of Illinois at Chicago.

Burgess, Ernest W. Papers. Joseph Regenstein Library, University of Chicago.

Chicago Area Project. Records. Chicago Historical Society.

Detroit Police Department Records—City Archives. Burton Historical Collection, Detroit Public Library:

"Complaints." Vols. 1, 3, 11, 18, 26. 1896–98, 1903–4, 1908, 1912–13.

"General and Special Orders." Vols. 3–4. 1894–1908.

"Incidental Events." 1887–89, 1899–1909.

"Record of Arrests." Volumes 16–18, 20–21, 23–24, 27, 30, 33. 1889–91, 1892–94, 1895–97, 1900, 1903, 1906.

Illinois Institute for Juvenile Research. Life Histories. Chicago Historical Society. Chicago Historical Society.

Juvenile Protective Association Papers. Department of Special Collections, University of Illinois at Chicago.

Lewis Larkin Papers, University Archives, Wayne State University.

Los Angeles County (CA). Juvenile Court. Case Files. 1940. Microfilm.

Merriam, Charles E. Papers. Joseph Regenstein Library, University of Chicago.

National Association for the Advancement of Colored People Papers. Part 12, Series C. United States Library of Congress. Microfilm.

Talbot, David J. Reminiscences. Chicago Historical Society.

## NEWSPAPERS

*Chicago Tribune*
*Detroit Free Press*
*Detroit News*
*Detroit Sunday News*
*Detroit Tribune*
*New York Times*

## ANNUAL REPORTS AND GOVERNMENT DOCUMENTS

California. State Emergency Relief Administration, Bureau of Research. *Project 1-E4–15: A Juvenile Delinquency Prevention Program.* 1934.

Chicago (IL). Police Department. *Report of the General Superintendent of Police of the City of Chicago, to the City Council.* 1890–1912.

———. *Annual Report.* Chicago, 1913–40.

———. *Book of Rules and Regulations of the Department of Police of the City of Chicago.* Chicago, 1905.

———. *Rules and Regulations of the Police Department of the City of Chicago.* Chicago, 1933.

Cook County (IL). *Juvenile Court and Juvenile Detention Home of Cook County, Illinois, Annual Reports.* For 1909–26.

Detroit (MI). House of Correction. *Twentieth Annual Report of the Officers of the Detroit House of Correction to the Common Council of the City of Detroit for the Year 1881.* Detroit: Post and Tribune Job Co., City Printers, 1882.

———. *Forty-Seventh Annual Report of the Officers of the Detroit House of Correction to the Common Council of the City of Detroit for the Year 1908.* Detroit: Post and Tribune Job Co., City Printers, 1909.

Detroit (MI). Mayor's Inter-Racial Committee. *The Negro in Detroit.* Detroit Bureau of Governmental Research, 1926.

Detroit (MI). Police Department. *Annual Report of the Board of Commissioners of the Metropolitan Police to the Common Council of the City of Detroit.* Vols. 25–31, 33–35. Detroit: Raynor and Taylor, 1890–1900.

———. *Annual Report of Commissioner of Metropolitan Police of Detroit, Michigan to the Common Council of the City of Detroit.* Vols. 36, 38–51, 53, 55–65, 67–75. Detroit, 1901–40.

———. *Story of the Detroit Police Department, 1916–17; 52d Annual Report of Commissioner of Metropolitan Police for the Twelve Months Ending June 30, 1917.* Prepared Under the Direction of James Couzens, Commissioner of Police. Detroit, 1917.

———. *Training School for Police Service.* 1911. Revised Edition. Detroit, 1921.

Los Angeles (CA). Police Department. *Annual Report of the Police Department.* For the Fiscal Years 1914–40.

———. *Law Enforcement in Los Angeles: Los Angeles Police Department (August Vollmer, Chief) Annual Report 1924.* Reprint. New York: Arno Press, 1974.

Michigan. Industrial School for Boys. *Biennial Report of the Board of Trustees of the Industrial School for Boys of Michigan,* 1894–1916. Lansing, MI, 1894–1916.

———. *Laws Relating to Board of Corrections and Charities, Juvenile Courts, and County Agents.* Lansing, MI: Industrial School Press, 1911.

———. *Laws Relating to Juvenile Courts and County Agents.* Lansing, MI: Industrial School Press, 1910.

———. Reform School. *Biennial Report of the Board of Control of the Reform School of Michigan,* 1888, 1890. Lansing, MI, 1888, 1891.

———. *Report of the Superintendent of the State Reform School at Lansing, Michigan, to the State Board of Inspectors for the Biennial Period Ending June 30, 1892.* Lansing, MI, 1892.

New York (NY). Police Department. *Annual Report for the Years 1929–1940.* New York, 1930–41.

U.S. Department of the Interior, Census Office. *Report on Crime, Pauperism, and Benevolence in the United States at the Eleventh Census: 1890,* Part II. General Tables. Washington, DC: Government Printing Office, 1895.

———. *Census Reports Volume II. Twelfth Census of the United States, Taken in the Year 1900. Population.* Washington, DC: Government Printing Office, 1902.

———. *Report of the Population of the United States at the Eleventh Census: 1890.* Part II. Washington, DC: Government Printing Office, 1897.

U.S. Department of Commerce and Labor. Bureau of the Census. *Special Reports: Occupations at the Twelfth Census.* Washington, DC: Government Printing Office, 1904.

U.S. Department of Commerce. Bureau of the Census. *Thirteenth Census of the United States, Taken in the Year 1910. Volume I: Population 1910.* Washington, DC: Government Printing Office, 1913.

———. *Fourteenth Census of the United States, Vol. II: Population, 1920: General Reports and Analytical Tables.* Washington, DC: Government Printing Office, 1922.

———. *Fifteenth Census of the United States: 1930. Population Vol. 2; General Reports Statistics by Subjects.* Washington, DC: Government Printing Office, 1933.

———. *Fifteenth Census of the United States; Abstract—Population.* Washington, DC: Government Printing Office, 1933.

———. *Sixteenth Census of the United States: 1940. Population. Vol. II: Characteristics of the Population.* Washington, DC: Government Printing Office, 1943.

———. *Sixteenth Census of the United States: 1940, Population. Vol. IV Characteristics by Age, Part 3: Maine-North Dakota.* Washington, DC: Government Printing Office, 1943.

## Printed Primary Sources

Abbott, Grace. "The Juvenile Courts." *The Survey* 72 (May 1936): 131–3.

Adams, Myron E. "Municipal Regulation of Street Trades." In *Proceedings of the National Conference of Charities and Corrections, at the Thirty-First Annual Session Held in the City of Portland, Maine, June 15–22, 1904,* ed. Isabel C. Barrows, 295–301. Fred. J. Herr, 1904.

Addams, Jane. *Twenty Years at Hull-House.* 1910. Reprint, New York: NAL, 1999.

Additon, Henrietta. "The Crime Prevention Bureau of the New York City Police Department." In *Preventing Crime: A Symposium,* ed. Sheldon Glueck and Eleanor Glueck, 215–36. New York: McGraw-Hill, 1936.

Alger, Horatio. *Ragged Dick, or Street Life in New York with the Boot-Blacks.* 1868. Reprint, New York: NAL, 1990.

Almy, Frederic. "The Economics of the Juvenile Court." *Charities* 13 (January 7, 1905): 337–39.

Altgeld, John Peter. *Live Questions; including Our Penal Machinery and Its Victims.* 3d ed. 1884. Reprint, Chicago: Donohue & Henneberrry, 1890.

Arnold, Victor. "The Juvenile Court." In *Proceedings of the 33rd Annual Convention of the International Association of Chiefs of Police,* 191. 1926. Reprint, New York: Arno Press, 1971.

Bates, Helen Page. "Digest of Statutes Relating to Juvenile Courts and Probation Systems." *Charities* 13 (January 7, 1905): 329–37.

Beam, Kenneth S. "The Coordinating Council Movement." In *Yearbook, National Probation Association, 1935,* ed. Marjorie Bell, 200–213. New York: National Probation Association, 1935.

Belden, Evelina. *Courts in the United States Hearing Children's Cases: A Summary of Juvenile-Court Legislation in the United States.* U.S. Children's Bureau Publication no. 65. Washington, DC: Government Printing Office, 1920.

Benjamin, Paul L. "The Pirates' Den." *The Survey* 48 (May 20, 1922): 277.

Bennett, Mrs. Mildred E. "New Dynamics and Philosophy in Detention Home Care." M.S.W. thesis, Wayne University, 1946.

Bigger, Mary. "A Study of the Factors Underlying the Behavior of Twenty Delinquent Girls in the House of the Good Shepherd." M.S.W. thesis, Wayne University, 1944.

Blake, Judge Samuel R. *Report on Conditions and Progress of the Juvenile Court of Los Angeles,* 1930, 1931, 1932, and 1933. Los Angeles: Rotary Club of Los Angeles, 1934.

Bolitho, William. "The Gangster Traumatism." *The Survey* 63 (March 1, 1930): 661–65.

Bolt, Richard A. *Juvenile Offenders in the City of Detroit, With Suggestions for the Establishment of a Juvenile Court and Probation System.* Ann Arbor, MI: Richmond & Backus, 1903.

Bowen, Mrs. Joseph T [Louise de Koven]. "The Policeman with a Wink: His Menace to Youth as Shown in the Present Chicago Administration." *The Survey* 43 (January 24, 1920): 458–60.

———. "The Early Days of the Juvenile Court." In *The Child, the Clinic, and the Court,* ed. Jane Addams. New York: New Republic, 1925.

Breckinridge, Sophonisba P., and Edith Abbott. *The Delinquent Child and the Home.* New York: Charities Publication Committee, 1912. Reprint, New York: Arno Press, 1970.

Broughton, James M. "Crime Prevention." In *Proceedings of the 35th Annual Convention of the International Association of Chiefs of Police,* 151–53. 1928. Reprint, New York: Arno Press, 1971.

Brown, Major Ernest W. "Cutting to the Core of Crime." In *Yearbook of the International Association of Chiefs of Police, 44th Annual Convention,* 153–54. 1938.

Bruere, Henry. "The Police as Social Workers." *American City* 10 (March 1914): 282.

Buckley, James M. "The Present Epidemic of Crime." *The Century Magazine* 67 (November 1903): 151.

Burgess, Ernest W., "Delinquency or Recreation." In *Delinquency and the Community in Wartime; Yearbook of the National Probation Association 1943,* ed. Marjorie Bell, 138–49. New York: National Probation Association, 1943.

Burgess, Ernest W., Joseph D. Lohman, and Clifford R. Shaw. "The Chicago Area Project." In *Coping with Crime: Yearbook of the National Probation Association,* ed. Marjorie Bell, 8–28. New York: National Probation Association, 1937.

Burgess, Ernest W., and Charles Newcomb, eds. *Census Data of the City of Chicago, 1930.* Chicago: University of Chicago Press, 1933.

Bush, Gillmore O. "Juvenile Delinquency." In *Proceedings of the 35th Annual Convention of the International Association of Chiefs of Police,* 111–12. 1928. Reprint, New York: Arno Press, 1971.

"Busting Gangs as They Blossom." *Literary Digest* 123 (May 29, 1937): 19.

Cabot, Richard C., MD. "1000 Delinquent Boys." *The Survey* 70 (February 1934): 38.

Campbell, H. M., John M. Flynn, and Elton Lower. "The Chicago Police: Report of the Chicago Civil Service Commission." *Journal of Criminal Law and Criminology* 3 (May 1912): 62–84.

Castendyck, Elsa. "Helping to Prevent Sex Delinquency." In *Proceedings of the National Conference of Social Work, Seventieth Annual Meeting,* 104–47. 1943.

"Chicago's Policewomen." *The Outlook* 104 (August 30, 1913).

Citizen's Police Committee. *Chicago Police Problems.* Chicago: University of Chicago Press, 1931.

"The City Child, Playgrounds, and the Police." *The Outlook* 113 (May 3. 1916).

"Cooperative Cops." *The Survey* 63 (December 15, 1929): 343.

"Cop Colleges." *The Survey* 66 (June 15, 1931): 318.

Cowles, Henry D. "Probation." In *Proceedings of the 18th Annual Convention of the International Association of Chiefs of Police,* 113–18. 1911. Reprint, New York: Arno Press, 1971.

"Crime Prevention Work by American Police Departments." *American City* 36 (March 1927): 387–89.

Davenport, Walter. "The Making of a Gunman." *Collier's* 85 (June 7, 1930): 12–13.

Davis, James E, and F. M. Slaughter. "Council Participation Recommended by Captain." *Coordinating Council Bulletin* 5 (April 1937): 4.

Davis, William. "Summer Recreation Camps Reducing Delinquency." *Coordinating Council Bulletin* 4 (August 1936): 3.

———. "L.A. Police Summer Camp Reduces Delinquency." *Coordinating Council Bulletin* 4 (September 1936): 3.

Desmond, William. "The Juvenile Court." In *International Association of Chiefs of Police; 10th Annual Session,* 72–74. 1903. Reprint, New York: Arno Press, 1971.

"Disciplining Chicago's Police." *The Survey* 23 (February 12, 1910): 695.

Downs, William T. *Michigan Juvenile Court: Law and Practice.* Ann Arbor, MI: Institute of Continuing Legal Education, 1963.

Eastman, Harry L. "The Juvenile Court Today." In *Yearbook of the National Probation Association 1934,* ed. Marjorie Bell, 76–80. New York: National Probation Association, 1934.

Farnan, Thomas F. "Is Crime a Disease?" In *Proceedings of the 15th Annual Convention of the International Association of Chiefs of Police.* 1908. Reprint, New York: Arno Press, 1971.

Folks, Homer. *The Care of Destitute, Neglected, and Delinquent Children.* Albany: J.B. Lyon Co., 1900.

Forman, Henry James. *Our Movie-Made Children.* New York: Macmillan, 1933.

Fosdick, Raymond B. *American Police Systems.* 1920. Reprint, Montclair, NJ: Patterson Smith, 1972.

"Gangs without Gangsters." *Literary Digest* 115 (April 8, 1933): 14.

Gerry, Elbridge T. "Some Causes of Delinquency in New York City, 1892." In *Juvenile Offenders for a Thousand Years: Selected Readings from Anglo-Saxon Times to the Present,* ed. Wiley Britton Sanders, 437–39. Chapel Hill: University of North Carolina Press, 1970.

Glover, Katherine. "Project I-E4–15, Los Angeles: How Unemployed Men and Women Met Juvenile Delinquency on Its Own Ground." *The Survey* 71 (November 1933): 362–63.

Glueck, Sheldon. "A Thousand Juvenile Delinquents." In *Yearbook of the National Probation Association 1934,* ed. Marjorie Bell, 63–75. New York: National Probation Association, 1934.

Glueck, Sheldon, and Eleanor Glueck. *One Thousand Juvenile Delinquents.* Cambridge, MA: Harvard University Press, 1934.

———, eds. *Preventing Crime: A Symposium.* New York: McGraw-Hill, 1936.

Goler, G. W. "The Juvenile Delinquent: The Causes that Produce Him; The Evolution of Modern Methods for His Reformation." In *Proceedings of the National Conference of Charities and Corrections,* 23rd Annual Session, 1896, ed. Isabel C. Barrows, 352–67. Boston: Geo. H. Ellis, 1896.

Grant, Glen O. "Recreation as Crime Prevention." In *The Offender in the Community; Yearbook, National Probation Association, 1938,* ed. Marjorie Bell, 256–73. National Probation Association, 1938.

Gray, Joshua B. "Probation Laws and Their Workings." In *Proceedings of the 18th Annual Convention of the International Association of Chiefs of Police.* 1911. Reprint, New York: Arno Press, 1971.

Harley, Herbert. "Detroit's New Model Criminal Court." *Journal of Criminal Law and Criminology* 11 (November 1920): 398–418.

Hart, Hastings H., ed. *Juvenile Court Laws in the United States.* New York: Russell Sage Foundation, 1910.

Healy, William. *The Individual Delinquent.* 1915. Reprint, Montclair, NJ: Patterson Smith, 1969.

———. "The Psychology of the Situation: A Fundamental for Understanding and Treatment of Delinquency and Crime." In *The Child, the Clinic, and the Court,* ed. Jane Addams, 37–52. New York: New Republic, 1925.

Henderson, Charles R. "Juvenile Courts: Problems of Administration." *Charities* 13 (January 7, 1905): 340–43.

Hinkley, Alice. "Venturing for Idle Boys and Girls." *The Survey* 69 (May 1933): 190–91.

Hoover, J. Edgar. "Criminals Are Home Grown." *The Rotarian* 56 (April 1940): 16–18.

———. "Wild Children," *American Magazine* 136 (July 1943): 40.

———. "Mothers . . . Our Only Hope." *Woman's Home Companion* (January 1944), 20; reprinted in *Women's Magazines 1940–1960: Gender Roles and the Popular Press,* ed. Nancy A. Walker (Boston: Bedford/St. Martin's, 1998), 45.

Hulbert, Henry S. "Detroit's Juvenile Court and Its Functions in the Community." *Detroit Saturday Night* (December 18, 1909): 22–23.

———. "Probation." In *The Child, the Clinic, and the Court,* ed. Jane Addams, 238–45. New York: New Republic, 1925.

Hurley, Timothy D. *Origin of the Illinois Juvenile Court Law.* 3d ed. Chicago: Visitation and Aid Society, 1907. Reprint, New York: AMS Press, 1977.

Hynd, Alan. "PALS—Cops and Kids." *Collier's* 126 (November 11, 1950): 20–21.

Inches, James W. "Increased Police Force Checks Crime." *The American City* 24 (June 1921): 589–90.

Jeter, Helen R. *The Chicago Juvenile Court.* U.S. Children's Bureau Publication No. 104. Washington, DC: Government Printing Office, 1922.

Johanboeke, Karl G. "Waging War on Juvenile Delinquency." *Recreation* 27 (November 1933): 382–85.

"Juvenile Crime Study Reveals Urgent Need for More Recreation." *American City* 39 (July 1928): 157.

Kahn, Alfred J. *Police and Children: A Study of the Juvenile Aid Bureau of the New York City Police Department.* New York: Citizens' Committee on Children, 1951.

Kelley, Camille. "Solving the Problem of Juvenile Delinquency." In *The Police Yearbook, 1944; Proceedings of the 46th Annual Conference of the International Association of Chiefs of Police,* 110–15. 1944.

"The Kid Cops." *The Literary Digest* 50 (February 20, 1915): 396–97.

Kingsley, Sherman C. *A Study of the Juvenile Court and Detention Home of Wayne County, Michigan.* 1928. Reprint, Glen Rock, NJ: Microfilming Corporation of America, 1976.

Kobrin, Solomon K. "The Chicago Area Project—A 25-Year Assessment." *Annals of the American Academy of Political and Social Sciences* 322 (March 1959): 19–29.

Landesco, John. "Member of the 42 Gang." *Journal of Criminal Law and Criminology* 23 (March 1933): 964–98.

Lathrop, Julia C. "The Development of the Probation System in a Large City." *Charities* 13 (January 7, 1905): 344–49.

———. "The Background of the Juvenile Court in Illinois." In *The Child, the Clinic, and the Court,* ed. Jane Addams, 290–97. New York: New Republic, 1925.

Lenroot, Katherine R. and Emma O. Lundberg. *Juvenile Courts at Work: A Study of the Organization and Methods of Ten Courts.* U.S. Children's Bureau Publication No. 141. Washington, DC: Government Printing Office, 1925. Reprint, New York: AMS Press, 1975.

Lexow, Clarence. *Report and Proceedings of the Senate Committee Appointed to Investigate the Police Department of the City of New York.* 1895. Reprint, New York: Arno Press, 1971.

Lindsey, Ben B. "The Juvenile Court of Denver." In *Children's Courts in the United States: Their Origins, Development, and Results,* ed. Samuel J. Barrows. Washington, DC: Government Printing Office, 1904.

———. "The Boy and the Court." *Charities* 13 (January 7, 1905): 350–57.

"Los Angeles Police Open Boys Camp at Valyermo." *Coordinating Council Bulletin* 5 (July 1937): 2.

Lossing, Elizabeth. "The Crime Prevention Work of the Berkeley Police Department." In *Preventing Crime: A Symposium,* ed. Sheldon Glueck and Eleanor Glueck, 237–63. New York: McGraw-Hill, 1936.

Lou, Herbert H. *Juvenile Courts in the United States.* 1927. Reprint, New York: Arno Press, 1972.

Lowden, Carl Schurz. "Chicago, the Nation's Crime Centre." *Current History* 28 (September 1928): 892–98.

MacDonald, Byrnes. "The Juvenile Aid Bureau." In *Police Yearbook; Proceedings of the 43rd Annual Convention of the International Association of Chiefs of Police,* 191–96. The Association, 1937.

Mack, Julian W. "The Juvenile Court." *Harvard Law Review* 23 (1909–10): 104–22.

Mandel, Arch. "Why Crime Decreased in Detroit." *The American City* 27 (August 1922): 149–52.

Matheson, Duncan. "Character Building and Crime Prevention." In *Proceedings of the 34th Annual Convention of the International Association of Chiefs of Police,* 119–21. 1927. Reprint, New York: Arno Press, 1971.

McLellan, Howard. "Boys, Gangs, and Crime." *Review of Reviews* 79 (March 1929): 54–59.

McMeans, Orange E. "Boy Scouts from Boy Gangs." *The Survey* 64 (July 1, 1930): 308–10.

Minehan, Thomas. *Boy and Girl Tramps of America.* 1937. Reprint, Seattle: University of Washington Press, 1976.

"Miss Deputy Commissioner Additon." *The Survey* 66 (July 15, 1931): 379.

Moehlmann, Arthur B. *Public Education in Detroit.* Bloomington, IN.: Public School Publishing Company, 1925.

Montgomery, Julian. "Boys Don't Want to Be Criminals." *The Rotarian* 47 (December 1935): 38–40.

Moore, William. "The Boy and the Policeman." In *International Association of Chiefs of Police, 9th Annual Session,* 46–47. 1902. Reprint, New York: Arno Press, 1971.

Morris, R. W. "Tomorrow's Criminals." *The Rotarian* 44 (April 1934): 29–30.

Moses, Earl R. *The Negro Delinquent in Chicago.* Washington, DC, 1932.

Murphy, Benjamin. "Prevent Crime—The Principal Duty of the Police." In *Proceedings of the 8th Annual Convention of the International Association of Chiefs of Police.* 1901. Reprint, New York: Arno Press, 1971.

Murphey, Bradford J. "Delinquency." In *Proceedings of the 35th Annual Convention of the International Association of Chiefs of Police,* 87–92. 1928. Reprint, New York: Arno Press, 1971.

Murray, Virginia M. "Policewomen in Detroit." *American City* 25 (August 1921): 209–10.

National Commission on Law Observance and Enforcement [Wickersham Commission]. *Report No. 11: Lawlessness in Law Enforcement.* 1931. Reprint, Montclair, NJ: Patterson Smith, 1968.

———. *Report No. 14: Police.* 1931. Reprint, Montclair, NJ: Patterson Smith, 1968.

National Probation Association. "Pinched for Stealing." Solicitation pamphlet, circa 1925.

Neumeyer, Martin H. "The Los Angeles County Plan of Co-Ordinating Councils." *Sociology and Social Research* 19 (May–June 1935): 460–71.

"The New York City Junior Police." *The Outlook* 113 (July 12, 1916): 588.

"An Over Night Hike for 570 Boys." *Juvenile Research Bulletin* 2 (Sept.–Oct. 1934): 2.

"Patrolmen Specializing Too." *Detroit Police News* 2 (February 1915): 5.

Pettit, M.L. "An Experiment in the Use of Recreation in the Treatment of

Delinquents." In *The Yearbook, 1931: Probation, Juvenile Courts, Domestic Relations Court, Crime Prevention,* 61–68. National Probation Association, 1931.

Pigeon, Helen D. "The Role of the Police in Crime Prevention." In *Trends in Crime Treatment: 1939 Yearbook, National Probation Association.* National Probation Association, 1939.

Pilides, A.P. "Detroit, Where Boys Went Bad." *Review of Reviews* 79 (June 1929): 69–71.

Piper, Alexander R. "Report of an Investigation of the Discipline and Administration of the Police Department of the City of Chicago, 1904." In *Chicago Police Investigations: Three Reports.* New York: Arno Press, 1971.

"Police Departments Install Crime Prevention Programs." *American City* 52 (December 1937): 103–5.

"The Police as Social Workers." *The Outlook* 108 (December 16, 1914): 861.

"Preventive Policemanship." *The Survey* 65 (October 15, 1930): 92.

Quinn, William J. "The San Francisco Police Department Big Brother Bureau." In *Yearbook of the International Association of Chiefs of Police, 43rd Annual Convention,* 196–204. 1936–37.

Rhoades, Mabel Carter. "A Case Study of Delinquent Boys in the Juvenile Court of Chicago." Ph.D. diss., University of Chicago, 1907.

Richards, Jerome E. "Juvenile Offenders." In *Proceedings of the Seventh Annual Convention of the International Association of Chiefs of Police.* 1900. Reprint, New York: Arno Press, 1971.

Rodenbaugh, W. H. H. "Juvenile Reformation." In *International Association of Chiefs of Police, 9th Annual Session.* 1902. Reprint, New York: Arno Press, 1971.

Roller, Anne. "Vollmer and His College Cops." *The Survey* 62 (1929): 304–7.

Rutledge, William P. "Police as a Preventive Agency in Juvenile Delinquency." In *Proceedings of the 34th Annual Convention of the International Association of Chiefs of Police,* 133–37. 1927. Reprint, New York: Arno Press, 1971.

Saunders, Margaret. "A Study of the Work of the City Mother's Bureau of the City of Los Angeles." M.S.W. thesis, University of Southern California, 1939.

Scudder, Kenyon J. "How California Anchors Drifting Boys." *The Survey* 69 (March 1933): 101–2.

———. "Drunken Children." *Juvenile Research Bulletin* 2 (July–August 1934): 1.

———. "Perverted Children." *Coordinating Council Bulletin* 3 (July 1935): 1–7.

———. *Life Anew: Annual Report, Los Angeles County Probation Department, for the Year Ending December 31st, 1935.* Los Angeles, 1936.

———. "The Los Angeles County Coordinating Council Plan," In *Preventing Crime: A Symposium,* ed. Sheldon and Eleanor Glueck, 25–45. New York: McGraw-Hill, 1936.

———. "Coordinating to Beat the Devil." *Rotarian* 51 (September 1937): 21–23.

Scudder, Kenyon J., and Kenneth S. Beam, *Who Is Delinquent: The Los Angeles County Plan of Coordinating Councils.* Los Angeles: Los Angeles County Juvenile Court and Probation Department, 1934.

Sharp, Roland Hall. "Checking Crime at the Source." *Christian Science Monitor Weekly Magazine* (July 3, 1937).

Shaw, Clifford R. *The Jack-Roller: A Delinquent Boy's Own Story.* 1930. Reprint, University of Chicago Press, 1966.

Shaw, Clifford R., and Earl D. Myers. "The Juvenile Delinquent." In *The Illinois Crime Survey,* ed. Illinois Association for Criminal Justice. 1929. Reprint, Montclair, NJ: Patterson-Smith, 1968.

Shaw, Clifford R., with Frederick M. Zorbaugh, Henry D. McKay, and Leonard S. Cottrell. *Delinquency Areas: A Study of the Geographic Distribution of School Truants, Juvenile Delinquents, and Adult Offenders in Chicago.* Chicago: University of Chicago Press, 1929.

Shaw, Clifford R., with Henry D. McKay and James F. McDonald. *Brothers in Crime.* Chicago: University of Chicago Press, 1938.

Shaw, Clifford R., with Maurice E. Moore. *The Natural History of a Delinquent Career.* Chicago: University of Chicago Press, 1931. Reprint, New York: Greenwood Press, 1968.

Shepherd, William G. "How to Make a Gangster." *Collier's* 92 (September 2, 1933): 12–13.

Siegel, Helene Freud. "A History of the Detroit House of Correction." M.S.W. thesis, Wayne University, 1940.

"Stealing Bases to Stop Theft." *Literary Digest* 113 (May 21, 1932): 18–19.

"Stop Reckless Shooting." *The Outlook* 149 (23 May 1928): 141.

Sutherland, Edwin D. "Crime." In *American Society in Wartime,* ed. William Fielding Ogburn, 185–206. Chicago: University of Chicago Press, 1943.

Sylvester, Richard. "Principles of Police Administration." *Journal of Criminal Law and Criminology* 1 (September 1910).

Taylor, Frederick Winslow. *The Principles of Scientific Management.* 1911. Reprint, New York: W.W. Norton, 1967.

Taylor, Graham. "The Police and Vice in Chicago." *The Survey* 23 (November 6, 1908): 160–65.

———. "Police Efficiency the First Effect of Vice Inquiries." *The Survey* 28 (April 12, 1912): 136–41.

Thrasher, Frederic M. *The Gang: A Study of 1,313 Gangs in Chicago.* Chicago: University of Chicago Press, 1927.

———. "The Problem of Crime Prevention." In *Yearbook of the National Probation Association 1934,* ed. Marjorie Bell. New York: National Probation Association, 1934.

Tillard, J. N. "The Child, the Home, and the State." In *International Association of Chiefs of Police; 14th Annual Session,* 38–41. 1907. Reprint, New York: Arno Press, 1971.

———. "The Juvenile Criminal." In *International Association of Chiefs of Police; Proceedings 23rd Convention,* 30–34. 1916. Reprint, New York: Arno Press, 1971.

Tuthill, Richard S. "History of the Children's Court in Chicago." In *Children's Courts in the United States: Their Origin, Development, and Results,* ed. Samuel J. Barrows. Washington, DC: Government Printing Office, 1904.

Vollmer, August. "The Policeman as a Social Worker." In *International Association of Chiefs of Police, Proceedings of the 26th Annual Convention,* 32–38. 1919. Reprint, New York: Arno Press, 1971.

———. "Aims and Ideals of the Police." In *Journal of the American Institute of Law and Criminology: Selected Articles,* 251–57. 1922. Reprint, New York: Arno Press, 1971.

———. "Predelinquency." *Journal of Criminal Law and Criminology* 14 (August 1923): 279–83.

———. "The Police (in Chicago)." In *The Illinois Crime Survey,* ed. Illinois Association for Criminal Justice, 357–72. 1929. Reprint, Montclair, NJ: Patterson-Smith, 1968.

———. *The Police in Modern Society.* Berkeley: University of California Press, 1936.

Warner, Florence M. *Juvenile Detention in the United States; Report of a Field Survey of the National Probation Association.* Chicago: University of Chicago Press, 1933.

Watkins, James K. "The Police and the Prevention of Delinquency." In *Yearbook of the National Probation Association,* ed. Marjorie Bell, 42–49. New York: National Probation Association, 1933.

———. "The Function of a Police Department in a Community Social Welfare Program." In *Proceedings of the National Conference of Social Work, 60th Annual Session.* 1933.

Westcott, Ethel M. "The Wayne County Juvenile Court." M.A. thesis. Wayne State University, 1936.

Wheeler, Charles A. "A Boy Scout Program as an Aid in the Police Juvenile Problem." In *Yearbook of the International Association of Chiefs of Police, 44th Annual Convention,* 209–12. 1938–39.

White, Walter. "Negro Segregation Comes North." *The Nation* 121 (October 21, 1925): 458–60.

Wilkby, A. J. "Crime Prevention in Cities under 25,000." In *Yearbook of the International Association of Chiefs of Police, 46th Annual Convention,* 135–38. 1939–40.

Williams, Mornay. "The Street Boy—Who He Is, and What to Do With Him." In *Proceedings of the National Conference of Charities and Corrections, at the Thirtieth Annual Session Held in the City of Atlanta, May 6, 1903,* ed. Isabel C. Barrows, 238–44. Fred. J. Herr, 1903.

Williamson, Mrs. E. E. "The Street Arab." In *Proceedings of the National Conference of Charities and Corrections at the Twenty-Fifth Annual Session Held in the City of New York, May 18–25, 1898,* ed. Isabel C. Barrows, 358–61. Boston: Geo. H. Ellis, 1899.

Wolf, Anna W. M., and Irma Simonton Black. "What Happened to the Young People." In *While You Were Gone: A Report on Wartime Life in the United States,* ed. Jack Goodman, 64–88. New York: Simon and Schuster, 1946.

Woods, Arthur. *Crime Prevention.* Princeton, NJ: Princeton University Press, 1918.

Zuck, John M. "The Junior Probation Camps of Los Angeles County." In *Current Approaches to Delinquency, 1949 Yearbook,* ed. Marjorie Bell, 76–89. New York: National Probation Association, 1949.

## Secondary Sources

Adler, Jeffrey S. "'On the Borders of Snakeland': Evolutionary Psychology and Plebian Violence in Industrial Chicago, 1875–1920." *Journal of Social History* 36 (Spring 2003): 541–60.

Alexander, Ruth. *The "Girl Problem": Female Sexual Delinquency in New York, 1900–1930.* Ithaca: Cornell University Press, 1995.

Appier, Janis. "Juvenile Crime Control: Los Angeles Law Enforcement and the Zoot-Suit Riots." *Criminal Justice History* 11 (1990): 147–70.

———. *Policing Women: The Sexual Politics of Law Enforcement and the LAPD.* Philadelphia: Temple University Press, 1998.

Austin, James, and Barry Krisberg. "Wider, Stronger, and Different Nets: The Dialectics of Criminal Justice Reform." *Journal of Research in Crime and Delinquency* 18 (January 1981): 165–96.

Ayers, William. *A Kind and Just Parent: The Children of Juvenile Court.* Boston: Beacon Press, 1997.

Baldwin, Peter C. "'Nocturnal Habits and Dark Wisdom': The American Response to Children in the Streets at Night, 1880–1930." *Journal of Social History* 35 (Spring 2002): 593–611.

Barnard, Harry. *Independent Man: The Life of Senator James Couzens.* New York: Charles Scribner's Sons, 1958.

Bennett, James. *Oral History and Delinquency: The Rhetoric of Criminology.* Chicago: University of Chicago Press, 1981.

Bernard, Thomas J. *The Cycle of Juvenile Justice.* New York: Oxford University Press, 1992.

Black, Donald J. *The Manners and Customs of the Police.* New York: Academic Press, 1980.

Black, Donald J., and Albert J. Reiss, Jr. "Police Control of Juveniles." *American Sociological Review* 35 (1970): 63–77.

Bottles, Scott L. *Los Angeles and the Automobile: The Making of the Modern City.* Berkeley: University of California Press, 1987.

Boyer, Paul. *Urban Masses and Moral Order, 1820–1920.* Cambridge, MA: Harvard University Press, 1978.

Brede, Richard M. "Complainants and Kids: The Role of Citizen Complainants in the Social Production of Juvenile Cases." In *Law and Order in American Society,* ed. Joseph M. Hawes, 77–100. Port Washington, NY: Kennikat Press, 1979.

Brennan, James J. "The Prevention and Control of Juvenile Delinquency by Police Departments: A Critical Study of Programs in Urban Police Departments." Ph.D. diss., New York University, 1952.

Brumberg, Joan Jacobs. *Kansas Charley: The Story of a Nineteenth-Century Boy Murderer.* New York: Viking, 2003.

Capeci, Dominic J., Jr., and Martha Wilkerson. *Layered Violence: The Detroit Rioters of 1943.* Jackson: University Press of Mississippi, 1991.

Carte, Gene E., and Elaine H. Carte. *Police Reform in the United States: The Era of August Vollmer, 1905–1932.* Berkeley: University of California Press, 1975.

Cavallo, Dominick. *Muscles and Morals: Organized Playgrounds and Urban Reform, 1880–1920.* Philadelphia: University of Pennsylvania Press, 1981.

Chauncey, George. *Gay New York: Gender, Urban Culture, and the Making of the Gay Male World, 1890–1940.* New York: Basic Books, 1994.

Chudacoff, Howard P., and Judith E. Smith. *The Evolution of Urban Society.* 5th ed. Upper Saddle River, NJ: Prentice Hall, 2000.

Clapp, Elizabeth J. *Mothers of All Children: Women Reformers and the Rise of Juvenile Courts in Progressive Era America.* University Park, PA: Pennsylvania State University Press, 1998.

Conot, Robert. *American Odyssey.* 1974. Reprint, Detroit: Wayne State University Press, 1986.

Cook, Philip J., and John H. Laub. "The Unprecedented Epidemic in Youth Violence." In *Crime and Justice: An Annual Review of Research,* vol. 24, *Youth Violence,* ed. Michael Tonry and Mark H. Moore, 27–64. Chicago: University of Chicago Press, 1998.

Dahlberg, Jane S. *The New York Bureau of Municipal Research: Pioneer in Government Administration.* New York: New York University Press, 1966.

Diamond, Andrew. "Rethinking Culture on the Streets: Agency, Masculinity, and Style in the American City." *Journal of Urban History* 27 (July 2001): 669–85.

Dodge, L. Mara. "'Our Juvenile Court Has Become More like a Criminal Court': A Century of Reform at the Cook County (Chicago) Juvenile Court." *Michigan Historical Review* 26 (Fall 2000): 51–89

Domanick, Joe. *To Protect and to Serve: The LAPD's Century of War in the City of Dreams.* New York: Pocket Books, 1994.

Dulaney, W. Marvin. *Black Police in America.* Bloomington: Indiana University Press, 1996.

Escobar, Edward J. "Zoot-Suiters and Cops: Chicano Youth and the Los Angeles Police Department during World War II." In *The War in American Culture: Society and Consciousness during World War II,* ed. Lewis A. Erenberg and Susan E. Hirsch, 284–312. Chicago: University of Chicago Press, 1996.

———. *Race, Police, and the Making of a Political Identity: Mexican Americans and the Los Angeles Police Department, 1900–1945.* Berkeley: University of California Press, 1999.

Farrington, David P. "Age and Crime." In *Crime and Justice: An Annual Review of Research,* vol. 7, ed. Norval Morris and Michael Tonry, 189–250. Chicago: University of Chicago Press, 1986.

Feld, Barry C. *Bad Kids: Race and the Transformation of the Juvenile Court.* New York: Oxford University Press, 1999.

Finestone, Harold. *Victims of Change: Juvenile Delinquents in American Society.* Westport, CT: Greenwood Press, 1976.

Flink, James J. *The Automobile Age.* Cambridge, MA: The MIT Press, 1988.

Fogelson, Robert M. *The Fragmented Metropolis: Los Angeles, 1850–1930.* 1967. Reprint, Berkeley: University of California Press, 1993.

———. *Big City Police.* Cambridge, MA: Harvard University Press, 1977.

Fragnoli, Raymond R. *The Transformation of Detroit: Progressivism in Detroit—And After, 1912–1933.* New York: Garland Publishing, 1982.

Freedman, Estelle B. *Maternal Justice: Miriam Van Waters and the Female Reform Tradition.* Chicago: University of Chicago Press, 1996.

Friedman, Lawrence M. *Crime and Punishment in American History.* New York: Basic Books, 1993.

Friedman, Lawrence M., and Robert V. Percival. *The Roots of Justice: Crime and Punishment in Alameda County, California, 1870–1910.* Chapel Hill: University of North Carolina Press, 1981.

Getis, Victoria. *The Juvenile Court and the Progressives.* Urbana: University of Illinois Press, 2000.

Gilbert, James. *A Cycle of Outrage: America's Reaction to the Juvenile Delinquent in the 1950s.* New York: Oxford University Press, 1986.

Gilfoyle, Timothy J. *City of Eros: New York City, Prostitution, and the Commercialization of Sex, 1790–1920.* New York: W.W. Norton, 1992.

Gish, Clay. "Rescuing the 'Waifs and Strays' of the City: The Western Emigration Program of the Children's Aid Society." *Journal of Social History* 33 (Fall 1999): 121–42.

Gordon, Linda. *Heroes of Their Own Lives: The Politics and History of Family Violence, Boston 1880–1960.* New York: Viking, 1988.

Graff, Harvey J. *Conflicting Paths: Growing Up in America.* Cambridge, MA: Harvard University Press, 1995.

Grossman, James R. *Land of Hope: Chicago, Black Southerners, and the Great Migration.* Chicago: University of Chicago Press, 1991.

Haller, Mark H. "Urban Crime and Criminal Justice: The Chicago Case." *Journal of American History* 57 (December 1970): 619–35.

———. "Civic Reformers and Police Leadership: Chicago, 1905–1935." In *Police in Urban Society,* ed. Harlan Hahn, 39–56. Beverly Hills, CA: Sage Publications, 1971.

———. "Historical Roots of Police Behavior: Chicago, 1890–1925." *Law and Society Review* 10 (1976): 303–23.

Haring, Sidney R. *Policing a Class Society: The Experience of American Cities, 1865–1915.* New Brunswick, NJ: Rutgers University Press, 1983.

Harris, Patrick, and Flavia Hodge. *A Dictionary of Surnames.* Oxford: Oxford University Press, 1988.

Hawes, Joseph M. *Children in Urban Society: Juvenile Delinquency in Nineteenth-Century America.* New York: Oxford University Press, 1971.

Hays, Samuel P. "The Politics of Reform in Municipal Government in the Progressive Era." *Pacific Northwest Quarterly* 55 (1964): 157–69.

Hine, Thomas. *The Rise and Fall of the American Teenager: A New History of the American Adolescent Experience.* New York: Harper, 1999.

Hirschi, Travis, and Michael Gottredson. "Age and the Explanation of Crime." *American Journal of Sociology* 89 (November 1983): 552–84.

Holl, Jack M. *Juvenile Reform in the Progressive Era: William R. George and the Junior Republic Movement.* Ithaca, NY: Cornell University Press, 1971.

Holt, Glen E., and Dominic A. Pacyga. *Chicago: A Historical Guide to the Neighborhoods: The Loop and the South Side.* Chicago: Chicago Historical Society, 1979.

Horn, Margo. *Before It's Too Late: The Child Guidance Movement in the United States, 1922–1945.* Philadelphia: Temple University Press, 1989.

Hurl, Lorna F., and David J. Tucker. "The Michigan County Agents and the Development of Juvenile Probation, 1873–1900." *Journal of Social History* 30 (Summer 1997): 905–37.

Jackson, Kenneth T., ed. *The Encyclopedia of New York City.* New Haven, CT: Yale University Press, 1995.

Johnson, David R. *Policing the Urban Underworld: The Impact of Crime on the Development of the American Police, 1800–1887.* Philadelphia: Temple University Press, 1979.

———. *American Law Enforcement: A History.* St. Louis, MO: Forum Press, 1981.

Johnson, Marilynn S. *Street Justice: A History of Police Violence in New York City.* Boston: Beacon Press, 2003.

Kelling, George L. "Juveniles and the Police: The End of the Nightstick." In *From Children to Citizens, Volume II: The Role of the Juvenile Court,* ed. F. X. Hartman, 203–18. New York: Springer-Verlag, 1987.

Kenney, John P., and Dan G. Pursuit. *Police Work with Juveniles and the Administration of Juvenile Justice.* 5th ed. Springfield, IL: Charles C. Thomas, 1975.

Kessler-Harris, Alice. *Out to Work: A History of Wage-Earning Women in the United States.* New York: Oxford University Press, 1982.

Kett, Joseph. *Rites of Passage: Adolescence in America, 1790 to the Present.* New York: Basic Books, 1977.

Klein, Joanne Marie. "Invisible Working-Class Men: Police Constables in Manchester, Birmingham, and Liverpool, 1900–1939." Ph.D. diss., Rice University, 1992.

Knupfer, Anne Meis. *Reform and Resistance: Gender, Delinquency, and America's First Juvenile Court.* New York: Routledge, 2001.

Lacey, Robert. *Ford: The Men and the Machine.* Boston: Little, Brown, 1986.

Lane, Roger. *Policing the City: Boston, 1822–1885.* Cambridge, MA: Harvard University Press, 1967.

———. *Murder in America: A History.* Columbus: The Ohio State University Press, 1997.

Lemert, Edwin M. "Diversion in Juvenile Justice: What Hath Been Wrought." *Journal of Research in Crime and Delinquency* 18 (January 1981): 34–45.

Levine, David Allen. *Internal Combustion: The Races in Detroit, 1915–1926.* Westport, CT: Greenwood Press, 1976.

Lindberg, Richard C. *To Serve and Collect: Chicago Politics and Police Corruption from the Lager Beer Riot to the Summerdale Scandal, 1855–1960.* 1991. Reprint, Carbondale, IL: Southern Illinois University Press, 1998.

Link, Arthur S., and Richard L. McCormick. *Progressivism.* Arlington Heights, IL: Harlan Davidson, 1983.

Liss, Julia, and Steven Schlossman. "The Contours of Crime Prevention in August Vollmer's Berkeley." *Research in Law, Deviance, and Social Control* 16 (1984): 79–107.

Lundman, Robert J., Richard E. Sykes, and John P. Clark. "Police Control of Juveniles: A Replication." *Journal of Research in Crime and Delinquency* 18 (January 1979): 74–91.

Macleod, David I. *Building Character in the American Boy: The Boy Scouts, YMCA, and Their Forerunners, 1870–1920.* Madison: University of Wisconsin Press, 1983.

———. *The Age of the Child: Children in America, 1890–1920.* New York: Twayne Publishers, 1998.

Manfredi, Christopher P. *The Supreme Court and Juvenile Justice.* Lawrence: University Press of Kansas, 1998.

McGerr, Michael. *A Fierce Discontent: The Rise and Fall of the Progressive Movement in America, 1870–1920.* New York: Free Press, 2003.

McNamee, Gwen Hoerr. "The Origin of the Cook County Juvenile Court." In *A Noble Social Experiment? The First 100 Years of the Cook County Juvenile Court, 1899–1999,* ed. Gwen Hoerr McNamee, 14–23. Chicago: Chicago Bar Association, 1999.

Mennel, Robert M. *Thorns and Thistles: Juvenile Delinquents in the United States, 1825–1940.* Hanover, NH: University Press of New England, 1973.

Meyerowitz, Joanne J. *Women Adrift: Independent Wage Earners in Chicago, 1880–1930.* Chicago: University of Chicago Press, 1988.

Miller, Donald L. *City of the Century: The Epic of Chicago and the Making of America.* New York: Simon and Schuster, 1996.

Miller, Wilbur R. *Cops and Bobbies: Police Authority in New York and London, 1830–1870.* 2d ed. 1973. Columbus: The Ohio State University Press, 1999.

Modell, John. *Into One's Own: From Youth to Adulthood in the United States, 1920–1975.* Berkeley: University of California Press, 1989.

Mohl, Raymond H. *The New City: Urban America in the Industrial Age, 1860–1920.* Arlington Heights, IL: Harlan Davidson, 1985.

Monkkonen, Eric H. *Police in Urban America, 1850–1920.* New York: Cambridge University Press, 1981.

———. *America Becomes Urban: The Development of U.S. Cities and Town, 1780–1980.* Berkeley: University of California Press, 1988.

———. *Murder in New York City.* Berkeley: University of California Press, 2001.

Moore, Joan W., with Robert Garcia, Carlos Garcia, Luis Cerda, and Frank Valencia. *Homeboys: Gangs, Drugs and Prison in the Barrios of Los Angeles.* Philadelphia: Temple University Press, 1978.

Myers, Tamara, and Joan Sangster. "Retorts, Runaways, and Riot: Patterns of Resistance in Canadian Reform Schools for Girls, 1930–60." *Journal of Social History* 34 (Spring 2001): 669–98.

Nasaw, David. *Children of the City: At Work and At Play.* Garden City, NJ: Anchor Press, 1985.

National Research Council and Institute of Medicine. *Juvenile Crime, Juvenile Justice,* edited by Joan McCord, Cathy Spatz Widon, and Nancy A. Crowell. Washington, DC: National Academy Press, 2001.

Odem, Mary E. "Single Mothers, Delinquent Daughters, and the Juvenile Court in Early 20th Century Los Angeles." *Journal of Social History* 25 (Fall 1991): 27–43.

———. "City Mothers and Delinquent Daughters: Female Juvenile Justice Reform in Early Twentieth-Century Los Angeles." In *California Progressivism Revisited,* edited by William Deverell and Tom Sitton, 175–99. Berkeley: University of California Press, 1994.

———. *Delinquent Daughters: Protecting and Policing Adolescent Female Sexuality in the United States, 1885–1920.* Chapel Hill: University of North Carolina Press, 1995.

Odem, Mary E., and Steven Schlossman. "Guardians of Virtue: The Juvenile Court and Female Delinquency in Early 20th-Century Los Angeles." *Crime and Delinquency* 37 (April 1991): 186–203.

Ousby, Ian. *The Cambridge Guide to Literature in English.* Cambridge: Cambridge University Press, 1993.

Pacyga, Dominic A. "The Russell Square Community Committee: An Ethnic Response to Urban Problems." *Journal of Urban History* 15 (1989): 159–84.

Pagan, Eduardo Obregon. *Murder at the Sleepy Lagoon: Zoot Suits, Race, and Riot in Wartime LA.* Chapel Hill: University of North Carolina Press, 2003.

Peiss, Kathy. *Cheap Amusements: Working Women and Leisure in Turn-of-the-Century New York.* Philadelphia: Temple University Press, 1986.

Philpott, Thomas Lee. *The Slum and the Ghetto: Immigrants, Black, and Reformers in Chicago, 1880–1930.* 1978; Belmont, CA: Wadsworth, 1991.

Platt, Anthony M. *The Child Savers: The Invention of Delinquency.* Chicago: University of Chicago Press, 1969.

Potter, Claire Bond. *War on Crime: Bandits, G-Men, and the Politics of Mass Culture.* New Brunswick, NJ: Rutgers University Press, 1998.

Powers, Richard Gid. *Secrecy and Power: The Life of J. Edgar Hoover.* New York: Free Press, 1987.

Rafter, Nicole Hahn. *Creating Born Criminals.* Urbana: University of Illinois Press, 1997.

Reed, Rebecca. "Regulating the Regulators: Ideology and Practice in the Policing of Detroit, 1880–1920." Ph.D. diss., University of Michigan, 1992.

Richardson, James F. *The New York Police: Colonial Times to 1901.* New York: Oxford University Press, 1970.

Robertson, Stephen. "Age of Consent Law and the Making of Modern Childhood in New York City, 1886–1921." *Journal of Social History* 35 (Summer 2002): 781–98.

Rothman, David J. *Conscience and Convenience: The Asylum and Its Alternatives in Progressive America.* Boston: Little, Brown, 1980.

Ruth, David E. *Inventing the Public Enemy: The Gangster in American Culture, 1918–1934.* Chicago: University of Chicago Press, 1996.

Ryerson, Ellen. *The Best-Laid Plans: America's Juvenile Court Experiment.* New York: Hill and Wang, 1978.

Sanchez, George J. *Becoming Mexican American: Ethnicity, Culture, and Identity in Chicano Los Angeles, 1900–1945.* New York: Oxford University Press, 1993.

Schlossman, Steven L. *Love and the American Delinquent: The Theory and Practice of "Progressive" Juvenile Justice, 1825–1920.* Chicago: University of Chicago Press, 1977.

———. *The California Experience in American Juvenile Justice: Some Historical Perspectives.* Sacramento: Office of the Attorney General, State of California, 1989.

———. "Delinquent Children: The Juvenile Reform School." In *The Oxford History of the Prison: The Practice of Punishment in Western Society,* ed. Norval Morris and David J. Rothman. New York: Oxford University Press, 1995.

Schlossman, Steven L., and Alexander W. Pisciotta. "Identifying and Treating Serious Juvenile Offenders: The View from California and New York in the 1920s." In *Intervention Strategies for Chronic Juvenile Offenders: Some New Perspectives,* ed. Peter W. Greenwood. Westport, CT: Greenwood Press, 1986.

Schlossman, Steven L., and Michael Sedlak. "The Chicago Area Project Revisited." *Crime and Delinquency* 26 (July 1983): 398–462.

Schlossman, Steven, and Susan Turner. *Race and Delinquency in Los Angeles Juvenile Court, 1950.* Sacramento: California Bureau of Criminal Statistics, 1990.

———. "Status Offenders, Criminal Offenders, and Children 'At Risk' in Early Twentieth-Century Juvenile Court." In *Children at Risk in America: History, Concepts, and Public Policy,* ed. Roberta Wollons, 32–57. Albany: State University of New York Press, 1993.

Schlossman, Steven L., and Stephanie Wallach. "The Crime of Precocious Sexuality:

Female Juvenile Delinquency in the Progressive Era." *Harvard Education Review* 48 (February 1978): 65–93.

Schneider, Eric C. *In the Web of Class: Delinquents and Reformers in Boston, 1810s–1930s.* New York: New York University Press, 1992.

———. *Vampires, Dragons, and Egyptian Kings: Youth Gangs in Postwar New York.* Princeton, NJ: Princeton University Press, 1999.

Schneider, John C. *Detroit and the Problem of Order, 1830–1880: A Geography of Crime, Riot, and Policing.* Lincoln: University Press of Nebraska, 1980.

Schulz, Dorothy Moses. *From Social Worker to Crimefighter: Women in United States Municipal Policing.* Westport, CT: Praeger, 1995.

Shoemaker, Donald J. *Theories of Delinquency: An Examination of Explanations of Delinquent Behavior.* 2d ed. New York: Oxford University Press, 1990.

Smith, Douglas A., and Christy A. Visher. "Street-Level Justice: Situational Determinants of Police Arrest Decisions." *Social Problems* 29 (December 1981): 167–77.

Snyder, Howard N. "Juvenile Arrests 2001." *Juvenile Justice Bulletin* (December 2003).

Springhall, John. "Censoring Hollywood: Youth, Moral Panic and Crime/Gangster Movies of the 1930s." *Journal of Popular Culture* 32 (Winter 1998): 135–54.

Starr, Kevin. *Material Dreams: Southern California through the 1920s.* New York: Oxford University Press, 1990.

———. *Endangered Dreams: The Great Depression in California.* New York: Oxford University Press, 1996.

Steffensmeier, Darrell J. et al. "Age and the Distribution of Crime." *American Journal of Sociology* 94 (January 1989): 803–31.

Steinberg, Allen. *The Transformation of Criminal Justice: Philadelphia, 1800–1880.* Chapel Hill: University of North Carolina Press, 1989.

Stinchcombe, Arthur L. "Institutions of Privacy in the Determination of Police Administrative Practice." *American Journal of Sociology* 69 (1963): 150–60.

Sugrue, Thomas J. *The Origins of the Urban Crisis: Race and Inequality in Postwar Detroit.* Princeton, NJ: Princeton University Press, 1996.

Suzik, Jeffrey Ryan. "'Building Better Men': The CCC Boy and the Changing Social Ideal of Manliness." In *Boys and Their Toys? Masculinity, Technology, and Class in America,* ed. Roger Horowitz, 111–38. London: Routledge, 2001.

Tanenhaus, David S. *Juvenile Justice in the Making.* New York: Oxford University Press, 2004.

Thomas, Richard W. *Life for Us Is What We Make It: Building Black Community in Detroit, 1915–1945.* Bloomington: Indiana University Press, 1992.

Trost, Jennifer. *Gateway to Justice: The Juvenile Court and Progressive Child Welfare in a Southern City.* Athens: University of Georgia Press, 2005.

Tyack, David, and Michael Berkowitz. "The Man Nobody Liked: Toward a Social History of the Truant Officer, 1840–1940." *American Quarterly* 29 (Spring 1977): 31–54.

Uys, Errol Lincoln. *Riding the Rails: Teenagers on the Move during the Great Depression.* New York: TV Books, 1999.

Von Hoffman, Alexander. "An Officer of the Neighborhood: A Boston Patrolman on the Beat in 1895." *Journal of Social History* 26 (Winter 1992): 309–30.

Walker, Samuel. *A Critical History of Police Reform.* Lexington, MA: DC Heath, 1977.

―――. *Sense and Nonsense about Crime and Drugs: A Policy Guide.* 3d ed. Belmont, CA: Wadsworth, 1994.

―――. *Popular Justice: A History of American Criminal Justice.* 2d ed. New York: Oxford University Press, 1998.

Watts, Eugene J. "Police Priorities in Twentieth Century St. Louis." *Journal of Social History* 14 (Summer 1981): 649–73.

―――. "Police Response to Crime and Disorder in Twentieth-Century St. Louis." *Journal of American History* 70 (June 1983): 340–48.

Wolcott, David Bryan. "Cops and Kids: The Police and Juvenile Delinquency in Three American Cities, 1890–1940." Ph.D. diss., Carnegie Mellon University, 2000.

Wolcott, David. "'The Cop Will Get You': The Police and Discretionary Juvenile Justice, 1890–1940." *Journal of Social History* 35 (Winter 2001): 349–72.

―――. "Juvenile Justice before Juvenile Court: Cops, Courts, and Kids in Turn-of-the-Century Detroit." *Social Science History* 27 (Spring 2003): 109–38.

Wolcott, Victoria W. *Remaking Respectability: African American Women in Interwar Detroit.* Chapel Hill: University of North Carolina Press, 2001.

Woods, Gerald. *The Police in Los Angeles: Reform and Professionalization.* New York: Garland Publishing, 1993.

Zimring, Franklin E. "The Common Thread: Diversion in the Jurisprudence of Juvenile Courts." In *A Century of Juvenile Justice,* ed. Margaret K. Rosenheim et al., 142–57. Chicago: University of Chicago Press, 2002.

Zunz, Olivier. *The Changing Face of Inequality: Urbanization, Industrial Development, and Immigrants in Detroit, 1880–1920.* Chicago: University of Chicago Press, 1982.

# FILMS

*Little Caesar* (Warner Brothers, 1931).
*The Public Enemy* (Warner Brothers, 1931).
*Scarface* (Howard Hughes, 1932).
*West Side Story* (Mirisch/Seven Arts, 1961).

# INDEX

# HISTORY OF CRIME AND CRIMINAL JUSTICE
David R. Johnson and Jeffrey S. Adler, Series Editors

The series explores the history of crime and criminality, violence, criminal justice, and legal systems without restrictions as to chronological scope, geographical focus, or methodological approach.

*Gender and Petty Violence in London, 1680–1720*
Jennine Hurl-Eamon

*Pursuing Johns: Criminal Law Reform, Defending Character, and New York City's Committee of Fourteen, 1920–1930*
Thomas C. Mackey

*Social Control in Europe: Vol. 1, 1500–1800*
Edited by Herman Roodenburg and Pieter Spierenburg

*Social Control in Europe: Vol. 2, 1800–2000*
Edited by Clive Emsley, Eric Johnson, and Pieter Spierenburg

*Policing the City: Crime and Legal Authority in London, 1780–1840*
Andrew T. Harris

*Written in Blood: Fatal Attraction in Enlightenment Amsterdam*
Pieter Spierenburg

*Crime, Justice, History*
Eric H. Monkkonen

*The Rule of Justice: The People of Chicago versus Zephyr Davis*
Elizabeth Dale

*Five Centuries of Violence in Finland and the Baltic Area*
Heikki Ylikangas, Petri Karonen, and Martti Lehti

*Prostitution and the State in Italy, 1860–1915,* 2nd Edition
Mary Gibson

*Homicide, North and South: Being a Comparative View of Crime against the Person in Several Parts of the United States*
H. V. Redfield

*Rethinking Southern Violence: Homicides in Post–Civil War Louisiana, 1866–1884*
Gilles Vandal

*Violent Death in the City: Suicide, Accident, and Murder in Nineteenth-Century Philadelphia,* 2nd Edition
Roger Lane

*Controlling Vice: Regulating Brothel Prostitution in St. Paul, 1865–1883*
Joel Best

*Cops and Bobbies: Police Authority in New York and London, 1830–1870,* 2nd Edition
Wilbur R. Miller

*Race, Labor, and Punishment in the New South*
Martha A. Myers

*Men and Violence: Gender, Honor, and Rituals in Modern Europe and America*
Edited by Pieter Spierenburg

*Murder in America: A History*
Roger Lane